“Because It Gives Me Peace of Mind”

SUNY Series, McGill Studies in the History of Religions, A Series Devoted to International Scholarship

Katherine K. Young, editor

"Because It Gives Me Peace of Mind"

Ritual Fasts in the Religious Lives of Hindu Women

Anne Mackenzie Pearson

State University of New York Press

The author and SUNY Press gratefully acknowledge the following persmissions granted for material used herein: the Bhandarkar Oriental Research Institute for material from *The History of Dharmaśāstra* (1974) by P. V. Kane; Motilal Banarsidass Publishers for material from *Heat and Sacrifice in the Vedas* (1985) by Uma Marina Vesci; the Royal Anthropological Institute of Great Britain and Ireland for material from "Death and Digestion: The Symbolism of Food and Eating in North Indian Mortuary Rites" (1985) by Jonathan Parry, *Man*, 20 (4), 613; the University of Chicago Press for material from *The Mahābhārata*, vols. 1–3, translated by J. A. van Buitenen.

Published by
State University of New York Press, Albany

Printed in the United States of America

For information, address the State University of New York Press, State University Plaza, Albany, NY 12246

Production by Christine Lynch • Marketing by Bernadette LaMama

Library of Congress Cataloging-in-Publication Data

Pearson, Anne Mackenzie, 1957–
Because it gives me peace of mind : ritual fasts in the religious lives of Hindu women / Anne Mackenzie Pearson.
p. cm. — (McGill studies in the history of religions)
Includes bibliographical references and index.
ISBN 0-7914-3037-5 (hardcover : alk. paper). — ISBN 0-7914-3038-3 (pbk. : alk. paper)
1. Vratas. 2. Hindu women — Religious life. I. Title. II. Series.
BL 1237.78.P43 1996
294.5'446 — dc20 95-39811
CIP

1 2 3 4 5 6 7 8 9 10

To my grandmothers Alice and Maryon
who died
and to my daughters Kira, Landon and Rachel
who were born
during the preparation of this book

CONTENTS

LIST OF PLATES

ABBREVIATIONS OF SANSKRIT TEXTS

AP	*Agnipurāṇa*
AitBr.	*Aitareya Brāhmaṇa*
ApDS	*Apastamba Dharmasūtra*
AV	*Atharvaveda*
Gītā	*Bhagavadgītā*
GP	*Garuḍapurāṇa*
LP	*Liṅgapurāṇa*
MP	*Matsyapurāṇa*
Mbh.	*Mahābhārata*
Manu	*Manusmṛti*
RV	*Ṛgveda*
ŚB	*Śatapatha Brāhmaṇa*
TS	*Taittirīya Saṁhitā*
VR	*Vratarāja*
Yāj.	*Yājñavalkya Smṛti*
YS	*Yogasūtra*

NOTES ON TRANSLATION AND TRANSLITERATION

I am responsible for all translations from Hindi, French and German sources, and for the translation of passages quoted from the Sanskrit Nibandha text, the *Vratarāja*. For other Sanskrit material, I relied on the translations of others, as indicated in the text. Many of these translations were checked against the original source to ensure relative accuracy. I sometimes indicate in square brackets what the Sanskrit word or phrase being translated is.

Diacritics are used with transliterated Sanskrit and Hindi following current standard usage. In general, I use the Sanskrit forms (e.g., *vrata*) when referring to the Sanskrit textual tradition, and Hindi forms when referring to modern contexts (e.g., *vrat*). Hindi versions of Sanskrit words are often marked by dropping a middle and/or final "a" (e.g., Skt. *devatā* is rendered in Hindi as *devtā*, *dharma* becomes *dharm*).

Indian place-names, the pseudonyms of individuals I interviewed, and words that are now familiar to Western readers (mantra, guru) as well as genres of texts that are used adjectively (vedic, purāṇic) are rendered into phonetic English and are not italicized. The names of gods and goddesses, authors, and characters referred to in Sanskrit and Hindi texts are rendered with diacritics.

The great majority of interviews with women were conducted in Hindi and taped. The remarks of women quoted in this book are based on my translations of the transcribed tapes. When inverted commas are used in a quote, they indicate that the word or phrase was used exactly as noted.

PREFACE

In the 1970s I had the good fortune of living and travelling in India for several years, first with my parental family, then alone, before I returned to undertake dissertation field research in the North Indian city of Banaras. This experience in my teens and early twenties set the stage for my scholarly interest in Indian culture and religious history. Occasionally while travelling, I came across women who were fasting. Fasting was clearly such a commonplace activity and women mentioned it so matter-of-factly that I did not pay too much attention to this phenomenon except to use it as an excuse to refuse food or hospitality from time to time when I felt ill at ease or ill of stomach. It was an immediately understood cultural idiom: "of course, she's fasting" *(vah vrat hi rakh rahi hai)*—nothing more need be said.

I mention this observation partly to suggest that one of the reasons *vrats* and the *vrat* tradition were largely overlooked by the mostly male Western scholarly community over the last century is that the very ubiquitousness of *vrats* and their close association with women's practices rendered this tradition almost invisible. The *vrat* tradition, if it was noticed at all, was seen to be largely inconsequential to an understanding of the foundations and "core" of Hinduism. When particular *vrats* were noticed and described in journals by early ethnographers, they sometimes appear as a curiosity: "Piriya—A Curious Folk Rite," or their aims depicted as superficial: "Bratas in Bengal: A Cult of Beauty."

Attitudes about the insignificance of the *vrat* tradition for an appreciation of Indian culture have persisted into the present. Some educated Hindu men I met looked at me with genuine puzzlement when I explained to them that I had come to India to study *vrats*. A typical response was: "Why would you want to study *vrats*?" meaning, what is there to say about them? Of course, other Hindus expressed a different view and understood vrats to be very important, laudable rites.

I first learned about the connection between the "fasts" which women had told me they were keeping, and which I sometimes told others I was observing, and the *vrat* tradition while researching a paper on Hindu women's rituals as a graduate student. Reading the Dharmaśāstra scholar P. V. Kane alerted me to the long and substantial Sanskrit textual tradition on *vrata*s, and so for my master's thesis I explored the treatment of *vrata* in a selection of medieval Purāṇas. After completing this study, however, I was left with a number of unanswered questions. The study of texts alone yields much information about how *vrata*s ought to be observed from an orthodox Brahmanical point of view, but tells us little about the contexts in which *vrata*s were and are actually observed, and tells us nothing about the functions that *vrat*s play in the religious lives of Hindus.

While the anthropologist Susan Wadley, among a few others, had provided some of this information, there was still lacking a comprehensive account of the *vrata* tradition which attempted to link the massive textual sources on *vrata*s with the lived tradition whose practice is dominated by women. For my doctoral work, then, I set out to explore the relation between text and practice, to investigate the factors that can account for the particular popularity of *vrat*s among women, and to learn more about the roles and meanings of *vrat*s in the devotional lives of Hindu women. This book is a product of that investigation.

ACKNOWLEDGMENTS

The preparation and completion of this book is also the result of the assistance and input from many individuals and it is my pleasure and heartfelt duty to acknowledge and thank them. For reading through and commenting on earlier drafts of this work I thank David Kinsley, Graeme MacQueen, Landon Pearson, Lynn Teskey Denton, Katherine Young, and especially Ellen Badone, who used her training as an anthropologist to help me shape the "telling" of my field work, and Paul Younger, whose support and confidence in me from the early years of graduate school contributed in no small measure to my reaching the end of that passage and to the crossing into a new one. I also thank the three anonymous readers who read and commented on the draft manuscript for the State University of New York Press.

For financial support during fourteen months of research in India, I thank the Shastri Indo-Canadian Institute, which granted me a junior fellowship.

Next, I express my profound gratitude to the many women in India who with inimitable hospitality welcomed an unknown foreigner in their homes; who not only received and considered my numerous questions and allowed me to observe their lives, but who also shared some very personal reflections and experiences with me, allowing me to catch glimpses of their ordinary, but always extraordinary, lives. A number of these women I would not have met without the help of my research assistant, Kalpana; and so I thank her for that and for all the other help she provided.

For other forms of assistance in Banaras, I would be remiss not to mention Srimati Dr. Vimla Karnatak, Professor of Sanskrit at Banaras Hindu University Women's College, and Virendra Singh for Hindi lessons and for rescuing me one night after an accident on Sonarpur Road. In Mussoorie, I thank Citranjan Dutt and Dinkar Rai of the Landour Language School for assistance both in transcribing the tapes of my interviews and in translating *vrat kathā* books. In Kerala, I thank George Jacob and Srimati Matthews, who arranged interviews with women in Trivandrum and Kottayam respectively and acted as interpreters.

In Hamilton, I thank Lakshmi Subbiah, Bimla Kaul, and Shobhana Bhargava for further assistance in the transcriptions of tapes and discussions about interpretation. And I thank my husband Mark—a true *pativrata*—for his sacrificial involvement in parenting our three daughters, born during the preparation of this work.

Lastly, I would like to thank the editors at SUNY Press, and in particular, Christine Lynch and Christine Worden for their assistance in the production of this book.

Introduction

> The outstanding impression my mother has left on my memory is that of saintliness. She was deeply religious. . . . She would take the hardest vows and keep them without flinching. Illness was no excuse for relaxing them. . . . To keep two or three consecutive fasts was nothing to her. Living on one meal a day during *Chaturmas* [the four months of the rainy season; a traditional period of fasting] was a habit with her. Not content with that, she fasted every other alternate day during one *Chaturmas*. During another *Chaturmas* she vowed not to have food without seeing the sun. We children on those days would stand, staring at the sky, waiting to announce the appearance of the sun to our mother. Everyone knows that at the height of the rainy season the sun often does not condescend to show his face. And I remember days when, at his sudden appearance, we would rush and announce it to her. She would run out to see with her own eyes, but by that time the fugitive sun would be gone, thus depriving her of her meal. "That does not matter," she would say cheerfully, "God did not want me to eat today." And then she would return to her round of duties. (M. K. Gandhi 1957, 4–5)

These words come from Mahatma Gandhi's autobiography. He speaks little of his parents, but most of what he says about his mother centers on her profound religiosity, and this religiosity in turn is expressed most vividly for Gandhi in her observance of vows and fasts. Gandhi's association with rigorous fasting is too well kown to warrant further description, but what may be less well known (to non-Indians at least) is that Gandhi's early forays into fasting were in imitation of his mother; her observance of *vrats* provided an early model for his religio-ascetic disciplines. In a chapter subtitled "Fasting" Gandhi writes about how he got started on his "experiments" with dietary discipline to further buttress the vow of celibacy which he had already taken: "Just about the time when I gave up milk and cereals, and started on the experiment of a fruit diet, I commenced fasting as a means of self-restraint. . . . Having been born in a Vaishnava family and of a mother who was given to keeping all sorts of hard vows, I had observed . . . the *Ekadashi* fast. As a rule Hindus allow themselves milk and fruit on a fasting day, but such fast I had been keeping daily. So now I began complete fasting, allowing myself only water" (1957, 330). He also started to keep "Pradosha," a *vrat* involving fasting until evening, which he says "some members of the family used to observe." In fasting according to his mother's practice Gandhi placed himself squarely within the long Hindu tradition of *vrat*s, the subject of this book.

Literature on *vrata* in English frequently refers to the term *vrat*a (or *vrat*) as a vow or fast, as did the translator of Gandhi's autobiography. The translation of *vrata* as fast is easily understood, as some sort of fast is characteristic of a *vrata*, and Hindus I spoke with during my stay in India in 1984–85 most often used this English word when I mentioned *vrata*. But fasting is only one aspect of *vrata*; there must also be some association with a vow. In English the word vow has a variety of senses, such as personal promise, pledge, and commitment.[1] It also evokes institutionalized vows, like marriage vows, monastic vows or the renunciatory vows of the ascetic. *Vrata*s share many of these senses, including the voluntary personal promise or resolve to undertake some course of action (in a secular or religious context), or the promise made in front of religious authorities to adhere to a specified code of conduct in rites of initiation.[2] Yet the English word vow has become generalized and somewhat abstract and it fails to bring to mind a specific form of observance. In Hindi-speaking India, however, the word *vrata* usually elicits an image of a particular observance involving fasting, worship *(pūjā)*, the listening to or recitation of a narrative about the efficacy of the rite *(kathā)*, and the giving of gifts *(dān)* consisting of money and items of food and clothing to another person, often a Brahman. A *vrata* is usually understood to be a rite that is performed on a regular basis to achieve particular objectives, following rules that have been transmitted from one generation to the next. Further, many Hindus, in my experience, immediately think of women in connection with *vrata*s. As Gandhi's reference to his mother suggests, *vrata*s are predominantly something *women* do and have done for generations.

CHARACTERISTICS OF *VRATAS*

Vratas are normally instrumental in nature. A response (usually believed to be effected by the deity to whom the *vrata* is directed) is expected by the votary, although she or he is fully aware that it may not be immediate or even tangible. *Vratas* do not usually take the form of bargaining pledges of the sort: "If you (God) will cure my son, I will go to shrine X." The form they take is, more commonly, "I will undertake such and such a regimen for this period of time and may you, O God, pleased by my devotions, protect my family."

There are different forms of instrumentality associated with *vratas*. It is interesting to compare *vratas* as practised by Hindu women with the forms of vows made by Catholic women in rural Spain described by the anthropologist William Christian. Thus, sometimes *vratas* are similar to Christian's description of a promesa, a kind of conditional vow made and observed primarily by women.[3] Essentially something is given up in order to secure something else, redemption or aid. In a *promesa*, a pledge is made involving some sacrifice of resources such as money or time, sacrifice of pride, denial of pleasures or the undertaking of hardships (e.g., pilgrimages on bare feet). These forms of self-imposed hardship may occur in a *vrata*. For both *promesas* and *vratas*, a specified proxy may be used (in certain conditions), but the vow must be fulfilled or dire consequences are believed to ensue.

Vratas may also resemble Christian's category of "petitionary devotions"—a subset of instrumental prayers. These are devotional acts which put God in "one's debt," in which one can "earn credit with the divine for divine actions on this earth" (1972, 128). For example, a novena might be performed for the sake of souls in purgatory. Underlying the devotional attitude expressed in the novena is the petitioners's hope that God may feel in some sense compelled to act favorably toward her at some later time.

Finally, certain *vratas* can also be like Christian's description of the "prayers for the fulfillment of the annual round" (1972, 117ff.). These are prayers in which no definite response is expected other than the continuation of the existing (positive) state of affairs. They are usually made by women, Christian notes, in the context of annual visits to shrines. He says these visits become something of a psychological necessity, a way of fulfilling a regular, calendrical contract (1972, 117). Likewise, certain annual *vratas* are associated with generalized purposes, but carry with them a sense of obligation such that if they were not observed a *pāp* ("sin") would be incurred or misfortune might strike in consequence.

To this point I have discussed *vratas* in the present tense, and have given some indication of their forms and function in contemporary religious practice, but *vratas* have been a feature of Hindu religious life for millennia. The word *vrata* emerges in the oldest extant literature of Hindu India—the Vedas. This means that the term itself, if not all its ramifications, goes back at least three thousand years. Nevertheless, it is not possible to demonstrate that the *vrata* tradition, consisting of the particular votive rituals discussed in this book, is much older than the beginning of the Common Era.

A fully comprehensive study of the history of *vrata* turns out to be an enormous task. Even P. V. Kane, the author of the indispensable five-volume *History of Dharmaśāstra,* who devoted 462 pages of his work to a discussion and description of *vratas* from Sanskrit Dharmaśāstra texts, admitted that the tabulation of all the sources of *vrata* (including all the regional and local variations, and all the *vratas* observed by women and by aboriginals) "would entail an enormous amount of labour" and "would require the co-operative effort of a large team of workers spread over many years," but which, when completed, would result in "a monumental [work] on the social anthropology of India" (1974, 5, 1: 60). This last phrase is appropriate because the observance of *vratas* is so common and widespread, and incorporates (or relates to) so many aspects of Hindu religious practice and thought. As a result, learning about *vratas* enables one to understand a great deal about Hindu religiosity in general, and Hindu women's religiosity in particular.

Today, *vratas* are found throughout India. Under different names (usually variations of the Sanskrit *vrata*), these rites are observed across regional boundaries, caste and *jāti* groups, sectarian affiliations and educational backgrounds, in both rural and urban localities. They are common to the young and the old; to the married, unmarried and widowed. Of course, *vratas* are not observed equally among these various groups. Young boys or men, low-caste persons, the very poor, or highly Westernized persons, for example, may observe very few as a group and many do none as individuals. Nevertheless *some* among them *do* observe *vratas*.

There are great variations in the actual practice of a given *vrata*. This variation affects not only those *vratas* known across India but also those *vratas* peculiar to small regions of the country. Personal predilections, family and *jāti* practices can all influence the way a *vrata* is performed. *Vratas* can be done for virtually any purpose concerning one's own or another's well-being. With few exceptions, a *vrata* is never observed for the purpose of harming someone. In the texts and in practice there are, for example, *vratas* for obtaining progeny or agricultural fertility, for ensuring the long life of husbands or brothers, for eradicating one's past sins, for averting snake bites and disease, and for securing a place in one of the god's *lokas* (heavens). New *vratas* are still being generated. The rise of the relatively recent goddess Santoṣī Mā and her *vrata* is already well documented.[4]

The performance of *vratas* intersects with a wide range of practices in Hinduism and governs a wide range of acts and behaviors, both ritual and ethical. These practices include worship, speech and silence, sleep, clothing, sexual activity, food (kind, preparation, amount, time when eaten), cooking (how, where, when and for whom), gift-giving and receiving, story-telling, singing, the creation of ritual art, and pilgrimage.

Finally, *vratas* encompass many different strands in Hindu culture, including those that in the past some scholars characterized as "oppositions." For example, *vratas* are part of both the orally transmitted, local folk (*laukik*, lit. "worldly") traditions and the written, *śāstrik* (brahmanical) pan-Indian traditions. *Vratas* share features of both the *bhakti* (devotionalistic, theistic) strand of Hinduism, where the deity's grace and boons are sought by the devotee, and the *smārta* ritualistic strand wherein correctly performed ritual is of itself efficacious. *Vratas* also share the form and worldview of both *gṛhastha-dharma* (prescribed duty of the householder), in which specific, worldly concerns, values and desires are expressed or sought out, and ascetic *dharma*, in which increasing detachment and finally release *(mokṣa)* from this same world is the goal. It is because the *vrata* tradition does touch upon so many features and aspects of Hinduism that its study is such a valuable key to both the Indologist's and the nonspecialist's understanding of this ancient living religion.

VRATAS AND THE SOCIAL CONSTRUCTION OF GENDER

In the Purāṇas and Nibandhas, the major Sanskrit textual descriptive and prescriptive sources for *vratas*, both men and women, of all castes, are deemed eligible to perform the rites. The textual descriptions of *vratas* in which it is clear men, and only certain men (such as a king or a celibate student), can perform the particular *vrata*, constitute a small fraction of the total *vrata* descriptions. One can find a few more *vratas* which single out women as the suitable performer of the *vrata* and this is usually marked by the addition of *saubhāgya* (the auspicious state of the married woman) to the list of goals or rewards accruing to the votary. Most *vrata* descriptions, however, do not designate the sex of the votary, though some may add that forest hermits or widows can perform the *vrata*. In reading these texts alone, one would not receive the impression that *vratas* were especially designed for women, nor could one predict that while both men and women observe *vratas* throughout India today, women observe far more of them and at more frequent intervals than do men.

In general, I found that in Banaras high-caste men, who come from observant families, tend to perform a handful of annual *vrats* that are part of their family's traditional practices. If they have a strong sectarian affiliation, they may perform *vrats* more often (for example the semi-monthly Ekadaśī Vrat if they are Vaiṣṇavite). Some men may take on a *vrat*, in the sense of altering or restricting their diet or some other behavior, just prior to and during a pilgrimage. In addition, men of all castes (and, as I found, Buddhists and Jains too) may take on a short-term weekly *vrat* on the advice of an astrologer to counter a prevailing malefic influence of a planet or a certain celestial configuration. In a few instances, I encountered men of lower castes (in one case, a rickshaw driver) who had taken on the Santoṣī Mā Vrat as a means of soliciting help from the goddess to solve a particular problem. Finally, I met a number of men who had taken on a *vrat* in honor of their favored deity *(iṣṭadevatā)*, as a demonstration of devotion or to seek the deity's blessings.

Women may observe *vrats* for all these same reasons, and in similar contexts. Nevertheless, while there are many regularly occurring *vrats* that only women perform, I did not discover any calendrical *vrats* performed only by men. Further, there are discernible differences between the sexes not only in the frequency of their performance of *vrats*, but also in the way the *vrats* are performed, in the purposes for which *vrats* are kept, and finally in the significance which male and female votaries attach to these rituals. One way by which these differences can be explained is by appealing to cultural constructions of gender that are woven into the ideological heritage (or cultural milieu) of every Indian. Indeed, it would be impossible to appreciate fully the significance of Hindu women's performance of and relationship to *vrats* without taking into account the implications of these cultural constructions of gender in India.

The scholarship on Hindu women in the last two decades has amply documented that women as a group have had ascribed to them, by dominant religio-cultural ideologies formulated largely by male Brahmans, different natures and functions than men as a group.[5] Views about the nature and roles of women have been, over a period of centuries, worked out fairly cohesively and set down in texts (in particular, Dharmaśāstras) the ideas of which remain influential to the present. In general, women's natures are depicted as unsteady, lustful and weak, and their functions depicted as centering on their roles as wives and mothers under the control of male kin. Such an ideology regarding women (expressed in both sacred and popular literature, films and common adages) informs and reinforces social conventions so that it is typical to find girls in India actively socialized to be modest, obedient, self-effacing and self-sacrificing for the sake of others in the family. In the context of *vrats*, we find girls trained to direct the performance of *vrats* for the attainment of a husband, or, for young married women, for the well-being of their husband and children; being trained, that is, to understand the purpose and meaning of *vrats* within a relational context. Men's rituals (including their performance of *vrats*) tend to be self-directed, that is, concerned with their own aims and well-being. In essence, the *vrats* that women perform are tied to domestic life and traditionally defined family and gender relationships in a way that the *vrats* men perform are not.

A number of researchers who have discussed women and *vrats* (e.g., Kakar 1978; Mazumdar 1981) have portrayed *vrats* as essentially normative practices which reproduce cultural values emphasizing (or reinforcing) the structural subservience of daughters to fathers and wives to husbands. It is from such a perspective that in 1986 the editors of the important investigative journal *Manushi: A Journal About Women and Society* disparaged *vrats* as rituals contributing to the subordination and disempowerment of women in India. Other scholars (e.g., Wadley 1975, 1976, 1980a; Freeman 1980; Bennett 1983; McGee 1987, 1991), while acknowledging that women's *vrats* reproduce cultural values that place women in a subservient role, have pointed out women's creative or self-affirming responses—revealed in their votive rites and in the stories they tell—to the strictures placed on their behavior. For example, while Susan Wadley placed women's *vrats* in the context of women's "duty" *(strīdharm)* and depicted the performance of these rites as constituting a "fundamental aspect of being a *pativratā*"—the ideal Hindu woman (1976, 164)—she also emphasized the positive aspects of *vrats* through which women express their roles. She suggested that rituals like *vrats* "may give psychological support to the women themselves, because they allow women to have active control of events rather than depend completely on their male kin. Ritually, only a wife or a sister can really save a husband or brother from death" (1980a, 109). And Freeman described the sense of comradery that Orissan women enjoy while observing the Habisha Vrat, and the fact that some women took advantage of the opportunity afforded by the *vrat* to go on a nearby pilgrimage without male kin. Such accounts showed that Hindu women are not just passive recipients of a hegemonic gender ideology, meekly colluding in their own subordination, but rather are humans exercising agency, interacting with tradition, even if within culturally prescribed constraints that define and limit the parameters of that action.

The explanation and significance of gender differences between men's and women's performance of *vrats* can be approached from another perspective besides social conditioning through a dominant ideology. The historian of religion, Carolyn Walker Bynum, has examined the issue of gender difference in socioreligious contexts from the premise that *all* experience is gendered. In response to Ortner and Whitehead's statement that women's (and men's) actions and "perspectives are to a great extent constrained and conditioned by the dominant ideology" (1980, x), Bynum argues that "Even where there is no hint of an alternative ideology to counter a dominant one, subordinate and dominant individuals [or women and men] will experience this accepted ideology in different ways" (1986, 5). Bynum argues that not only gender-related symbols (which can be about values other than gender) but all symbols arise out of the experience of gendered users and that no theory of symbol (or one could add, religious practice) can be adequate unless it incorporates women's experience and discourse as well as men's. She says further that

> If we take as women's rituals and women's symbols the rituals and symbols that women actually use, and ask how these symbols mean, we may discover that women have all along had certain modes of symbolic discourse different from those of men. Even where men and women have used the same symbols and rituals, they may have invested them with different meaning and different ways of meaning. (1986, 16)[6]

Certainly *vratas* can be viewed as symbolic constructions expanded into ritual and narrative, and it is possible to demonstrate through a study of *vrats* that Hindu women have "modes of symbolic discourse different from that of men's." For instance, in the *vrats* that only women perform, there are a number of elements appearing in their *pūjās*, ritual art and stories that are expressive of women's responsibilities and concerns: reproductive fertility, the health of their children and familial well-being in general, the problems of a "co-wife," as well as the values of auspiciousness and *saubhāgya*. Such values and concerns are often transposed by women onto the *vrats* that are normally observed by both men and women, though these values and concerns in the shared *vrats* may be ritually far less explicit. It is not the gender symbolism in women's *vrats* as such, however, that I will be focusing on in this book, but rather the "different ways of meaning" that women have drawn from their performance of *vrats* based on their experience and perspectives as women.

Gloria G. Raheja and Ann G. Gold have argued that if we fail to hear Indian women's self-affirming voices or to appreciate their own sense of what constitutes a good life or to see how they skillfully negotiate their chance for such a life, we perpetuate the mistaken assumption that these women have completely internalized conventions of female subordination and fragmented identity (1994, xxxiv). I found that while women often spoke initially of *vrats* as being for [maintaining] *suhāg* (Hindi for *saubhāgya*)—the auspicious married state—they also spoke directly or indirectly about the psychological, social, physical and spiritual benefits for *themselves.* For many women, these were not just residual benefits, but primary benefits. For a significant number of women whom I interviewed, *vrats* are an important (even central) vehicle for developing and expressing devotion and religious fervor, in short, faith in God. Furthermore, the phrase "*vrats* give me peace of mind" turned up repeatedly in my interviews. While "peace of mind" includes the feelings of satisfaction, calmness and contentment implied in a surface reading of the phrase, it often had deeper levels of meaning for the women I spoke with. These are meanings connected directly with the Hindu yoga and ascetic traditions, for women also spoke of *vrats* as a form of *tapasyā* (transformative "heat" generated through austerities) and as a means to help them to control their minds and bodies. Women's reflections on what keeping *vrats* does for them give voice to alternative ways of understanding the purposes for which women keep *vrats*, the meanings and significance they attach to them, and the functions *vrats* play in their lives.

The reasons for the vitality of the *vrat* tradition among women in India, then, would appear to be more complicated than has hitherto been suggested. Though from one angle *vrats* may be portrayed as a means by which a conservative androcentric gender ideology is both expressed and transmitted to Hindu women—and thus one way in which Hindu men can indirectly control women—I would argue that women use *vrats* as a way to gain control over their own lives. *Vrats* have become (if they were not always) a source of empowerment for women, providing them with a degree of personal autonomy in an environment in which women frequently lack control and self-determination. Paradoxically, Hindu women who are culturally placed in a position where they must practice self-denial (for example, as a young daughter-in-law in her husband's home) manage to achieve a measure of control over their own lives by practising further forms of self-denial. Asceticism brings power *(tapas* and *śakti)* both in a religiously prescribed sense, and in the sense that it provides these women with a feeling that they are in control. Through practising *vrats*, they can control at least some aspects of their lives; essentially, they are controlling their own bodies (through modifying eating, sleeping and other physical acts). They can also control men's use of their bodies—by legitimately refusing sexual activity while fasting. Because *vrats* are religiously sanctioned and are ostensibly performed for the benefit of male family members, there is little resistance to a woman's performing as many *vrats* as time, resources and her stamina allow. While researchers have been documenting the ways in which Hindu women's lives and their rituals are expressive of their domestic social milieu and of the values of the householder, they have for the most part neglected to consider how women, traditionally denied access to formal asceticism, have found a way to tap into this powerful realm for their own benefit through the performance of *vrats*.[7]

FORMAT OF THE BOOK

The first chapter introduces my research population (consisting primarily of urban women, mostly from the city of Banaras in the state of Uttar Pradesh) and profiles six *vrat* observing women. Chapter 2 provides a text-historical review of the usage and development of the term *vrata* in Hindu sacred and authoritative (*śruti* and *smṛti*) literature. Such an historical review of the long textual tradition on *vrata* is, in my estimation, essential to enable one to make full sense of the current practice of *vrats* in India and of the meanings women have culled from the richness of this tradition. The last section of chapter 2 also draws connections between the practice of *vrats* and general ideas about being a good wife which are articulated in the *smṛti* literature. Chapter 3 situates *vrats* within the annual cycle of seasons and other divisions of time in the Hindu calendar and begins to explore how knowledge about *vrats* is transmitted. Chapter 4 investigates the contours or parameters of *vrats* (what makes a *vrat* a *vrat?*), and chapter 5 their procedures (what exactly does one do when one does something called a *vrat?*). To help set the parts back into the whole, the chapter ends with a detailed account of two currently observed *vrats* in Banaras. In both of these chapters, "precepts" as expressed in the Dharmaśāstras and Nibandhas are juxtaposed with the "practice" (the actions and comments) of the women I interviewed. Such a format allows us to explicitly compare what the texts say one (or in some situations what women) *ought* to do when keeping a *vrat* with accounts of what some women actually do or think ought to be done when keeping a *vrat*.

The last two chapters are both concerned with addressing the questions of the role of *vrats* in the lives of Hindu women and the reasons women give for observing these rites. Since *vrats* can be construed as one of the central ritual expressions of *strīdharm* and the means of fulfilling *strīdharm* alters somewhat according to women's marital status and stage in life, chapter 6 examines the practice of *vrats* within the context of the life cycle or life stages of Hindu women. In the process I address the questions of how *vrats* function as agents of socialization and conveyors of normative values. The final summary chapter examines the less explicit dimension of women's *vrat* observance—their appropriation of ascetic values: self-control, self-discipline and spiritual power—values which lend their practice of *vrats* a more personal and self-developmental significance than the normative ideology of "duty" alone would assume or allow. Each chapter, then, presents data on the *vrat* tradition from a different perspective, though the issue of "how" *vrats* mean to women remains a constant theme.

1

Six Women

Banaras, also called Varanasi and Kashi (the "city of light"), is an ancient and densely populated city of over one million situated on the banks of the holiest of India's rivers, the Ganges, in the eastern part of the state of Uttar Pradesh. All over the country Gaṅgā *jal*, or Ganges water, carefully brought home by pilgrims or purchased in the bazaar in sealed copper pots, is used in home *pūjās*. As the Ganges is the holiest of India's rivers, Banaras is the holiest of Hindu India's many *tīrthas*, literally, "sacred crossings," that is, pilgrimage centers.[1] It is a commonly held belief among Hindus that to die in Banaras is to achieve *mokṣa* (liberation) instantly, or at least a sure place in Śiva's heaven, since he presides over the city. Consequently, there is an unusually large number of elderly pilgrims who come from all over the country to spend their last days in Banaras. There is also, at any one time, a large number of ordinary visitors who have come to take "auspicious viewing" (*darśan*) at the better known of Banaras' innumerable temples. As the city of Śiva, the preeminent ascetic god, Banaras also hosts a high concentration of resident and visiting male and female ascetics of various orders, as well as ascetic institutions. Many famous "renouncers" (*sannyāsins*) and learned gurus have lived in Banaras or have regularly passed through, offering public discourses. A good number of the Hindus I became acquainted with in the city had either heard these gurus directly or were keenly aware of their life-styles, if not of their teachings. Comments about gurus and ascetics often came up in my conversations with women about *vrats*, leading me to speculate that the general population of Banaras may be more affected by the ascetic tradition(s) than the populations of most other Indian cities.

The antiquity of Banaras and its ancient status as an important *tīrtha*, as well as center of traditional learning and the arts, have given the city a richly diverse resident population. In addition, Banaras now houses a large national university, with students and faculty from around the country. For these reasons many of the women I met and some of those I interviewed, while having lived in Banaras throughout their lives and speaking Hindi, came from families originating in other parts of India.

The majority of the fifty-eight Hindu women with whom I conducted formal interviews in Banaras and its environs were Brahman, about one-sixth were of Kshatriya castes and the remainder were from other classes and castes.[2] The women's ages ranged from seventeen to seventy-two years, and their educational backgrounds ranged from illiterate to a doctorate level. Just over two-thirds of the women interviewed were married, and the others were either unmarried or widowed. Nine of the women had no children.

Interviews usually took place in women's homes, after appointments were scheduled in advance. Not infrequently appointments were cancelled or indefinitely delayed or interrupted by the demands of small children, husbands, or by any number of situations requiring the immediate attention of the woman I was interviewing. It was not always possible to complete my interviews or to speak exclusively to one woman. In particular, husbands who happened to be present in the home during the interview found it difficult to restrain themselves (no doubt from lack of practice[3]) from adding comments, interjecting a response to a question, or simply answering on behalf of their wives. By force of habit, inculcated through years of socialization, wives often deferred to their husbands' views. There was also a concern that I, the visiting foreign "scholar," should be sure to get the "correct version of the facts." This concern, and the belief of many women that they did not know anything about *vrat*s worth communicating to me, made it difficult for me to persuade women that I genuinely wanted to talk to them, rather than to "panditji" down the street (or in the next room), or to some professor at Banaras Hindu University. Some women were also shy and unaccustomed to reflecting on their beliefs and practices and articulating those reflections to a foreigner. In these cases, a certain amount of encouragement, prompting and rephrasing of questions was required. Overall, however, I was pleasantly surprised at the willingness and in some cases eagerness of women to answer my questions and to allow me to look at their places of worship, watch their rituals, and from time to time, participate with them in their *vrat* observances.

I learned something new about the lore, practice and function of *vrat*s with each interview, and it became clear to me that this learning could go on indefinitely. Almost every time I formed a conclusion or a generalization about some aspect of *vrats*, it would be challenged in the next interview. Information I received from a woman one day might be contradicted by her in the next interview. These experiences contributed to my privileging the particularity of individual voices in the context of individual lives. Thus, while I have drawn general conclusions from my fieldwork, I have sought to do so without losing sight of the rich complexity of women's religious experience.

To begin examining the place and function of *vrats* in the lives of contemporary Hindu women, six women of various ages, castes and marital statuses from Uttar Pradesh are profiled below. In each profile I have included information about the woman's family and religious background, her education, and her religious activities such as daily worship practices, visits to temples, pilgrimages, and, of course, her performance of *vrats*. The interviews I conducted with these six women constitute my "core" interviews such that in the ensuing chapters, while describing and discussing women's views on various issues—from the question of the difference between a *vrat*, a fast and a festival to the meaning of *vrat*—the responses of some or all of these six women will be provided. Material from the remaining interviews will be drawn upon more selectively. Throughout, I have preferred to quote a woman directly rather than paraphrase or construct a summary in order to hear as much as possible from the women themselves, and, in the case of these six core interviews, to provide continuity in the remaining chapters.

A number of the topics and themes concerning Hindu women's religiosity and their performance of *vrats* which emerge perhaps fleetingly and without comment in this chapter will be pursued in greater depth later. Nevertheless, I have also taken the opportunity in each profile to consider a particular point or issue in more detail and, in the process, bring in the voices of other women interviewed.

Important in the selection of women to profile was the presence of a rapport between myself and the woman interviewed.[4] The establishment of such a rapport or sense of friendship and openness in our relationship was important because it gave me greater confidence to extrapolate later from the material at hand (drawing out implications from what was said or not said), and to form some general conclusions. A sense of confidence is essential when one cannot go back to the field to double-check one's findings. At the same time, I am conscious that in one sense I have also "created" these women, even as they "created" themselves to me as they talked about their lives and reflected on my questions. Whatever the "reality" of their lives is, it is refracted through several lenses—their lens, my lens and the lens of the reader. That does not mean, however, that we cannot learn something that approximates a truthful vision of some aspects of their lives, and the significance of *vrats* to these women, even while, as James Clifford has described, such ("ethnographic") truths are "inherently partial—committed and incomplete" (Clifford and Marcus 1986).[5] I can only hope that the women profiled here would easily recognize themselves in these chapters.

KAMALA

Kamala is a highly educated and religious middle-class woman who identified her caste as "Parmar Kshatriya." She was thirty-eight when I interviewed her, and her main occupation was looking after her household and three children. She was one of the first women I interviewed in Banaras and also one of the most articulate. Her answers to my questions were often expansive and thoughtful. Kamala welcomed me warmly into her home, took a genuine interest in my project and quickly grasped the meaning and intent of my questions. Although she had travelled little outside of Uttar Pradesh, her education and keen sense of sociological observation lent her responses an unusual perspicacity. She was more aware than most women whom I encountered of the possible cultural and ideological differences of our respective backgrounds, and this awareness had an influence on the way she answered some of my questions. She built analogical bridges to "my world" as I tried often to do with all the women I interviewed. For example, aware that I came from North America—"the land of science and technology"—she made statements like "in other respects *vrats* are very scientific," and she proceeded to outline their scientific aspects. With respect to women's roles and gender arrangements, however, Kamala expressed conservative views. On the topic of "woman's duty," for instance, she explained that:

> *Strīdharm* begins at the point at which we become married. The meaning of this is that one should give support to one's husband

> and family. She should give all respect to her mother and father, she should run the family, bring up the children and educate them. Then she must fulfill the duties of arranging marriages. As long as we are in the householder stage (*gṛhastha āśrama*) we should fulfill it properly, which is *strīdharm*. . . . [Yet] *strīdharm* changes according to [one's] stage in life. In old age we do work for society. Now I am fully devoted to my husband and family, but when the children grow up and stand on their own then I will have the time to do a little for my country and society [like Lakshmibai,[6] one of her heroines].

We met over several days in her white-washed cement bungalow in a relatively new section of Banaras. I interviewed her on my own over biscuits and tea, sitting on a hard sofa, underneath the ubiquitous rotating fan. Since her Hindi was impeccable, it was easy to understand her and she graciously offered corrections to my own phrasing of questions, which assisted me in later interviews.

Kamala was born in Banaras but her family was originally from Malwa, in northern Madhya Pradesh. Though she was married young—at age sixteen—her husband encouraged her to continue her studies in Hindi, which she did, up to the Ph.D. level. Despite her high level of education, there did not seem to be any thought that she should find employment or seek a career outside the home. It was not financially necessary and she had the important responsibility of looking after three young children. And, as she intimated above, she was thinking of doing some sort of volunteer social work after her children married. It appeared that both Kamala and her husband (who worked in administration at the university) considered education valuable for its own sake and both were proud of her educational accomplishments . At one point I was shown some of the books on history, religion and philosophy they kept prominently displayed in the living room. Kamala's husband was also pleased to have me interview his wife, and on the first afternoon I visited, after showing me the books and sharing tea and formalities, he slipped away after telling us to "carry on."

Kamala's parents' family protective deity (*kuldevtā*[7]) is Durgā and that of her husband's family is Śiva. She identified herself as a Sanātani, and said that this meant belief in and worship of all the deities. But the place where Kamala does daily *pūjā* in her home bears only Hanumān's image, her own personal or preferred god (*iṣṭadevtā*). Her husband performs a daily *pūjā* as well, but separately, as is commonly the case. For spiritual instruction and inspiration Kamala tries to read a little from the *Gītā*, *Purāṇ* or epics daily, as time permits. She visits various temples on inclination or on some special occasion, but favors the largest Hanumān temple in Banaras, Sankat Mochan. She has been on pilgrimage with her husband's family to Rameshvaram (southern India), Puri (eastern India) and Haridvar (northern India). These three sites are known and venerated across India.[8] Kamala said that she does not believe in the existence of unhappy ghosts and spirits (*bhūt-pret*),[9] or at least not in their capacity to interfere in human affairs. Like the vast majority of Hindus, Kamala does accept the doctrines of *karma* and rebirth (*punarjanma*).

Kamala observes fifteen different *vrats* and celebrates nine additional annual festivals, so her year is frequently punctuated by religious fasts and feasts, observances and celebrations. We went through a pocket calendar I had listing all the religious holidays, observances and *vrats* and she briefly explained what she knew about them. Like many women I encountered, she had an impressive storehouse of knowledge about the details of many rites and rituals beyond the ones that she actually observed herself.

Kamala started observing the family *vrats* (that is, those *vrats* which the whole family observes)—Kṛṣṇa Janmāṣṭamī, Śivarātri, Naurātri, Rāmnaumī—when she was very young, "two or three years old." "Haritālik Vrat I started at the age of eleven . . . because mother did them, grandmother also does them—so girls also start to do them." She began most of the other *vrats* she now keeps after her marriage: Vaṭ Sāvitrī, Ṛṣi Pañcamī, Karvā Cauth, Śravaṇ Somvār, Mahālakṣmī, Kārtik Pūrṇimā and Ānant Caturdaśī. After the birth of her children (two boys and a girl) she began to keep the Halṣaṣṭhī, Gaṇeś Cauth and Jīvitputrika Vrats—each of which is traditionally directed to the well-being of children.

Since she observed so many *vrats*, I asked Kamala which ones were the most important to her, and she responded:

> All the *vrats* I do are important. Haritālikā is for one's husband, Gaṇeś Caturthī and Jīvitputrika are for one's sons. In my view all my *vrats* are important in their respective places. Therefore I want to do the maximum number of *vrats*. The effect of each

> *vrat* is different. Somvar (Monday) Vrat is for Śiv, Maṅgalvār (Tuesday) is for Hanumān, Ravivār (Sunday) is for Sūrya—so each [*vrat*'s] effect, significance and its results are also different. [Yet] from every *vrat* the *ātma* (Self or soul) receives contentment. *Vrat*s are such that one would not get angry [as one might ordinarily]. One does not bring problems to others. The heart becomes pure. Mere fasting does not constitute a *vrat*.

In her response, Kamala began by saying that she considered *all vrat*s to be important because, as eventually became apparent, it is the effect of observing *vrat*s on *herself* that is of lasting spiritual and personal significance to her. She next mentioned the conventionally laudable reason for women to keep *vrat*s, that is, for husbands and sons, and stressed that, therefore, one (a woman) *should* observe as many as possible. Then she stated that the effect of each *vrat* is different, and by the examples she gave it is clear that she was referring to the weekday *vrat*s—those which are usually taken on or prescribed for specific reasons, including protection from the malefic influence of certain planets. Her final comments returned to the results that each *vrat* produces on the person observing it—peace of mind or contentment, the restraint of negative emotions, the cultivation of purity of heart—regardless of who is keeping the *vrat* or why. As I noted earlier, Kamala was among the first women I interviewed, and comments such as these on the personal spiritual benefits arising from the performance of *vrat*s alerted me to this dimension of women's relationship to the *vrat* tradition. Clearly, for some women, it was the self-disciplinary features of the *vrat* tradition, the ascetic values, that they found most meaningful.

Towards the end of our second interview I asked Kamala if she thought that women are naturally (*prakṛtik rup se*) more religious (*dhārmik*) than men. This question was asked because I had often come across statements to that effect in articles or books written by Indians and I also had heard such assertions from both Indian men and women. For example, from A. S. Altekar we hear that, "Women are by nature more religious and devotional than men. They can visit temples with greater regularity, perform sacred rites with higher faith and submit to religious fasts with more alacrity than men" (1956, 206). I wanted to explore what this meant and wondered what bearing it had on women's performance of *vrat*s.

In my question about women's natural religiosity, the term *dhārmik* (for "religion" or "religious") was usually equated by my respondents, including Kamala, first with *pūjā-paṭh*—meaning the multitude of religious rituals and related observances (*pūjās* to household deities, *vrats*, hymn [*bhajan*] singing, observances of festivals, temple visitation, the sponsoring of sacred story [*kathā*] recitations) that occupy the religious praxis of many Hindu householders. *"Dhārmik"* was only secondarily equated with *"dharm"* in its moral dimensions or in its sense as duty to god, one's family, *jāti,* and so on. The question I asked women about *strīdharm* brought out this distinction because in this case *"dharm"* was understood as the person and gender specific code of morally and socially responsible behavior.

The question concerning the differential religiosity of men and women was posed to the majority of women interviewed. Three-quarters felt that women are naturally more religious than men. Among those women who felt that women are not naturally more religious than men, each had male family members who were very pious or observant, or a husband who was a pandit or *pujārī.* Thus, as one woman put it: "Women are not necessarily more religious than men. It depends on the individual and (his or her) families. . . . My father-in-law is extremely religious." Yet some women who had told me about observant male relatives nevertheless put personal familial experience aside and reflected on their impressions of the larger social picture. "Yes, women are more religious than men—look all around you," said one. Who stays at home? Who has more time? Who does the *vrats*? Who goes to the temple to hear religious discourses? Who goes to the *bhajans?* "It is women, after all," summarizes the statements of several others. For many, then, being "religious" was a matter of having the time—and of being at home. What does this mean?

It should be noted at the outset that in these responses the "naturally" part of the question was disregarded. Women are viewed as being more religious than men as a matter of social fact. First, for women especially, the locus of their religious praxis is in the home—tending the place of *pūjā,* worshipping, performing the *vrats*, celebrating the festivals, and observing the purity/pollution codes. Much of this activity revolves around the kitchen—the place one often finds the household shrine, the place where the *pūjā* items and special fasting and feasting foods are prepared. The kitchen is the place from where women govern the household. If men (or women for that matter) are not at home—because they are "at work"—then they are not able to "be religious."

Second, do women have more time than men? Certainly that was the perception of the women I talked with, even when women tend to get up before the men and children, are busy all day long, and go to bed after them. Again, what was understood by "time" (in this urban setting) was that men had the allocation of their time dictated to them by the constraints and demands of their work, whereas women saw themselves as having greater freedom to allocate their own priorities. This meant that they could "take the time" to focus on their religious or ritual activities, if they so desired. But further, as one woman put it, "men go about here and there; women remain in the home—so they follow the rules (*niyam*)." Some *vrats*, for example, must begin and end at a certain *tithi* (defined as the time or period required by the moon to gain twelve degrees on the sun to the east) which may arrive at any time of the day or night. Time is by no means homogeneous for Hindus. Women, being at home, can follow the rules; they can attend to the discrete and qualitatively appropriate times or moments when the performance of certain rituals will render them more auspicious and efficacious.

These remarks may help to explain why several women suggested, as one put it, "though women today are still more religious than men, both (men and women) are less so than in times past." She attributed this fact to a "lack of religious instruction" and the intrusion of "the modern world" with its imposition of an impervious secular time. "There are fewer religious activities and they are less effective," she concluded.

Kamala's response to my question about women's natural religiosity, below, reiterates some of the points made by other women, but it also introduces further dimensions. She felt that women are more religious than men because "they are more emotional." She paused and then continued:

> From childhood we are socialized [within the home] this way. We have seen that grandmother and mother kept *vrats* but "fatherji" did not. The girl remains more in contact with her mother so her influence must be the strongest. So even from childhood the traditions have been created in such a way that girls become religious. But the category of men's activities is mostly outside [the home]. Women's [activities] are mostly linked with the home. . . . That is where the major portion of her time is

> spent. Therefore everything is connected with the home, for instance, *vrats*, festivals; [women] learn and [they] do [them] all. Thus the influence of religion continues to affect mostly women, [and] so we are more religious than men. Then, in old age—because no work remains—how are we to spend our time? So we turn ourselves towards God.

Initially, I had thought that Kamala was going to pursue the theme that women are more "naturally" religious than men because they are inherently (or have a stronger proclivity to be) more emotional—as other women were to tell me. Instead, Kamala suggested that women's "emotionalism," as their greater involvement in *dhārmik* activities, was a result of the way girls are brought up and the sociocultural reality of women's lives being centered in the home. Women are *encouraged* to be more religious (than men) in Hindu society, and so women become more religious. Nevertheless, Kamala has introduced into the women: home: religion equation the idea that women are more emotional, whatever the source of this difference from men, and that being emotional is significantly relevant to being religious. I shall pursue this dimension in some of the following profiles and chapters.

SARITA

Sarita is a pious middle-class Kanyakubja Brahman housewife. She was fifty when I interviewed her and her widowed, childless, older sister-in-law, Rani. The two women are close (or, it seems, dependent on one another) and they visit each other frequently. Over several visits to Sarita's home I had the opportunity to interview both women. While asking questions to one, the other would interject comments from time to time, although it was usually the elder sister-in-law "correcting" Sarita. It was Sarita, however, who appeared most interested in answering my questions, and who had the most definite opinions. For example, when I asked her such questions as when a formal *saṅkalp* was necessary or which *vrats* required the reading of or listening to a *kathā* she had quick answers. She also readily distinguished between "men's *vrats*" and "women's *vrats*" and between "*laukik vrats*" and "*śāstrik vrats*." Certainly not all women I interviewed had such decisive views on these questions.

Sarita was deferrent to her husband. He was present in the house during my visits "doing *pūjā*," but I never actually met him because he remained in his study—his *pūjā* room. Nevertheless, he was frequently making demands on her ("Bring tea!," he would shout), and did not seem happy or comfortable with the idea of my interviewing his wife and sister-in-law. Our first meeting was cut short because he required his wife's full attention for some apparently urgent matter. Sarita told me that "he does eight to ten hours of *pūjā* a day . . . mostly in sitting meditation." She characterized her husband's *pūjā* as *"dhyān"* and *"samādhi"* (both terms refer to meditation) oriented. I expressed surprise that he would engage in such a lengthy *pūjā* every day—but she insisted that this was so. Evidently he could spend his time in this fashion because they received sufficient rental income to keep them comfortable. For all his meditative *pūjā*, he remained a domineering and cantankerous husband.

Hearing about how much *pūjā-paṭh* her husband performed, I asked Sarita if *she* thought that women were naturally more religious than men and she replied in the affirmative, arguing that:

> Women are more emotional [*bhāvuk*]. They are kind-hearted; women always have compassion in the heart [*man*]. Where there is compassion there is *dharm*. In men there is hardness (or severity). If the hardness were not there then a man will not be called a man. Therefore, men could not be more religious [than women].

For Sarita, being religious is a quality of the heart, manifested in one's ability to show compassion to others.[10] This quality is inherently greater in women than in men. Though her husband was engaged in religious practice to an unusual degree for a householder, this kind of practice did not seem to her to constitute being "religious." While Sarita was not the only woman who expressed the view that women were more religious than men on the grounds that they were more emotional, it was especially poignant to hear it from a woman whose life experience (and marital experience in particular) apparently so strongly supported this view.

Since Sarita had said that men can and do keep *vrat*s as well as women, I asked her what the difference was. She answered succinctly: "It is like this. Women take the desires of their husbands and sons (into account) when they do *vrats*, and men do *vrats* for God; they do *vrats* for *mokṣa.*" Why don't men observe *vrats* for their wives and daughters?, I persisted. "Men are capable of doing what they want," Sarita answered. "Men are men. [But] it is wives who do *vrats* for their (men's) own well-being. For men it is not necessary [there is no need] to perform worship for their wives. Men and women are different." This perceived difference in function and duty between the sexes and its manifestation in the performance of *vrats* was echoed time and again by men and women I encountered in India.

Sarita was born in Allahabad (about 100 miles west of Banaras) and received her matriculation there. She moved to Banaras when she was married at the age of twenty-four. She has two married sons who live outside of Banaras. Her parents' lineage or family deity was Rām; her husband's family's deity is Śaṅkar (Śiva), to whom her husband directs his *pūjā*, and for whom he observes a weekly Monday Vrat (fast)—the only *vrat* he keeps. Sarita's own favored deities are Śiva and Śakti (or, Durgā). She also performs a daily *pūjā*, slotted in before her husband begins his own worship. Her *pūjā*, done in front of images of the "Sanātan *devas*," she characterized as *"mantrik"* oriented, which she explained by saying that she had been initiated in a mantra some years earlier from a guru[11] (named Paravajrakacarya) of the Udāsin order. He gave her a *śakti* mantra, to be kept secret. She uses the mantra in daily prayer and also whenever she feels the need. She affirmed that women can say all mantras.

Sarita also reads the *Rāmāyaṇ* every day, and goes to the Sankat Mochan and Durgā temples on special occasions. When I asked her if she had gone on pilgrimage, she was the only one of the women I interviewed in Banaras who said, "I live in a *tīrtha*—Kashi; there is no need to go anywhere else." In fact this is what the Kashi Mahātmyas (texts extolling the city of Kashi—Banaras) insist on. Since Banaras is *the* pilgrimage center *(tīrtha)* par excellence, there is no reason to go anywhere else for those who already live in "the abode of the gods."

Sarita said that she accepts the doctrines of karma and *purnarjanma*, but she does not, however, believe in the existence of *bhūt-pret*. She occasionally consults an astrologer; he had prescribed a *vrat* for her three years previously, the Tuesday Vrat, because "the planet Maṅgal was too strong in my ruling house." *Maṅgal* also means "auspiciousness;" but too much of a good thing can become a bad thing, and this, she felt, was the case with her. Auspiciousness in her family life had been replaced by discord and tension. Women see themselves as being responsible for maintaining auspiciousness in the home and the *vrats* they perform are a means to achieve this end. When Sarita was told by the astrologer that the planet Maṅgal (Mars) was exerting a negative influence on her, she felt she had found the source of the discord, the inauspiciousness, in her family life. It was her responsibility to remedy the situation and so she gladly took on the Tuesday Vrat. She observes the *vrat* in the conventional way—offering a simple *pūjā* with flowers, lights and incense to a picture of Hanumān at home. (Hanumān is one of the principal deities associated with Tuesday.) She then goes to a small Hanumān temple[12] for *darśan* (auspicious sight of the deity). For her fast she abstains from salt, and eats mostly *phalāhar* (literally, "fruit-food") and sweets. The benefits of observing this *vrat*, she said, have been that there is more peace in her home; "less argument or problems with my husband."

Altogether Sarita has observed eleven different *vrats*, including several before her marriage. As three of these have been weekly *vrats* and one is a semi-monthly *vrat* (Pradoṣ), Sarita's yearly total of *vrat*-observing days is fairly high. In addition to some family *vrats*, she kept the Monday Vrat before marriage "for the pleasure of Śaṅkarji," her favored deity. The Monday Vrat when kept by unmarried girls is usually observed to secure a "good husband"; but Sarita did not mention anything about a good husband. The only premarriage *vrat* which she continues with is Śivarātri. Other regular *vrats* which she does now (yearly and semi-monthly) were "started all at once right after marriage." Her mother-in-law (now deceased) instructed her. Sarita said that she had not felt pressured by her mother-in-law to keep *vrats* for she believed in them already. In answer to a question about the issue of taking permission for observing *vrats* from one's husband (which the Dharmaśāstra texts require), she replied: "I have kept *vrats* since childhood when I hadn't even seen my husband's face! . . . I have followed my *own* heart."

At several points in our conversations Sarita stressed the importance of, indeed the necessity of, having confidence or belief (*viśvās*) in the *vrats* that one keeps. "It is *viśvās* itself that is fruitful," she said.

> A *vrat* is . . . that in the name [of a god] on that [particular] day one lives according to a rule [*niyam*]. For example, assume you

> did a Monday Vrat—that day is Śaṅkarji's day; you believe in Śaṅkar, you will do his *pūjā*; you will make a food offering (to him). . . . Any *vrat* should be observed with *viśvās*. . . . Whether you do a *pūjā* with the *vrat*, or not it doesn't matter . . . you [make] a resolve that "today I will give up salt," "give up grains," [or] "give up water"—the meaning of this is just this that by that name [in the name of such and such a deity] something is given up.

Because the terms *viśvās* and *śraddhā* ("faith") came up frequently in my interviews with women about *vrats*, I want to comment on how these terms are used. Women usually used one or both of the terms *viśvās* and *śraddhā* sometime in our conversation. Initially, I assumed that the two words were being employed interchangeably (and sometimes they are). But, on closer scrutiny, I realized that there were differences in usage. The word *viśvās* was used more often than *śraddhā* and seemed to have the freest meanings. Though the word *viśvās* is often used in a religious context, this is not always the case. (I heard Hindi speakers use *viśvās* in relation to "belief" in actions [*karya meṁ viśvās*], in science, in a political philosophy, or in oneself. A phrase meaning self-confidence is *"ātma viśvās.")* The word *śraddhā*, on the other hand, was always used by women in a religious context, to indicate relationship to God. *Śraddhā* is thus "faith" in the sense of piety, veneration, devotion; and *viśvās* is "belief" in the sense of confidence, trust.[13]

One way in which the distinction became clearer as I examined women's usage of the two words in relation to *vrats* is that when a few women spoke of stopping particular *vrats* because they lost belief in them—it was the word *viśvās* that was used. None spoke of "losing *śraddhā*" in particular *vrats* because *śraddhā* is something larger. If one spoke of losing *śraddhā* it would mean losing one's religious faith (one's connection to God, and to one's family traditions) altogether. In this case, *vrats* would also largely lose their meaning; unless, that is, *vrats* had become a *niyama* only—a form of discipline independent for meaning of its mooring in faith.

Under what circumstances did women "lose confidence" in particular *vrats*? "I stopped observing several *vrats*—Santoṣī Mā Vrat, Monday Vrat, Thursday Vrat, Pūrṇimā—because I lost belief in them," said Savitri, a forty-three-year-old mother of five, and wife of a temple attendant *(pujārī)*. "Observing *vrats* comes from the heart," she continued. "You have to follow your heart." When

I asked her why she lost confidence in these *vrats* (all of which, significantly, were not part of her family tradition, natal or affinal, but were ones that she tried on the advice of friends for various reasons), she said that in one case "something bad" kept happening on the *vrat* day, and she was afraid to continue it. In the other cases she was not getting "good feelings" about the *vrats*. As she became half-hearted about them, she realized that she should just drop them. "There are many reasons for keeping *vrats*," Savitri concluded. "Sometimes without any reason except devotion [*bhakti*] people do *vrats*."

Indeed, for many women, *vrats* (or, certain *vrats*) are preeminently an expression of *bhakti*—a demonstration of faith in God, and a means of getting "closer to God." "Vrat is a kind of worship of God," said twenty-nine-year-old Archana. "It is like this," explained fifty-seven-year-old Siddheshvari. "By keeping a *vrat* I will be closer to God. On the *vrat* day meditation on God is heightened, for one eats little, so we remember God more often. The heart remains pure that day."

Some of Sarita's remarks about her observance of *vrats* made it clear that for her too some of the *vrats* that she performs are an important means of expressing her faith and devotion to God, a faith that in turn is a source of solace and strength. When discussing the importance of faith and of adopting the right attitude while keeping a *vrat*, Sarita quoted from the *Bhagavadgītā* to provide a scriptural explanatory context. Such discussions further enlarged the dimensions of Sarita's *vrat* observance beyond those circumscribed by a *pativratā* ideology.

MIRA

Mira, like Sarita, is a Kanyakubja Brahman. Her family originally came from the Lucknow area, but moved to Banaras before she was born. She was married at the age of fifteen. When I met her, Mira was seventy-two and had been a widow for twenty years. While she was educated up to middle-school level, her three children, two boys and a girl, all have university degrees. She lives alone on the second floor of her large, older two-storey house which surrounds an inner courtyard. Mira rents out the first floor and this provides her with sufficient income for her needs. She employs a sweeper woman, but otherwise looks after herself. She lives simply, always wearing a white sari without any ornamentation, and eats plain food twice a day, which she cooks with care and full consideration of the various purity rules. (She was careful not to let me enter her kitchen.) From all appearances she is a model Brahman widow.

I met with Mira on several occasions. Two of those occasions were spent interviewing her at some length. During another meeting I had the opportunity to interview her daughter, Jyoti, who was visiting from Delhi and whose profile follows. I found Srimati Mira to be somewhat formal and initially a little suspicious of me. The formality remained, but her natural warmth soon emerged. Like most women I met in Banaras, she wanted me to wear a sari which, since it is the conventional dress of Hindu women, seemed to make her feel more at ease with me. Wearing a sari, demonstrating appropriate manners and speaking in Hindi were often met with verbal appreciation by women and helped to dissolve some of the barriers that separated us. Wearing a sari also has the effect of rendering one more invisible to men.

Mira's parents' lineage deity was Katyāyanī Devī (Kṛṣṇa's sister) and "Kanyakubja Brahmā." Her husband's lineage deity was Durgā, and her own favored deities are Sītā and Rām. She identified herself as a "mostly Vaiṣṇavite Sanātani." She has thus retained her natal family's Vaiṣṇavite leanings. Indeed, Mira observes all twenty-four Ekādaśīs as any devout Vaiṣṇavite (and widow) should. She performs a daily *pūjā* in her home—in front of pictures of the five *sanātani devas* (Brahmā, Śiva, Viṣṇu, Gaṇeśa and Devī), as well as a picture of Sītā and Rām. The *pūjā* consists of salutation *(praṇam)* to the deities, decorating them with flowers, lighting incense and meditating briefly. Like Vaiṣṇavites all over India, she keeps a *tulsī* (basil) plant on her balcony, from which she periodically takes leaves, using them in her *pūjā* and putting them in her food "to increase its purity." She also celebrates Tulsī Vivāha (the marriage of the goddess Tulsī and Viṣṇu), for which occasion she draws a ritual diagram *(ālpanā)* under the plant and performs *pūjā* to it (see plate 3).

Each day, Mira reads from the *Rāmcaritmānas*—Tulsi Das' famous version of the Sanskrit *Rāmāyaṇa*, and Hindi translations of the *Bhagavatapurāṇa* or the *Mahābhārata*. She visits several temples in Banaras, particularly during festivals celebrating occasions devoted to Viṣṇu, Kṛṣṇa or Rām. Several times in conversation she emphasized that all the deities are the same. "Any person at all can do *pūjā* to God and do *vrats*—whatever *jāti* or religion they belong to—God is one, but God's forms are many. I give respect to all forms of God—whether [He] be Rām or Kṛṣṇa, whether it be the Muslim's God, or the Christian's—why not? These are all the many forms of the one God." This affirmation of the essential oneness of God underlying a multitude of forms is common among Hindus, and was reiterated by several of the women I interviewed.

Mira accepts the doctrines of karma and *punarjanma* and has a practical "reap what you sow" understanding of them. "What I do in this life, I will reap in the next; what I did before I reap now." And so, from one point of view, her widowhood was foreordained.

Thirty years previously, while on pilgrimage to Brindavan (the place where Kṛṣṇa supposedly spent his childhood), Mira took *"mantra dīkṣa"* (was initiated with a mantra) from a guru there. Her husband, who accompanied her, was not himself initiated—but his permission for her to take *dīkṣa* was required and he obliged. Mira sees her mantra as a kind of protective amulet. She said that with her mantra (recited in her mind) no *bhūt-pret* can harm her. This is different from Sarita who viewed her mantra as a kind of meditative and calming aid. As for the guru who initiated her, Mira said she rarely saw him after her trip to Brindavan, unless he happened to come to Banaras. Because this guru lived far away, Mira did not develop any kind of personal relationship with him. However, she mentioned later in the interview that she went to hear "many famous *svāmis* [learned holy men] who came to Banaras." She would most often go to Malviya Bhavan at Banaras Hindu University to listen to them. She said she received much inspiration from them, but now she is old and weary and does not go much. Based on these statements and on the fact that she was widowed for so many years and lived alone, it seems likely that if she had found a guru with whom she could develop a rapport she would have established a close relationship, even becoming his disciple, as so many older women do.[14]

Besides initiating her with a mantra, Mira's guru gave her general instructions on how she should conduct her life. He prescribed four *vrats* for her to follow. Mira had already been observing two of these—Rāmnaumī and Kṛṣṇa Janmāṣṭamī—since childhood. The other two—Vāman Dvādaśī and Nṛsiṃh Caturdaśī—are currently rarely observed. Mira herself said that "Nṛsiṃh Caturdaśī and Vāman Dvādaśī have almost vanished. Here very few people know about these *vrats*." The central rite of Vāman Dvādaśī involves feeding a Brahman boy and giving him gifts.

The day of the *vrat*, the boy represents Viṣṇu in his dwarf *avatār* ["descent" or incarnation]. Mira described it this way:

> [We fast on that day and then] any young boy, between eight and ten years old, who has gone through the sacred thread ceremony *(upanāyaṇ saṁskār)* [from] a Brahman family is called to our home and having cleaned his feet with our own hands we put a sandalwood *tīka* (mark) on his forehead and make him sit on a [handwoven pure cotton or wool] mat—and we do *pūjā* to him. We put a garland on him and place in his right hand a *kamaṇḍal* [brass vessel used by mendicants] and in the left hand a staff [*daṇḍa*]. Then we give him at least twenty-one rupees. We believe that Vāman god has come [in the form of the young boy]. . . . One time Lord Viṣṇu went to King Bali and took the form of a dwarf in order to deceive him and went to his palace to ask for *dān*. To remember that story we do this *vrat*.

Mira has observed seventeen different *vrats* during her life, including the ones mentioned above. When I asked her when and how she learned them she said she began to do *pūjā* when she was very young. Her grandparents told her to go into the house with the older ladies and do *pūjā*. Thus by observation and practice she learned from her own family the significance of *vrats* and how to perform them. She recalls:

> I started to do Rāmnaumī in my childhood because when I was very small on the Rāmnaumī day the elders of the house said to the children, "Today you will get a meal only after 12:00 because at noon Rāmcandraji took the form of an *avatār* [on the ninth day of Caitra]. So children were given fried bread and rice pudding to eat—and the older people sustained themselves on just fruit and milk. . . . Lord Rāmcandraji took the form of an *avatār* on the earth in Ayodhya because at that time the tyranny of the Rakṣaṣas was excessive. He came in order to protect the Brahmans and the cows. So all the people celebrated happily and did a *vrat* in Lord Rām's name. People especially go to Ayodhya because it is the birthplace of Rām. They take a bath in the Saryu River there; it is very meritorious. They stay there eating fruit.

Mira went on to recount in more detail the story of Rām, and she ended, "This is our belief. I sometimes go to Ayodhya too."

When she was a little older, her grandmother encouraged Mira to start observing the Sunday Vrat in the month of Māgh for seven consecutive Sundays with the other women in the family. A couple of years before her marriage was arranged, she started the Tīj Vrat, as her socialization into her impending wifehood was augmented. After marriage, she took on several more *vrats*—"for my husband's welfare; so that he'd be respected, blessed, prosperous and healthy." After her first child was born (when she was sixteen), she began *vrats* for children: Gaṇeś Cauth, Bahulā Cauth and Lalahī Chaṭh. She said that, in her day, all married women observed *vrats* as a matter of course. She said that widows usually stop keeping (most) *vrats*. Their "job is to teach young girls [about *pūjā* and *vrats*]—especially with regard to marriage preparation."

Concerning men and *vrats* Mira said that, "Men aren't involved with the different *vrats* and *pūjās*—they only worship God and read religious books." "So are women more religious than men?," I asked. Mira felt that women have more interest in worship than men. She said it is women's nature (to be more religious). God gave it to them. From this worship women gain success *(siddhis)*. Mira explained that a *siddhi* is the outward manifestation or fruition of a wish expressed in a sincere prayer (literally, "what is prayed for on the inside will appear on the outside").

When I asked Mira on another day about consulting astrologers, she replied that she did consult them, but only well-reputed ones. "There are a lot of quacks around," she told me; a sentiment echoed by many of the women I interviewed. Mira explained to me that she consults astrologers when bad circumstances arise. With the astrologer's help she finds out what stone she should wear and what mantra she should say. "But God, after all, knows what my wishes are. I don't need to specifically ask." This last, somewhat gratuitous comment reflected Mira's growing unease or perhaps impatience with astrology, or any elaborate rituals. She puts greater weight now on the efficacy of personal faith in God expressed in the simplest of devotional rituals—especially since her husband died. "Since the death of my husband I don't have that much belief [in rituals]. Now I believe only in God." And yet there was a slight sadness in her voice when she was commenting on the apparent gradual disappearance of *vrats* in the modern world. "My grandparents did more (*vrats*) than my parents did; my parents did more than I; I have done more than my daughter—and my daughter-in-law doesn't do any at all."

JYOTI

Jyoti, the forty-six-year-old daughter of Mira, lives with her husband and one of her four children in Delhi. She was born in Banaras and married at nineteen but continued with her studies, finishing with two master's degrees, in philosophy and in music. Her husband is a government servant and his work has taken them to several places in India, including Chandigarh and Madras. Like Kamala, despite her education Jyoti did not express a need or a desire to work outside the home. Even with a servant or two, there is plenty to do in the home and she feels that this work is a woman's primary duty. I found Jyoti to be commonsensical in her attitudes toward religion and *vrats* and something of a realist. For example, she said she does *vrats* to please her husband and the gods "and because this is a male-dominated society."

Jyoti told me that she does not have a preferred deity. Nor would she care to identify herself in any sectarian way. She has a shrine in her home with images of Śiv, Rām and Kṛṣṇa, and she performs a simple *pūjā* daily at this shrine. The rest of her family, Jyoti said, does not take much interest in religion—with the exception of her father-in-law in Lucknow who does a three-hour daily *pūjā*. Jyoti has been quite impressed with this demonstration of piety and discipline. She tries to read a portion of sacred text every day "but time is sometimes a problem." As for visiting temples, aside from special occasions, she goes to a Hanumān temple on Tuesdays, often accompanied by her daughter-in-law. She goes to this temple because she has taken on the *vrat* that was prescribed to her husband; a *vrat* which he had given up observing after a few weeks. He had long days at the office and was getting headaches from the partial fasting required. "Women have more resistance," she explained. As well, although she did not say this, it is typical for women to take up *vrats* for male family members who are unable to perform them. In several such cases that I encountered, the *vrats* that the women assumed had been prescribed to their male relatives upon examination of their horoscopes by pandits or astrologers.

With regard to pilgrimage, Jyoti mentioned that she saw many famous temples in the south of India on a tour she took with her mother, brother and daughter.[15] Jyoti has also been to the famous Vaiṣṇo Devī temple near Jammu. Her husband had taken mantra *dīkṣa* in Haridvar, but Jyoti said that she is still keeping her eyes open for a personal guru with whom she would be inspired to establish a connection.

Jyoti has observed ten different *vrats* during her life; nine are the same ones her mother has observed and one is new, the Tuesday Vrat, which she has taken over from her husband. There are several factors that help explain the continuity and discontinuity in *vrat* observance between mother and daughter. First, there is a strong relationship between *vrats* done by a woman and her natal family tradition. Four of the *vrats* that both Mira and Jyoti keep (Śivarātri, Rām Naumī, Navarātri, and Kṛṣṇa Janmāṣṭamī) are familial *vrats* that both have celebrated since childhood. Jyoti felt a desire to maintain these family *vrat* celebrations and encountered no resistance from her husband. She and her husband never lived with the rest of his family so she did not have to contend with competing traditions. Three other *vrats* that both mother and daughter keep are well-known *vrats* observed for the sake of a woman's husband: the Sāvitrī Vrat, the Tīj Vrat and the Karvā Cauth Vrat. The first two are known in the texts and are popular in many parts of central and northern India. Karvā Cauth is widely observed in the states of Uttar Pradesh, Haryana, Rajasthan, and the Panjab.[16] When she was still living in northern India, particularly in Delhi and Chandigarh, Jyoti experienced general reinforcement from neighbors, friends and others to continue with these *vrats*.[17] The Gaṇeś Cauth Vrat (in Māgh) is also well-known and observed by many women for their children.

The final *vrat* that both mother and daughter keep in common is the sixteen-day Mahālakṣmī Vrat. Jyoti said, however, that she only keeps this *vrat* "sometimes." This too is a woman's *vrat*, and keeping it alone—that is, without the company of other female relatives—would require a strong commitment. Clearly Jyoti was not so sure about her commitment and she admitted that she might abandon it in the near future.

As for the other *vrats* that her mother has performed which Jyoti herself has not taken up, two, Vāman Dvādaśī and Nṛhsiṃh Caturdaśī, are "out of fashion," as Jyoti put it. Indeed, I did not meet anyone else who kept these two *vrats*, though they both can be found in some modern *vrat kathā* books and in the Nibandhas. One may recall, however, that these *vrats* were prescribed by Mira's guru and so had no family tradition behind them. Three of the remaining *vrats* observed by Mira, Lalahī Chaṭh, Ānant Caturdaśī, and Śravaṇ Somvār, do not appear to be as widely observed by women as the Sāvitrī, Tīj, and Karvā Cauth *vrats*. While Lalahī Chaṭh is kept by women for the sake of children, the other two (directed to Viṣṇu and Śiva respectively) are performed by both men and women for generalized purposes. So again, without close relatives nearby to share in the performance of these *vrats*, there was less incentive for Jyoti to keep them. Finally, there is Ekādaśī—a *vrat* Mira keeps assiduously twice a month, but for which Jyoti feels no inclination nor does she feel she has the time right now to take it up.

Jyoti's mother, Mira, had consulted a religious almanac *(pañcāṅga)* as had her mother and grandmother. However, Jyoti has not done so. She gets information about *vrat* and festival days and times from weekly magazines such as *Dharm Yug* and *Saptahi Hindustan*. In 1984, she bought her first *vrat kathā* book to refamiliarize herself with the procedures and stories of *vrats*—since she does *vrats* mostly alone in Delhi and felt that she could not always rely on her own memory to do them properly.

At one point in our discussions, Jyoti began to tell me in a mixture of English and Hindi what she thought most women gained from observing *vrats*:

> Vrats and festivals [*tyauhār*] are connected. In the villages there isn't any entertainment, isn't any picture-hall, no club. So these *vrats* and festivals are also a form of entertainment. One *vrat*, which comes in the cold season, goes [like this]: [women] would go to a garden, sit under an *āṅvla* tree,[18] prepare food and eat it. Normally everybody's life was so busy they wouldn't go [and do that sort of thing], but because of that day [a *vrat/tyauhār* specially marked] they would cook food under the *āṅvla* tree and by eating there it became a kind of picnic; so in this way festival and *vrat* were mixed. For ladies especially it became an amusement. Men could listen to music, they could watch dance or folk theatre [*nautaṅkī*]; other entertainments were also allowed; but ladies could not go out, they were in *pardā* [seclusion]. So whatever entertainment they got was by doing this *vrat* or that festival.
>
> In certain festivals there is a stipulation that until you bathe in the Gaṅgāji or in some river you can't finish the *vrat*. So a whole group of women will go, bathe and come back. It was a big change for them. Thus on the one side . . . it was monotonous to daily make food, [look after] children—and in the middle of this came a break. A festival came and in the festival there was also a *vrat* with it; so in that they obtained some change [got a break from daily routine].

Kamala expressed a similar view about one of the important functions that *vrat* observances have among village women; that is, these rites provide the opportunity for women to socialize and escape from the monotony of daily routines.

Jyoti also mentioned the benefit she perceived for herself in observing a *vrat*: "It is good for self-discipline. It is good for one's health—both mental and physical." Although Jyoti had felt obliged to take on the *vrat* that her husband had left, Jyoti never spoke of keeping *vrats* "for *suhāg*." Rather, it was a combination of wanting to keep a connection with her mother's tradition and, as in Kamala's case, the value Jyoti found in the self-disciplinary features of *vrats* that appeared to be the strongest source of motivation for observing the *vrats* she keeps. Here again, my evidence contradicts the argument that all women's *vrats* are directed toward domestic and familial concerns.

SHYAMDEVI

> There was once a woman who made *uraḍ dāl ki kacaurī* [fried cakes made out of split peas] on a festival day and sat down to eat it. Nearby a crow was cawing; it kept circling around hoping that she would give him some. She ate but did not give any to the crow. She went inside the house. While cleaning the *kacaurī* [pan] whatever could not be removed [to eat] she threw out [into the courtyard]. The poor crow searched and took out only one grain. Up to the end of her life the woman didn't offer food. When she went to the other world she was very hungry; everyone received food except for her. She reported to Yamrāj [the lord of the underworld] that she was hungry. So he said, "Go, go. In that *nālā* [ditch] many seedlings may be found—you eat that." She went there and found black gram sprouts. She thought that she would husk them and eat a lot of *dāl*. But when she husked them she got only one grain. She ate it and then returned. Then she said, "Oh Lord, when I husked all the grains I only got one." He replied—"All right, have you not taken it? You gave one grain to the crow when you were eating *kacaurī*—that was written in the 'file,' so you got what you gave. You didn't give more so you didn't get more."

This story was offered as part of a response to a question I asked Shyamdevi (a Camar [Harijan] widow, aged around fifty-five) about giving *dān*. It also clearly illustrates the "reap what you sow" theme characteristic of the doctrine of karma. Like Mira,

Shyamdevi accepts that the reaping of karma takes place in the next world or life rather than in this world. She said, "Everyone wants to think that 'I have acted rightly'—but justice is [actually] meted out in the other world; here nothing happens. When God takes out your 'file'—on there itself will be seen that your actions were such and such; you have given this and that. . . . You can't fool around [alter the file] there." Shyamdevi's mentioning of Yamrāj (or later, Brahmāji's) "file" was, incidentally, the only time that she used an English word in her Hindi-Bhojpuri dialect. She went on to explain further about how the act of giving is related to one's karma:

> Say today in our house it is a festival so I will make *pūrī* [fried bread] and cooked foods; but we are very poor so it is not possible to give much. If there are four people I will have to give two [*pūrīs*] to each [person]; so there will have to be eight *pūrīs*, no? My child will eat, I will eat, so how many blessings will you get? For, I don't have anything [much]—so whatever I can give I will give. . . . Suppose you give your old *dāl*—you give one but it will be written as two . . . [in your file]. You will certainly receive that. [And] to whomever I have given, he too will have a contented *ātma*. So here [in this world] it [my action] may not be noted, [but] it is written there [in the next world]. When one goes from here then Brahmāji takes out one's 'file' and [sees that] such and such has been noted. Whatever I gave that will be noted and if I didn't give—that also will be noted. . . . Suppose here I said to others, "I gave that much"—but there it will be shown precisely *who* has given [and how much].

The duty to give to others—*dān* to Brahmans, feeding guests, giving alms to beggars—and the merit that can be acquired thereby is powerfully reinforced in India by narratives such as these told by Shyamdevi. In this case, miserliness, especially on festive occasions, is condemned.

Shyamdevi is illiterate. She is nonetheless gifted in storytelling and has a large repertoire of narratives which children and other women flock to hear when an occasion arises. Yet (perhaps because of her illiteracy) she is self-deprecating when it comes to her own years of accumulated wisdom which in fact she passes on through her stories.

> There are very great texts [literally *rāmāyaṇas*], and very great sayings [*kavitā*]. Old people know. You and I, what do we know?

> [We] are ignorants. . . . [My brother] has so many books, and he also studies a variety of things. Hearing all these things—so much has entered my own mind. Otherwise, how would I know this much? . . . At this advanced age I use my mind [*buddhi*] to learn.

Shyamdevi lives in a Harijan village, adjacent to Banaras Hindu University. She was born in Shukulpura in the west of Banaras, and was married at the age of twelve. She had three children, one of whom died, and she was widowed in her early thirties. She has had a hard life, exacerbated by the early death of her husband. "I had three small children when my husband died, therefore I had much trouble. Daily the whole day I did work in someone's field, [worrying], 'Can I earn 50 paise a day doing fieldwork? With 50 paise, can I feed three children?' . . . At home I also kept [grew] vegetables and going to the bazaar I used to sell them. By this means we lived." Her life is now somewhat easier since she makes a decent wage as a cook/housekeeper for foreign residents and her two surviving children have married. However, her work is still precarious, since her employers never stay in Banaras for more than a year or two. She also complained that the prices of basic groceries have risen dramatically in recent years, making it still difficult to make ends meet.

My interview with Shyamdevi was incomplete because of several interruptions and the limited spare time available to her during the day. Nevertheless, I have chosen to profile her because of the richness of her comments, anecdotes and stories and her practical common sense. In addition, profiling Shyamdevi provides an example of a low-caste woman's *vrat* activities and reflections. Certainly Shyamdevi, and her niece whom I interviewed as well, gave me the impression that most women in their village kept at least a few *vrat*s. According to Shyamdevi and her niece, many women in their village observed the same *vrat*s as they. The occasional sweeper, washerwoman and fruit-seller I asked also told me she did *vrat*s, and Tīj and Jiutiyā were specifically mentioned.

Shyamdevi's favored deity is Vindyācal Durgā Devī, a local form of Durgā whose worship is centered in a well-known temple about an hour's bus ride away. But it is to Gaṅgā Māī—"Mother Ganges"—that she seems to turn to frequently for help, judging by the many references Shyamdevi made to her. For example, she said at one point that sometimes when she is beset by some problem or other she goes to the river (a fifteen-minute walk away) and in Gaṅgā Māī's presence she prays: "O Gaṅgā Māī! May you cut loose this trouble [*kaṣṭ*], may my children live well. And then I will offer you lighted lamps or I will offer a pot [*kalaś*]. . . ." She does *pūjā* to the goddess every Monday. If she has time she goes to the temple; if not she offers water and flowers to a tree outside her home. Each month, on the Pūrṇamāsī (full moon) day, she "takes a *vrat*," bathes in the Ganges, listens with other women and men to a formal recitation of the Satyanārāyaṇ Kathā, and gives *dān* to the Brahman pandit who reads the story.[19] She has done the five-day Pañcakroś pilgrimage around Banaras four times and she said she will undertake it one more time.[20] She does both the monthly observances and the pilgrimage as a form of spiritual discipline, to acquire religious merit, and because, as she said, she enjoys it. She has a strong belief in the existence of *bhūt-pret* and recounted vivid stories about her own and others' experience with them.

Shyamdevi has kept nine different *vrat*s in her life.[21] However, she stopped all but two: Jiutiyā and the Pūrṇamāsī, when her husband died. She said one did not have to discontinue *vrat*s when one became a widow, but now as the principal breadwinner, she had little time and energy for *vrat*s. She said that she still does *pūjā* "sometimes" on the *vrat*-festival days, such as on Rāmnaumī and Naurātri. She said that she had performed an ending ceremony *(udyāpan)* for the *vrat*s that she abandoned, "otherwise I couldn't give them up because having kept *vrat*s it is difficult to abandon them." In other words, it seems she had grown attached to keeping these *vrat*s, and only gave them up reluctantly.

As for Jiutiyā—which she considers the most important and efficacious *vrat* "because it is the most difficult"—she said that she would keep it for as long as she remains alive, or as long as it is possible for her to do. She has kept it, as is the custom, for the sake of her children. She learned this *vrat* and its stories from her mother, and is passing it on to her daughter-in-law. "Sometimes my *bahū* will keep [this] *vrat*, so on that day, after doing the *pūjā*, I take out [the Jiutiyā threads] from my neck and put them on hers. My *bahu* will take it over fully when I can't do it anymore." Unlike some others, Shyamdevi had no sense that *vrat*s as a whole were going out of practice. She was confident that these traditions would continue.

Like Sarita, Shyamdevi said that the most important element in a *vrat* observance, the "first thing," is *viśvās*. For her, the observance of *vrat*s, which in her descriptions amounts to a kind of bartering with the gods, is one way, and an important one, of trying to alleviate or keep at bay the difficulties thrown in one's path. By pleasing the gods and attracting their attention, one compels them to respond to one's acts of worship and self-sacrifice.

> [When I keep *vrat*s I say] "O God, I am keeping a *vrat*—I have to endure some difficulties for a little while," so the one who is above [God] will solve my problems. "Because this woman underwent some hardship, let us help, give some assistance." Whichever goddess or god we may do a special *pūjā* to or keep a *vrat* for, they will come to our aid, and they will help our children too. Suppose some trouble afflicts us—"O my god! My life will leave me!" [During] whatever *pūjā* I do I will [recite in my mind]: "I am daily remembering you, I am doing your *vrat*—so make my troubles go away." I don't know who [which god] stands up and answers my call, makes my troubles go away.
>
> [In our village] children, after taking a bath, daily give one vessel [*loṭa*] of water to Sūrya Nārāyaṇ. So he also then blesses our children, wherever they may be, [saying] "May you remain happy, may no enemy kill you, may no confrontation take place, may you not be cheated, may you come and go peacefully." For that alone everyone does *pūjā*, gives water; for that alone they keep *vrat*s too—to cast off sorrows.

KIRAN

Kiran, aged twenty-two when I met her, was an unmarried Pahari Brahman living at home in the hill town of Mussoorie, north of Delhi. She has a master's degree in English and was teaching Hindi at a private school while her parents sought to find her a suitable husband. Kiran was one of my Hindi teachers during a summer I spent in Mussoorie. She helped correct the translations of *vrat kathā* books that I was working on at the time. Inevitably there transpired discussions about *vrat*s and eventually I undertook formal interviews with both Kiran and her mother.

Kiran and her mother described themselves as "Sanātani." Her own favored deities are Śiv and Rām (while her mother said that she had no favored deity). Her family has a shrine in their home—to "all the gods" (Rām, Kṛṣṇa and Radhā, Śiv and Pārvatī,

Viṣṇu and Laksmī, Brahmā, Gaṇeś, Devī [Durgā], and Sarasvatī). She does not perform a regular *pūjā* at home because both her parents, separately, do a *pūjā* for between fifteen and forty minutes morning and evening. She says the Gāyatrī mantra (one of the most sacred and revered verses of the *Ṛgveda*[22]) occasionally, "when tired, tense or when having problems—but not often." She said that this mantra brings her inspiration and peace of mind. Kiran learned the mantra from her mother and neither of these women subscribed to the orthodox view that women are not authorized to utter a vedic mantra like the Gāyatrī. Kiran goes to the closest Hindu temple on Tuesdays and festival days. When she was younger, she went on pilgrimage with her parents to the nearby towns of Rishikesh and Haridvar. Both towns are the site of many temples and ashrams, and both have attracted numerous pandits and ascetics. When I asked Kiran if she had or wanted to have a guru, she replied that her parents were her guru—and so were books.

Kiran said that she believes in the existence of *prets* and *bhūts*, and "very much" in the doctrine of karma and *punarjanma*. She and her family also believe in astrology; "I'd like to consult an astrologer to know about my future," she said. But she did not think that there were any "good" astrologers in the area and she asked me to refer her to one in Banaras. Kiran's family was especially concerned about her slightly mentally-retarded sister and they wanted some good advice about how to help her, and forecasts for her future. Their family pandit of ten years had not proved to be sufficiently helpful to them in solving this daughter's problems.

Kiran has observed four different *vrats*: Śivarātri, Navarātri, and Kṛṣṇa Janmāṣṭamī on a regular basis since childhood, and Śravaṇ Somvār from time to time. At the time, Kiran rated all the *vrats* she had kept as equally important. After she gets married, she said she would take up more *vrats* for her husband and any children she might have.

Since I was interested in the perceptions that women had of any correlation, positive or negative, of frequency of *vrat* observance and age, I asked Kiran (and other women) if they thought older women observe more *vrats* than younger women. Kiran thought that older women probably do keep more *vrats*, "widows especially." While certainly not uniformly the case, the general perception of the younger women whom I interviewed, both married and unmarried, is that older women perform more *vrats* than younger women. However, this perception is not consistent with the responses of older women. For example, Nirmala (sixty-five) and Gulab (sixty-six), both widows, and Sartarji (seventy-one), still married, said that they had observed more *vrats* when they were younger. Gulab explained that she is weaker now; "most *vrats* I keep nowadays are for my sons." In analyzing the comments of women on this issue I found that many of the younger women, still in the midst of caring for children and managing a household, experience the relentless limitations on their time and look to the future when some leisure time may reemerge and they can focus on the pursuit of self-directed religious activity. Besides this, their own deaths seem remote. Other women, especially the older ones, understand that as a woman ages and begins to experience physical infirmities, activities like fasting become more difficult. Observing *vrats* is no longer within the realm of their abilities, even if the time is there. While widows are expected to concern themselves primarily with such religious practices, those I knew had turned more to prayer and meditation. Some women, however, spoke not about older or younger women observing more or less *vrats*, but about the importance of persevering with those *vrats* that for women (married and widowed) are felt to be reflective of their responsibilities as women.

Kiran gave me a detailed description of Śivarātri, a *vrat* which she said had always been observed in her family. She started when she was very young—watching her parents do it and then gradually beginning to participate. Kiran saw that "it was part of *dharm*, and that it brought a different kind of peace and satisfaction" to her parents. On the morning of Śivarātri, when they get up, each family member takes a bath and puts on clean clothes. Then each person does his or her own *pūjā* (Kiran initially sat with her mother, and then when she became a teenager she started to do it herself). The *pūjā* involves lighting incense and sometimes small oil lamps *(dīp)*, and then sprinkling a little water, milk, sandal, red tumeric, flowers, fruit, woodapple leaves and sweets on the image. This is followed by a circling of lights *(āratī)* accompanied by the uttering of verses in praise of Śiva. Kiran learned some of the verses from her mother, and others she learned from a book. After the *āratī* Kiran goes to the temple in the morning or afternoon with her family. One person brings a steel platter *(thālī)* filled with the *pūjā* offerings and a copper *loṭa* of water. They are not supposed to eat anything before going to the temple. They do exactly the same *pūjā* at the temple. The reason they go to the temple and repeat the *pūjā*, she said, is because the food and money that is offered can then be redistributed by the temple committee to poorer people. The family receives some *prasād* (consecrated food) and goes home. At home they can drink tea and milk and in the evening, after saying a few more prayers, they can eat only fruit, potato, coconut and *caulai* (a green leafy vegetable). The main food restriction for any *vrat*, Kiran affirmed, was that one could not eat *anāj* (literally "grain," but in the context of *vrats* usually understood to include a wider array of foods). She provided a rationale for not eating *anāj*, explaining that "it is good for the stomach to have a break from these harsher foods."

When I asked Kiran how she would define a *vrat* she said that it was for *santoṣ* (satisfaction, happiness). "It involves sacrifice, which is connected to *dharm*." "Yes, it is following *dharm*," she concluded.

Each of the six women profiled in this chapter takes the *vrat* tradition seriously and has confidence in the efficacy of these rituals. *Vrats* form a significant part of their cultural (as Indians and Hindus) and social (as women) identity. Kamala is well-educated and perceptive. While her experience of the non-Hindu and non-Indian world is limited, she is aware of other possibilities; other ways of life and points of view. She is firmly committed to the traditions of her ancestors, which include the observance of many calendrical *vrats* and festivals. Yet that commitment is not blind, for Kamala tries to find explanatory models from within Hinduism that give a rational basis for the various rituals and religious practices. She has thought deeply about the meaning of the *vrat* tradition, and has found their self-disciplinary features to be of great significance to her own spiritual development.

Mira's spiritual formation and self-understanding are shaped by centuries of brahmanic traditions which she does not seriously question, even if, as she has aged, she has begun to feel some unease with these traditions. She adopted her performance of *vrats* as a matter of course; these rituals were expected of married women, so she performed them. However, Mira sees, through her daughter and daughters-in-law, that drastic changes are occurring in the "way of life" for women, and she is not certain that rituals such as *vrats* will survive such changes.

Mira's daughter, Jyoti, educated in a large national university, speaking some English, living with a relatively secular husband in a nuclear family, and in several different urban localities, is between two worlds—but seems comfortably so. The environment of her childhood undoubtedly continues to exert a strong influence on her so that she still feels an attachment to rituals like *vrat*s, and feels respect for genuine piety. Yet, unlike her mother, Jyoti has had to make an effort to relearn some of the *vrat*s and for the most part has to perform them on her own, without the support and companionship of other women. Thus, while she observes fewer *vrat*s than her mother did, she may well keep them with greater conviction.

Sarita is probably the most pious woman among those profiled. Since her mother-in-law died and her children have now left home, there is no longer a buffer between herself and her difficult husband. In drawing on her own resources to cope with the strained marriage and the demands of her husband, Sarita has turned to her faith as a source of strength and consolation. While she claimed that women do not perform *vrat*s for their own desires, it became clear that the *vrat*s she keeps have come to be predominately an expression of her faith in Durgā and Śiv; and that such faith is rewarded with feelings of peace and satisfaction.

Shyamdevi is illiterate, poor, and has been confronted with continual hardship; but her sense of humor, the support of kin and the esteem in which she is held in her village community have helped to develop her self-confidence. She has a clear sense of herself and her place in the religiously defined cosmos. Shyamdevi is impelled neither by a particularly strong sense of tradition or of piety or faith in God. Rather, it is the practical and instrumental nature of *vrat*s that she emphasized: *vrat*s are a means to solve, lessen or prevent various problems that arise in one's life, due in large measure to the workings of karma and fate. The point of *vrat*s is to please the gods so that in turn they will feel inclined to help one out.

Kiran is, in some ways, a young version of Kamala. She is well-educated though, unlike Kamala, she has had extensive contact with foreigners. She comes from a religious and fairly orthodox Brahman family. Kiran does not now question that her primary role will be that of wife and mother, and she sees *vrat*s as very much a part of that role. But with her rationalistic mind, *vrat*s will have to prove themselves a "good" thing in various ways for her to assume more of them, and to continue performing *vrat*s down the years. That is, Kiran will have to find an intellectually and personally satisfying meaning in the *vrat* tradition for her to follow through their performance.

More will be learned about these women in the ensuing chapters as I continue to explore their understanding of the nature of *vrat*s and of how *vrat*s are situated for them within the continuum of related Hindu religious practices. In particular, it will become apparent that these women are not merely motivated to observe *vrat*s for *suhāg* or from a sense of duty, but that *vrat*s provide an opportunity for women to achieve individual spiritual development. How the observance of *vrat*s is linked to individual spiritual development, ethical (and material) concerns, and the larger social good, as well as to ascetic disciplines are all elaborated in the textual tradition treating of *vrata*. It is to this textual tradition, then, that I now turn in order to investigate the history of ideas and practices that have informed and shaped the current practice of *vrat*s by Hindu women.

2

The Concept of *Vrata* in the Hindu Textual Tradition

VRATA IN THE EARLY LITERATURE: *ṚGVEDA* TO DHARMASŪTRAS

Like many other important Sanskrit words, "*vrata*" appears in the earliest and most revered group of texts of classical Hinduism, the Vedas. In the *Ṛgveda*, the oldest of the Vedas, *vrata* occurs just over 200 times alone or in combination with other words (Kane 1974, 5,1:4), and it continues to turn up with some regularity in the later vedic Saṃhitās, Brāhmaṇas, Upaniṣads and Sūtras. However, while the word *vrata* occurs often enough in this literature, its meaning is far from clear.[1] Indeed, there has been some lively controversy among scholars about the etymology (and hence early meanings) of this term. The controversy has centered on the problem of which root *vrata* is derived from.[2] P. V. Kane, following the lead of the St. Petersburg Dictionary,[3] preferred the root *vṛ*—"to choose, select" as the best derivation for *vrata*, and in fact this derivation is approved very early in the classical Hindu tradition as it is given by the influential lexicographer Yāska in his *Nirukta* (c. 6th to 5th century B.C.E.). It is the one that will probably remain the most widely accepted.[4]

In general, one can say that the concept of *vrata* in the *Ṛgveda* is closely connected with the larger metaphysical concept of the cosmic order *(ṛta)*, with *dharma* (perhaps the key concept in the Hindu tradition, but whose full ramifications have yet to emerge in the *Ṛgveda)*, and with the governed and governing activity of the gods. In many contexts the word has the sense of "immutably fixed ordinances" that keep the universe in order (keep or support the *ṛta)* and to which *all* beings are subject. In one passage, RV 9.112.1, it is stated that the various vocations in which men engage are their various *vratas*. A person's *vrata* may be "that of priest, or of warrior or ruler, or of some humbler occupation—physician or bard or artisan or agriculturalist" (Brown 1978, 112).[5] It is also not surprising to find that "the sacrifice, which is the single most important activity that vedic man could perform, is described as a *vrata* at RV 1.93.8" (Heckaman 1980, 57). Some *vratas* seem to be related to individual status and primary roles—so that one god's *vrata* may be quite different from another's, the *vratas* of humans different from those of the gods, or the *vrata* of a male cowherd different from that of a female teacher. Other *vratas* seem to have universal application. In all cases failure to comply with one's specific *vrata* or with the *vratas* decreed by the gods for all to observe is portrayed as a moral offence against the gods and against Order *(ṛta)* and Truth *(sat)*.

As is well known, a number of passages from the *Ṛgveda* reappear in later Saṃhitās, and these include some with the word *vrata*.[6] With respect to the usage of *vrata* in the later Saṃhitās, Brāhmaṇas and Upaniṣads, Kane notes that while *vrata* appears "here and there" in the sense of "ordinance of a god or of gods" the usual senses of *vrata* in these texts are two:

> (1) religious observance or vow, or restrictions as to food and behaviour when one has undertaken a religious vow, or (2) the special food, that is prescribed for sustenance when a person is engaged in a religious rite or undertaking such as cow's milk, *yavāgā* (barley gruel) or the mixture of hot milk and curds (called *amikṣā*). (1974, 5,1:23)

What Kane means by "religious observance" or "vow" are prescribed ritualistic obligations incumbent on the sacrificer *(yajamāna)* before, during or after a vedic sacrifical ritual. These may include general ethical injunctions ("He should not speak what is untrue"), behavioral restrictions (not to eat meat, not to sleep, not to have sexual intercourse with a woman), and specific kinds of injunctions ("he should not wash his clothes in salt water").[7]

The Āraṇyakas and Upaniṣads offer new nuances for the meaning of *vrata*—as well as carrying over older senses. This is not surprising, considering the radically different orientation and intended audience of these texts. The new significations reflect the interest in metaphysical, ascetic and meditational themes characteristic of this literature. M. Bhagat in his book on ancient Indian asceticism mentions the "Arunaketuka Vrata" in the *Tait-*

tirīya Āraṇyaka (I.1.32) prescribed for *ṛṣis* (mendicants) where the *vrata* seems to be an open-ended course of behavior for the seeker of knowledge. The *ṛṣis* "should live on water or every day eat whatever is obtained by begging—should worship Agni; they should not have any possession; they should live in [the] forest; wear '*Kśauma*' garment[s], either yellow or white[,] and carry on the pursuit of knowledge" (1976, 120–21). While such a "vow" anticipates the *sannyāsin*'s (renouncer's) *vratas* of later Hinduism, it also anticipates the introduction of ascetic behavior and values into the concept of *vrata* as we find it in the Purāṇas and Nibandhas.

Typically, the Upaniṣads go further in their rarefaction of the idea of *vrata*. The statement of the *Bṛhadāraṇyaka Upaniṣad* (1.5.21–23), writes Terrance Day, "that 'one should perform only one *vrata*,' namely, one should only breathe in and emit breath 'for fear that Death may seize him' reflects a yogic specificality in the usage of the word *vrata*." But, he goes on,

> since in the Taittirīya Upaniṣad (3.7–10) several *vratas* are mentioned—namely, one should not speak ill of food; one should not shun food; one should not refuse accommodation to a needy stranger, etc., it appears that *vrata* applies not only to strictly religious or liturgical procedures, observances, and obligations, but to propriety itself in the sense of the conduct proper to each situation which arises. (1982, 254n5)

Of course, "proper conduct" frequently *is* religiously prescribed, but the point is that some of these examples reveal a moral dimension to the concept of *vrata* that, while perhaps implicit in its vedic usage, becomes increasingly explicit in the later (especially dharmaśāstric) literature, as we shall see.

Kane also observed that the sense of "a proper course or pattern of conduct for a person"—in a more secular sense—is a "secondary" meaning of *vrata*, though he obtains this from the Brāhmaṇas rather than the Upaniṣads. Kane cites an example from the *Aitareya Brāhmaṇa* which is essentially advice—called a *vrata*—for the proper conduct of a king vis-à-vis his enemy (1974, 5,1:25). Brief mention should also be made of another "secondary" meaning of *vrata* which Kane derived from certain contexts in the Brāhmaṇas—that of *upavāsa* or a fast.[8] The connection of *vrata* with *upavāsa* or fast will continue to evolve in the literature up to the present day.

It is the second of Kane's two "ordinary senses of *vrata*," that is, food or sustenance when a person is engaged in a religious rite, that is taken up by Keith and Macdonell in their *Vedic Index of Names and Subjects*. They say that *vrata* in the Saṃhitās and Brāhmaṇas "has the peculiar sense of 'milk' used by one who is living on that beverage alone as a vow or penance."[9] These references, as the ones cited by Kane, often refer to the *dikṣita* (one undergoing a *dīkṣa* or consecration ceremony for a vedic sacrifice). During the ceremony the *dikṣita* undergoes purificatory rites and milk is considered one of the substances that is particularly pure and suitable for the sacrificer. In this case *vrata*, identified with the milk, may symbolize the purifying process which the initiand is undergoing—as *dīkṣa* has also been construed as an initiation rite.[10] Interestingly, the ritual practices involved in the *dīkṣa* ceremony have a number of parallels with *vrata* rites as described in later literature such as the Purāṇas. For example, the *dikṣita* must eat only certain foods or refrain from eating particular types of food, he makes a series of oblations into the fire *(homa)*, recites certain mantras, and feeds and gives gifts to Brahmans.

The link between *vrata* and *dīkṣa* appears again in both the Śrautasūtras (aphoristic texts on vedic sacrifices, based on the Brāhmaṇas) and the Gṛhyasūtras (texts detailing domestic rituals for the householder, c. 600–400 B.C.E.). Gonda has pointed out that the Gṛhyasūtras generally use the term *vrata* in connection with the *dīkṣa* of the young boy about to become *brahmacārin* (a celibate student under the tutelage of a Brahman preceptor), but also with the *dīkṣa* of a *snātaka* (one who has finished his studentship and is ready to become a householder) and of a householder (1965, 329–31). The *vratas* as part of the *dīkṣa* are intended to prepare the initiand for the study of sacred texts and to make him a recipient of its fruits. Yet even after the *dīkṣa* a student was expected to undertake particular *vratas* when he studied a new section of vedic literature.[11] So, for example,

> before a student began to study the *Mahānāmnī* or *Sakvarī* verses forming a supplement to the *Sāma-Veda*, he has to prepare himself by keeping a vow, the *sakvarī-vrata* for twelve, nine, six, or at least three years. . . . Among the many duties connected with this vow, the student was required to wear a single [dark] cloth . . . and eat dark food; he should keep standing during the day time, and pass the night sitting; when it rained he should not seek cover; . . . After he has prepared himself by

> these and other austerities, the verses were recited to him. (Chakladar 1962, 569–70)

The Śrautasūtras also mention *vrata* in connection with, for example, the special initiation restraints on behavior during the preparatory period of the new paterfamilias' first kindling of the *gārhapatya* (home) fire.[12] His *vrata*, which may be in effect for up to a year, consists of the sort of behavioral restrictions we have previously described.[13]

In the early Dharmasūtras (c. 600–300 B.C.E., religio-juridical texts), the term *vrata* continues to have the sense of restrictions concerning food and behavior during a certain stage in one's life, that is, as a *brahmacārin*, *gṛhasthin*, *vānaprasthin* or *sannyāsin* (what McGee has called "*āśrama vratas*"), or as part of the purificatory and initiatory rituals in connection with vedic rites and sacrifices. The *Āpastamba Dharmasūtra*, for example, has a section on the *vratas* of *snātakas* regarding garments, answering calls of nature, scandalous talk, not seeing the rising or setting sun, and avoiding moral faults such as anger. This text also "specifies the observances [*vratas*] to be followed by the husband and wife from the day of their marriage such as eating only twice in the day, not eating to satiety, fasting on *parvan* days."[14]

Before we leave these texts, it is worth recording McGee's observation about certain rituals for ensuring worldly success in the Gṛhya and Dharmasūtras that may well have also contributed to the shape of the later Purāṇa and Nibandha *vratas*. She writes:

> These include the *śanti* rites for averting evil, the precautionary *puṇyāha* rites for removing inauspiciousness preceding or during religious rituals, the *svastyayana* ceremonies for ensuring safe journeys, the *āyuṣṭya* rites for long life, and the *māṅgala* rites for increasing one's wealth.[15]

In the *Manu* (c. 100 B.C.E.–100 C.E.) and *Yājñavalkya* (c. 100–300 C.E.) Dharma Smṛtis—texts which are frequently quoted as sources of authority on *dharma* by later digest writers—*vrata* is identified primarily with the prescribed rites of expiation or penance *(prāyaścittas)*.[16] This identification of *vrata* with penance continues to hold throughout the Dharmaśāstra literature as a secondary meaning of *vrata* or, put differently, as a certain kind of *prāyaścitta*. An example from *Manu* is: "But after he has fully performed the penance [*vrata*], he must give to

[Brahmanas] learned in the Veda ten cows and a bull, [or] if he does not possess [so much property] he must offer to them all he has" (11.117).[17] And, *Yājñavalkya Smṛti* 3.254: "Wearing a woollen garment and matted locks he [one who drinks liquor] should perform the penance of Brahmanicide [*brahmahatyā-vratam*]; he should eat, in the night, cakes of sesame seeds or particles of rice for three years."[18]

The preceding review of the usage of the word *vrata* shows that the term shifted its meaning from its earliest usage in the *Ṛgveda* to its use in the Smṛtis of Manu and Yājñavalkya. In the *Ṛgveda*, *vrata* seems to have denoted the fixed functions or duties of all beings (be they god, human, or animal) which preserve and support the *ṛta* (cosmic Order or Truth) through the power of *dharman* ("righteousness"). In the later vedic Saṃhitās and Brāhmaṇas, the concept of *vrata* (as Kane suggests) gradually came to be restricted as the concept of *dharma* became more all-embracing, while the term *ṛta* disappeared from usage altogether. In certain contexts the term *vrata* came to refer to the restrictions of food and behavior undertaken by a particpant in a rite such as a sacrifice or a *dīkṣa*. But, it also came to be applied to the special food prescribed during such a religious rite. In the early Smṛti texts a *vrata* included not only rules of conduct in particular circumstances, but also referred to the prescriptions for expiating the negative effects of breaking those (and other) rules of conduct.

VRATA IN THE EPICS: THE MAHĀBHĀRATA

The word *vrata* appears numerous times in the *Mahābhārata*[19]—chronologically the first and the lengthier of India's two great Sanskrit epics. Its usage here reveals a wide array of meanings some of which are found in earlier texts and others which portend later usage. One reason for this wide array may be due to the fact that the epic itself was orally transmitted for many centuries and so reflected the shifting meanings of *vrata*. Later Smṛti writers (authors of the Purāṇas and Nibandhas) quote from sections of the epic as authoritative statements on *vrata*. In particular, the Śanti and Anuśāsana *parvans* are quoted most frequently, two books which are now considered to have received the most recent interpolations.

In the *Mahābhārata*, *vrata* as a kind of rite or vow, whether in a "religious" or "secular" context, begins to come to life. For the first time, particular individuals are associated with the observance of a *vrata*, including women. The *vratas* themselves range from a simple vow not to refuse to play dice when challenged (Yudhiṣṭhira's vow, Sabhāparvan 58.16) to nondescript, almost monastic vows (general self-restrictive behavior) accordant with a Brahman status and way of life. Finally, there are vows that sound more like present-day *vratas*. Sometimes what the *vrata* entails is described, but often it is not. Sometimes a specific purpose for the rite or vow is given, other times it is not.

In notes on his translation of the *Mahābhārata*, van Buitenen wrote:

> 'Vow' or 'life-rule' will consistently translate *vrata*, a self-chosen life-rule involving abstinences, usually vowed for a particular term; it cannot be broken except to the detriment of a person's 'truth'. Since especially the brahmin way of life involves *vratas* of various kinds, the description 'strict vows' can be applied to almost any brahmin. (1973, 1:436)

While his comments are not incorrect, they do not properly describe the full range of usage of *vrata* actually found in the text.

The most common usage of *vrata* (thirteen out of twenty-five times in the Adiparvan) occurs, as van Buitenen notes, in the context of a description of a Brahman—priest or *ṛṣi*—who is of good character and action; in other words, one who acts in ways deemed appropriate to the Brahman *varṇa*. For example,

> At this feast, son of the bard Lomaharṣaṇa, the learned family chieftain has taken the office of the *brahman* priest, capable, keeping to his vows, . . . An invariably truthful man, given to serenity, austere and strict in his vows [*dhṛta vrata*], he is esteemed by all of us. (1.4.5)
>
> He was a great seer who never spilled his seed, . . . well-versed in the Law and relentless in his vows. (1.13.9)
>
> [N]o one was to surpass him [Kṛṣṇa Dvaipāyana = Vyāsa] in austerities, in the study of the *Veda*, in the observance of vows and fasts, in progeny, or in temper. (1.54.4)

The specifics of these vows are rarely spelled out in the epic. Yet from their contexts one can surmise that the *vratas* were indeed a kind of self-imposed and hence "chosen life-rule" involving various behavioral restrictions observed for particular periods of time, serially or indefinitely. Though some of the vows may be chosen, others were evidently prescribed (as part of the observance of vedic rituals). In many examples it is unclear whether the vows are performed for any particular purpose other than to submit oneself to the now generally esteemed (though in the *Mahābhārata* ambivalently viewed)[20] "culture of austerity"; that is, the practices of self-restraint and the cultivation of its creative power *(tapas*, see below). One can at least say, without doubt, that the observance of *vratas* was considered praiseworthy behavior.[21]

In other contexts we can see that male Brahmans were not the only ones to observe vows. The Kshatriyas Dṛtarāṣṭra, Pāṇḍu and Vidūra are said to have undergone the "life-cycle ceremonies" *(saṃskāras*), *vratas* and studies until they reached manhood (1.102.16). Here again the *vratas* may refer to those indicated in the Brāhmaṇas and the Sūtras in conjunction with vedic study.[22] A king's people are said to do *vratas*, among other things, in the following passage: "Bent upon sacrifice and vow, wont to pursue liberality, ritual, and Law [*dharma*], . . . the people were prosperous then" (1.102.5). Not surprisingly, Shudras are denied the *vratas* and observances of the three upper *varṇas*: "obedience to the twice-born is declared to be the [*dharma* of Śūdras], as it is of those who study with a guru, though the former are denied the mendicancy, oblations, and vows of the latter" (3.149.37). This does not mean, however, that Shudras could not engage in *any vratas*, for another passage from the late Anuśāsanaparvan (106.11 and 13), echoing *Manu* and other Dharmaśāstras, "provides that brāhmaṇas and kṣatriyas should not engage in a continuous fast for more than three days and that vaiṣyas and śūdras can observe a continuous fast for two days only."[23]

The description "of good vows" *(suvrata)* or "of strict vows" *(niyatavrata)* could also apply to women, as in these passages:

> [A]nd Satyavatī of the good vows bade Bhīṣma farewell and departed for the forest with both her daughters-in-law. They did awesome austerities, and at last the princesses shed their bodies . . . and went the great journey. (1.119.10)
>
> This Pṛthā, Kuntibhoja's daughter, was gifted with beauty and character; she rejoiced in [*dharma*] and was great in her vows [*mahāvratā*]. (1.105.1)
>
> What beauty did Princess Śantā of strict vow possess that she seduced his heart when he lived like a deer? (3.110.8)

Or, in the case of a mother-in-law, Kuntī, who in exhorting her daughter-in-law, Draupadī, to good behavior says: "Be thou the wife at their sacrifices, strict in thy vows, and gifted with joy!" (1.191.5). Once more, it is not clear whether specific sorts of *vratas* are being exhorted or whether the phrase once more refers to a general attitude and conventionally prescribed and esteemed self-restrictive behavior. What *is* significant is that women, no less than men, were expected to subject themselves to this sort of self-restrictive behavior in this form. In later Sanskrit didactic literature women's vows and fasts are increasingly channeled explicitly to the service of husbands.

Demons *(asuras*—the confounders of *dharma)* are also portrayed as performing (ascetic) vows and mortifications. The reasons for undertaking such a course of behavior are, of course, usually sinister rather than benign. But even if their intentions are sinister, the power *(tapas)* arising from such self-mortification is still available to them.[24]

Specific *vratas* in the sense of expiation *(prāyaścitta)* can be assigned in given circumstances. For example, Arjuna says to King Dharma (Yudhiṣṭhira), "Assign me my vow [*vratam ādi śyatāṃ mama*]. I have violated the covenant by looking at you" (1.205.24) [when Yudhisthira was occupied with Draupadī].

Observing a *vrata* for particular ends such as having children also appears in the epic, ends which are very familiar to contemporary *vrata* observers. For example, "It was at this very time that the radiant Goddess, Dakṣa's . . . daughter Vinatā, was wishing for a son. Her austerities performed, her vows for the birth of a son faithfully fulfilled, the pure woman lay with her husband" (1.27.25). Or, in the description of the birth of the Paṇḍavas (fathered by five gods), Pāṇḍu wants a fourth son through Indra and he says:

> I shall obtain from him a powerful son when I have satisfied him with austerities. The son that he will give me shall be my choicest. Therefore I shall mortify myself greatly in acts, thoughts and words. Thereupon the lustrous Pāṇḍu Kaurava took counsel with the great seers and enjoined on Kuntī a holy, year-long vow. The strong-armed prince himself stood on one foot and with supreme concentration undertook awesome austerities. (1.114.17-21)

Pleased with the demonstration of devotion, Indra obliges Pāṇḍu with a boon.[25]

In the story of Sāvitrī (3.42.277–83), a story which is the basis of a three-day annual *vrata* still widely observed by women in India,[26] we find a description of a rigorous *niyama* (bodily and mental self-restraints) performed for the purpose of begetting a child. This *niyama* is, in essence, a *vrata*, which is why van Buitenen translates the word as "vow." This is an early example of the conceptual relationship between *vrata* and *niyama;* a relationship which is clearly established in the Purāṇas. In the episode King Aśvapati, the father-to-be of Sāvitrī, undertakes a severe vow to beget a child. "At mealtimes he restricted his food, he was continent and subdued his senses, he offered oblations a hundred thousand times with the *sāvitrī* formula [mantra] . . . and forewent his meal every sixth time." He observes this life-rule for eighteen years at which time the goddess Sāvitrī (after whom he later names his daughter) grants him a boon, being well pleased with his "continence, purity, restraint [*niyama*], and self-control [*dama*]," as well as with his "whole-hearted devotion" to the goddess. He asks for offspring, and is granted a daughter in due time. It is remarkable that the description of this *niyama* undertaken for the purpose of having a child is not so very different in broad outline from current *vrat* practices among women in India: the kind and amount of food is curtailed, *pūjā* is performed, behavior is altered in certain self-restrictive ways for a (predetermined) period of time.

Sāvitrī—The Ideal Wife as Practitioner of Severe Austerities *(Tapasvinī)*

The Sāvitrī story, in fact, offers us more that can shed light on the concept of *vrata* as it was developed in literature subsequent to the epics, as well as on related ideas about Hindu women. Later in the story, the "Śṛī-like" daughter Sāvitrī, who has married a prince (Satyavat) whom she knew was fated to die within a year, undertakes a three-night vow (*vrata*) just prior to her husband's appointed death. In this vow she stands all night each night. Her father-in-law tries to dissuade her because he thinks Sāvitrī's austerities are too severe. However, she remains firm and her reply is interesting: "Do not feel sorry, father, I shall finish the vow; for it is done with resolve [*vyavasāya*], and resolve is the reason" (280.6). In other words, her fixed determination (or resolution) is her support during her self-imposed acts of austerity, and is what makes these acts of austerity a vow. On the morning of the third day of the *vrata*, her parents-in-law encourage her to eat. Evidently, then, her vow also involved fasting of some sort, and the breaking of the fast would signal the *vrata*'s completion. But she refuses, saying, "I shall eat when the sun is down and I have fulfilled my wish. This is the intention [*saṅkalpa*] and covenant I have conceived in my heart" (280.17). Her intention, of course, is to save her husband's life, which, unknown to both him and to his parents, is under mortal threat that day.

Sāvitrī's resolve may or may not have been formally spoken (as it should be according to the much later Sanskrit digests on *vratas*). What is important for Sāvitrī is her resolve to fulfill the vow she had made to herself, so that the vow in turn fulfills her wishes. It is the firmness of her intent, despite being "gaunt from [her] fast and vow" as her husband remarks, that further gives her the stamina to follow Satyavat into the woods. ("I am not weak from my fast, and I do not feel fatigue. I have set my heart on going, please don't stop me!" [280.21].) Her singleness of purpose lends her the courage to confront the terrifying god of death, Yama, when he arrives to take away the soul of the unconscious Satyavat. Finally, it is her knowledge of *dharma* (the Law) together with her nimbleness of mind that eventually outwits Yama and wins back her husband's life and more.

Sāvitrī herself declares to Yama that her course shall be unobstructed through "the power of my austerities, my conduct toward my elders, my love for my husband, my vow, and by thy grace" (281.21). Significantly, these are more or less the same elements (including her resolve, determination and faith) to which women votaries in present day India attribute the efficacy of their *vrats*.

One of the most important ideas found in the story of Sāvitrī is that of the power of *tapas* (literally "heat," but it came to include in its meanings the practice of austerities) in relation to *vrata*. Though intent on performing his own duty, Yama deigned to reply to Sāvitrī's initial supplications because, as he says, "you are a devoted wife, Sāvitrī, and possess the power of austerities." A few verses later the text itself describes Sāvitrī as, "this stately, devoted wife, perfected by her stressful vow."[27] What is this power of austerities which Sāvitrī is credited with having? How does it function in the context of a vow? And what is its relation to the power of the devoted wife, the *pativratā* so extolled in Indian literature? While much has been written about the role of women as *pativratā*, and on the intriguing concept of *tapas* in Hindu, Buddhist and Jain religious history,[28] their interconnection with the concept of *vrata* has not been seriously investigated. I would like now to draw attention to certain ideas and connections that I believe have informed the *vrata* tradition (both its expounders and its practitioners) on implicit if not always explicit levels. In particular, I want to consider first some of the vedic antecedents to and implications of the idea of one being "perfected" by a "stressful vow"; that is, I would like to look at *vratas* as (self-sufficient) agents of transformation and spiritual power juxtaposed with earlier conceptions of the transformative "cooking" (= perfecting) of the vedic sacrifice through the heat *(tapas)* of the fire.

In her book tracing the role and function of heat in the brahmanic sacrifice, U. M. Vesci (1985) argues that in the Brāhmaṇas sacrifice came to be absolutized as self-sufficient action, the center and source of creation itself, an effect of which was the relegation of the gods to a position as dependent on it as humans. At the risk of oversimplifying some of her carefully constructed arguments, let me extract a few ideas and quote several passages from Vesci's book that have a bearing on our subject; that is, that illustrate the evolution of certain ideas that I would argue passed over into the *vrata* tradition and continue to inform women's understanding of the significance of their practice of *vrats*.

As is well known, fire and sacrifice assumed an unusual prominence in the religion of ancient (vedic) India. Ritual and speculative attention focused on the power of fire and heat to change that with which it came in contact. Cooking, Vesci writes, became "so significant [in the Vedas] that what [was] not cooked [could not] even be considered either as a proper offering to the Gods or a suitable portion for a meal, to such an extent that to eat raw food [was] a way of eating without breaking ritual fast" (1985, 19). In fact, the suitability of raw food (roots and fruits) as fasting food has continued to the present day in *vrata* (and other) rites. Heat *(tapas)* was understood to purify *and* equip that which is heated with a kind of divine energy. ("Soma, thus, rises up to the gods, only when transformed, purified and fully endowed with energy" [Vesci 1985, 32].) In this early conception, Vesci argues, the divine world "seems to receive power from the offering, not so much in the form of nourishment (as common elsewhere) but by welcoming in their midst a 'friend' who gives them power by his very presence full of energy" (1985, 38). Further,

> The discovery of the sacred properties of heat, exhibited in the sacred fire enables the Vedic priest to make use of this energy

> to surmount through using the transformation of the victim the distance between Heaven and Earth and to overcome the difference between Divinity and Humanity. . . . It is the sacrificial fire, with its heat, which transforms, prepares, "cooks" the offerings, consecrating into the very "substance" of the Sacred. (Vesci 1985, 51)

When a correlation is made between the results of sacrifice and the sanctifying heat, a shift in the understanding of the ritual occurs, such that the sacrificial offering becomes the center of liturgical action and the "Sacrifical Act" acquires "Absolute Power" insofar as it is identified with the Divine on a creative and universal level. At this point, the power of the gods in relation to the efficacy of the sacrifice begins to wane, for:

> If it is the sacred action itself, which effects the transformation and the immortalization of the victim, it is natural that it tends to become self-sufficient and independent of the whole Ultimate Reality, absorbing in its own sphere of action both men and Gods. Sacrifice becomes a vivifying force independent of any other agent superior to it, and acts directly first of all on the victim itself and then on the whole universe. Thus it gradually becomes the sole guarantee for the fulfillment of what is asked of it (from the continuation and maintenance of the cosmic order to the granting of progeny and wealth) independently of any eventual intervention by Gods. Thus, the whole sacrificial Action is divinized, by being made to represent the divine activity par excellence, and later on by being absolutized in such a way that it itself becomes cosmic and eternal. (Vesci 1985, 55)

The role, function and power of the individual divinities diminish, although the gods "continue to exist and even to remain the recipients of the Sacrifice at least for a certain time."[29] In certain texts man is depicted as dependent on the Sacrifice in and of itself for desired aims and for the attainment of immortality, "detaching himself from the necessity of having to ask for graces and favours from the divinities."[30] The gods become "models to copy" because of their perfect way of performing the ritual, and guarantors (but not the source) of ritual power (Vesci 1985, 70, 96).

However, although the "independence of the Sacrifice" had the effect of "liberating" the sacrificer from the uncertain response of the gods to his desires,[31] it also had other consequences,

consequences which eventually led to the virtual obsolescence of the vedic sacrifice. One consequence was that the rituals of the sacrifice became increasingly complicated, leading to the need for more specialized personnel and to an efflorescence of texts and commentaries produced by various schools of method and interpretation. The performance of the sacrifice also became more dangerous for a mistake made in the ritual, every action of which was now equally important, could have devastating consequences. Hence certain Brāhmaṇas (e.g., AitBr. 32, ŚB 13) are replete with expiatory formulas to counteract such mistakes, and require the increasingly rigorous training of the ritual specialists. There was also the danger of the priest not being able to regulate the "thermic energy" *(tapas)* of the sacrifice. Excess heat could psychically as well as physically burn the priests and possibly threaten the very order of existence.[32]

To sum up, Vesci's central thesis is that the heat used to prepare the sacrificial offering for the gods was already in the *Ṛgveda* understood to be a unique and sacred power. After a correlation is made between the results of sacrifice and heat, the sacrifical rite is understood to acquire its own power from heat, a power which transforms the ingredients of the offering, endowing it with energy to "ascend to the immortal sphere of Reality." In the end, the gods become secondary to the sacrifice itself which, through the energy of heat, becomes the source of cosmic power.

Returning to the depiction of *vrata* in the epic, let me now use this conceptual background against which to consider the possible meanings of the description of Sāvitrī as being "perfected" by her "stressful vow." We need to remember that in its speculative developments the energy produced by the sacrifice became interiorized through ascetic discipline as *tapas*. In the epics, many beings—gods, demons, men, women—are depicted as performing austerities for a number of different reasons, for example, for obtaining spiritual power, *mokṣa*, or children. The word *tapas* is often used to describe both the act and the rewards of self-mortification, as it earlier described both the heat and the results of the heat in the sacrifice. Such performance of austerities is often portrayed as generating heat[33] which "cooks," perfects, purifies, and transforms the actor, producing spiritual energy (and also, at the extreme, magical powers—*siddhis*). Through the internal heat which Sāvitrī generated by her ascetic practices, she, too, purifies, transforms and endows herself with a powerful energy which enables her to accomplish her goal. Thus too she says that it is the "power of my austerities" and "my vow" (among other factors) that will prevent obstructions to her purpose.

Vesci writes that the Brāhmaṇa texts explicitly recognize "three functions of Sacred Heat namely, purification, transformation, and the bestowal of energy to the victim that it may reach its goal" (1985, 88). The transformative function of heat "can be found in a term of comparison which the exegete [*brahmavādin*] uses to clarify the effects on the priest or on the sacrificer by his consecration [*mahā-vrata*]." In the *Gopatha Brāhmaṇa* (1.4.13) the priest or sacrificer is compared to "an earthen vessel baked by the heat of his ascetic power *(tapas,* already in the sense of heat obtained by personal effort and abstinence)" (Vesci 1985, 93). The consecration *(dīkṣa/vrata)* the *yajamāna* or *dikṣita* undergoes transforms and protects him from "being melted" (as the text puts it), just like the raw clay vessels are first purified and transformed (hardened) by heat so that they can then withstand the heat of the sacrifice itself. The presence of the right amount of heat "is a condition *sine qua non* for the sacrifice to be efficacious," whether to obtain "wealth, or interior change, or ascension to the higher worlds" (Vesci 1985, 90,94).

The resonance of these ideas in the *vrata* tradition as it emerged centuries later and is practised and understood today is striking. For, already in the Purāṇas *vratas* are described as a form of *tapas.* Thus they have a transformational power on the votary brought about through the purifying and perfecting of her or himself by the austerities she or he performs, just as *tapas* transformed the vedic sacrifice from the raw material of the offering to the energy which finally (re)creates and sustains the universe, and which gave to the sacrificer the power to achieve desired goals without the help of the gods. The idea of the efficacy of self-mortification alone achieving one's desired aims, while usually subsumed under a devotional cast, persists today in the performance of certain *vratas* where the gods are apparently secondary or almost irrelevant to the success of the rite. Such ideas regarding the power of *tapas* also offer one explanation to why it is, for example, that, as I was told in so many words, the harder the fasting and other abstinences, the greater the *tapas* generated, and the more assured the results.

Having explored the power of austerities and its functioning in the context of a vow, I now briefly turn to my third question, the relationship of *vratas* and *tapas* to the *pativratā*. In the story of Sāvitrī there are two other (related) elements that make her, and women who behave in the same sort of way, powerful. One is Sāvitrī's feminine *śakti*, often described as a kind of raw generative energy present in the world as a whole, and in women in particular. The other is her truthful chastity, her sincere single-minded/hearted devotion to her husband Satyavat. To the chastity of women (that is, faithfulness to one man, rather than celibacy) the epics and later literature ascribe all manner of marvelous properties. Bhagat writes: "The epic eulogizes *tapas*, its efficacy and power. There is nothing superior to it. Its might enables a person to achieve great results. The ascetic through *tapas* acquires supernatural power. . . . But such powers are accessible to women also if they are chaste" (1976, 2). While some commentators have suggested that such praise of the *pativratā* by male Brahmans occured in large measure in order to recommend such behavior to women, I think there is more to it than that. On the one hand, the power of chastity derives from the cultivation of *tapas* in the self-restraint and single-mindedness involved. On the other hand, taking on the *vrata* of *pati-śuśruṣa* (service to the husband) has a connection to the power of truth, *satya*.

In commenting on the themes of book 3 of the *Mahābhārata* (the Āraṇyaka *parvan*), van Buitenen draws attention to the firmness of Yudhiṣṭhira's pledge to remain in the forest for thirteen years and not avenge his deceitful cousins before that time had elapsed. He says, "From this point of view the *Book of the Forest* is the celebration of the highest value in the moral code of the ancient Indians, truthfulness and faithfulness under all circumstances" (1972, 1:177). While Yudhiṣṭhira is the main male model for this, there are a number of women who also model this behavior in their capacity as *pativratās*, as for example Sāvitrī. Interestingly, even though it is Sāvitrī's husband who is named Satyavat, meaning "truthful,"[34] it is Sāvitrī herself who demonstrates these qualities in the story by word and action. Indeed, after Satyavat has been given back his soul and wakes up, immediately becoming fearful of finding their way back in the encroaching darkness, and weepy over his parents' possible worry, Sāvitrī consoles him and then utters a "truth-vow": "If it is true that I have practised austerities, if I have given, if I have offered up, then this night shall be safe for my parents-in-law and my husband. I do not recall that I have ever spoken a lie, even in jest—by that truth [*tena satyena*] my parents-in-law shall live today!" (281.97).

It is in looking at such truth-vows (wherein the word *vrata* may or may not be used) that one can arrive at the clearest sense of what van Buitenen meant, when he was quoted earlier as saying that vows cannot be broken except to "the detriment of a person's truth." Truth-vows usually involve appealing to the truth of one's prior conduct in order to dramatically prove one's fidelity (as in Sītā's case) or otherwise effect a curse, clear an obstruction, or resolve a seemingly unresolvable difficulty. They are, as W. Norman Brown noted, rare in the literature.[35] They are also, in the epics at least, far more often uttered by women than by men.[36] And when women utter them, they often appeal to the trueness of their chastity, their fidelity in deed, word, and thought to their husbands. In keeping with the general emphasis on Sāvitrī's austerities in this whole episode, however, Sāvitrī appeals not to her fidelity (a given) but to the fact that she has undertaken austerities and that she has never lied. The truth of her *(pativratā)* behavior, as well as her austerities (her self-sacrifice for the sake of another) performed with the right intentions, then, makes her positively powerful in this story; a story which women tell to each other each year when they perform the three-day Vaṭ Sāvitrī Vrat and become temporary *tapasvinīs*.

In the literature we have examined so far, *vrata* has been linked to such central concepts and practices in Hindu religious history as *ṛta* (cosmic order), *satya* (Truth), and *dharma* (Law), *yajña* (sacrifice), *dīkṣa* (initiation), and *tapas* (heat, austerities), *niyama* (restraints) and *prāyaścitta* (penance), and, more obliquely in relation to women, *pativratā*. Though the idea of *ṛta* is encompassed by the concept of *dharma*, and *yajña* and *dīkṣa* assume less prominence in later religious practice, each of these concepts and practices to which *vrata* is related remain important in some form or other to the present day. The next section follows the historical course of *vrata* as it emerges as a fully developed votive rite in the literature of the Purāṇas and Nibandhas.

VRATA IN THE PURĀṆAS AND NIBANDHAS

The Hindu medieval Sanskrit religio-juridical texts, the Purāṇas and the Nibandhas, constitute an immense literature, and *vratas* figure as a prominent topic.[37] Here I will concentrate on two particular aspects of the śāstric *vrata* tradition as depicted in this literature: the "*dharma* of *vrata*" (or, the code of conduct for the performer of *vrata*), and the implications for female votaries to be found in this literature written by, and predominately directed to, high caste males. There are several points about the depiction of *vrata* in this literature that are noteworthy.

First, the mention, description, and discussion of *vrata* effloresces in the Purāṇas and Nibandhas. This efflorescence indicates that *vratas* as a specific kind of votive rite had come to be considered a form of religious observance worthy of lengthy disquisitions sustained by pandits over many centuries. In these texts, we find the first relatively consistent portrayals of *vrata* as a votive rite normally involving at least fasting, *pūjā*, and *dāna* (the giving of gifts). We receive descriptions, sometimes detailed, sometimes perfunctory, of their purposes and procedures, of who was eligible to observe them, when, and under what circumstances. We also find attached to many of the *vrata* descriptions (or even comprising the description itself) the *vrata-kathā*, *vrata* stories that serve to demonstrate the efficacy of the rite. These stories, many of whose episodes and characters come from the epics or from other Purāṇas themselves, first emerge in literary form in the Purāṇas.

Second, the fact that *vratas* are included so prominently in works on *dharma* suggests that these rites were embraced and shaped by the Purāṇa and Nibandha editors as a means to inculcate dharmic (dharmaśāstric) values and socially responsible behavior. The ethical dimension in the concept of *vrata* implicit in earlier Śruti and Smṛti literature is now more clearly articulated and emphasized.

Third, congruent with the rise to prominence of sectarian theism in the first millennium C.E., *vratas*—especially in the Purāṇas—are given the devotional cast still characteristic of present day *vrats*. *Vratas* become a recommended way of expressing faith and devotion to one's chosen deity, as well as a way of soliciting blessings and favors from a god. Fourth, most of the *vratas* are depicted in these texts as *kāmya* rites. That is, they are set out as optional rites that a householder (or person of any social category) can choose to observe in order to obtain some specific *phala* (fruit). This distinguishes them from their predominately *nitya* (or obligatory) orientation in earlier vedic and Smṛti literature.

Finally, it should be noted that women are clearly secondary, if not virtual silent players with regard to *vratas* in these texts. Although women often figure prominently in the *vrata* stories, and a few *vratas* are slated specifically for women to observe, one does not get the sense that women have any special connection to these rites. Rather, women and Shudras are discussed as having the privilege of observing these vows, while they were disenfranchised from other rituals. But even here, there are various restrictions placed by the male upper-caste *(dvija* or "twice-born") authors on when and under what circumstances women and Shudras could actually keep the *vratas*.

The *vratas* are effusively praised in these texts, and favorably compared with vedic sacrifices, among other important religious acts. The merit and rewards for performing (or, as some Purāṇas would have it, even just hearing about) these rites are lavishly detailed. The *vratas* are portrayed as a means of achieving not just *bhukti* (earthly enjoyments—wealth, beauty, learning, long life) but also are given a prominent place among the means of attaining *mukti* (salvation) for those living in the Kali Yuga, the fourth and decadent stage of the grand cycle of the cosmos.

Descriptions and discussions of *vratas* appear in almost all the Purāṇas—usually in one section of the text, but sometimes scattered here and there. Rules for procedures can be extremely elaborate, and some are even made to sound like the ritual details for the complicated vedic great sacrifices described in the Brāhmaṇas.[38] Here the *vratin* (votary) is called a *yajamāna* (sponsor of the sacrifice) and the *vrata* a *yajña*, leaving us no doubt that *vratas* are to be considered the direct heirs of vedic sacrifices.

The Nibandha literature essentially took over from the earlier Dharmaśāstras in form and content. There are whole Nibandhas devoted to a discussion and description of *vratas*, and this discussion is far more detailed than all earlier literature on the subject. The writers of the Nibandhas *(nibandhakāras)* were often trained as *mīmāṃsā* specialists (trained in the categories and applications of vedic ritual exegesis) and one sees this training surface in their discussions of *vratas*. As McGee has pointed out, it sometimes emerges with curious results, manifested, for example, in the manner whereby the pandit-authors have had to manipulate the rules to accommodate—not always successfully—the involvement of women and Shudras. For, by this time, the traditions of ritual exegesis were quite accustomed to excluding women and Shudras from any direct participation in the central features of vedic/brahmanic rituals because of their *amantravat*[39] status.

The number of *vratas* described in such early Purāṇas as the *Viṣṇupurāṇa* was not very large. Gradually, however, their numbers increased until they proliferated almost exponentially in the works compiled in the ninth to the fourteenth centuries, as in the *Padmapurāṇa*. Similarly, in the Nibandhas one finds an explosion of *vrata* descriptions from such earlier treatises as Lakṣmidhāra's *Kṛtyakalpataru* (first half of the twelfth cent.), to Hemādri's *Caturvargacintamāṇi* (end of the thirteenth century) and finally to the works such as Viśvanātha's *Vratarāja* (early eighteenth century), a work devoted exclusively to *vrata*.[40] As Kane says: "There is no topic on Dharmaśāstra except probably that of *tīrthayātra* [pilgrimage] and of *śrāddha* [funerary and memorial rites] on which the Purāṇas [and Nibandhas] wax so eloquent as on *vrata*" (1974, 5,1:57). Though the *vratas* listed in the works may be counted in the thousands many of them are repeated from one work to another, or different names are given to the same *vrata*. One commonly finds in the later Purāṇas whole sections lifted out of earlier texts, sometimes reformulated with a different sectarian angle. Similarly, in the Nibandha literature authors often took portions of earlier works verbatim and added them to their own. The *Vratarāja*, for example, contains long passages borrowed from Hemādri and many others.

The predominately Vaiṣṇava *Garuḍapurāṇa* makes the following statement on *vratas* which describes in a general way the model purāṇic *vrata*:

> Suta said: I shall now deal with the mode of practising those vows [*vratas*] and penances, O Vyasa, by which a man may win the good graces of the god Hari to the extent that he may be pleased to answer all his prayers. The god should be worshipped in all months of the year and in all days of the week, and under the auspices of all lunar phases and astral combinations. The votary shall observe a fast or take a single meal in the night, or live upon a fruit regimen on the day of the vow, and make gifts of money and paddy for the satisfaction of the god Viṣṇu, for which he will be blessed with the birth of a son and the ownership of fresh landed estates.[41]

The person who supplicates his chosen deity, then, with fasting and *pūjā* may be granted his wishes and more if the deity is well disposed. The passage recommends constant devotion to God.

Indeed, many of the Purāṇas advocate *bhakti* (devotion) alone as a means of getting what one wants—whether spiritual rewards or a material object. Though statements such as this advise the observance of *vratas* on any and all days of the week, month and year, they also stress the correct astrological calculation. The gods may be powerful in their own right, but the movement of the planets and stars at all costs must be taken under consideration for they also exert their powers on humans.

Following an introductory pronouncement on votive rites the typical specific *vrata* description may add a further sentence on the merit that the *vrata* will confer on the votary such as wealth, prosperity, health, beauty, progeny, *saubhāgya* (marital felicity), the removal of the effects of one's (or one's ancestors') sins, or a place in the god's *loka* (heaven). Next comes the account of how to practice the *vrata*; when to begin and end it, what deity(ies) should be worshipped and in what manner, what mantras, if any, should be said, and what offerings given in the *pūjā*. Lastly, the description will specify how many Brahmans or others are to be fed in the ending ceremony, the sort of food to be given and the amount and nature of the gifts to be donated. Fasting, either complete or partial, is always a central feature of a typical *vrata*, as is the giving of gifts. Many Purāṇa *vrata* descriptions do not include all of these features and indeed some descriptions are extremely short, while others dwell on aspects of the *pūjā*, the nature of the *dāna*, or the *kathā* (which itself may contain the information of when to do the *vrata* and the basics of the procedure) to the virtual exclusion of other details.

The Nibandha sections on *vrata* usually begin with the praise of *vrata*, general rules for *vrata* and then the description of individual *vratas*, often arranged by a time category like month, weekday or *tithi*.[42] Topics which are addressed in these statements and descriptions, all elements that may be included in the performance of a *vrata*, are: *saṅkalpa* (statement of intent); *snāna* (ritual bathing); *japa* (meditational recitation); *homa* (or *agni havan*—fire sacrifice); *pūjā*—including fashioning the *mūrti* (image) and the ritual enclosure *(maṇḍapa)*, performing the *upacāras* (rites honoring the deity) and/or the rite of *nyāsa* (ritual projection of divinities into various parts of the body),[43] and making ritual designs *(maṇḍalas*, *yantras*, or *ālpanās*); *upavāsa* (fasting); *kathā; dāna;* and *udyāpana* (the final concluding rite of a *vrata*).

The *Dharma* of *Vrata* and Votary: The Taming of *Tapas*

The phrase, the *dharma* of *vratin* (votary) or the *dharma* of *upavāsah* (faster) comes from the Nibandhas themselves, for the discussion of *vratas* is usually prefaced by statements on the nature of *vrata* indicating that the observance of *vratas* is dharmic action; action conducive to the moral well-being of the individual and society at large.[44] These statements also spell out the specific physical and mental (or moral) patterns and rules of behavior that the votary should observe in order to render the activity dharmic. It is in these dicta that we receive the best picture of how the Purāṇa and Nibandha writers conceived of *vrata*, for the Hindu pandits rarely offered a comprehensive definition of *vrata*.

In the prefatory statements made about *vrata* in these texts there are several terms which emerge repeatedly and which are clearly central to our understanding the concept of *vrata* in the Purāṇas and Nibandhas as well as to the current practice of *vrata*. These terms are *dharma*, *saṅkalpa*, *niyama* and *tapas*. The first, *dharma*, is the overarching concept under which *vrata*, as well as the other concepts, have been subsumed, shaped and assigned their place. This is entirely consistent with the nature of these texts, since they, and especially the Nibandhas, are concerned above all with the practical elucidation of the brahmanic ideals of *varṇāśramadharma* and *puruṣārtha*. *Varṇāśramadharma* comprises the duties and responsibilities *(dharma)* of the four castes *(varṇa)* and in each of the four stages *(āśrama)* in life (student, householder, forest dweller and renouncer). The *puruṣārtha* are the four aims of life: *dharma* (duty), *artha* (wealth), *kāma* (sensual pleasure) and *mokṣa* (spiritual liberation). The Nibandha texts on *vrata* make a point of showing that *vratas* fit in with each of these stages and aims of life. In theory, *vratas* are an appropriate practice for a person of any caste, of either sex, at any stage of life to achieve each of the four aims provided that other relevant conditions are met.[45]

Vrata as resolve *(saṅkalpa)*

Nibandha statments on the meaning of *vrata*, where they occur, tend to focus on *vrata* as *saṅkalpa*,[46] the votary's mental resolve to undertake the rite. In reference to *vratas* (and other rites) the term *saṅkalpa* is used in two ways. The first way refers generally to the act of making a choice, that is, to the intention, determination, resolution, the vow formed in the mind of the votary which leads him or her to undertake a set of actions. Making the vow commits one to fulfilling this set of actions, and the votary is warned that serious negative consequences are in store for the one who intentionally breaks the vow. The second way refers to the specific ritual act of formally making a *saṅkalpa* following a standard formula in front of a deity or priest at the commencement of the rite.[47]

The twelfth-century Nibandha author Bhatta Lakṣmidhāra, for example, in his *Kṛtyakalpataru* says that a *vrata* is a resolution [*saṅkalpa*] based on the śāstra whereby one contemplates what to do and what to abstain from.[48] Similarly, Raghunandana in his *Vratatattva* (c. 1520–75) holds that a *vrata* means various rites about which a resolve is made and also that a *vrata* is a *niyama* enjoined by the śāstra, characterized by *upavāsa* and the like.[49] The *Vratarāja* (p. 2) qualifies the identification of *saṅkalpa* with *vrata* saying: "*saṅkalpa* is part of a *vrata*. It is included in all the *vratas*, but *saṅkalpa* by itself refers primarily to the *nitya* (daily religious duties)."

The Nibandha definitions conform to statements made in earlier Smṛti texts, notably the *Manusmṛti* (2.3) which says: "Desire is the very root of the conception of a definite intention [*saṅkalpa*], and sacrifices are the result of that intention; all the vows [*vratas*] and the duties of restrictions [*yamas*] are traditionally said to come from the conception of a definite intention" (Doniger, tr. 1991). This statement is made in the context of a discussion on *dharma* and the role of desire in motivating humans to act. While acknowledging the sort of message found in the *Gītā*, for example, which advocates the doctrine of "desireless action" *(niṣkāma-karma)*, the *Manusmṛti* argues that "here on earth there is no such thing as no desire" (2.2), thus one should rather aim to foster and act on "good" (dharmically ordained) desires and abjure others. In this sense, for the *nibandhakāras*, a *vrata* is a resolve to undertake good actions, as determined by the Dharmaśāstras.

Vrata as austerity and restraint *(tapas* and *niyama)*

While the Nibandhas tend to focus on the resolve—the vow aspect of the rite—the Purāṇas tend to focus on the *niyamas*—on the discipline and restraint aspects of the *vrata*. One emphasizes the votary's intention, the other the aspects of the votary's behavior that ensue from that intention. For example, the *Agnipurāṇa* (175, 2–3) says:

> A restrictive rule [*niyama*] declared by the sastras is called *vrata*, which is also regarded as *tapas*; restraint of the senses and other rules are but special incidents of *vrata*; *vrata* is called *tapas* because it causes hardship to the performer (of the *vrata*) and it is also called *niyama* since therein one has to restrain the several organs of sense. (Kane 1974, 5,1:33)

Earlier in this chapter we saw how the term *tapas*, which originally meant heat in the *Ṛgveda*, came to be associated with the inner heat generated by effort *(śrama)* on the part of, for example, the *yajamāna*, the *brahmacarya* or the ascetic, and then with any act of self-imposed austerity, as in the *Mahābhārata*. The term was also used in connection with rites of expiation *(prāyaścitta)* where sometimes severe forms of privation were demanded. In the text the *Yogasūtra tapas* is named one of the *niyamas*. By the time the Purāṇas are set down (prior to the Nibandhas), the concept of *tapas* had become inextricably bound with the concept of *vrata*.

The *Garuḍapurāṇa* (128, 1–2) stipulates that a *vrata* "should be performed together with the observation of Niyamas (restraints) mentioned in the scriptures. A Vrata is a form of penance [*prāyaścitta*]. Yamas . . . along with Niyamas . . . should be equally observed." The word *niyama* comes from the root *yam* with the prefix *ni*, and in *Manu* and in the *Mahābhārata* and other sources of around the beginning of the Common Era it means "to restrain, check, hold back, prevent, control" (Monier-Williams 1984, 552). The concept of *niyama* as disciplinary practices involving various forms of self-restraint has its roots in the ascetic rules and practices of the early *śramaṇas* (wandering mendicants). These practices and values were adopted and diversely developed by various streams of brahmanical religion and philosophical schools, as well as by the Buddhists and Jains. Patañjali systematized yogic techniques and placed them within a coherent philosophical and theistic framework in his *Yogasūtra*, a treatise of around the first century. The *Yogasūtra* recommends both *yamas* (abstinences) such as nonviolence *(ahiṁsa)* and continence, and *niyamas* (observances) which inculcate the performance of meritorious deeds (Yardi 1979, 42). Patañjali calls *niyamas* one of the eight yogic "limbs" (2.32)[50] and says they consist of five observances: bodily and mental purity *(śauca)*; contentment *(santoṣa)*; austerities (*tapas*); study of sacred texts *(svādhyāya)*; and devotion to God *(īśvarapraṇidhāna)*. In his commentary on this verse, Yardi says that there is external cleanliness—washing the body, eating pure food, and so on—and internal cleanliness "brought about by the removal of [such] mental impurities" as attachment and aversion by the cultivation of attitudes such as friendliness and serenity. "Contentment is the absence of desire to acquire more than the means at hand. Austerities include . . . [subjecting oneself to] hunger and thirst, heat and cold,... silence . . . and includes the observance of vows" (for which he lists in a note such examples as *kṛcchra, cāndrayāṇa,* and *sāntapana*—all also expiatory rites). "Sacred study means the reading of scriptures and includes the repetition of the sacred syllable *Om.*" Devotion or "surrender of works to God" is the dedication of all actions to God (1979, 186–87).

The five abstinences *(yamas)*, namely, nonviolence, truthfulness *(satya)*, continence *(brahmacarya*[51]), not stealing *(asteya)*, and not taking more than one needs, or aquisitiveness *(aparigraha)* are called by Patañjali the *mahāvrata*, or great vow, which is binding on all who wish to be yogins.[52]

The Purāṇas and Nibandhas incorporated the idea of *yamas* and *niyamas* into their discussion and description of Hindu dharmic observances such as *vratas*, accepting them (in modified form) as models for the virtuous conduct of a householder *(gṛhasthin)*. The *Agnipurāṇa* (175.10–11), for example, mentions the ten *niyamas* which are to be practised while observing a *vrata*: "forgiveness or patience *(kṣma)*; truthfulness *(satya)*; compassion *(dāyā)*; charity *(dāna)*; purity *(śauca)*; control of the [six] sense organs *(indriyanigraha)*; *deva pūjā;* fire sacrifice *(homa,* or *agni havan)*; contentment *(santoṣa)*; and not stealing *(asteya)*. This tenfold *dharma* is declared as common to all *vratas*."[53] The similarity of this list to the that of the *Yogasūtra* list of *yamas* and *niyamas* is obvious. It is also clear here that the term *niyama* is being used in the *Agnipurāṇa* in a larger sense than external restraints—indeed *"dharma,"* used in the last sentence, *is* the more appropriate term to cover the range of psychological and moral qualities, behavioral restrictions and ritual actions mentioned in the list. In the theistic context within which *vratas* were now usually placed, the ultimate purpose of these *niyamas* was the cultivation of inward and outward purity, and physical and spiritual discipline required to take a votary or devotee closer to God, or to union *(sayujya)* with God. This is the goal, also, of the yogin, described not only in the *Yogasūtra*, but also in such texts as the *Bhagavadgītā*.

It is clear that there is a long history of interconnection between the concepts *vrata, prāyaścitta, tapas, upavāsa* and *niyama*. Though each term may have had a separate and specific meaning in its earliest usage, we find that by the period that the Purāṇas were being set down, all five terms are brought together, not quite as synonyms, but as closely related elements in religious observances. These are all elements which serve to discipline and spiritually develop the householder for whom these texts are intended. In the case of the Purāṇa *vratas*, the *vrata* may be viewed as being the "subject" and *tapas, niyama* and *prāyaścitta* its "modifiers." In other contexts, these terms may be constituted or interrelated differently.[54]

Vrata Dharma in Practice

We have seen, then, that according to the Purāṇas and Nibandhas, a person undertaking a *vrata* should follow a series of guidelines and rules which discipline and purify the mind and body. These rules include observing the *niyamas*, not sleeping in the day, reading or listening to the śāstras and religious stories, performing auspicious work, curbing one's temper, and sleeping on the floor at night. Some texts also recommend avoiding contact with "low," "bad," or ritually impure persons which may involve also shunning contact with women in general.[55] The rules and prohibitions governing the behavior of the votary, however, get much more detailed than indicated to this point. For the broad principles and norms of *vrata-dharma* are translated into the practical minutiae of mundane activities like bathing and eating. This is a task at which the Dharmaśāstras excel. The texts provide us with long lists of the multifarious foods, articles and practices that are to be strictly avoided. The *Garudapurāṇa* (chap. 128) for example says that a votary

> . . . should not take anything out of a bowl of Indian bellmetal, nor consume any potherbs, nor take honey, grain, and koradushaka [?], nor chew any betel leaf on the day of breaking his fast. . . . A fast is vitiated by using flowers, perfumes, unguents, collyrium, a toothbrush, a new cloth, or an ornament. A vratee should wash his mouth with pancagavyam in the morning before breaking his fast. The merit of a fast is destroyed by gambling, by indulging in day sleep or in sexual intercourse, and by constantly drinking water.

The *Agnipurāṇa* (chap. 175) has much the same list but adds wine and boiled rice belonging to others as items to be avoided while fasting and includes garlands, bright-colored clothes, fumes of burning incense, sandalpaste and "suchlike articles of luxury" as forbidden things to use.[56] Oily or cooked foods are also often proscribed in the *vratas*.

There are many possible reasons for these specific prohibitions, but I will confine myself to a few general comments. In the first place the votary is supposed to be undergoing a form of *tapas* and general restraint, so sense enhancing or luxurious items like perfume, ornaments and betel leaf are to be avoided. However, exceptions to some of these items, like collyrium and ornaments, are made for married women because the primary *vrata* of married women is *pativrata* and so she should try to remain beautiful to her husband. Unless, that is, he is away, in which case these prohibitions against the use of toiletries and ornaments apply whether or not she is observing a *vrata*. Second, as is well-known, foods (as well as utensils, activities, kinds of employment, etc.) are divided by Hindus into categories of pure, less pure and impure according to their *guṇas* (qualities). The *pañcagavyam* (cow dung and urine, milk, ghee, curd) and *pañcāmṛta* (milk, curd, honey, sugar and ghee) mixtures are considered *sattvik* (conducive to lightness and calmness), extemely pure *(śuddha)* and purifying to the imbiber and are commonly used in religious rituals. Salt, wine, meat, onions, spices, certain vegetables and legumes are generally *rājāsik* (conducive to excitability). Some of these items are potential conductors of pollution, like someone else's boiled rice, if not polluting in themselves. Thus these items must naturally be avoided if one wishes to be in both a calm and a ritually pure state. Ritual purity is, after all, "the path to *dharma*, the resting place of the Veda, the abode of prosperity *(Śrī)*, the favourite of the gods."[57]

Bellmetal as an inferior metal is also considered impure for religious purposes though not for daily purposes for it is frequently named among the gifts to be given at the end of a *vrata*. Traditionally vessels used in a sacrifice are made of silver or gold as these metals are thought to be more pleasing to the gods.[58] Abstention from the use of flowers, sandalpaste, unguents, and toothbrushes refers to personal use as these items are central to the *devapūjā*. Not using a toothbrush[59] helps one, presumably, to remain sexually chaste.

Even though the above items are generally prohibited, some of the items are nonetheless prescribed in the ritual of certain *vratas*. At first glance there are plain contradictions and many inconsistencies in these lists of prescriptions and proscriptions. On closer inspection, however, one realizes that despite the plethora of rules it is the particular context (the *vrata*, the condition of the votary, and other such variables) which finally determines the application of those rules.

There are also many rules governing *vratas* and time, of which the votary must be (made) aware, since, according to the texts, attention to these rules is crucial to achieving a positive outcome for the *vrata*. From an early period, *vratas* have been intimately related to India's elaborate systems of time reckoning. In the Purāṇas and Nibandhas the systems of time reckoning to which *vratas* are related most closely are the celestial configurations—especially those based on the lunar cycles—*tithis* and *nakṣatras* (lunar asterisms). Thus descriptions of *vratas* are frequently arranged according to the *tithi* on which they fall, from one to fifteen for each *pakṣa* (half of the lunar month). The solar calendar and its cycles are referred to and configured with lunar cycles when particular points of time are deemed especially auspicious or inauspicious for beginning or ending certain *vratas* or for observing certain ritual aspects of *vrata*: starting a *pūjā* or breaking a fast. In general, it is acceptable to begin a *vrata* any time provided that the time is auspicious, that is, the correct *tithi* or conjunction of *tithis*, an auspicious month or time of the year, and so on. Since it can be complicated to determine the correct or auspicious time, votaries in the past would have had to depend on the expertise of a pandit or an astrologer. Today, votaries may refer to printed *pañcāṅgas* or to special religious calendars.[60]

After undertaking a *snāna* or ritual bath, the votary should perform the *saṅkalpa*, the formal ritual declaration of resolve, which marks the beginning of the *vrata*. If subsequently there is a birth or death in the family, or if a female votary begins menstruation, the *vrata* is not considered compromised. However, these states of ritual impurity do affect the ritual procedure (e.g., the *pūjā*) of the *vrata* and modifications or alternative arrangements have to be made. According to the *Kṛtyakalpataru*, "danger (to the observer of a vrata) from all beings, disease, forgetfulness, the command of one's guru do not break a vrata provided these occur only once (during the period of the particular vrata)."[61] One's guru has the final say and overules all other rules for the disciple. Since the husband is the guru of the wife, then of course he can also dictate the terms of her *vrata* if he so wishes.

Breaking a *vrata* before its appointed completion without sufficient reason, however, was said to have grave consequences. The *Vratarāja* (p. 11) quotes the Smṛti writer Chagaleya as saying in the *Madanratna:* "Who does not fulfill a *vrata*, having already made a *saṅkalpa*, on account of various desires, becomes a *cāṇḍāla* [an "untouchable" caste] in the present life and a dog in the next life."

There are also lengthy statements in the Nibandhas about actions and foods that will and will not break a fast, and so affect the efficacy of the whole *vrata*. Some of the items that will break a fast have already been mentioned. But, just as the writers of the Nibandhas were aware that not all votaries had the same means for collecting the required *pūjā* items, nor for offering *dāna*, so they recognized that not all votaries could always fast in the stipulated manner. Thus for those unable to keep a complete fast when required, the following foods could be taken (in moderation) without incurring any demerit: water, roots, fruits, ghee, milk, any food with the permission of one's preceptor, and medicine.[62] Of course, the foods mentioned are the most *sattvik* and pure foods (referred to as *phalāhar* in Hindi). If one cannot fast completely *(nirjalā)* and one is in doubt about the fasting requirements, one can always count on *phalāhar* as being acceptable fasting food.

Classification of *Vrata*

Various attempts have been made to classify *vratas*, both within the Sanskrit texts and by researchers for either organizational or descriptive/analytical purposes. The fact that *vratas* can be and have been classified in so many different ways speaks to the phenomenological, sociological and symbolic richness of *vratas*. Some classifications are based on objective factors like the time and date on which a *vrata* begins. Others are based on more subjective criteria (e.g., "spiritual" versus "familial"[63]), criteria which may reveal as much about the attitudes or points of view of the classifier as of the *vratas*.

On the whole, the Purāṇas do not concern themselves with classifying *vratas*, at least not in any consistent or formal way. The Nibandha writers, on the other hand, were more meticulous about arranging their material in an orderly manner, following established principles. Thus one can tease out categories repeatedly found implicitly within the textual descriptions themselves such as time[64] (e.g., *tithi-vratas*, seasonal *vratas*, annual *vratas*); deity (*vratas* directed to Śiva, Gaṇeśa, Kṛṣṇa, or Devī); reward or desired fruit (*vratas* for progeny, *vratas* for health, *vratas* for vanquishing a king's enemies); or the fasting requirement (waterless, eating only once a day). The Purāṇas and Nibandhas are not often explicit about who the votary should be, but in some descriptions of particular *vratas* a category of persons—"married women," "mendicants"—are listed as suitable votaries. The male votary's marital status is not significant with regard to classification of *vratas* in the texts or in practice, but it is for the female votary. Thus some *vratas* are for unmarried girls *(kumārī)*, some for married women *(nārī)*, and some are designated as suitable for widows *(vidhvā)*.

Vratas have been categorized according to whether the *vrata* is conditional or not (Ward 1817, 1:75]), "purificatory/expiatory" or "devotional" (Banerjee 1946), "active" *(pavṛtti)* or "passive" *(nivṛtti)* (Banerjee 1946). And, *vratas* have been categorized according to origin or form, as in *"śāstrik"* (from the śāstras) or *"laukik"* / *"jyoṣit"* (folk or local) (Tagore 1919; Robinson 1985).

A very old classification applied initially to vedic rituals by *mīmāṃsā* scholars, but also applied to other rituals such as *vratas* by *nibandhakāras*, is one that has a tripartite division: (i) *nitya*, (ii) *naimittika*, and (iii) *kāmya*. The first two terms literally signify a period of time—*nitya* meaning perpetual or constant and *naimittika* meaning occasional. The third term refers to desire. Applied to *vratas* the term *nitya* refers to those *vratas* which are to be performed regularly and are held to be necessary or obligatory.[65] These include the initiation *(dīkṣa)* and life-stage *(āśrama) vratas* of the vedic Sūtra literature. One does not perform *nitya vratas* for merit or any reward, but rather as a duty or out of a sense of obligation and to avoid demerit.[66]

"Naimittika" is applied to occasional rites and refers to *vratas* undertaken occasionally, for a specific reason, or at a special time or place.[67] Dīpavālī, Navarātri and the Kumbha Mela, among other pan-Indian festivals, are classified as *naimittika* events, McGee notes, and so too are "the birth anniversaries of the deities [such as Rāmanavmī], even though they occur annually on fixed lunar days" (1987, 304). Expiatory *vratas* are also classified as *naimittika*. A *naimittika* rite, like a *nitya* rite, "has no positive fruit; it is done simply because the occasion calls for it" (McGee 1987, 304).

Thus *nitya* and *naimittika vratas*, following McGee's terminology, are "rites of maintenance" rather than "rites of acquisition."

The designation *kāmya* is applied to optional *vratas* observed for a limited time and for the purpose of attaining some specific object. The desired "object" of a *kāmya vrata* may be something intangible like spiritual merit or auspiciousness or something tangible like achieving wealth or healing a sick child. Or the desired object may be something that can only be secured in the "next" world such as eternal reunion with loved ones or a blissful place in one of the god's *lokas*.

A closer look at the application of this formal ritual classification by *nibandhakāras* to *vratas* reveals both its limitations and the orientation of its users. Its limitations are exemplified in the fact that while some *vratas* are labeled as *kāmya* and others as *nitya*, these labels are relative (as the texts themselves sometimes acknowledge). For, in practice, individual *vratas* can be *nitya* for some and *kāmya* for others, or both *kāmya* and *nitya* or *kāmya* and *naimittika* depending on context and player—who is to observe the vow and why. In the case of the extensively discussed Ekādaśī Vrata, for example, there are numerous statements made about for whom and under what conditions this *vrata* is to be considered *nitya*, and for whom and under what conditions it is optional *(kāmya)* based on such considerations as whether the votary is an avowed Vaiṣṇavite or not, his stage in life, and so on.[68] But the texts fail to mention other sorts of conditions that can determine the circumstantial and motivational category of the *vrata*. Family tradition, for example, may render a *naimittika vrata* into a *kāmya* or *nitya vrata*, as McGee and I found in our fieldwork.

To conclude this overview of *vrata* in the Purāṇas and Nibandhas, it is clear that *vratas* as specific types of votive observances, involving at least *saṅkalpa*, *upavāsa*, *pūjā*, and *dāna* first appear in these texts (though we can see their beginnings in the epics), and that descriptions and discussions of them multiply as the texts become more recent. While *vrata* procedures contain many parallels to vedic rituals they also contain nonvedic elements such as the inclusion of local or nonvedic deities for worship, the use of ritual diagrams and rites like *nyāsa*. The Purāṇas, in general, absorbed and integrated a number of nonvedic features as the process of compilation and editing continued over the centuries, not only from "popular religion" but from Tantrism and Buddhism as well.

There are several probable reasons as to why the discussion and description of *vratas* proliferated in later Purāṇas and in the Nibandhas. While in the Gṛhyasūtra literature there were *vratas* that marked the passage from one *āśrama* to another, the Purāṇa and Nibandha literature rarely mentions these sorts of initiatory rites in the context of *vratas*. Instead, most of the *vratas* are now depicted as optional householder rites available to all classes *(varṇas)* and both sexes. They are available to help achieve any or each of the four "aims": *dharma, artha, kāma,* and *mokṣa.* Thus, from its various applications and connotations in earlier literature, as well as quite likely from existing folk rites, the concept of *vrata* was shaped by the Purāṇa and Nibandha writers into the ideal ritual for the householder to express his or her duties, devotion and spiritual aspirations. Within the context of these spiritual aspirations the doctrines, practices and *dharma* ("yogic" values) of the ascetics are "tamed" and harnessed under the control of the this-worldly *dharma* of the householder. While *mokṣa* is a legitimate aim of *vratas*, spiritual discipline as a principle of *dharma* is emphasized. At the same time, *vratas* were presented as rites over which Brahman pandit-priests ought to preside (ritually control), and from which, therefore, they could economically benefit. Indeed, the description of suitable gifts to be given as *dāna* to the Brahman officiant sometimes occupies a majority of the textual description of particular *vratas*.

To encourage their practice, the purāṇic *vratas* were made accessible: they were available for everyone (in theory) to perform at any stage of life. Though the texts do not support the view that *vratas* were especially directed to women and Shudras, there is no doubt that some of the restrictions normally imposed upon these groups primarily because of ritual impurity were lifted in the case of *vratas*. Widows and menstruating women, females considered either inauspicious or polluting, were yet eligible to continue to perform certain aspects of the *vratas*, like the fasting requirements and the *niyamas*. As well, other ritual impurities that normally affect religious observances, such as a death in the family, did not jeopardize the *vrata* rite provided the rite had already begun.[69]

In these texts *vratas* were rendered sufficiently feasible and flexible to accommodate a person's means, in contrast to the greater rigidity of vedic rituals. One did not have to be particularly rich to observe them, for, though *pūjās* and the giving of gifts were always required, concessions were made for those unable to afford the stipulated items. In many *vrata* descriptions, a choice of considerably simpler procedures is given after the details of the more complicated procedure have been outlined. Of course, the texts probably assume that a Brahman would have to oversee the application of these alternatives.

The range of purposes for which a *vrata* could be performed was wide—from progeny, beauty or learning, to a higher station in the next world or in the next life. "A woman will be reborn as a man," one *vrata* promises. It is conceivable that any problem that one wanted alleviated or any desire that one wished to be fulfilled could be sought through the observance of a *vrata*. However, the Nibandha writers apparently sought to temper the pursuit of purely selfish or material desires by placing an emphasis on the ethical conduct of the votary during the course of the *vrata*.

The Purāṇa *vrata* descriptions dwell on the merits promised to votaries at some length and often in rather exaggerated terms. P. V. Kane, in particular, focused on this point and expressed the opinion that this was one of the main reasons *vratas* became so popular. It revealed the "materialistic attitudes and expectations" put "under the garb of religion" (1974, 5,1:55). The Brahmans pandered to the "ordinary human cravings" through *vratas*, to which S. C. Banerjee adds, "as a means to gain income." What Kane does not say is that the vedic sacrifices (of which he has a higher opinion) as described in the Brahmanas also promised cows and sons and worldly rewards.[70]

It is easy to see why the *vratas* over the course of centuries so increasingly garnered the attention of the Purāṇa editors and the *nibandhakāras*, and why they came to be so exuberantly extolled in this literature and by their descendents in the popular *vrat-kathā* literature of modern times.[71] Representing a more typically enthusiastic view than Kane's on the significance or value of *vratas* is C. S. Venkateswaran who, writing on ethics in the Purāṇas, says of *vratas*: "These have great spiritual and ethical value. They discipline, purify, and sublimate the mind. Hence they are given a prominent place in the scheme of religious duties" (1962, 297). Or Madhvācarya, the editor and commentator (in Hindi) of the *Vratarāja*, who waxes lyrical in his 1984 introduction with such comments as:

> When one is absorbed in *vrat* then one believes in the truth that, "before I was wasting my valuable time and now I am truthfully using it—and getting rid of the wastage. As much time as I may take up (observing) *vrat*, it is truthful time, the remainder then is falsehood, that is, its use is false." The time not used for *vrat* is time not useful for one's life.

"I DO *VRATS* FOR *SUHĀG*": *VRATA* AND THE IDEOLOGY OF *PATIVRATA*

In what way is the time devoted to performing *vratas* "useful time" for women in the Hindu tradition? Why do the Purāṇas and Dharmaśāstras, while theoretically allowing women to perform any *vrata*, slate those *vratas* which pertain to furthering the well-being of family members as ones specifically suitable for women? In short, what is the relationship between women's performance of *vrats* today and traditionally construed gender ideology in Hindu India? Indeed, why would *vrats* suit the vision of the role of women articulated by the dominant male brahmanical culture? With these questions in mind I asked thirty-eight-year-old Aruna one humid afternoon in Banaras why men don't keep *vrats* for women.

The thick turbulent monsoon clouds darkened further the already gloomy front room of Aruna's second-storey decaying flat adjacent to the Ganges. "Well," she responded while nursing her youngest daughter (and sixth living child of the ten children she has borne), "for women the first [husband] is the divine marriage blessed by the gods. If a man loses his wife he can get another without too much problem; if a woman loses her husband it is much more difficult. If she does get another husband she might be called a concubine—he might have other women. . . . Women perform *vrats* for *suhāg* [Hindi for *saubhāgya;* to preserve the auspicious married state]."

Aruna's response brings to focus the social reality shaping the lives of at least high-caste Hindu women, and the continued force of a gender ideology which informs that reality: wives must keep *vrats* to preserve the longevity of their husbands. The early death of a husband means hardship and varying degrees of societal opprobrium for the widow. Men are not under such constraints. Ideologically and socially, it does not matter how many times a man is widowed.[72] He is not stigmatized by the death of a wife; nor is the widower put under permanent suspicion because of his status, as is the widow, even (or especially) if she remarries. It is not difficult for a man to obtain a new, "untainted" wife, as well as mistresses. Thus men do not need to observe *vrat*s for the well-being of their wives simply because they are not expected to—"there is no need for them," as Sarita put it—and practically there is much less at stake.

To understand the relationship of women's performance of *vrat*s to gender ideology it is necessary to situate them within the framework of the dominant cultural construction of gender, that is, within the ideology concerning women's natures, roles and functions formulated over two millennia by the orthodox Brahman elite. It should be noted that while this gender ideology may be found expressed most succinctly in those texts—the Dharmaśāstras—that this elite is responsible for producing, it turns up in varied forms in other literary genres (e.g., in the epics, Purāṇas, and *vrata-kathā* literature), and appears in folk sayings, films and other media. This task involves reviewing the orthodox conception of *strīsvabhāva* (the inherent nature of woman), the development of the *pativratā* ideal, and the practical elucidation of both concepts into *strīdharma* (the duties of women).

In a 2,000-year period from approximately 600 B.C.E. to 1400 C.E., orthodox brahmanical religion gradually excluded women from significant or independent participation in virtually all (vedic) ritual activity.[73] Though it would be naive if not incorrect to say that women originally enjoyed equal status with men in some early vedic "golden age," scholarship has fairly conclusively shown that (at least some) "twice-born" or upper-caste women received vedic instruction and as wives were considered essential and even honored participants in the prescribed duties of sacrifice, feeding and propitiating the ancestors, and producing sons, all of which took place in the home.[74] Such terms for women as *sahadharmanī* truly meant "partner in *dharma*" rather than merely "ritual assistant" as it came to mean later on. Other terms which appear in vedic literature such as *yajñopavitinī* (a woman who has undergone the sacred thread ceremony), *brahmavādinī* (a woman learned in scripture) and *paṇḍitā* (a female pandit) posed explanatory problems for later Smṛti writers who could no longer tolerate or perhaps even fathom the obvious implications of these terms.

Though debates about women's need for vedic education and hence about their ritual authority to receive *upanāyaṇa*, say mantras, and offer independent sacrifice long preceded the infamous *Manusmṛti*, it is in this text that the more conservative view regarding women found its most influential champion. Here women are not only relegated to the ritual status of Shudras, but now the first reasons given are that they are weak and impure and only secondarily that they are ignorant of vedic literature.[75] According to Leslie the logic went like this: "Since being born a woman or a *śūdra* is the result of particular sins in a previous birth [cf. Mbh. 13.120.9; Manu 12.3.9], the mere fact of femaleness is seen as proof of sin. Being sinful, a woman is *amantravat;* being *amantravat*, she cannot purify herself of sin; she therefore remains sinful all her life" (1989, 246). With this sort of thinking, then, the view of *strīsvabhāva* that tended to prevail was one that stereotyped women in general as inherently sinful, fickle, untruthful, promiscuous and, of course, weak and impure. Thus it is that this text calls for the "protection" of women at all stages of her life under the authoritative guidance of her male relatives. Thus it is, too, that the *Manusmṛti* (5.154) includes a declaration that no sacrifice, no *vrata* and no fast may be performed by a woman independently of her husband. (This would appear to be the first specific prohibition against women observing *vrata*s alone in the Dharmaśāstra literature.)

Yet, at the same time, women in their roles of wife and mother continue to be praised (as they were in vedic texts) as bringers of good fortune; the very embodiments of the goddess Śrī (or Laksmī)[76] in the household. They are also called *ardhāṅganī*—"half the body" (of the male)—because, among other reasons, the fulfillment of two of man's three primary debts—to the gods, ancestors and society—depend on his having a wife; and the *trivarga*, the triple goal of the householder *(dharma, artha* and *kāma)*, can only be met through the cooperation of the wife.[77] Thus the wife is essential to the well-being and to the dharmic responsibilities of the male householder.[78]

While not true in the wider Hindu tradition, which associates the mother (and in some contexts all females) with the powerful and pervasive goddesses, the Dharmaśāstras tend to pay little attention to the category of woman as mother. They concentrate instead on the woman as wife. The reason for this is essentially that from the religio-legalists' point of view the category of mother is relatively unambiguous and unproblematic. In general, the mother is eulogized; she is to be honored and respected by her children for she is the "guru of gurus." The wife, on the other hand, can wreak havoc on the purity of her husband's ancestral line *(gotra* and *jāti)* and possibly deprive him of the son which he needs to fulfill his own ritual obligations by sexual indiscretions and transgressions. The wife, then, must be carefully selected and guarded (controlled). To make this task easier, among other reasons, women as wives are exhorted to be *pativratās*. The term *pativratā* is a compound made up of the noun *pati,* meaning "lord" but in this context understood "husband," and *vrata.* A woman's *vrata*—her duty, her function, and her overarching vow—is devoted service to her husband-god. This is the essence of women's *dharma (strīdharma),* irrespective of caste and class. According to Manu, "for women the marriage ritual is held to be the equivalent of initiation *(upanāyaṇa),* serving one's husband that of residing in the teacher's house [and similarly serving him], and the household duties that of the worship of the sacrificial fire."[79] Thus "household tasks become part of the . . . *vrata* or religious observance of the wife [and thus] the high tone in which these apparently mundane tasks are [often] described" in later treatises on *strīdharma* (Leslie 1989, 50). Eulogistic expositions on and illustrations of this *pativratā* ideal were soon to be found in (probably interpolated parts of) Hinduism's great epics. As the ideal became virtually normative, these illustrations and such epic goddess/women as Satī or Pārvatī, Sītā, Draupadī, Sāvitrī, and Anasūyā found their way into the later Purāṇa and Nibandha *vrata* stories accompanying descriptions of these rites. The *pativratā,* then, is the "perfect wife," as Julia Leslie has cogently demonstrated in her book of the same name. In the most conservative view, to rigorously follow *strīdharma* and to strive to become a true *pativratā* should be a Hindu woman's only goal; it is her only legitimate aspiration; the only option that can result in spiritual merit, and the only means by which she can save herself from her inherently flawed womanly nature.[80]

Though, as was mentioned, such goddess/women as Satī/Pārvatī, Sītā, and Sāvitrī—insofar as they exemplify *pativratā* behavior—continue to be held up as role models for women today, these are not role models that ordinary women can easily follow (as women I interviewed told me). Furthermore, the very existence of these model women does not challenge the orthodox view of *strīsvabhāva,* for the texts make it clear that these women were *exceptions* to the general class of women. (See Leslie 1989, 262, 272.)

There are dozens of didactic passages in the epics and Purāṇas, often placed in the mouths of goddesses or important male or female characters, describing how the perfect wife is to comport herself. For example, in the *Mahābhārata* (3.222, 15–35) Draupadī explains to Satyabhāmā how she manages to be the perfect wife to her five husbands; and in another place (Anuśāsana Parvan.134.6,10.30–55) Pārvatī is asked by her husband Śaṅkara to explain what constitutes ideal womanhood and the duties of the faithful wife. Similar in tone and wording, but without the background color of characters and stories, one finds the *pativratā* ideal detailed in sections of the Dharmaśāstras and Nibandhas under some such heading as "*strīdharm.*"[81] What is interesting is that many of the qualities of mind and the self-restrictive behavior that are required of a *pativratā* are precisely the ones required of the votary as described by the Purāṇa-Nibandhas under the "*dharma* of *vratin.*" But this should not be surprising because a woman's (a *pativratā*'s) behavior toward her husband-god is patterned on the worshipper's ritually prescribed behavior before his *kul* or *iṣṭadevatā.* Furthermore, one could imagine that the ideal wife herself, as depicted, for instance in *Manu* 5.165–66 or Mhb. 3.196.6, where the virtuous woman is described as one who restrains and controls her mind, speech and body, could have been the model for the Purāṇa-Nibandha writers' description of the *dharma* of the votary. *Pativratās* would have been the ideal candidates for the performance of *vratas* since they were already trained in all the appropriate *niyamas*.

Aruna's comments quoted earlier—"For women the first husband is the divine marriage" and "I do *vrats* for *suhāg*"—demonstrate how inextricably the concept of the *pativratā* has become intertwined with the *vrat* tradition for women today. Ritual and gender ideology have been powerfully blended in the *vrata* tradition, each reinforcing the other. A woman's primary *vrata* is the vow of service and fidelity to her husband/god which she assumes at marriage. Particular *vrats* that she performs are to promote his well-being, and secondly, that of his sons. Though perhaps not initially the case or the intention, women's *vrat* observance, then, has come to be seen by both men and women as a ritual extension of their "*pativratā*-ness." It is in this context that the most conspicuous omission in the Nibandha writers' application of the *kāmya, nitya,* and *naimittika* classification of *vrata* is to the peculiar situation of women—a situation itself ideologically constructed by these same authors. One of Mary

McGee's important contributions to our understanding of the *vrata* tradition in text and practice is to demonstrate, as she puts it, the "gender-related implications of these distinctions as they are understood by theorists and by the women votaries" (1987, 301). McGee found that women she interviewed persisted in calling (or in so many words describing) certain of the *vratas* they performed as *nitya*, while the texts would label them *kāmya*. In "their treatment of desire *(kāma)*," she concludes, "the *nibandhas* fail to provide a clear slot for the selfless desire"; and secondly, "the nibandhakāras persist in classifying as personal desires *(kāma)* goals such as *saubhāgya* that pertain exclusively to women" (1987, 317). When the Dharmaśāstras defined women's primary *vrata* as *pati-vrata*, and when particular *vratas* that women perform—with the permission of their husbands—are to be directed to *his* well-being, they asked women to submit to a perpetual state of unselfishness. McGee thus calls women's *vratas* (in the main) "rites of maintenance," rites that serve to maintain the well-being of the family, rather than "rites of acquisition," with the usual implication of material benefit or aggrandizement. Today, women continue to (be socialized to) feel obliged to maintain the state of marital felicity, to secure the well-being of their husbands in order to fulfill their prescribed duty as wives. The more *vrats* a woman does, the more devoted (to husband and family) she is seen to appear. Hence the pride and satisfaction that some husbands expressed to me in the number of *vrats* that their wives performed, even when they were not really sure what exactly the women did during these rituals.

It is not difficult to see how *vrats* suit the vision of the role of women articulated by the dominant male brahmanical culture. While some women's rituals, perhaps early folk versions of votive rites, may have been appropriated by Purāṇa-Nibandha author-compilers, the new transformed Dharmaśāstric *vratas* were molded to serve Brahmanical visions of the proper ordering and functioning of society. In this ideal society, women's place and function are made plain. The view of woman's nature as tending toward weakness, sensuality, distraction, idleness and disorder and the need therefore to control women would lend itself to the recommendation of *vratas* to women. That is, pandits and high-caste men in general may have felt inclined to encourage women to perform *vratas* because they saw these rites not only as a way of providing a regular means to instil in women the values associated with the *pativratā*, but also as a mechanism of self-control.

The particular forms of moderate self-restraint, the ritual care for maintaining purity, and the moral behavior prescribed in the Dharmaśāstric *vratas* would all have been seen as contributing to the aims and welfare of men, and by extension, women themselves. Taking the viewpoint of a conservative pandit, then, *vratas* could be seen to be ideally suitable for women to observe. As *vratas* are supposed to be voluntary or optional meritorious rites, women who "choose" to perform *vrats* for the benefit of their families act as self-regulators. Men can indirectly control women by "allowing" women to control themselves; and to control themselves in a way that promotes the interests of a patriarchal social structure.

Yet one must not forget the other sort of lesson that Sāvitrī in the *Mahābhārata* offered. She did indeed act as the perfect *pativratā:* she protected her husband, in fact, wrested his soul back from the god of death. But she accomplished this feat by first refusing to acquiesce to fate, and then by exercising her wit, by perseverence, and by engaging in a powerful vow. "*Vrats* make one strong," some women were to tell me, and "with self-control" and "purity of heart" all things are possible, "all things are obtained." These sort of statements reflect the "posture of confidence" that Sandra Robinson referred to when she compared images of the female in orthodox gender ideology ("brahmanical paradigms") with images of women in what she calls the "Hindu devotional configuration." In both paradigms, she argues, "women are powerful but subordinate, but in the women's traditions their powers are used directly and resourcefully and their subordination is reduced, in effect, to a symbolic level. Instead of consigning their powers and efficacy to male agents as brahmanic consort goddesses do, women in devotional Hinduism exercise their powers themselves for purposes they themselves choose. The purposes in the end do reflect values of self-sacrifice, but the selflessness involved in performing rites for one's family welfare proceeds from a posture of efficacy and confidence" (1985, 209).

3

Vrats, The Seasons and the Festival Calendar in Banaras

Every religious culture has some sort of calendar which sets apart "sacred time" when special rites, observances and festivals occur (Leach 1984; Eliade 1958). Because India is the birthplace of several religions with a rich cultural diversity, and has had a long history of interest in astronomy and astrology, there are several such calendars operating simultaneously. Events are configured with solar and lunar cycles, astrological considerations and the agricultural seasons. The topic of *vrata* is bound up with discussions of time *(kāla)* and the Nibandhas in particular are very concerned with setting out in great detail the appropriate astrological conditions and most auspicious times for the observance of religious rites and the celebration of festivals and other important occasions. As a result, much of the discussion on *vratas* is devoted to determining which are the most auspicious times for their effective performances according to these astrological calculations. Such considerations continue to inform the contemporary *vrat* tradition. This chapter is concerned with describing the articulation of *vrats* with the various orchestrations of time in Banaras.

I arrived in Banaras in mid-October or the end of the month of Āśvin 1984, as the intense heat and humidity of the monsoon season was starting to ebb and the autumn festival season was reaching its peak. Across the river, still high from the rainy season flooding, the Ramnagar Rāmlīlā, a highly elaborate annual ritual reenactment of the *Rāmāyaṇa*, sponsored by the former Maharaja of Banaras, was nearing its finale after a month of nightly performances by well-trained actors. There was no question among the thousands of viewers (or what Richard Schechner has called "participant-pilgrims") that these elaborately costumed actors were indeed the deities (Rām, Sītā, Hanumān) incarnated each evening to play out the divine drama (see Schechner 1993). They had come, not just to watch a spectacle, but to "take *darśan*" (auspicious viewing) of the actor-gods. Around the city, local neighborhood renditions of the Rāmlīlā were also taking place, although these were much shorter and less formalized versions than the grand Līlā across the Ganges.

Throughout the city Durgā Navarātri (also known around India as Durgā Pūjā)—a twice-yearly pan-Indian nine-night religious festival in honor of the goddess Durgā—was about to start. Local "clubs" and other sponsoring groups were setting up *paṇḍāls* (small stages or pavilions) in the narrow cobbled lanes of the old city or near busy intersections. These stages would house brightly painted and decorated larger-than-life images of Durgā in her most famous pose, slaying the buffalo demon. Smaller images of Kālī on the right side and Sarasvatī on the left of Durgā are also often included. For nine days and nights these consecrated images would be the locus of *pūjā* by priests and of prayer and *darśan* by hundreds of reverent Hindus. On the eleventh day, following Vijayā Daśamī ("Victory Tenth"—the day the goddess is victorious over the buffalo demon and Rām is victorious over the evil Rāvaṇ), the goddesses would leave their *mūrtis* and these now lifeless images would be taken in procession to the river to be immersed and washed away.

Amma, a lively seventy-two-year-old South Indian and a longtime Banaras resident—who gave me several afternoons of coffee, spicy snacks and generous conversation—reiterated the popular dictum that "Navarātri is the festival and *vrata* [in the sense of prescribed observance] of the Kshatriyas, as Yama Dvitīya is for Brahmans, Dīpavālī is for Vaishyas, and Holi is for Shudras." Of course, she added, "all the four *varṇas* observe the [Navarātri] *vrata* and do *pūjā* for nine days. Some fast only one or two of these days. Some observe a fast the whole day." Unlike the three other festivals mentioned, Navarātri is also observed as a *vrat* (fast) by many Hindus of all castes and sectarian backgrounds.[1]

Another elderly woman, Hardevi, a seventy-year-old Banarsi Brahman who had founded and directed a girls' school, told me that she started observing Navarātri as a *vrat* on a regular basis in 1940. At that time she was thirty-five, and she had refused marriage in order to be a full-time activist for Mahatma Gandhi. She began the *vrat* because Durgā was her *iṣṭadevtā*, her favored deity. Hardevi learned the *vrat*'s procedure from her family, who were instructed by a pandit. She still observes the *vrat* for the full nine days. In 1940, she initially began the *vrat* with a formal *saṅkalpa* made in front of a *purohit* (a local priest) who told her what to say. This included Sanskrit mantras from the *Durgāsaptaśatī*.[2] In recent years a priest has not been involved in the observance, except, as she explained, when "I don't have time and then I'll call a pandit to do the *pūjā*." Each morning of the *vrat* Hardevi takes a bath first thing, "for purification." This is followed by a simple *pūjā* in which she reads out the *Durgāsaptaśatī* and "all the important mantras." She may also read different verses *(ślokas)* from the *Rāmāyaṇ* and the *Gītā*. The *pūjā* is concluded with an *āratī*. Throughout the nine days she consumes only fruit and milk, the most common fasting regimen during Navarātri.

Hardevi may also, as is customary for all those keeping Navarātri, go each evening to the particular Devī temple singled out that day for a special *pūjā* and where the *darśan* of that facet of the goddess is particularly auspicious. The designation of these nine temples and goddesses is prescribed and the circuit remains the same each year.[3] At the end of the observance of this annual *vrat* Hardevi gives *dān* to a Brahman (the pandit, a neighbor or friend): clothes, money and sometimes food.

The month following the Rāmlīlā and Navarātri is Kārtik, when Viṣṇu "wakes up" and the gods descend to earth. As such, it is an especially holy month, hosting another spate of festivals, *pūjās* and *vrats*. These include Lakṣmī *pūjā* and the festival of Dīvalī (the festival of light). At this time, women clean and whitewash the house, and with rice powder draw the footprints of Lakṣmī, the goddess of prosperity, from the doorstep to the center of the home in order to entice Lakṣmī to bring her good fortune into the home for the year. (See plate 1.) Other late fall observances include Bhaiyadūj ("Brother's Second"), when sisters honor their brothers, and the popular women's Karvā Cauth Vrat observed for the welfare of husbands. During the cold winter months of Mārgaśirṣ and Pauṣ, festival activity slows down, only to pick up its pace in the next month, Māgh. Māgh is another particularly holy month which hosts Banaras' major Gaṇeś festival on the fourth day of the "dark" (waning moon) half of the month, and later the spring festival of Vasant Pañcamī. The month of Phālgun is fairly quiet except for the important *vrat-pūjā*-festival of Mahāśivarātri, the "Great Night of Śiva," celebrated all over India. Festival activity increases significantly in the following month (Caitra), beginning with the exuberant, if not riotous, festival of Holī, the last festival of the religious calendar. In North India the New Year starts halfway through Caitra and the festival cycle turns again beginning with the spring Navarātri, the last day of which is the important *vrat*/festival of Rāmānavamī.[4]

THE *VRAT* CALENDAR

Today in Banaras, if one wanted to find out what *vrat*s were being observed and on what days, or more specifically at what exact time they were to be commenced, the easiest way would be to go to a bookstall specializing in religious material (these are readily found near temples), and buy a wall calendar such as the "Hṛṣikeś Jantri." This particular calendar, published locally in Hindi, is in the same format as any Western calendar—with the days of each solar month beginning in January listed—but it is packed with other information. On each square is given the North Indian Pūrṇimānta system date (the lunar month, the *pakṣa* or fortnight, and the *tithi),* as well as several other time-system dates.

On the right side of the calendar, for each month, are listed all the *vrat*s and festivals and their dates for that month. Included are national holidays and major Muslim, Buddhist, Jain and Christian holidays or observances. The bottom of the calendar explains how to translate dates from one era to another (e.g., Vikrama to Śālīvāhana Śāka), and also provides a summary of the "fruits of the year" (events that may occur). In addition, one finds a listing for each month of the "auspicious moments" for such activities as harvesting grain, preparing medicines, opening a shop or performing the *saṃskār* (life-cycle ceremony) of the infant's first feeding of solid food. On the back of the calendar for each month is given: (1) a list of *nakṣatras* (asterisms or lunar mansions) for the month and phases of the moon; (2) the exact time for starting a particular *vrat, śrāddh* (rite for the dead) or *parv* (festal day or occasion for the performance of religious rites); (3) the monthly horoscopes for each sign of the zodiac; (4) *māsphal* (the "fruit of the month")—a list of predictions on a range of subjects from the weather to grain prices;[5] (5) *mantra-auṣadhi*—local medicines and their uses, for instance, snake venom remedies; and (6) *najar-jharaṇa-mantra*—mantras to avert the evil eye.

This calendar is basically an adaptation (to the contingencies of a Western-calendar-based international business and civic world) of the *pañcāṅga* (lit. "five limbs"; almanacs). As the name suggests, the *pañcāṅga* deals with five topics: *nakṣatra, vāra* (the seven solar days of the week), *yoga* (addition or conjunction), *karaṇa* (a half *tithi*), and *tithi*. The almanacs are prepared from different astronomical texts and are printed today in vernacular languages for local use principally by pandits, priests and astrologers. Aside from personal use, *pañcāṅgas* are consulted by pandits and astrologers to advise clients on when, for example, to set a marriage date, build a house, open a new business, observe a festival, and begin or end a *vrat*. Few Hindus are able to "read" these almanacs easily. Some of the women I interviewed said, however, that they did consult them for their *vrat* observances, as their parents and grandparents had. A calendar like the Hṛṣikeś Calendar just described, however, is more accessible as well as more informative than the almanac—and serves as the layperson's *pañcāṅga*. I saw them hanging in most of the homes of the families I visited.

There are approximately 134 *vrats* listed in the Banaras Hṛṣikeś calendar. I say "approximately" because in some cases where two *vrats* fall on the same day, one encompasses the other. For example, Durgānaumī Vrat falls on the last day of Navarātri. Some people only observe the first day of the autumn Navarātri, some people observe two days of both spring and autumn Navarātri. It is somewhat arbitrary whether one counts these as one *vrat* or several *vrats* from the calendar description alone. Of the *vrats* listed, seventy-two are regularly occurring semi-monthly *vrats*—namely: Gaṇeś Cauth, occuring on the fourth *tithi* of each *pakṣa* (or "half": the waxing moon half is called "bright" and and the waning moon half is "dark") of each month; Ekādaśī, occuring on each eleventh *tithi;* and Pradoṣ, occuring every twelth or thirteenth *tithi* (depending on when the *tithis* start and end). And twenty of the *vrats* listed fall under two monthly *vrats*, namely: Śivarātri, occurring on the thirteenth *tithi* of the dark half of each month; and Pūrṇimā (full moon day), occurring on the fifteenth *tithi* of the bright half of each month. Thus there is a large, almost bewildering number of regularly occurring *vrats* that, in theory, one could choose to observe each year. In fact, however, most people assume or choose the majority of the *vrats* that they perform on the basis of local and family traditions.

It is only a minority of the *vrat*-observing population that actually keeps all the Ekādaśīs or Pradoṣ or Śivarātris in a calendar year. Those who would observe the full twenty-four or twelve of these semi-monthly or monthly *vrats* are generally (though not necessarily) those who have a strong sectarian affiliation; Vaiṣṇavite or Śaivite respectively. Pradoṣ and Śivarātri frequently overlap in the calendar, so, because both *vrats* are directed to Śiva, those wishing to observe a monthly *vrat* as an act of devotion to Śiva would ordinarily do one or the other. About one-fifth of those I interviewed kept all twenty-four Ekādaśīs. In the textual tradition, the Ekādaśī Vrat is probably the most frequently mentioned and extolled *vrat* in the whole Purāṇa-Nibandha corpus.[6]

I did not encounter any person in Banaras who observed all Gaṇeś Cauths except, not surprisingly, a Maharashtrian priest of a local Gaṇeś temple. No doubt other Maharashtrians living in Banaras and many in the state itself, where Gaṇeś has assumed such prominence in the last century, would observe all twenty-four Cauths in honor of the elephant-headed "Remover of Obstacles."

All Pūrṇimās are auspicious days (except if an eclipse occurs) and because of their inherent auspiciousness, observing a *vrat* on this *tithi* may augment the likelihood of a favorable result. But, again, I encountered very few people who observed a *vrat* on all Pūrṇimās. Since the "deity" in front of whom, or in light of whom, the *vrat* is observed is the moon, there is no particular religious affiliation indicated. Indeed, the observance of Pūrṇimā (or certain Amāvasyās [new moon days], or eclipses) underscores the fact that attention to certain celestial configurations is in some cases more relevant to the efficacy of a *vrat* than the show of devotion to a particular deity. This becomes clearer in some of the weekday *vrats* where it is the power of the (divinized) "planets" *(grahas)* that are appeased, softened or channeled through the observance of the rite.

Instead of observing all twenty-four or twelve of these regular *vrats* many people will keep only certain Cauths or Ekādaśīs, totalling between one and four in the calendar year. The special Cauths are those which fall in the months of Māgh, Śravaṇ, Bhādrapad and Kārtik. The special months for Ekādaśīs are Jyeṣṭh, Āśaḍh, Kārtik and Māgh. There is no special month for Pradoṣ—evidently one does them all or not at all. The special months for Pūrṇimā are Māgh and Kārtik. For Śivarātri the special month is Phālgun—the time of Mahāśivarātri—often observed by whole families in Banaras. A full three-quarters of those I interviewed observed Mahāśivarātri, a not surprising finding perhaps for Śiva's city. Many of those observing Mahāśivarātri do not hold Śiva as their *iṣṭa* or *kul* (family) *devtā*, but they keep a *vrat* or fast in Śiva's honor nonetheless. This situation is paralleled in the

Kṛṣṇajanmāṣṭamī Vrat, the other most frequently observed *vrat* in Banaras.

The months of Māgh and Kārtik stand out as the months when particular occasions of the semi-monthly or monthly *vrats* are observed by much greater numbers of votaries. These two months, along with Vaiśākh, are also considered special months as a whole with respect to *vrats* and other religious observances. That is, if one chooses to do a month-long *vrat* for the sake of others or one's own welfare, then Māgh, Kārtik and Vaiśākh are the usual months in which to carry out the observance. In the Hṛṣikeś calendar they are called "Māgh-*snān-vrat*," "Vaiśākh-*snān-vrat*" and "Kārtik-*snān-dān-vrat*" respectively. Those choosing to observe one of these month-long *vrats* (mostly older women and widows in Banaras) would take a daily dawn bath in the Ganges, perform a simple *pūjā*, perhaps listen to the recitation of religious stories *(kathā)* by a priest, perhaps give money or food *(dān)* to the poor, and adopt a fasting regimen—such as eating only once a day or eating only *phalāhar*. Some votaries will also try to get to Allahabad for the important annual month-long Māgh bathing festival and religious gathering.

There is the twice yearly *vrat*-festival, described above, the spring (in Caitra) and autumn (in Āśvin) Navarātri. Almost three-quarters of those I questioned observed a *vrat* either for the whole festival or for certain days (the first and last being the most important) in both Navarātris or just one (usually the autumn).

Cāturmās

In addition to the three special months when it is especially efficacious to observe a month-long *vrat*, there is also, each year, a four-month period known since antiquity as "Cāturmāsa," literally, "four months." This period corresponds with *barsat*, the rainy season, from June through September, or from Āśaḍh bright 11 (Mahā or Śayanī Ekādaśī) to Kārtik bright 11 (Prabodhinī or Devotthani Ekādaśī). It also demarcates on either side the end of the hot season and the beginning of the cold season (i.e., it includes monsoon and postmonsoon). In Hindu mythology this is the time of the dissolution of the world *(pralaya)* when Viṣṇu reclines on his serpent Ananta—floating on the primeval waters—and withdraws into sleep (Viṣṇu *sayanī)*. Viṣṇu's awakening (Viṣṇu *prabodhini)* occurs Kārtik bright 11. Traditionally, Cāturmās was the period during which travel and agricultural work temporarily came to an end—and the period during which wandering ascetics and monks (Hindu, Buddhist and Jain) would stop in villages and towns for an extended stay and hold discourses. It was, and remains, a time for listening to religious stories such as *vrat kathās*. A Banarasi pandit told me that there are more *vrats* and *vrats* are more frequently observed during Cāturmās than at any other time of the year. "Even Buddhists, Jains and Muslims observe more *vratas* during this time," he said. Certainly I found that the women I interviewed kept a greater number of *vrats* during Cāturmās than during any other season or period of the year. The number of *vrats* listed in calendars, almanacs and Sanskrit digests is also higher during this time.

There are various possible reasons for the existence of more *vrats* during Cāturmās. One reason may be connected to the agricultural year. The Cāturmās period is critical for the agricultural cycle because if the rains come in adequate but not overwhelming amounts, the newly planted crops—rice and corn—will flourish and the ground will be ready for the next crop planting in the fall—wheat and barley. If the rains are very late or inadequate, the crops can fail and scarcity or famine result. In her book on Bengali women's *bratas* (Bengali for *vrat*), E. M. Gupta (1984) categorizes the *bratas* according to purpose, one of which is concerned with agricultural themes. *Bratas* such as the Rone-Eyo *brata*, the Kojagaru-Lakṣmī *brata*, the Kṣetra *brata*, the Puṇyipukur *brata* aim to ensure rain, the fertility of the soil, rich harvests, to protect crops and so on. Many of these *bratas* take place during Cāturmās. In Banaras, however, I did not come across any *vrats* that are currently performed specifically for such purposes. While one can certainly detect "harvest themes" in some of the *vrats*, such as the use of the sugar-cane stalk *paṇḍāls* (called *kosi varṇa)* in Ḍala Chaṭh, which I was told symbolizes the new harvest and by extension "fertility" or "fruition," the harvest or the rains themselves are not the object of the *vrats*. It is probable that the urban environment has made such purposes largely irrelevant.

A reason that is possibly more compelling to many urban Hindus today for the existence of more *vrats* during Cāturmās has to do with the effects of climate on health. This was emphasized by the same pandit mentioned above. He accentuated the "scientific" (his word) basis of *vrats*; much of what he said is derived from popularly accepted principles of Ayurvedic medicine. He told me that "Cāturmās is a time of illness" because the "climate becomes polluted, the humours are out of balance and in particular the wind humour [*vaṭa*] is defective." "When it rains," he continued,

> the *vaṭa* increases. The air is full of moisture and carries diseases—especially infectious ones. The "fire" of the stomach is dampened and weakened and so the digestive system becomes weak. . . . Yama [the god of death] "bites" people at this time. . . . Thus to maintain health, less food should be eaten and it should be of a purer—*sattvik*—variety. Hence all the *vrats* prescribed at this time;

vrats which, of course, require fasting or the eating of *sattvik* and seasonally specific foods (foods that are easier to digest and which contain the right balance of nutrients).[7]

A number of other Hindus reaffirmed to me that Cāturmās was a time of increased danger to health and that children are especially vulnerable. In fact there are a greater number of *vrats* (kept predominately by women votaries) which single out children as the primary beneficiary during Cāturmās than at any other season of the year. Examples of these are: Lalahī Chaṭh (Bhādrapad dark 6) for sons; Sūrya Ṣaṣṭhi (Bhādrapad bright 6) for sons, children; Jīvitputrika (Āśvin dark 8) for sons; Aśok Aṣṭamī ("Ahoī Vrat," Kārtik dark 8) for sons; and Ḍala Chaṭh (Kārtik bright 6) also for sons. There are additional observances that parents keep (especially but not exclusively) for children at this time that are not *vrats* as such. For instance, Nāg Pañcamī (Śravaṇ bright 5) is an ancient observance involving the propitiation of snakes which are forced out of their holes in the monsoon and which often end up in people's homes. There is also Kajali Tīj (Bhādrapad dark 3), a ritual in which sisters tie newly sprouted barley behind the ears of their brothers to protect them. Some women told me they also performed a *pūjā* for the sake of their daughters on this day.

Completing the description of the cycles of *vrats* in the calendar year in Banaras, mention should be made of the seasonal monthly *vrats* which include the four Śītalā Saptamīs in the hot/dry season and the four Āśunya Śayanas during the monsoon. Only two women among those I interviewed observed Śītalā Saptamī, a *vrat* whose main purpose was to avert smallpox. Since smallpox is no longer a threat, it is not surprising that this *vrat* is apparently losing its place. I could not find anyone who observed the Āśunya Śayana Vrat, a *vrat* that according to the texts is associated with averting widowhood (for both men and women). It is possible that this *vrat* has also largely gone out of practice in Banaras. Certainly this is not the only *vrat* listed in the Hṛṣikeś calendar for which I could not find practitioners. For example, no one I talked to observed Śravaṇ Tuesdays, the Svarṇ Gaurī Sukṛt Vrat, the Kapilā Ṣaṣṭhi Vrat or the Upāṅga Lalit Vrat. There is little doubt that *vrats* go in and out of practice and that the almanacs and calendars are slow to reflect such trends. In addition, like the Nibandhas, the Hṛṣikeś calendar also tends toward inclusiveness. Thus it contains in its listings some *vrats* that are performed predominately in other parts of India, such as the Kokila Vrat (which McGee mentions as one which Maharashtrian women keep [1987, 490–92]), and the Upāṅga Lalit Vrat, which some women characterized as a "South Indian *vrat*," the Svarṇ Gaurī Vrat as a "Rajasthani *vrat*," and so on. It is clear, then, that referring to a Hṛṣikeś calendar alone is not sufficient for discovering which *vrats* are current in a particular place at a particular time, and that *vrats* while astonishingly resilient as a class of religious practice, are individually susceptible (or responsive) to social and environmental changes. In fact, this may be a reason why *vrats* have proved so resilient.

Tithi (Lunar Day) *Vratas*

While Nibandhas usually arrange their description of *vratas* according to the *tithi* from the first to fifteenth for each "wing" of the month, modern vernacular *vrat* books and calendars usually list *vrats* following the solar calendar (months), though the lunar *tithis* remain as an important (and in most cases crucial) reference. Some *tithis* are much more likely to have *vrats* associated with them than others,[8] although (with the exception of the *pūrṇimās* and *amāvāsyas*) it is not the *tithi* itself so much as its affiliated deity that is relevant to the nature and number of *vrats* falling on it.

Like certain seasons and times of the year, certain *tithis* and weekdays *(vāra)* are associated with certain deities, which in turn may bear upon particular aims and desires of votaries. For example, the third *tithi* is associated with goddesses like Pārvatī and Lakṣmī who respectively preside over marital and material well-being. The fourth *tithi* is associated with Gaṇeś, the remover of obstacles. The sixth *tithi* is associated with both the god Sūrya and the godess Ṣaṣṭhī—a goddess linked with human fertility and children who is worshipped during *vrats* only on particular sixths (and who is especially popular in Bengal). The eighth *tithi* is associated with the fearsome Bhairava aspect of Śiva and the "darker" facets of the goddess, for example, Kālī, Durgā and Śītalā. The eleventh is associated all over India with Viṣṇu, and the twelth conjoined with the thirteenth is associated with Śiva.

Days of the Week—*Vāra Vratas*

Regular solar weekly *vrats* that can be taken up and left off are not, of course, mentioned by the Hṛṣikeś calendar since it gives listings only for the solar months. Many individuals, men and women of different marital, caste and educational backgrounds, observe or have observed a weekly *vrat*. I also met non-Hindus who had kept a weekly *vrat*. Just over half of the women I interviewed had done so. Unlike a large portion of the annual or seasonal *vrats*, weekly *vrats* are not normally handed down in a package of family traditions. They are usually observed for specific periods of time for specific reasons. I found that astrologers play an important role in the prescribing and dissemination of the weekly *vrats*.

Two astrologers *(jyotiṣi)* I interviewed at some length in Banaras gave me more or less the same information (presented in table 3.1) on the ruling planet, and number, color, character, stone and herb or plant associated with each solar day of the week, plus the *rakṣa grahas* ("demon planets") Rāhu and Ketu.[9] Each ruling planet and Rāhu and Ketu have areas of influence, physical and dispositional, on humans. For example, the sun (Sunday) affects blood pressure and people "dominated" by the sun have hot temperaments; Ketu makes people more susceptible to accidents, Rāhu to insanity.

Most Hindus, if they can afford it, will try to have horoscopes or birth charts *(janma kuṇḍali)* done on their newborn babies. The moment the head appears out of the birth canal the prevailing positions of the stars, moon and planets are thought to "imprint" their energy pattern on the person, making him or her susceptible to certain personality traits, behavioral patterns and physical conditions. Horoscopes are thus consulted for such important decisions as finding a suitable spouse and, for those with the means and opportunity, making a career choice. But they are also consulted when things are not going well—for one's

Table 3.1. Days of the Week and Associated Phenomena

ENGLISH	HINDI	RULING PLANET	DEITY	NUMBER	COLOR	CHARACTER	EFFECTS
DAYS OF THE WEEK							
Sunday	Ravivār/ Itvār	Sun	Sūrya	1	red or white	warm	blood pressure
Monday	Somvār	Moon	Śiva	2	white	cool	nervous system, chest, lungs
Tuesday	Maṅgalvār	Mars	Hanumān Durgā	9	red or orange	hot	lower parts of the body
Wednesday	Budhvār	Mercury	Viṣṇu	5	green	cool	skin diseases
Thursday	Bṛhaspativār/ Guruvār	Jupiter	Bṛhaspati	3	yellow	cool	liver
Friday	Śukravār	Venus	Devīs	6	white	cool	urinary tract, genitals
Saturday	Śanivār	Saturn	Śani	8	black	tepid	abdominal region, nervous system
THE *RAKṢA GRAHAS*							
Ketu	(ascending nodes of the moon) "dragon tail" (falling star)			7	ash		susceptibility to accidents
Rāhu	(descending notes of the moon) "dragon head" (eclipse)			4			abodominal region, head, legs

dominant or ruling planet can have both beneficent and malefic influences. A person may be affected in different ways at any one time according to the current astral configurations combined with the individual's ruling stars and planets. The astrologer's job is to determine which astral configurations are operative, what the effects are, for how long this situation will endure, and what, if anything, can be done to maximize any positive effects, or counteract or neutralize any negative effects.

One way the malefic influences of the planets and stars are neutralized is through the use of specific stones which are associated with each planet and which one must wear on certain fingers touching the skin. As one astrologer explained to me, "Take for example the ruby—it absorbs the rays coming from the sun [and] the body absorbs these rays through the stone." The stone can lesson or neutralize the effects of the sun. "Now when the stone is touching the skin it may change the frequency of the blood pressure or absorb the rays which are falling on the body. If the stone is not the right size—if it is too small for the level of the affecting planet's rays—it might break. So one has to consider the weight and height of the person and the age." There are also herbs which have the same effects as the stones. "The herbs have to be changed every fortnight on the full moon and new moon days," the same astrologer told me. "Men wear the herbs on the right hand or arm, women on the left." He then explained that these herbs are tied with threads of a color appropriate to the planet.

Finally, there are special *vrats* which can be prescribed to offset, although not necessarily to eliminate, the negative influence of a planet. As one *jyotiṣi* put it, "My experience is that what is to happen will happen—but wearing gems or herbs or doing *vrats* acts like an umbrella."

The two astrologers regularly prescribed *vrats* to their clients. Because the *vrats* prescribed (usually weekly ones) were geared to achieving very specific ends, they were labeled "*sakām,*" literally, "with wishes" (in mind). Many aspects of the *vrat*—the color(s) the votary is to wear, the color or kind of food to be consumed or avoided, the sex of the votary are all variously correlated with the characteristics and associations of the planets or deities governing the days of the week. Mondays, Thursdays and Fridays are considered auspicious days while Sundays, Tuesdays and Saturdays are ambiguous, or "cruel" as one astrologer put it, because the potential effects of their governing planets are more often than not malefic.[10] Wednesdays seem to be more neutral than other days and *vrats* are rarely prescribed for this day.

According to these astrologers, Monday, Thursday and Friday are the days particularly suitable for women to observe *vrats*. "Friday," said one, "is considered to be female." Indeed, Friday *vrats* in honor of various goddesses (Santoṣī Mā, Annapūrṇā, Sankatā Devī) are especially popular among women in Banaras.[11] The next most frequently observed weekly *vrat* (one-fifth of women interviewed) was the Tuesday Vrat, contrary to this same astrologer's comment to me that "only men do Tuesday Vrat to offset the bad influence of Mars—because men are more 'ferocious' [and] aggressive." However, a number of the women who told me they kept a Tuesday Vrat did so in honor of Durgā or Hanumān—deities associated with Tuesdays—not specifically because Tuesday is "Mars' day." On the other hand, Hanumān is in fact a god who is especially popular with young men because of his association with strength and "manliness." Yet he was also a "favored deity" of several women that I interviewed. One middle-aged woman, who had assiduously kept a Tuesday Vrat directed to Hanumān for most of her life, told me that when she first started the *vrat* as a teenager, her father (and later, when married, her father-in-law) tried to dissuade her from keeping this *vrat* because, they said, "Hanumān is a bachelor; he is not attracted toward women. How is he going to listen to your requests?" She said that that is the reasoning that is given to women. "The menfolk worship Hanumān, but because I had faith in him, I still went ahead" (with her *vrat* for Hanumān).

Bṛhaspati (Jupiter) is generally considered to be the giver of knowledge, prosperity, male offspring and the peace and happiness of the family. The Thursday Vrat, said one astrologer, "is particularly prescribed to married women for the protection of husbands. In marriage the two bodies and souls are tied together with mantras so they will be in a happier condition. Now suppose a malefic influence of a planet is on the husband and the husband's life is in danger—then the Bṛhaspati Vrat is prescribed *to the wife* to help remove the danger" (my emphasis). Again it may be noted how a woman is *expected* to "fix" problems in her family, and to use *vrats* as a means to accomplish this task.

I myself was prescribed a Thursday Vrat by an astrologer. The purpose was to help me "get a good husband," a going concern among many Indians I met since I was already past my mid-twenties and quickly becoming unmarriageable. I was to avoid salt and eat fruit, milk and (milk-based) sweets each Thursday. I was to garland a banana tree "as if a husband," circle around it with lit earthen lamps seven times and have a Brahman say mantras. I was also to give bananas and money to beggars or Brahmans at a temple. No *pūjā* to a specific deity was prescribed to me possibly because it was assumed that I would do some sort of *pūjā* anyway or because I was a non-Hindu, or possibly because the *vrat* is efficacious without *pūjā*.

Śani, or Saturn, who rules Saturday, is the most troublesome planet, especially for those whose fortunes fall beneath his shadow (see Eck 1982, 256). Men and women are equally susceptible, and thus the Saturday Vrat is prescribed to both sexes. "The Śani Vrat is for mental problems" which the planet Saturn (and the figure of Rāhu) can cause. Saturn, like Rāhu and Ketu, is particularly associated with bad luck and difficulties of all kinds. "Rāhu and Ketu are 'shadows'—their effect is like Saturn. When under the influence of Rāhu things are only accomplished with difficulty. [It] affects the body with mental tension and bad dreams—especially full of snakes and demons; and affects the urinary tract," explained one of the astrologers. He then averred that those under the influence of Śani, Rāhu or Ketu "are proud people."

Sūrya, the sun, rules over Sunday. He can be propitiated by men and women for any sort of reason, though one astrologer told me that he usually prescribes the Sunday Vrat in relation to illness. Indeed, in a particularly telling example illustrating both the short-term remedial use so often associated with the weekly *vrats* and the explicit connection made between the characteristics of a divinized celestial body and human bodies, one woman told me that she had been prescribed a Sunday Vrat to help her with a recurrent eye infection. In propitiating Sūrya with her fast and *pūjā*, the sun restored her impaired sight.

SOURCES FOR THE TRANSMISSION OF *VRATS*

An outsider like myself, or a non-*vrat* observer, can learn about *vrats* by reading texts and looking at religious calendars, visiting an astrologer and, of course, talking to those who do perform *vrats*. But these are not the primary sources for the transmission of *vrats* to Hindu women. Sarasvati, a fifty-year-old matron of a large, orthodox Brahman family on the outskirts of Banaras explained to me one pleasant February afternoon in the receiving room of her large house, when, why and how she started to observe *vrats*.

> Since I was a little girl I wanted to do *pūjā* and I used to pick up any stone or leaf and if I had some *gūr* (raw sugar) or offering I would give it and sprinkle water on it. Later, I noticed my mother and grandmother kept a Monday Vrat. At age sixteen I got married and my mother and grandmother showed me how to do this [and other] *vrats* during the year before I went to live with my husband. When I came to my husband's house, there was no house shrine and so I started to do Śiva *pūjā* to a picture . . . by offering it eleven *bel patra* (wood apple leaves), and kept the Monday Vrat. . . . Now I do *pūjā* to the Śiva-*liṅg* behind the house. When I came to my husband's house I saw that my mother-in-law kept the semi-monthly Pradoṣ ("Theras"—13th *tithi)* Vrat to Śiva, plus did daily *pūjā* to Kṛṣṇa (her own *iṣṭadevtā).* She advised me about other *vrats* to keep. . . . I started to do many more *vrats* until my husband told me I was doing too many. I then did *udyāpan* [the formal ending ceremony performed when one discontinues a *vrat*] for several of them and continued with a few. . . . I had three daughters. Meanwhile my mother-in-law started to make special prayers to Harṣi-brahm (their *kuldevtā)* that I may have a son. . . . My fourth child was a son, and when he was born a pandit told me to start keeping the Pradoṣ Vrat. He told me to do this *vrat* because my son's horoscope revealed that the two planets Maṅgal and Cāndrama were ruling—(so I needed) to offset any ill effects that they might cause. [This] pandit told me to do this *vrat* but did not tell me anything except that the planets needed to be (counterbalanced). A second pandit examined (my) son's chart in more detail and told me to keep a Maṅgalvār [Tuesday] Vrat as well. I decided not to do this . . . because I had too much work to do and could not go (so often) without food.

Instead, her son was prescribed a silver ring with a coral to wear on his right hand as a protective amulet. He was also instructed to keep the Maṅgalvār Vrat when he got older. When I met Sarasvati her son was seventeen, but Sarasvati had not told him to do it because she wanted to wait "until he is older and understands the significance of the *pūjā*."

In Sarasvati's case, while pandit-astrologers (would) have played a role in the transmission of *vrats* by prescribing a *vrat* for Sarasvati and her son, it is clearly her mother, grandmother and mother-in-law who have exerted the strongest influence both in encouraging Sarasvati to perform *vrats* and in affecting which ones she has kept. That she chose not to observe the *vrat* prescribed by the astrologer confirms the fact that *vrats* are a voluntary observance. The specific *vrats* that a woman will perform over the course of her lifetime, and the manner in which she will observe them, then, is still determined principally by family traditions—of both her natal and affinal families. In some cases there may be considerable pressure to keep these traditions. In these circumstances the "voluntariness" of *vrats* for the woman remains in the realm of theory rather than social reality.

Women often begin observing *vrats* while children, living in their natal families, as Sarasvati did. They start copying the rituals of older women relatives on their own or are instructed by grandmothers, mothers, aunts and older sisters. They thus learn, through oral transmission and observation, about the names and ostensible purposes of particular *vrats* and the details of their attendant *pūjās* and fasting requirements. "In this way," said one woman, "our traditions and practices regarding *vrats* continue to be passed on. And before doing *vrats* we learn from a pandit or the family that by observing this *vrat* one obtains that fruit. For this one doesn't need to learn anything new because for centuries this has been the custom in regard to *vrats*. For example, everyone knows that Karvā Cauth is for *suhāg* [well-being of one's husband]." In the same fashion, girls learn how to make the ritual diagrams *(cauk, ālpanā)* that accompany many *vrats*, and they memorize the *vrat-kathās*. By the time an older, unmarried girl is ready to start observing *vrats* seriously and on a regular basis, she will be well prepared.

Once a new wife *(bahū)* goes to her in-laws *(sasurāl)* she will quickly discover which calendrical festivals and what *vrats* are part of that family's tradition *(saṁskār, paraṁpara)* and the ways in which they are observed. Sometimes there is very little difference and sometimes there is a great deal of difference in which *vrats* are observed by the families of the bride and groom. There may also be a difference in the manner in which the same *vrat* is performed. In most cases a *bahū* will be expected to adapt herself completely to her affinal family's practice for at the time of marriage, she takes on her husband's lineage *(gotra)*. Yet, while she has to change her *kuldevtā*, she may retain her *iṣṭadevtā*, and continue her own private worship of that deity, at home or in a temple. In Sarasvati's case, her *iṣṭadevtā* is Durgā, and she continued to worship the goddess while also worshipping Śiva and Harṣi-brahm.

A woman may learn additional *vrat*s from friends, neighbors or colleagues who have found one particular *vrat* to be especially efficacious for them. This mode of transmission (as well as a popular film rendition of the *kathā)* has been characteristic of how the relatively new (and decidedly nonpurāṇic) Santoṣī Mā Vrat has been spread throughout India. The elderly unmarried school headmistress, Hardevi, mentioned earlier, told me that she had observed the Santoṣī Mā Vrat for a few months: "I started it . . . because I had some slight trouble where I was working . . . there was a staff teacher around and she told me about it." The procedure of this weekly Friday *vrat* involves rising at dawn and, either at home or in a Santoṣī Mā temple, lighting a small ghee lamp to the goddess, adorning her with a flower garland, and reading or listening to the *vrat-kathā* while holding small quantities of unrefined sugar and chickpeas in one's hand. At the end of the *kathā*, an *āratī* is performed before the image of the goddess while the votary sings Santoṣī Mā's *āratī* song. (The words of the song, in praise of the goddess, are painted on the wall of the Santoṣī Mā temple in the Khojwan section of Banaras.) The fast for this *vrat* requires the votary to abstain from eating anything sour.

I asked Hardevi how she had benefited by keeping this *vrat* and she replied: "The benefit is just here—that I received peace of mind and I feel that I have achieved something." She felt that her troubles had seemed easier to overcome after performing the *vrat*. Whatever the involvement of the goddess had been in alleviating the problems, the lasting benefit for Hardevi in keeping this *vrat* was the satisfaction that she received in taking the problem in her own hands and having successfully strengthened her self-discipline in the process.

Sarita, the married Brahman woman in her fifties (profiled in chapter 1), had also observed the Santoṣī Mā Vrat. Her brother and his family were having some difficulties. A friend of Sarita's told her about this *vrat* so she went to the bazaar and bought the *kathā* pamphlet containing the procedural instructions as well as the story.[12] She said that this *vrat* can only be kept for three months or three years, after which time it should be stopped with a formal ending ceremony *(udyāpan)*. "I did it for the sake of my brother and his family—to help him get a good job, a good house and for his health. I feel it was successful."[13] Buoyed by her apparent success in assisting her brother, she encouraged her son to observe this *vrat* for his studies. She bought him the *kathā* pamphlet and he performed the *vrat* for three months.

A guru may also advise his or her devotee to keep particular *vrats* as part of their religious regimen. This was the case with Mira, where, in the town of Brindavan, the guru who initiated her with a mantra also prescribed four *vrats* for her to follow (see chapter 1). Apparently a "shaman" too may fulfill this role. In describing the activities of an Ahir shaman in the village of Senapur (outside Banaras), Mildred Luschinsky mentions that the shaman told one client "that evil spirits were troubling her and that she should not eat meat or fish for six months, should fast on Sundays, and should offer water to a god (whom he named) after her Sunday bath. He gave her cloves and ash from his holy fire, telling her to eat the cloves and some of the ash and to rub the ash on her body. 'Come back in six months if you are not well,' he said" (1962, 700). While Luschinsky does not specifically use the term *vrat* for this ritual it certainly conforms to a *vrat* format.

Finally, a woman (or a man) may learn on their own accord how to do a new *vrat* through the locally published, inexpensive *vrat* booklets so readily available now in the bazaars and in the bookstalls outside temples.[14] This may happen more frequently in present-day India because of factors such as increased literacy, availability of these published materials, and the breaking up of the large extended families in which older women were able to teach and guide younger women. A woman may purchase a *vrat* booklet, then, when she has heard about a particular *vrat* and wants to try it but has not found someone to show her how it is done. Alternatively, a woman may find that her natal or affinal family do not do any or very few *vrats* and she wishes to observe more.

In sum, traditionally the main body of knowledge about *vrats* and specific information about which *vrats* to keep and how to perform them are transmitted from mother or grandmother to daughter or granddaughter, and mother-in-law to daughter-in-law with the occasional introduction of new *vrats* to a woman by a friend, a family pandit, astrologer or guru. The pandits (caretakers of the Sanskritic tradition and its plethora of rules and regulations) and the astrologers (specialists in the activities of the celestial bodies and their inexorable influences on human affairs) largely depend on written sources for their knowledge of *vrats*: Sanskrit Dharmanibandhas like the *Vratarāja*, various astrological texts, and, to a lesser extent, the *vrat* booklets written in vernacular languages. Greater literacy among women along with the mass publication and availability of *vrat* booklets is allowing women to select new *vrat*s to observe, as well as inevitably leading to an increasing and unprecedented standardization of *vrat* practices. New media like the mythological films and the televisions and video cassette recorders which show them are also helping to popularize previously unknown *vrat*s and spread knowledge of them at unprecedented speeds and to ever wider audiences, including the diaspora Hindu communities abroad.

4

Precept and Practice: The Contours of a *Vrat*

This chapter explores the "contours" of a *vrat* as a particular form of religious or cultural practice from two points of view: the "precepts" as represented by a selection of Dharmaśāstras, and the "practice" as represented by a selection of mostly Banarsi women. Specifically, the chapter addresses such questions as what the difference is between a *vrat* and a festival, a *vrat* and a fast, and one *vrat* and another; who is "entitled" to perform a *vrat*, and the circumstances under which *vrats* may be and are in fact discontinued. The following chapter then describes in detail the individual components that make up a *vrat*. In both chapters precept and practice are juxtaposed so that we can see points of convergence and divergence between what has been prescribed by male pandits and exegetes of "the tradition" and what is accepted and practised by some women in northern urban India today. If the written Sanskritic tradition on *vratas* is not altogether homogenous (itself being largely a product of the interplay between observed practice and ideologically informed prescriptions developed over centuries by various schools of "religious legalists": Dharma-nibandhakāras), the "practice" I speak of is all the more heterogenous. The voices and perspectives of the practitioners, then, are multiple, contextually shifting, and at times perhaps also, to borrow Gloria Raheja's phrase, "strategically deployed" (Raheja and Gold 1994, 3) to take account of who was present when the conversation occurred and what messages may have been wished to be conveyed. Thus, if a husband or father-in-law (or mother-in-law) was present during one part of the interview, some women would respond to certain questions with answers that they felt would meet with their (or my) approval. Later, if I pursued the same question(s) when we were alone, earlier answers might be modified or contradicted. These are not "facts" about *vrats* I am presenting here, then, but rather views, perspectives, understandings given by, on the one hand, a group of (for the most part) long-dead male exegetes, and on the other, a group of living women practitioners of votive rites about the nature of *vrats*, the rules for keeping them, and the reasons and methods for starting and stopping them.

VRATS, FASTS AND FESTIVALS

In one of her comments quoted in chapter 1, Jyoti emphasized the "interconnectedness" of *vrat* and *tyauhār* (festival), describing *vrats* as a form of "entertainment for the ladies." But she also later affirmed that they were "different"; "a *tyauhār* is a 'festival'—one puts on nice clothes, makes nice food. But there may be a *vrat* on the *tyauhār* day, or the other way around." Modern vernacular literature on *vrats*, just like its Dharmaśāstra antecedents,[1] often groups together festivals and *vrats* under the same descriptive rubric *("vrat, parv aur tyauhār")*. In many instances, the actual descriptions of either rite are virtually indistinguishable. Since men and women I met, like Jyoti, also often spoke of them together, I wanted to know how the women I interviewed would explain the difference or relationship between *vrat* and *tyauhār*. "There is a strong connection between *vrat* and *dharm*," Kamala began:

> *Vrat* is a personal thing. Look, what worshipping is done, what fasting is done—these are all for one's own life. But festivals are more social; we celebrate [festivals] by mingling together. . . . The primary difference is this: *vrats* are personal, festivals are social *(sāmājik)*. And then some [*vrats* and festivals] are together. Take, for example, Śivarātri—it is celebrated on the occasion of Lord Śiva's wedding, so everyone celebrates with joy. The birthday of Kṛṣṇa is also a (major) event, so everyone celebrates it. But, for instance, Tīj, Karvā Cauth, Jīvitputrika, Gaṇeś Caturthī—all these are [observed] out of one's desire for [specific] wishes. There is no compulsory rule that everyone should observe a *vrat* on Janmāṣṭamī and Śivarātri . . . everyone gets together and celebrates [these occasions] joyfully.

Kamala opened by associating *vrat* with *dharm* and emphasizing the personal nature of *vrats*: "for one's own life" (even while the ostensible beneficiary is someone else). In other words, *vrats* are an extension of one's personal religious obligations, or an expression of one's personal faith. By contrast, festivals are social; an expression, perhaps, of collective faith. They are occasions to celebrate together with one's family and larger community. Some of these occasions, however, are both *vrats* and festivals. Kamala mentions Śivarātri and Kṛṣṇa Janmāṣṭamī—both of which are usually called *vrats* because observing some sort of fast on these days is traditional. (The texts consider fasting on these occasions obligatory for Śaivas and Vaiṣṇavas respectively, but optional for others.) The tone of the day is one of joy and festivity. Together with one's family one honors and celebrates the deity whose birthday or special day it is. As Kiran's family does, one often goes to the temple on these occasions to give *dān*, participate in another *pūjā* and receive *prasād*. This *prasād* may then be distributed to guests invited to one's home that day or evening for a meal and for all night *bhajan* or hymn singing. These acts underscore the "*sāmājik*" or public and social dimension of these *vrat*/festivals. Through such voluntary acts and also by fasting, one may hope to receive general (or specific) blessings from the deity so honored; or, one may simply perform these acts as offerings of praise without any expectation of return. On the other hand, *vrats* such as those which are primarily observed by women (Karvā Cauth, Jīvitputrika) are often understood to be performed with an expectation of return; a positive outcome to specific wishes. These may involve festivity and group participation in some of their aspects, but they are not considered festivals as such.

For Mira, the main difference between a *vrat* and a festival centered on food. "In a festival we make attractive meals—special meals. In a *vrat* there is a fast. For instance, on the day of the Nāgpañcamī festival we must eat rice pudding and *pūrīs*, and we must do Nāgdevtā *pūjā*."[2] While some *vrats* do not require particularly difficult fasting, and some *vrat* fasts are broken with sumptuous feasts, it is generally the case that *vrats* are most obviously characterized by a complete or partial restriction in one's food intake. This is the one behavioral change that is most readily noticeable. The *vrats* that Mira was observing—like Ekādaśī—were ones in which complete abstention was required.

Such comments on the relationship between *vrat* and *tyauhār*, and others I received, may be summarized as follows. *Vrats* are connected to *dharm;* they are dharmic acts. Women did not mention *dharm* with respect to *tyauhār*. *Vrats* are voluntary and personal; they are performed for some thing or some desire. Festivals are familial; observed for generalized purposes. *Vrats* are mainly kept by women; festivals are celebrated by everyone, "celebrated all over India by all people." In contrast, as one woman pointed out, "Only those who have belief in *vrats* observe them." They may be kept alone or with others. Festivals are always celebrated with others. Festivals are marked by "cleaning and decorating the house." *Vrats* involve fasting—"less or no eating." Festivals involve eating, "making attractive meals," and festivity; everyone "celebrates joyfully," "visits one another." *Vrats* involve performing *pūjā*; in festivals, *pūjā* may be performed or viewed at the temple, but it is not always a part of a festival.

Just as *vrats* and festivals are seen to be interconnected, so are *vrats* and fasts, but to an even greater extent. Among English-speaking Hindus that I encountered, the terms *vrat* and fast tended to be used interchangeably. This is true in the literature on *vrats* published in English in India as well. One women I spoke with invoked Gandhi as an authority on this matter: "Gandhiji used the word *vrat* usually to mean fast," she said. I wondered then whether the Hindi word *"upavās"* conjured a different image from the word *"vrat,"* and so I asked women about the difference. Just under a quarter of the women, including Kiran and Shyamdevi, simply declared that there was no difference between *vrat* and *upavās*. The answers of other women tended to fall into three groupings. In one group of responses *vrats*, again, were seen to be a religious activity while fasts were related to health and healing: "An *upavās* is for health *(svāsth);* a *vrat* has specific *niyams* (ritual and self-disciplinary rules); it is also a religious observance," said one woman, while another explained: *"upavās* is for purification of the body—especially if there is a disease; a *vrat* is observed because of belief in God." "A *vrat* is religious stuff," Kalpana said in English, *"upavās* is unreligious—you can keep a fast when you are sick. *Upavās* is to purify the body," as opposed to a *vrat* which is primarily to "purify the mind."

The second grouping of responses to the question about the difference between a *vrat* and a fast centered on the restricted consumption as opposed to the nonconsumption of food as the essential difference between the two activities. *"Upavās* is complete abstention from food; in a *vrat* there are different kinds of food restrictions"; *"upavās* is fasting, no food; in *vrat* one can usually eat fruit, et cetera." Some women also suggested that a fast, being complete abstention, is more difficult than a *vrat* (where some food may be allowed)—so its result will be greater. That is, total fasting was seen to be more powerful, even outside of a "religious" context.

Finally, a third group of responses affirmed that the relationship between a fast and a *vrat* was that of part to whole; that is, a fast is *included* in a *vrat*. One woman first remarked that "on a *vrat* day there is special *pūjā-paṭh* and one also fasts; this is a *dhārmik* thing." She then went on to explain the special circumstances that require fasting: "when an accident happens in the house—such as someone dies or someone becomes terribly ill or some other terrible mishap occurs—then on that day one doesn't eat or drink anything. That is called *upavās*."

Jyoti's comments on this issue summarize some of the previous points but also make evident the variable meanings of *vrat:*

> Generally a *vrat* is observed as a fast, but a *vrat* is not like a fast, not the same as a fast. Some say "on this day we don't eat"—that may be a *vrat*; or some say, "we don't put on colorful clothes"—that too is a *vrat*; or some time having [first] fed food to some poor [person] one will [then] eat food—that too is a *vrat*. . . . [So *vrat*] has extended meanings. . . . For instance, you may take a *vrat* [resolve] of anything—but a fast is purely your own decision on any day not to eat food. This is *upavās*.

Jyoti began by attending to the fact that in the usual understanding of the term *vrat*, a major and obvious component of the rite is the (variously qualified) fast that one undertakes during its course. She immediately moved on to suggest that the term *vrat* understood in the wider sense as a declared resolve (to modify one's behavior in any number of ways, for any number of reasons, connected or not to *dharm*) may result in, but often does not result in, complete fasting. Thus a *vrat* has "extended meanings" or describes several sorts of activities. As the particular religious observance that we have been discussing, it includes the taking on of some sort of fast. A fast, on the other hand, unqualified by religious contexts, is the specific action of abstaining from taking food, and there may be any number of reasons for this.

DIFFERENCES AMONG VRATS

Women I interviewed sometimes informally distinguished among their *vrats* in various ways. Particular *vrats* were categorized according to whether they were difficult or easy, simple or expensive, or observed alone or with others. However, I also formally asked women specifically what differentiated one *vrat* from another. Some women, while suggesting that differences did exist, insisted that these differences were in fact negligible; others disagreed. The various deities to whom *vrats* are directed was the most commonly suggested source of difference among the *vrats*. Kiran, for example, stated that "One *vrat* is for Devī, another for Śiv, another for Kṛṣṇa—they are different that way." One woman referred to the implications of the worship of one god as opposed to another on different *vrat* days: "For instance, on Bṛhaspativār [for the Thursday Vrat]," she explained, "one should wear yellow clothes, use yellow flowers [in the *pūjā*], eat yellow foods." Kamala extended the implications that the worship of specific deities had on the observance procedures of particular *vrats*. She was speaking in the context of a general discussion on fasting and *vrats*, when she began to point out varying fasting requirements:

> There are several differences between one *vrat* and another. Take Ṛṣi Pañcamī.[3] This occurs after Nāg Pañcamī and Pañcya Tīj. In this there is a special leafy green vegetable that one must eat and one special kind of rice and curd; only these are to be eaten. In Haritālikā nothing is eaten. In Gaṇeś Caturthī, sesame, curd and fruit are eaten. In Janmāṣṭamī one also can take but little. . . . In Ekādaśī, and Jīvitputrika there is a waterless fast. In each *vrat* the importance [= difficulty and requirements] of fasting is different. So the manner of celebration is also variant. Their aims and purposes are also different; and which deity we believe in [worship at that time] [is different]. Each *vrat* has its own presiding deity to be worshipped—so one has to see what that deity likes. For example, we offer *belpatra* [wood-apple leaves] to Śiv, *tulsī* [basil] to Viṣṇu, and *laḍḍu* [sweet chickpea flour balls] to Gaṇeś. We offer Kṛṣṇa milk products. So in a *vrat* we eat that which the deities like. (Also), in the waterless *vrats* there are different timings. For example, in Gaṇeś Caturthī from morning time until the moon appears one keeps a fast, then, having done *pūjā*, one can eat *phalāhar*.

Sarita, among many others, also mentioned that the *pūjā* and fasting requirements of some *vrats* were tailored to the particular "likes" of the presiding deity and she also gave as an example the Bṛhaspati Vrat in which "everything is yellow." I asked her why only yellow things are used and she explained:

> Bṛhaspati especially likes yellow. For instance, say you like white. If you were given black or yellow clothes to wear then you will take them but you won't be as happy as if you got white. Whichever god is there one acts accordingly [pleases that god with appropriate colors, etc.]. Santoṣī Mātā is pleased only by chickpeas and *gūr*—so these things are offered (to her), and red flowers and red clothes too. Hanumānji is also pleased with red flowers and red clothes, but not with *sin̄dūr* [which is only appropriate for goddesses, since it is a symbol of femininity and *saubhāgya*]. . . . You perform the *pūjā* of whichever god or goddess according to their different interests.

According to Sarita and other women, then, an important way to enhance the possibility of achieving a favorable outcome to one's desires is by pleasing the deity to whom one is directing one's *vrat* in this way — paying attention to their *ruci*, or "interests."

Time or a combination of time and deities was mentioned the next most often as the central feature distinguishing one *vrat* from another. Kalyani put it this way: "*Vrat*s are prescribed according to the dates—time, day, month—this is what differentiates them." Significantly, Kalyani is the wife of the Hṛṣikeś Pañcān̄ga publisher, who is himself an astrologer, and as was pointed out in chapter 2, time-date categories are the primary basis upon which *vrat*s are distinguished and presented in the Nibandhas.

Some women focussed on a different aspect or measure of time, length rather than date. That is, certain *vrat*s are supposed to be performed for particular periods of time. For example, the Santoṣī Mā Vrat is supposed to be kept for three months or three years; the Sola Somvār Vrat for sixteen consecutive Mondays. Usha, aged twenty-nine, however, came from a different perspective. She explained that "length of time (of the *vrat*) is an important factor that separates *vrat*s. For Pradoṣ, Gaṇeś Cauth, Tīj—these one should perform for as long as possible or necessary. Others one may choose to do for a specific purpose and limited period of time." While the Dharmaśāstras might consider the last two examples Usha gave as *kāmya* ("desire-born") because they are explicitly for the well-being of sons and husbands respectively, Usha considered all three of these *vrat*s to be long term; as a regular and, to a significant degree, obligatory and necessary practice. These three *vrat*s were contrasted with "other" *vrat*s which were evidently optional, that is, were taken on to address a particular problem or situation.

Vrats are also differentiated according to their aims and purposes. Under this last umbrella category can be placed responses that variously referred to the purpose, motive or intention of the *vrat* or of the votary. The category can encompass a wide range of possibilities. As women's motives and purposes or intentions for keeping *vrats* will be discussed in depth in the following chapters, for the moment it may simply be noted that some women discussed the difference between one *vrat* and another principally by distinguishing among the intended recipients of the benefits of the *vrat*. One such response came from Padma, a Brahman mother of two teenage sons. Her response describes what has been typified as "women's *vrats*" because of the nature of their (women's and their *vrats*') concerns.

> There is a lot of difference between one *vrat* and another; some are Śiv *vrats*, some are Gaṇeś *vrats*, some are Pradoṣ, some are Chaṭh—all are different. The Chaṭh *vrat* is for the god Sūrya and one does it keeping the desire of sons in one's mind. There are only two kinds of *vrats*: one is for *suhāg* and *saubhāgya*, the second [kind] is for one's sons. Worship of Śivji is done for one's husband; Tīj *vrat* is also for one's husband. Gaṇeś Cauth in [the months of] Māgh, Vaiśākh and in Bhādrapad—these (three) are all for desires of sons.

Padma was married to a well-known pandit in Banaras and, while not afraid to forcefully express her opinions, was strongly influenced in those opinions by her observant and orthodox husband. My impression was that her entire identity was bound up, to an unusual degree, by the ideology of traditionally construed *strīdharm*. Thus many of her responses to my questions were shaped by what she considered to be the appropriate answer within the framework of the "good wife" ideal. In other words, as she herself so succinctly put it, there are two kinds of *vrats* that women observe: those which serve the well-being of sons and those which serve the well-being of husbands. For Padma, these stated reasons were exhaustive. We might recall here Sarita's comment (quoted in chapter 1) that "Our *vrats* are for husband and sons; there aren't any for our own desires." These kinds of statements (which were made to me by a number of women) bear strong testimony to the power of an ideology which instructs the "good" wife to submerge her desires under those of her husband. Women are not supposed to express personal desires. Of course, women do have personal desires, though early on they learn to express them obliquely. In Padma's case, she was much younger than her husband and different in temperament and interests. To capture her husband's attention and respect, she had learned Sanskrit and enjoyed showing off to me the many verses *(ślokas)* she could quote to illustrate a point. But the many *vrats* she chose to perform had also captured his attention and respect, for he admired the fact that she could fast so often (for him and their sons), and I observed that Padma always found ways to make it known to him when she was keeping a *vrat*. Thus, Padma had found in *vrats* a means to achieve some of the regard from her husband that she apparently craved.

PERCEIVED DIFFERENCES IN METHODS OF *VRAT* OBSERVANCE

> *Vrat* is just one thing—but the Ahirs [milksellers] do it this way, the Brahmans do it that way. . . . The manner of observing all the *vrats* is different—different in the hill areas, different in Gujarat, in U.P. . . . in each province everyone does the *pūjā* according to their own way. . . . For instance, I do the Mahālakṣmī Vrat with *ālpanā* [wet rice paste]; some do it with dry flour; some don't do [these designs] at all. . . . This is a vast country. Before there wasn't the means for going here and there [travelling]; everyone was on their own [whatever they thought correct, they did].

Almost all the women to whom I asked the question of whether they thought there were differences in the way they observed *vrats* from the way people of other *jātis* or communities did, had ready opinions to offer like Bina's, above.[4] As an educated woman who had travelled a little and who lived in a cosmopolitan city, Bina had noticed differences in methods of *vrat* observance not only from one caste or *jāti* to another, but from one province to another. She speculated that this variation was due to the huge size of India and the historical fact of centuries of relative isolation at the local level. Other women also suggested that there were regional differences but insisted that there were not intercaste differences at the local level.[5]

Jyoti felt that "people in the South observe *vrats* in a more 'pure' original way." Although she did not elaborate, I believe she meant that Southern women followed the textual descriptions and guidelines more closely than Northern women did; and in fact two other women I interviewed, whose families came from Maharashtra and Tamil Nadu, also believed this to be the case. In my own experience speaking with women in Kerala, it seemed that they were more aware of the "correct" (read textual) rules for the observance of *vrats*, even if they did not always adhere to them.[6]

Kamala had also noticed some regional and caste differences:

> In Tīj women [observe] a waterless fast while others take water. Some people conclude the *vrat* at night but we don't do that; we observe the *vrat* for a full twenty-four hours. We conclude it on the next day. In North India, in South India, there are of course *vrats*, but the manner in which they are observed is different. The method is different. Women from the Ahir *jāti* and those who sell vegetables do so even during the [Tīj] day so they take water [during Tīj]. There is a difference in the manner of keeping *vrats* among Brahmans, Kshatriyas, Vaishyas and Shudras. Some don't do certain *vrats*, for instance, Shudras don't do Ekādaśī, et cetera. They mostly do *laukik vrats*. They don't do śāstric *vrats*. Śāstric *vrats* are observed mostly by Brahmans and Kshatriyas.

In response to my suggestion that Shudras do not do śāstric *vrats* because they have not studied the śāstras, Kamala replied that this was not the case. "Now anyone can read the śāstras but the traditions are such that they don't do them. One feeling is that, 'we don't observe these *vrats*; for us they are not necessary. There isn't any benefit.' In ancient times Shudras could not undertake the study of the Veda; but now it is not like that."

Later in our discussion, Kamala explained that "*laukik vrats* are related to people and society" while śāstric *vrats* are "concerned with spiritual things—with the Self [*ātman*] and the Supreme Spirit [*parameśvar*]." While Kamala was trying to say that it is custom and tradition that dictate which *vrats* a person will observe, rather than any intrinsic limitation based on caste specified by the texts (or the keepers of the texts, Brahmans), her explanations of the meaning of the terms *śāstric* and *laukik*, transposed on her earlier comments, suggest that she thought that lower castes tend to be more interested in mundane rather than "spiritual" aims.[7] Kamala implied that one (family or *jāti* group) should not take on new *vrats* that are not part of one's tradition *(saṁskār)* because "there is no benefit." In her view it seems that a *vrat*'s usefulness relates to its suitability to the person observing it.

Apart from asserting the existence of some differences in which *vrat*s are observed among different caste or *jāti* groups, Kamala pinpointed differences in the fasting practices. Deriving their knowledge from personal experience, other women who positively identified differences among castes also focused on the varying fasting practices as the basis for these differences. For example, twenty-six-year-old Sandhya, a well-to-do married Brahman, said:

> Yes, there are differences. Others might eat *prasād* on the *vrat* day, then later take a meal, but I will eat *prasād* only with the meal after the *upavās* is over. There are differences between *jāti*s—within each caste there are certain traditions of observing *vrat*s; the rules are different. . . . The *vrat*s I keep were done by my mother; there is little difference in the method of observing—however, each person gives a personal stamp to them.

And Shanti, the illiterate wife of an indigent *pujārī*, commented that "other" communities do differ in the way of observing *vrat*s from her own:

> They do [*vrat*s] according to their own methods and we do [them] according to our methods. Sometimes people take grains once [a day]; sometimes people take only fruit. Some want to really purify their body, mind and thoughts so they take only Gaṅgā *jāl*. One time I saw a woman taking only cloves for eight or nine days.[8] It depends on their strength; how much stamina one has to bear it.

In both responses, caste or *jāti* custom is acknowledged, but so is individual inclination and ability. Thus, some differences in *vrat* observance are due to the modifications an individual will make to any *vrat* (or fast). In some cases the modifications are made out of necessity, as in the case of the Ahir women described by Kamala who drink water during Tīj because they are outside in the hot sun all day selling vegetables. Nowadays, women may be making more and more modifications out of convenience—to accommodate the practice of *vrat*s to the exigencies of the modern world. Nevertheless, in other cases a woman may choose to be even more self-restrictive than required in order to demonstrate her devotion, or maximize the efficacy of the rite, proving her impressive stamina in the process. For example, Poonam told me about her mother who, at age seventy-five, still observes a waterless fast for each of the two dozen *vrats* that she performs each year. She has maintained this rigorous practice since she first started keeping *vrats* as a young woman. Though Poonam had a rather complicated relationship with her mother, she spoke of her mother's religiousness and stamina with a mixture of pride and awe.

WOMEN'S VIEWS ON THE ORIGIN OF *VRATS*

Scholarly debate in this century about the origin of the mass of Purāṇa and Nibandha *vratas* has resulted in two polarized sets of views. One set has argued that these textual *vratas* were essentially constructed from Brahmanical literature, the other has claimed that the texts borrowed rites from popular practices and "brahmanized" them (with some of these rites remaining both current and "unbrahmanized" to the present day).[9] These views are largely reflected in the variety of opinions expressed by women I spoke with concerning the origin of *vrats* currently performed.

All women were agreed that the *vrat* tradition was very old, transmitted through countless generations. "*Vrats* were originally given by the gods," Sandhya asserted. "One finds them even in the epics." Mira said that "all *vrats* have been made on the basis of the Purāṇ," but their forms have deteriorated. Her daughter, Jyoti, agreed, explaining: "all *vrats* were originally śāstric, but many have become corrupted over the centuries. Those with the original stories (found in the śāstras) are more in their pure form." Gita, on the other hand, held the contrary view that all *vrats* "began from *lokācar* (popular practices)—they are not śāstric." While many women felt that all or most of the *vrats* that people observe are śāstric (as Sarasvati, from an orthodox Brahman family put it, "because a pandit has to tell you how to observe it properly anyway, and he got that from the śāstras"), others expressed a different viewpoint. A number of women said that certain *vrats* are definitely *"laukik"* and others definitely "śāstric," and examples of both were provided.[10] Most women understood "śāstric" to mean "based on the śāstras," "given by the śāstras"; and many took *laukik* to mean "created out of someone's imagination." Sarita explained *laukik vrats* this way:

> Sankaṭ Cauth, Har Chaṭh, Bahulā Cauth, Karvā Cauth—these are concocted. These depend on our successes. . . . How they get concocted is that somebody does a *vrat* and it is successful; [the person] gets what she wants. Then she says [to others], "This is what you should do"—and the *vrat* is made popular. If I come on a Wednesday to Gaṇeśji and do a *vrat*, and I am successful in what I am asking for, then I will tell you how to perform the *vrat* and you may be successful too.

Sarasvati felt that this process is exactly how the Santoṣī Mā Vrat (the only *vrat* which she labeled *"laukik")* caught on. The Santoṣī Mā Vrat, she exclaimed, "came up like the wind and people caught on to it." Sarasvati does not give much credence to the kind of observances practised for the following kind of reasons, "you have to do this [rite] otherwise something bad will happen to you." "This sort of thing usually comes up when someone gets possessed by the Devī; the person who gets possessed utters the threat [literally, fear] that if you don't do such and such, a bad thing will happen to you."[11]

Finally, several women, like twenty-eight year-old Archana, felt that any *vrat* can be observed in a *laukik* way or a śāstric way. "All *vrats* can be śāstric or *laukik,"* Archana explained, "because there are the descriptions of them in the śāstras, then family tradition and personal variations which add the *laukik* content." In śāstric *vrats*, Anjali reflected, "the pandit does the *pūjā* and recites the *kathā* , et cetera. In *laukik vrats* people perform [their own] *pūjā-paṭh* following their heart, and recite *kahānīs* [stories] themselves." Anjali's comments summarize my own reading of the *vrat* landscape.

In order to get a sense of the malleability of *vrat* procedures in the eyes of the women votaries, I asked women whether they thought one could invent a *vrat* or modify its procedures. The great majority of women emphatically responded that one cannot simply "make up" a *vrat*. "Those rules [*niyam*] which have been made," Kamala explained, "to those we must give respect." Mira agreed that one cannot perform a *pūjā* to a method made up in one's own mind. "The rules which have been made in olden times through the Dharmaśāstras—by those very methods [*vidhi*] [*vrats*] are observed; otherwise it will be fruitless." Mira then added, "Sometimes there will be bad effects [from not doing *vrat pūjā* in the proper manner]. There won't be any merit." "You can choose which *vrats* you want to observe or a pandit will advise, but you can't make up new rules," Premlata said, continuing "one has to follow established rules and *śuddh* [proper or pure] practice."

The few women, like Jyoti, who felt that one could change a *vrat* understood the question in terms of modification. "One can modify existing [rules] to our 'convenience.'" Since Jyoti had lived in different parts of the country she could not always do things the way she had done them before, and she did not have her extended family around with whom she could consult. She felt less strongly about the fixedness of the Dharmaśāstra rules than most other women I interviewed. Usha, a married Brahman in her twenties, also initially responded, "Yes, why not?" to which my research assistant, Kalpana, eyebrows raised, queried: "If you were to offer vegetables instead of sweets, could this be done?" "No," Usha replied, "that can't be done. No, according to our own hearts, no; but we do what is both in the śāstras and in our families." She then went on to elaborate how one *vrat* observed in her rural *maike* (natal family) differed in procedure from the way she encountered the same *vrat* being observed in her urban *sasurāl* (husband's family's home). Usha's response stemmed from her awareness of the possible differences between one family and another, between village and city, and between less orthodox and more orthodox practices.

I believe that these women, both those who felt that one could not change a *vrat* and those who accepted varying degrees of procedural modification, were responding to dual messages from the textual tradition that have permeated conventional practice. One message comes from the late vedic and early Smṛti literature and says that the efficaciousness of a ritual depends precisely on the exactitude with which one follows every detail of established method, with possible perilous consequences ensuing from any mistakes made. The other message emerges in the Purāṇa and Nibandha literature and it says flexibility in ritual implements and procedures is permissible when taking into account the votary's circumstances, resources and intentions. Such substitutions and modifications, of course, are usually carefully prescribed, and the texts would seem to assume that a specialist (priest or pandit) would be overseeing the ritual. In the Sanskrit textual *vrata* descriptions, at the end of the section on rules *(vidhi)*, the formula, "if not that [e.g., gold image] than this [silver or clay image]" is often given for each item or action for which substitution is permitted. Neither in the textual tradition nor in practice, then, is there a standard method strictly defined for the correct observance of a *vrat*. The authors of the Sanskrit and vernacular texts on *vratas* reflect their own regional practices; but, aware of other possibilities, they sometimes furnished alternative methods. Women were also aware, as we saw earlier, that the same *vrat* could be performed in different ways.

ENTITLEMENT IN THE OBSERVANCE OF *VRATS*

The issue of *adhikāra* (right or entitlement) to observe *vrats* is a topic that always concerned the Dharmaśāstra writers. While it was not a problematic issue for the women with whom I spoke in the same way that it is in the śāstras, there are several points of convergence between text and practice here. First, I will give some background on the textual discussion of *adhikāra*.[12]

It has been suggested by some scholars (e.g., P. V. Kane and R. Hazra) that the Purāṇa writers opened the doors of brahmanical religion to all members of Hindu society as part of their effort to attract more adherents (see note 9). Basing much of their material on the Purāṇas, the Nibandha writers followed suit. Kane and other scholars have stated that rites like *vratas* were available to all to perform, in contrast to the restricted access imposed on most *smārta* rituals (rituals derived from the Smṛti texts). Indeed, the texts themselves give the strong impression of an "open door" policy with regards to *vratas*. For example, Kane quotes the Smṛti writer Devala concerning who could benefit from observing *vrata*: "There is no doubt that [people] of all varṇas are released from sins by observing *vratas*, fasts and restrictive rules of behaviour [*niyama*] and by mortification . . . [*tapas*] of the body" (1974, 5,1:51; also quoted in the VR, p. 6). According to the *Vratarāja* (p. 6), the *Skandapurāṇa* says:

> those who have the authority to observe *vratas* are the non-greedy, the truth-speaking and those who are actively engaged in the welfare of all living things. Others would find that their *vrata* efforts were fruitless. Those having faith, who have fear of sin, who are without anger and pride, who follow through on decisions, who are not against the Veda, and who have knowledge are authorized to observe *vratas*. Those in all four *varṇas* and all four *āśramas* have the authority to observe *vrata*.

The *Vratarāja* then continues: "The *Devīpurāṇa* [quoted in] Hemādri says . . . those who are daily bathers, who believe in performing *vrata* and who have no jealousy, Brahmans, Kshatriya, kings, Vaishyas, Shudra, Bhaktivan, *mleccha* (outcasts, foreigners), and women all may listen to the rules of *vrata*." In other words, the primary qualifications for observing a *vrata* are being law-abiding (as mandated by the Dharmaśāstras) and being of noble intent. With these qualifications, anyone is entitled to keep a *vrata*.

Yet, while some of the restrictions normally imposed on women and Shudras because of their assigned low (or variable) ritual status were lifted in the case of *vratas*, the door was still not as open as the texts themselves would have us believe in their general statements on entitlement. In the case of women, although one can find a number of *vratas* prescribed specifically for women (including courtesans as one category of female votaries[13]), these *vratas* tend to underscore a by now well established *strīdharma* ideology. Furthermore, the injunctions of Manu (2.66) and others (e.g., Yāj.Sm. 1.13) regarding restrictions against women performing aspects of rituals (like vedic mantras) or any religious rites *on their own* continued to prevail, if not become further entrenched.

As McGee writes: "Since entitlement to perform *vrata* implied the right of ownership and enjoyment of the fruit of the ritual, the *nibandhakāras* [had to take] special care to explain women's and *śūdras*' rights regarding the performance of *vrata*" (1987, 77). A second type of restriction, she explains, "results from the fact that the rite in question may include or depend upon activities that in themselves are not open to everyone; in such an instance the entitlement to the rite in question is limited by implication to those entitled to perform the activities that it presupposes" (1987, 78). A third type of restriction relates to capacity—"physical, intellectual, financial or otherwise—to carry out the ritual activity in question" (McGee 1987, 79). For this reason there are rules in these texts restricting the length of time that Vaishyas, Shudras, and women can fast. For example, the same *Devīpurāṇa* quoted in the *Vratarāja* above stipulates that "Vaishyas and Shudras can fast for only two nights; if they do more their effort will be fruitless." Women in like manner are prohibited from fasting for too long with similar consequences if they do. As McGee correctly argues in this regard, there is no realistic basis for supposing that lower-caste groups or women are physically (or mentally) less sturdy than Brahmans or Kshatriyas, but, "it is likely," she continues, "that the *brāhmaṇas* did not wish to have the services of either group endangered by the weakening or distracting effects of prolonged fasting" (1987, 80).

Finally, the Purāṇa and Nibandha texts reiterate the old injunction (following Manu 5.147) that married women do not have the authority to observe *vrata* (or other ritual activity) without the permission of their husbands. Both Kane and the *Vratarāja* quote the *Viṣṇudharmasūtra* (25.16), which says that "a woman who fasts without the permission of her husband will reduce the longevity of his life and herself will go to hell." The *Śaṅkhadharmaśāstra* is quoted as saying that: "*strīdharm* is [the observance of] *vrata* and fasting performed with the permission of the husband." Yet, again, the author of the *Vratarāja* says (p. 7), "it cannot be said that only the permission of the husband is necessary for widows can do *vrata* too. As the *Mārkeṇḍeya-purāṇa* says, women can get permission from husbands, fathers or sons."

In regard to women and entitlement for *vrata*, then, it would appear that first the Purāṇa and Nibandha writers *wanted* to make sure that it be known that women had the right to observe *vratas*. However, the pandits' liberal declarations (whatever the true motivation) when translated into practice kept getting entangled in the somewhat inflexible *mīmāṃsā*-generated rules—rules and injunctions that were not meant to apply to women or to "popular" religious practices. The equivocation or ambivalence about women's right to perform *vrata* among Smṛti writers is illustrated in some of their statements on *vrata* which would appear to exclude women and Shudras altogether from observing them. For example, the *Vratarāja* (p. 13) quotes Dakṣa as saying that "he who does not do (the twice daily) *saṃdhya* is impure and therefore has no authority to observe any religious work. If this person should do a *vrata*, no benefit will accrue." Women were not supposed to perform *saṃdhya*. Or again, the *Vratarāja* (p. 13) quotes the *Chandogapariśiṣṭa* as saying, "one should wear a sacred thread and have a topknot—and those who do not cannot receive the benefit of a *vrata*." Again, obviously, this would exclude women and Shudras.

Second, the Purāṇas and Nibandhas continued to insist that men be given control over women's religious activity, even when this activity was to be directed for the benefit of the men themselves. The apparent need to reassert Manu's injunction may suggest that many women were already observing *vratas* (or similar rituals) regardless of fathers', husbands' and sons' approval.

Most women readily asserted that anyone can observe a *vrat*, as the texts suggest. To this many added further comments such as: "even non-Hindus do," or, alternatively, "*if* you are a Hindu," again coinciding with the different opinions of the Dharmaśāstras. Other women qualified their affirmations that anyone can perform a *vrat* in one of three ways. In the first way the "can" was understood as "should," as in: "if you have belief *(viśvās)* in them"; "if you have the feeling in your heart"; "if there is a desire inside." Or, as Sarita put it: "To me it doesn't matter. Anyone may do a *vrat*. God is one for everybody. Whoever has belief in these (*vrats*) . . . whether they be a Hindu, a Muslim, a Christian . . . it is no problem." In the view of these women, genuine faith in the deity to whom the *vrat* is directed, or belief in the efficacy of the ritual, is an essential prerequisite to the performance of a *vrat*. Otherwise the ritual would be meaningless, mere imitation. Anyone, then, who has such faith or conviction may perform a *vrat*. Shyamdevi emphasized this, as did many other women. These sorts of statements again underscore the *bhakti* or devotional orientation of *vrats*, an orientation which, while present in the texts, has been particularly embraced by women.

Still other women interpreted the question of entitlement to refer to the *ability* of specific individuals to perform *vrats*. Jyoti's comment reflects this understanding:

> Yes, anyone in the Hindu Dharm; people of all *jātis* and anyone can observe. This depends on one's *śakti* and how much ability [one has] in that. For example, in the Tīj Vrat one starts the *vrat* without taking any water, but it depends on how much ability you have [to carry the *vrat* through to its conclusion].

Looking at the experience of her husband, and perhaps others, Jyoti saw that not all people who wanted to do *vrats* or who started them were in fact able to carry them through to their conclusion. Although this is not strictly an issue of entitlement, the Dharmaśāstras in other places also acknowledge the varying ability that individuals may have to undertake fasts, and they stipulate acceptable concessions in the fasting requirements. Significantly, many men and women with whom I spoke seemed to think that women were more *able* to fast than men on a regular basis, due to greater stamina. Some scholars writing about *vrats* have also commented on women's apparently greater proclivity if not ability to fast. For example, the anthropologist

R. S. Khare admitted: "Actually, women pursue more varied forms of fasting and practice greater austerity on more occasions in feeding themselves than men under the spiritual fasts. They go without salt, without ghee, without oil, without 'plough-grown' . . . rice, without milk and milk-products, and sometimes without any food or drink for twenty-four hours or even more" (1976, 149).

The third way in which women I interviewed reflected on the issue of entitlement was in terms of the question "can anyone observe *any vrat?*" It was from this angle that Kamala commented that:

> Ekādaśī, Pradoṣ, Amāvāsya, Pūrṇimā, Janmāṣṭamī, Śivarātri, Rāmnaumī—these *vrats* can be observed by all. But Karvā Cauth, Jīvitputra and Sāvitrī Vrat—all these are observed by women. And all other *vrats* anyone can do, whether they are male or female. For these there isn't any stricture against sex, age, et cetera.

And Kiran, making even finer distinctions among the women's *vrats*, said:

> Only women can observe Karvā Cauth, Vaṭ Sāvitrī; girls do Candra Vrat (and) Surāj Cauth. Some *vrats* can only be done by women with sons, for the sake of their sons, like Ahoī Vrat [Aśok Aṣṭamī]. Widows with sons can observe these, but not others.

As we have seen elsewhere, women themselves often readily make a firm (and usually consistent) distinction between what I have termed "familial *vrats*" which the whole family can observe (and some of which are also festivals often connected to visits to temples and larger community celebrations), and then the "women's *vrats*," some of which are only for unmarried girls, some for married women, and some for mothers of sons.

Lastly, I present Mira's response to my question; a response that anecdotally expressed her self-consciousness of "outside" perceptions of Hindu women's rites:

> Anyone [can observe a *vrat*]. Believers in Hindu *dharm* keep *vrats*. They [*vrats*] won't catch on to the hearts of other people; it has come through the family traditions of Hindus [who] do [these things] with faith and devotion. Other people will think

> that all these things are useless. Outside people will not do [these things]. For example, on the second day of Dīpavāli we worship the Govardhan mountain, which we make out of cowdung, and in that we tuck in many small pieces of cotton and plant a small tree. When my daughter-in-law who is a reader at B.H.U. Medical College saw all this, she was astonished and began saying, "What foolishness is all this? Can anyone really worship cowdung too?" When my daughter-in-law who is an Indian says such things then what will others and foreign people say? They won't believe it!

Related to the issue of "entitlement" is the question of "permission." Did women feel that they had to ask permission from their husband, other male relatives, or a pandit in order to observe a *vrat* as the śāstras stipulate? Most women felt that it was not necessary to ask permission, and they gave a variety of comments and explanations as to why this was so.[14] "I never had to ask permission," exclaimed the elderly school mistress, Hardevi; "In my [natal] family we were all free." Kavita, a fifty-six-year-old widowed Brahman, stated that "*vrat*s are performed from personal inclination; it comes from the heart" (so permission from someone else is not needed). And Sudha, a twenty-four-year-old well-educated single Brahman whose father had died a few years previously, explained that there are days for every god and so "it is not necessary to ask [permission or get instruction] from the pandit. For instance, I observe the Durgā Vrat [every Tuesday] for myself alone; it comes from the heart." Lakshmi, aged nineteen and newly married, said much the same thing as Sudha, adding that one could ask a pandit if one needed to know how to observe a particular *vrat*, "about the details of the *vrat*." But later, Lakshmi told me that her father had urged her to stop the few *vrat*s she kept when she got married so as not to weaken her body (and possibly compromise her ability to get pregnant, which would reflect negatively on him).

Lakshmi's grandmother, whom I interviewed separately, told me that if the *vrat*s follow the family tradition, it is not necessary to ask permission from one's husband or elders, but if a woman wanted to start a new *vrat*, she would have to ask first. This is probably because performing a *vrat* takes up a woman's time and energy and may incur expenses that draw from the joint family's shared resources. For a young daughter-in-law in particular, the use of her valuable time and energy is usually strictly controlled by her elders. Even if the new *vrat* the woman wished to take up was to be directed to benefit others in the family, the time, energy and resources needed to observe the *vrat* would require that senior members of the family give their assent. As she got older and established her authority, permission would become perfunctory. And obviously, with respect to the *vrats* that members of the extended family are already keeping, permission is assumed. Indeed, as I discuss in chapter 6 the new daughter-in-law will be expected to take on the family's regularly kept *vrats* as a matter of course.

An elderly Brahman woman, Sartarji, whose husband had beat her and from whom she is presently estranged said that she used to ask his permission to keep *vrats* "so that later he won't get angry and possibly upset the *vrat*." Here it was clear that Sartarji was not simply conforming to a traditional rule, but was trying to avoid the possible negative practical consequences to herself and to her *vrat* if she acted alone or without his agreement.

Finally, Premlata, who comes from a fairly traditional and well-to-do Brahman family, revealed something of her manipulative strategy with respect to her (late) husband when she answered: "From a pandit I don't believe it is necessary, but from my husband I certainly used to ask [permission to keep a *vrat*]. And when he forbade it then I said that the Lord of lords [i.e. husbands] is God. He was religious minded so in the end he would agree with me. I kept some *vrats* even without asking him," she ended with a smile.

VRATS AND MALE FAMILY MEMBERS

I did not normally ask women specifically what *vrats* their fathers or husbands or brothers performed. Instead I asked the general question; "who in your family observes *vrats*?" Typically the reply was "all do," or "all the women do," but not infrequently a male family member was mentioned as well as the particular *vrat*(s) he did. Here, Kṛṣṇa Janmāṣṭamī and Mahāśivarātri were cited most often; and among the weekly *vrats* the Tuesday Vrat was named the most frequently, with the occasional mention of other weekday *vrats*, excepting Friday and Wednesday ones. Kiran, for example, said that all family members observe Janmāṣṭamī and Śivarātri, and that "father also sometimes does Śravaṇ Somvār. My oldest brother always keeps the Tuesday

Vrat; and second oldest brother sometimes does the Monday Vrat." She then went on to the much lengthier list of the *vrats* that her female family members kept.

Kamala commented that everyone observes *vrats* in her family, but some keep one *vrat*, and others keep another. "For example, my son observed Hanumānji Vrat on Tuesdays [for his studies]. When he started to [leave home] then I said, 'Son, now you must give up the *vrat* because alone it will be difficult for you to do the *vrat* properly.'" Keeper of the hearth and the *vrat* tradition in her household, Kamala was anxious that her son in his juvenile (and perhaps masculine) ignorance of these matters would compromise the *vrat*, at the very least by not knowing how to prepare the requisite fasting foods. He said he would stop. This attitude toward men's performance of *vrats* is not unusual. As we saw in chapter 3, Sarasvati was also concerned about her son's ability to keep a weekly *vrat*. Even though he was already seventeen at the time of our meeting, she was still not prepared to pass the *vrat* on to him, submitting that he may still not "understand its significance." It is clear that women view the performance of a *vrat* as a very serious matter. A *vrat* must be done properly or not at all. Jyoti, too, felt obliged to take on the *vrat* that had been prescribed for her husband when he began to be delinquent in its performance. Since the *vrat* had been prescribed, she feared the consequences of its not being continued to its conclusion.

Aside from a certain possessiveness that Hindu women seem to feel about the *vrat* tradition, these examples demonstrate women's pressing sense of responsibility for the mental and physical health and safety of family members. As Veena, a twenty-two-year-old woman married to one of the sons of a large joint family, positively and succinctly put it: "women do the protection of their families." When *vrats* are prescribed to husbands (as in Jyoti's case) or to sons (Kamala and Sarasvati) it is the wife or mother who takes it upon herself to ensure that the *vrat* is properly performed (or not prematurely abandoned) so that it will help bring about the desired state of affairs.[15]

When I asked Annapurna, a forty-year-old and illiterate married Brahman, if men could observe women's *vrats*, she replied that men could observe all the *vrats* that women do if they had time or were inclined to. She then cited as proof some of the men (mostly relatives) she knew who observed *vrats*. The conversation continued:

> *So men can observe* vrats *in the same way that women do?*
>
> Yes, they can. For instance, women have their monthly "*dharm*" [period], so men can do the *vrat*. . . . My maternal grandfather and maternal uncle observed Pradoṣ Vrat. My father-in-law used to do the Monday Vrat. Any man or woman can do a *vrat*. My grandfather and uncle both also used to observe Dvitīya Vrat, Gaṇeś Cauth, Lalahī Chaṭh. If a child has no mother then a man can do the *vrats*. He *should* do them.

The Lalahī Vrat is in fact normally a woman's *vrat* done for the sake of children; but in this woman's maternal family some of the men had conjointly observed *vrats* with their wives for the sake of their children. Among the women I spoke with about this matter, this practice was considered unusual, but not strange or preposterous. Some *vrat* observances require the joint participation of husband and wife. For example, Lolark Chaṭh (Bhādrapad bright 6), considered by many Banarsis I spoke with to be a "country-folk" *(deśi-log) vrat*, requires that husband and wife together make the pilgrimage to Lolarka Kund in Banaras, bathe together in the *kuṇḍ* with sari tied to dhoti, make offerings to Sūrya, and fast for the sake of obtaining sons. Alternatively, these things may be performed in gratitude for having obtained a son in the previous year and to seek such blessings for the son's continued well-being.

Nevertheless, as Shyamdevi emphasized, men simply do not do many *vrats*, and certainly not many in comparison to women. "Menfolk keep Śivarātri," she explained, "and when they do '*kanyā-dān*' [gifting their daughter the bride] then men keep *vrats*. The father does it. If the father does not keep it then the brother can do it or the father's brother can." She continued:

> If a child is born womenfolk are in bed for a full twelve days, if not for about a month and a half—so men can observe their [the women's] *vrat*(s) [during this time]. They are eligible, but they don't usually do it.
>
> *But if some man is in trouble, what does* he *do?*
>
> Well, men may also keep doing [rites]. Oh! they are growing a beard? Some trouble is there; they decide they have some problem; they will do some *pūjā*. When the problem is solved then they will shave; or, if men have problems, they will do *pūjā* in the temple.

So the wife does the vrat *for him.*
Yes, it is like that.

Sarita agreed that men can and do keep *vrats*, but the difference was that men keep *vrats* "for God," "for *mokṣa,*" not for the sake of their families as women do. According to Sarita, this is not their role and is not expected of them, "though they are capable."

DISCONTINUING *VRATS*

Women offered a number of reasons for giving up certain or even all *vrats* that they had been keeping. One woman stopped her weekly *vrat* when she got married because she knew she would have to begin several others in her new home and she did not want to overburden herself. Another said that she had been observing the Pūrṇimā Vrat for her own benefit, but stopped it when she had children, because she needed to start new *vrats* for their sake. In both these cases *vrats* that were kept for the benefit of the women themselves (for personal reasons) were given up in favor of taking on *vrats* for the sake of others. Some women said they had to end certain of their *vrats* because there was too much household work to do. Other women said the objective or desire *(kāmana)* of the particular *vrat* had been fulfilled and so the *vrat* could be formally ended. Responses that pinpointed the fulfillment of a specific objective as the reason for stopping a *vrat* were offered almost exclusively in the context of the discussion of a weekday *vrat* or the Santoṣī Mā Vrat. Several widows said they stopped some of their *vrats* (those specifically slated for *saubhāgya)* when their husbands died. The most frequently mentioned reason for giving up *vrats*, however, was poor health.

There are also circumstances under which a *vrat* should not be observed. Bajanti told me that she had to leave the Gaṇeś Cauth Vrat (for sons) because she had inadvertently eaten on the day the *vrat* was to be observed. She explained that once her mother was in hospital and (while staying with her) Bajanti could not find out when the *vrat* was, and so she ate food, thereby breaking the fast. She felt that she could not start this *vrat* again because it would be inauspicious. Usha stated that, "When someone in the family dies on a festival or *vrat* day then the family will cease to observe the festival or *vrat* for the rest of their lives, unless a son happens to be born on that very day." The birth of a son is such an auspicious occasion that it will reverse any misfortune associated with a particular day previously so tarnished. In corroboration, Bimla mentioned that "around here no one can observe a *vrat* on the fifth [*tithi*] . . . because my brother-in-law's son died on that day." Other women spoke about being unable to observe *vrat*s for varying numbers of days immediately following child-birth, or following a death ("for thirteen days"). These periods of impurity (referred to in Sanskrit as *sutaka aśauca* and *śava aśauca* respectively) do not break the *vrat*, but they do postpone its performance.

The injunctions regarding women performing any ritual during times of impurity (i.e., menses or childbirth) are elaborated at length in the Dharmaśāstras, as are the stipulations regarding the use of and the authority to be a proxy *(pratinidhi)*. Generally, if a *vrat* that a woman has been keeping comes during the time of her menses, she may observe the fast and other self-restraints, but must refrain from performing a *pūjā*, going near the place of *pūjā*, or giving *dāna*. In short, a woman is to avoid any part of the *vrata* in which her polluted state can be adversely transferred.[16]

A few women said they could not do the *vrat* at all if menstruating; they would take it up again later. Most said they would continue with the fast, but they could not do the *pūjā*, some adding: nor touch the *mūrti* or any religious book, or the *tulsī* plant, or go to the temple. "But you would still receive the full merit," Sandhya affirmed. Shyamdevi's niece, Lakshmi, was the only woman who thought menstruation should not make any difference: "We can do *pūjā* during menstruation time—after all, these things are given by the gods and the goddesses are women, aren't they?"[17]

For most women sickness did not seem to compromise the *vrat* either. "If [I was] really sick," said twenty-six-year-old Sandhya, "I will leave the *vrat* and start again later, no problem." "If sick, and I needed to drink medicine (during the *vrat*) that would be alright," Chandralekha, aged thirty-five, reflected. And indeed, the texts do allow *"auṣadha"* (medicine) during a *vrat*. Lastly, nineteen-year-old Lakshmi who, like many women, was not familiar with the detailed injunctions of the texts, nor in her case was she particularly concerned about what the pandits might say, stated matter-of-factly: "If one is sick and can't finish or do the *vrat* properly, Bhagwan (God) will not get angry, he will understand."

According to the Dharmaśāstras, *vratas* (though not *prāyaścitas*) may be practised through a proxy. "The performance of a *vrata*," the *Agnipurāṇa* (chap. 128) says, "may be delegated to one's son in the case of ill health." Other texts say that a substitute for a *vrata* could be a wife, husband, elder sister, brother, pupil, *purohita*, and a friend.[18] Some texts insist that the proxy be a Brahman. But whoever the proxy, the votary still reaps the fruit or merit of the *vrata*, if the *vrata* is *nitya* or *naimittika*.

While women generally agreed that a votary could use a proxy to complete the worship portion of a *vrat* if she was menstruating or was otherwise incapacitated, most seemed to think that this was unnecessary.[19] Forty-one-year-old Bajanti, from an orthodox Brahman family, informed me that: "You can't leave the *vrat* [if sick]; you may use [your] husband as a substitute; if he can't, then a *kanyā* [prepubescent girl] will do."[20] Annapurna, a middle-aged, poor Brahman woman commented that, "A husband should be the first substitute. If not then another Brahman woman who is more respected than me, or girl [*kumarī* or virgin] can do it. [But] I have not done this; despite illness I always keep a *vrat*. Once started I don't want it to stop." Whether one uses a substitute or completes the fast and *pūjā* even when sick, the majority of women interviewed asserted that "not completing a *vrat* [when one can] is very inauspicious."

In this chapter, we have seen that there are many points of convergence between the dharmaśāstric presentation of the *vrata* tradition and women's practice of *vrats*. Women view *vrats* as strongly connected to *dharm;* both as an expression of personal religious obligations and of faith. Because of their ritual and spiritual context, *vrats* are distinguished from mere fasting *(upavās)*, and because of the self-sacrifice (principally in the form of noneating) and discipline required in *vrats*, they are distinguished from festivals. Some women located differences among *vrats* principally in their differential fasting requirements, and differences among individuals or group *vrat* observers in terms of their varying ability to fast. Indeed, many women and men I spoke with felt that women as a group were more able to fast than men as a group. Unlike the Dharmaśāstras, women made a point of associating *vrats* with women; this was contrasted with the situation obtained in festivals, which do not have such gender-specific associations.

Coincident with the Dharmaśāstras, women felt that anyone could perform a *vrat* (even non-Hindus) provided that he or she did so with genuine conviction. But, contrary to the stipulation of the texts, most women felt that asking permission to observe *vrats* from pandits or husbands was not necessary. Women usually followed their own heart on this matter, assuming that husbands would not forbid it. In fact, if anyone were to be asked, it would be the mother-in-law, the person who usually wields the real authority over the daughter-in-law. The vast majority of women I spoke with did take the guidelines governing their worship practices during periods of impurity very seriously: avoiding *pūjā* while menstruating, for example. A number of reasons were offered by women for giving up all or certain of the *vrats* they had been keeping. Fufillment of the *vrat*'s purpose, overwork and especially ill-health were prominent among these reasons. Many married women expressed a marked sense of obligation to continue with their regular *vrats* whenever possible; especially those specifically related to the maintenance of familial well-being. While this sense of obligation testifies to the power of an ideology which locates women's value and function in terms of their adherence to *strīdharm* as well the success of the socialization that brings it about, it also speaks to women's positive self-affirmation of the significance of their responsibilities and abilities—for it is women who "do the protection of their families."[21]

Plate 1. Preparations for Lakṣmī *pūjā* in a home shrine. Stylized feet have been drawn with rice paste on top of an ochre base from the door of the house to the home shrine (in Lucknow). Beneath the rice bowl and other vessels on right is a *śrī yantra*, a geometric design symbolizing the body of the goddess.

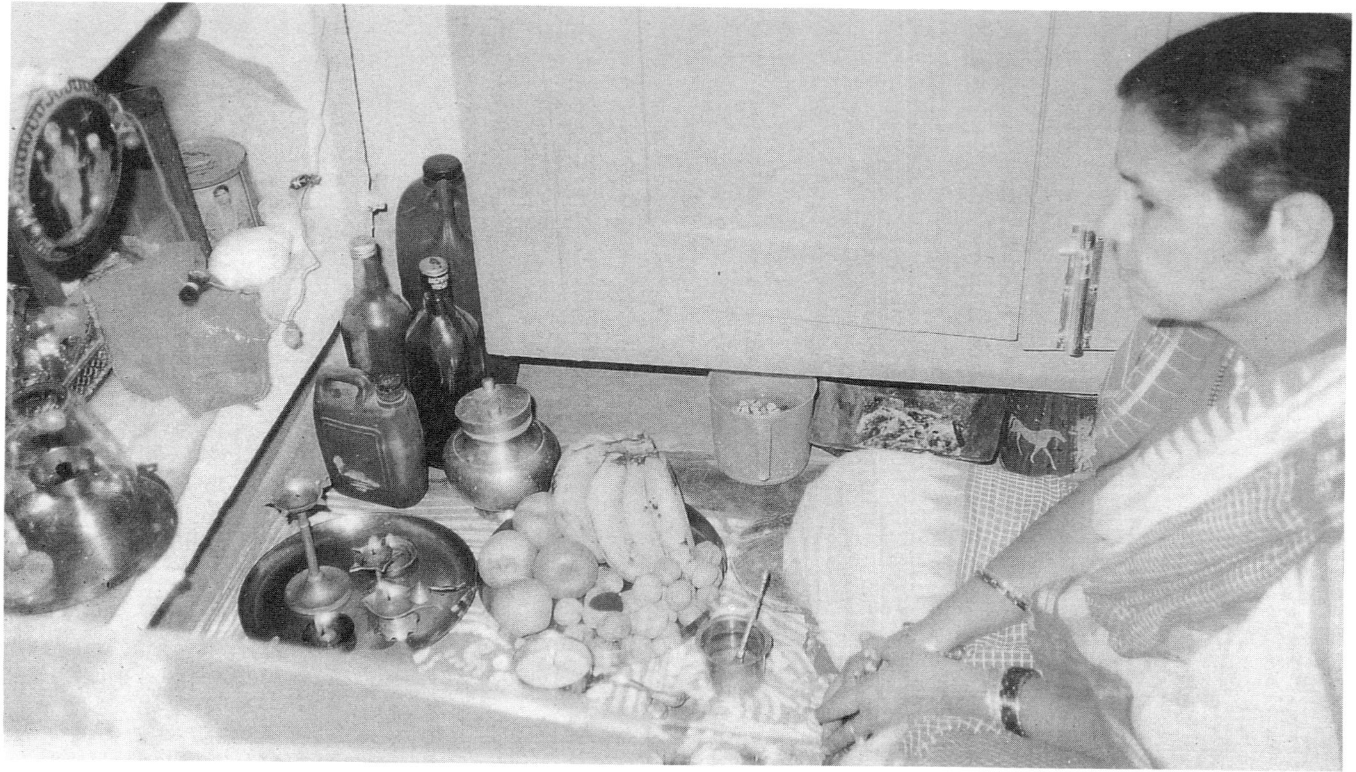

Plate 2. A woman about to start Lakṣmī *pūjā* in her home shrine

Plate 3. Auspicious rice-paste designs below pots of sacred *tulsī* (basil) plants in Mira's courtyard (in Banaras).

Plate 4. Fading *ālpanā* design prepared on a clay tablet on a balcony (in Haridvar)

Plate 5. Women offering milk and *bel patra* (wood-apple leaves) to a Śiva *liṅga*, with a bull (Śiva's "vehicle") promptly consuming the offerings (in Banaras)

Plate 6. Women performing *pūjā* and taking *Gaṅgā-snān* on Kārtik Ekādaśī in Banaras)

Plate 7. Vendors selling *pūjā* items on a *vrat* day in Banaras

Plate 8. A *mūrti* seller in Banaras

Plate 9. Women preparing to do *pūjā* and recount stories on Jiutiyā Vrat day, Lakshmi Kund, Banaras

Plate 10. Lakshmi Kund on Jiutiyā Vrat day

Plate 11. Asi Ghat (Banaras) on Jiutiyā Vrat day

Plate 12. Women gathered to do *pūjā* and tell stories on Ḍala Chaṭh Vrat day (Photo courtesy of David Kinsley)

Plate 13. Women gathering for *pūjā* and bathing next to their bamboo ritual enclosures on Ḍala Chaṭh Vrat day in Banaras

Plate 14. Women with their baskets of *pūjā samāgri* along the *ghaṭs* of the Ganges River, on Ḍala Chaṭh Vrat day in Banaras

Plate 15. Cover of a contemporary Hindi *vrat* pamphlet featuring the Haritālika Tīj Vrat

Plate 16. Cover of a Hindi *vrat-kathā* pamphlet featuring the Ṛṣipañcamī Vrat

Plate 17. Cover of a Hindi *vrat-kathā* pamphlet featuring stories for each of the seven days of the week

5

Precept and Practice: The Constituents of a *Vrat*

What exactly is involved in the observance of a *vrat*? While several brief descriptions of various *vrats* that women perform have been included in earlier sections of this book, this chapter examines the mechanics of *vrat* procedure in greater detail. Eight features or constituents, at least some of which are common to all *vrats*, have been selected for discussion. These are: the statement of intent, the *pūjā*, the role of pandits or ritual officiants, gifting, the ending ceremony, the fast, the *vrat* story, and the ritual art. This description is once more informed by both the precepts laid out in the Purāṇas and Nibandhas, and by women's actions in their performance of *vrats*.[1] To bring all the constituents back into a whole picture, the chapter concludes with a detailed description and analysis of two of the most commonly performed women's *vrats* in Banaras: Haritālikā or "Tīj," conventionally observed by women for *saubhāgya* (that is, marital felicity and the long life of husbands); and Jīvitputrika Vrat or "Jiutiyā," observed by married women for the sake of their children.

There is a difficulty in generalizing about *the* basic ritual components and form of *vratas*. McGee observed that each *vrata* seems to have one, sometimes two, procedural elements which stand out as the central characteristic of that *vrata*. In one case it is the particular form of the fast; in another it is the *pūjā* rite; in another it is the *vrata* story or a special ritual bath *(snāna)* which is the distinctive feature of the *vrata*. She called that distinctive or central feature the *"vrata pradhāna"* (1987). When looking at the textual *vrata* descriptions, one can often pick out "the central feature" as that which the text pays most attention to in its description. In practice, the *pradhāna* is not always obvious from observation. One must ask the votary what she considers to be the most important feature of *that* particular *vrat*. Although I did not in fact ask this specific question of the women I interviewed, some women offered statements that seem to support the idea of a *vrat pradhāna* for at least some of the *vrat*s which are observed. One woman, for example, told me that, "on the Somvati Amāvāsya day the *snān* is the most important" (element of the *vrat*).

Possibly because there are different *vrat pradhāna*s for different *vrat*s, the women I interviewed found my question, "what is the central feature of a *vrat*?" too general. Even when I prompted "the *saṅkalp*?, the *pūjā*?, the fast?," the responses were usually short or simply affirmative of whatever I suggested. Several women singled out the *pūjā* as being very important, which is understandable as the *vrat pūjā* is the primary ritual form of the votary's devotional expression. But others refused to say of *vrat*s in general that one feature was of central importance, or more important than another. However, in analyzing the longer responses, "faith" or "belief" emerged as pivotal because it provided the impetus for or made sense of all the other ritual components. This is why several women had told me that anyone could keep a *vrat* (including those of other faiths) as long as they had genuine belief in them.

EIGHT FEATURES

The *Vrat Saṅkalp*

One of the first ritual components of the *vrat* is the *saṅkalp*.[2] A *saṅkalp* is the formalized rite of self-identification—uttering the full details of one's lineage—and the statement of intention. The historian of religion C. Diehl, in his important work on Hindu ritual, explained that the *saṅkalpa* (Sanskrit for the Hindi *saṅkalp*) "preserves to the *karma* (ritual act) a character of efficient instrument (the formulation of the 'intention' comprises also the result the worshipper has in mind), even if surrendered to the will and pleasure of [the deity]" (1956, 85). According to the *nibandhakāra* Devala, "If no sankalpa is made the person secures very little benefit from the *vrata* and half the merit is lost" (quoted in Kane 1974, 5,1:81).

Ordinarily, the votary is to perform the *saṅkalpa* on the morning of the first day of the *vrata*, after bathing. The *Vratarāja* (p. 8) quotes the method of *vrata saṅkalpa* as described in the *Mahābhārata* as follows: "After observing a fast [i.e., before breakfast] the wise should make a *saṅkalpa* facing north and holding a copper vessel full of water [with the right hand]. Those who have no copper vessel may make a *saṅkalpa* with just cupped hands full of water." The *saṅkalpa* is to be declared before the sun, other deities or a Brahman priest. "In the morning before taking food, and after bathing and *ācamana* (ritually sipping water three times), one should offer water to Sūrya and other gods, and then one may start the *vrata.*" (Devala, cited in the VR, p. 9.)

Most of the Purāṇa *vrata* descriptions do not actually state the contents of the *saṅkalpa* for a particular *vrata*, probably because there were regular formulas used. Underscoring their devotional orientation, some of the Purāṇa *saṅkalpas* found in the context of particular *vrata* descriptions require the votary to express his or her realization that the desired results are ultimately dependent on the beneficence or grace of the deity. For example:

> I salute Nārāyaṇa, I throw myself under your protection. On the Ekādaśī day, I shall keep a fast and worship Nārāyaṇa and keep a vigil at night, have a bath early in the morning (i.e. on the dvādaśī day) and make an oblation of [ghee] to [Agni]. Pundarikakṣa, I shall, with mind controlled, eat rice cooked with milk, with a few good Brahmans. May that be fulfilled by thy grace, without any obstruction.[3]

Among the women I interviewed, I soon discovered that the term *saṅkalp* as a ritual was usually understood in one or the other of two general ways: (1) as just described in the texts—the formal statement of self-identification or intent made by the votary at the commencement of the *vrat*; or (2) as a rite connected with *dān* (gifting) performed either at the *end* of the *vrat*, or, separately from a *vrat*, during ritual bathing in the Ganges, or during a sponsored *kathā* (as in the Satyanārāyaṇ-Kathā).[4] Both forms of *saṅkalp* usually involve the presence of a Brahman priest or pandit, but not necessarily.

Rani, an elderly Brahman, summarizes current uses and meanings of the term *saṅkalp:*

> In this [practice one says] one's name, *gotra* [lineage] and one says: "O Lord Viṣṇu—I am keeping your *vrat.*" Taking [some] Ganges water, unhusked rice [*akṣat*], and flowers [in the hand] one releases them while saying the name of God. For all *vrats* the *saṅkalp* is necessary. [It] solemnizes the *vrat*—because of that [vow] you are bound to fulfill it. [But] we also do *saṅkalp* with *dān-dakṣina;* in feeding Brahmans [during some special occasion] there is also *saṅkalp.* And, if in the name of your

> [deceased] grandmother you serve a meal—in that there is *saṅkalp* too. In the fortnight of *śrāddh* [first half of the month of Āśvin] one remembers the names of one's ancestors—and then do *dān*. All these [practices] are called *saṅkalp*.

Rani did not say whether a Brahman priest had to be present in the first "traditional" example of *saṅkalp;* but certainly for others who described *saṅkalp* in this form a priest was required. For instance, Bina said:

> For those *vrats* in which a pandit must come, for example, Pūrṇimā, Mahālakṣmī, Ṛṣi Pañcamī, Satyanārāyaṇ—a *saṅkalp* is done. It is said by the pandit and I repeat some of it [when told]. Water and flowers are put in the right hand and offered [to the deity]; one's name, family and *gotra* are said, as well as the name of the *vrat* and the reason for doing it, plus mantras.

Another elderly woman, Sartarji, who had kept some seventeen *vrats* in her life, wanted to explain to me why she had not done a formal *saṅkalp:* "You need a *pakka* [proper] Brahman to do formal *saṅkalp* and one was not easily available to do these things in my village [Azamgarh]." So, she had not bothered to engage a Brahman priest for such a purpose even when she moved to Banaras, and simply kept a mental resolve for her votive rites.

Lelauti and Shyamdevi's descriptions of their observance of *saṅkalp* exemplify the second meaning of the term, that is, *saṅkalp* connected with *dān-dakṣina* at the end of a *vrat* or as part of a ritual like Gaṅgā-*snān*. After keeping the Tīj Vrat, Lelauti said that she goes to the bank of the Ganges and [to a Brahman priest] offers flour, rice, lentils, vegetables, spicy salt, sweets, and money—"following my own peace [= whatever it takes to make me feel satisfied], and [I] perform the *saṅkalp*. Then I return home and eat and drink a little," indicating that the *vrat* has formally ended. "One can [also] do a *saṅkalp* every day," she continued, "after [taking] Gaṅgā-*snān*," as a meritorious act that garners blessings. Shyamdevi explained that in her family *saṅkalp* is usually performed in the home, without the involvement of the "pandit community." During Naurātri, for example, she said that "we bring pure, good ghee and light a fire. We mix ghee, barley, black sesame and rice, offer it to the goddess and ask [her] for blessings." On other occasions, she noted, "we will offer a garland for Gaṅgā Māī to one very poor Brahman. I gave [as *saṅkalp*] one sari, and a petticoat [for the wife of a Brahman] on the bank of the Ganges. . . . In Satyanārāyaṇ [*kathā*] too there is *saṅkalp*. When the *pūjā* takes place then at the [specified] time for offering the *saṅkalp* [we] straight away give to the pandit rice, lentils, wheat flour, and money—half a rupee. In Pūrṇimā [on which day she always keeps a fast] it is necessary to give to the pandit—[no matter] how rich he may be and how poor we may be—still we have to give something." For Shyamdevi, then, *saṅkalp* is a matter of ritual gifting and includes a wide variety of formats depending on the occasion and on what is customary in her family or on what she has been advised to do by local pandits or *pujārīs*. Shyamdevi's niece gave a similar account, noting that when she takes a ritual bath in the Ganges, she first gives the priest some paise (coins) and he will say some mantras and put water in her hand. Then she bathes and the priest puts sandalwood paste on her forehead (as a blessing). She claimed that this action "is necessary" on certain *vrat* days (on Rāmnaumī, Śivarātri, Tīj and Ekādaśī), but optional for other *vrats*.

Some women felt that making a formal *saṅkalp*, in the sense of ritual of intention, was not necessary for any *vrat*, while others made distinctions among those *vrats* which required such a *saṅkalp* and those which did not. Among those who made distinctions, the most commonly held opinion was that "regular" or "family" *vrats* (one woman referred to them as *"nitya")* did not require a *saṅkalp* because these are to be performed for one's whole life. Those *vrats* which one took up to achieve a specific and personal end, and which were perhaps time limited, however, did require a ritual resolve—to formalize the pact, as it were, between votary and deity. Sarita referred to these latter as the *"kāmana vrats."* "Those which are family *vrats*," she continued, "don't require a *saṅkalp*. We just know that this is the fruit-bearing day for this particular *vrat*."

It is worth noting what Kamala said about the whole point of the *saṅkalp* as resolve. She emphasized that making a *saṅkalp* was important for all *vrats*. "For the *saṅkalp*, before doing any *vrat*, I take the decision in my mind that, 'I must do this work/action [*karm*]. Today, by performing the *vrat*, I should worship this god.' When we have made the decision in our own mind then we do the *pūjā*." Kamala further explained that it is not necessary to make the resolve in front of a deity *(mūrti)*:

> one does it in one's mind. This much is enough. After observing the *vrat* when the *udyāpan* [final ending ceremony] is being done then it is because of the resolve that one has completed it. For example [take] the Haritālikā Vrat. In this one fasts, performs *pūjā*, and then breaks the *vrat*—all these one does successfully because of the resolve. When our resolve is carried out then we will fast as long as twenty-four hours. We won't drink water for twenty-four hours, so the resolve for each *vrat* is essential.

For Kamala, the formal śāstric *saṅkalpa* had no place in her *vrat* observance. Clearly, however, she viewed the making of a mental resolve as psychologically crucial to the successful completion of the rite, though not, of course, a guarantor of its fruition.

In the end, then, women were agreed on the point that by taking a *saṅkalp*, one's determination to follow through on the rite is strengthened; that if a *saṅkalp* is made, the *vrat* has to be finished; and that making a formal or even informal resolve, binds one to follow the rite to its conclusion, at the risk of inviting serious negative consequences to oneself or to others if one intentionally breaks the vow.

The *Vrat Pūjā*

As the central ritual expression of worship and devotion, *devapūjā* is at the heart of theistic Hinduism. "The purpose of *pūjā*," explained the thoughtful and pious Brahman patriarch of a family I was visiting, "is to bring us closer to God—by purifying ourselves and creating an atmosphere of good feeling *(bhāvanā)*. . . . God is not himself affected by *pūjā*—we are. Its purpose is to transform us." He went on to say that there are different *pūjās* for different occasions, and while the method may vary from one *pūjā* to another or from person to person, all *pūjās* have certain elements in common, namely, the *upacāras* ("attendances," see below).

A *pūjā* of some sort to the deity or deities is mentioned either specifically or vaguely in virtually all the Purāṇa and Nibandha *vrata* descriptions. The *pūjā* can be elaborate and expensive and comprise a major part of the *vrata* or it may involve a simple procedure like offering flowers to an image of the deity. The practice of *devapūjā* (the worship of images kept in the home) was first recognized and described by Smṛti texts in the first few centuries of the Common Era. In popular practice, *devapūjā* gradually took over the vedic *homa* ritual—offering ghee into the consecrated home fire as an oblation to the gods.[5] Whereas by this period *homa* with vedic mantras could not be performed by women and Shudras, *devapūjā* could be performed by all. Jan Gonda argues that "the Hindu *devapūjā* originally and essentially is an invocation, reception and entertainment of God as a royal guest. In its full form it normally consists of sixteen 'attendances' *(upacāra)*" (1970, 77). Many of these *upacāras* were originally offered to Brahmans who had been invited to officiate at a vedic ceremony such as a *śrāddha* (funeral rite).[6]

There are various opinions among the Smṛti-Nibandha authors concerning the number of "attendances" and their order of offering.[7] The first *upacāra* is usually invocation *(āvāhana)* or reception *(svāgat)* of the deity, signalled by ringing a bell, blowing a conch or beating a drum. Next comes providing a cushion for the deity to sit on *(āsana)* and washing the feet of the deity *(padya).* Water is used throughout a *pūjā.* "It is the symbol and means of purification, physical and mental," said "Panditji," a middle-aged Brahman preceptor from Lucknow who offered to discuss the significance of *pūjā* with me at length. It is used in the rite of sprinkling pure water on the deity *(arghya);* in the rite of sipping water three times *(ācamana),* and for a ritual bath/ablution *(snāna).*[8] Following this, the deity is clothed *(vāstra);* and anointed with unguents *(anulepana)* or perfumes *(sugandha).* Also pleasing in fragrance, incense *(dhūpa)* and sandalwood *(candan)* may be offered, followed by flowers *(puṣpa)* or garlands *(mālās).* Earthen lamps with ghee and cotten wicks *(dīpa)* are lit,[9] and *naivedya*—cooked or uncooked food, usually sweets—are offered.[10] Rice is frequently used in the *pūjā* and has a number of symbolic meanings. It is considered the basic food; "an essential part of life"; as *anna* or "grain" it has "the power to satisfy a human being." *Akṣat,* or "not destroyable" (unhusked) rice, is the most commonly used kind of rice in *pūjās.* Important among the last attendances are circumambulation of the image *(pradakṣina);* circling lamps in front of the image *(āratī),*[11] and salutation *(namaskāra).* Some texts suggest that if only one *upacāra* can be offered by the devotee, he may use flowers alone.[12]

Only a few of these *upacāras* are normally named in individual Purāṇa *vrata* descriptions. Bathing the deity (with ghee, water, milk, *pañcagavyam* or *pañcāmṛta*[13]), anointing the image with sandalpaste or perfumes, and offering the deity flowers, incense, sandalwood and food (milk, ghee, sesame, rice, fruits, sweets) are the most commonly mentioned items in connection with the *devapūjā*. They are also the attendances which women most commonly offer in their daily *pūjās* and during their *vrat* observances.

In current practice *vrat pūjās* are not normally complicated, though again, there is a range from the exceedingly simple procedure of dripping water from a small pot *(loṭa)* on to a basil plant *(tulsī*, an emblem of Viṣṇu) with a few prayers, to far more detailed and time-consuming *pūjās*. These more complicated *pūjās* may be ones over which a pandit presides, complete with the *upacāras* and the rites of dripping ghee into the sacred fire *(homa)* or pouring a mixture of herbs into the fire *(havan)*—both rites accompanied by vedic mantras. Complex *pūjās* may also be presided over by women themselves and have little to do with śāstric prescriptions.

Essentially, the *pūjās* that women do both on a regular basis in their homes or during their *vrat* observances are considered by themselves or by the orthodox as "devotional" or "purāṇic," that is, as nonvedic. When "Mataji," the sixty-five-year-old wife of a local *pujārī*, and other women (usually, but not only, from observant Brahman families) told me such things as "ladies are not allowed to do *pūjā*" nor "touch the *pūjā* place," or "women can't do *āratī* nor touch the *mūrtis*," or "women ordinarily do not have the authority for *havan*," or "women can't say mantras," they are referring to the strictures governing women's involvement in vedic rituals laid down by conservative pandits many centuries ago. Some women, like Mataji, take these strictures seriously.[14] Others pay them lip service or openly disregard them. Of course, these same women do perform *pūjās* all the time, but without the *havan* and the vedic mantras, they are not "official" *pūjās*. The clay images which they often make or buy for their *vrats* are not official *mūrtis*. The mantras that they say are purāṇic, or they are not really mantras, but prayers (expressing both praise of the deity and the votary's wishes for herself). In these ways, by distinguishing between official (my word) ritual procedures and unofficial (or nonvedic) ones, women from orthodox families do not see any contradiction between what they say and what they do.

There are elements which distinguish women's *pūjās* from those of men during *vrat* observances. These include women's worship of household items or the inclusion of symbols of such items (winnowing baskets, combs, bangles, toys) in their ritual art, and their far greater use than men of *roli* (lime and tumeric paste), *haldi* (tumeric) and red powder or *kuṁkuṁ*, which as *sindūr* (vermilion, applied by married women to the part of their hair), is that preeminently married women's symbol. Accompanying many women's *vrat pūjās* are the creation and use of ritual designs *(ālpanā)*—as I shall discuss below—and the singing of songs and the telling of folk stories *(kahānīs)*.[15]

Pandits, *Pujārīs* and *Vrats*

In the Purāṇas and Nibandhas the role of the Brahman priests with respect to the *vratas* is rarely spelled out except as recipients of (often lavishly prescribed) gifts, food and honor. Occasionally the Brahman is to be honored and worshipped as a god—but always he is to be fed and is to receive gifts *(dāna)*. The expression of the idea of Brahmans as gods can be found in some of the earliest texts of vedic Hinduism.[16] In the Purāṇas, Brahmans are frequently eulogized and divine powers ascribed to them. As Hazra says, Brahmans are called the "visible gods on earth and are identified with Viṣṇu or some other prominent deity, so that any ill treatment of them means the same to these deities. The Brahmans are also often directed to be utilized as one of the mediums of worship" (1975, 258).[17]

In practice, learned Brahmans are certainly accorded much respect and their inherited ritual status and authoritative knowledge of "correct" ritual procedures is recognized in its place. I did not, however, encounter Brahmans being divinized or worshipped the way the texts suggest, though Brahmans—men, women and children—more than any other category of people are fed, honored and given gifts in many, if not most, of the *vrat* ending ceremonies observed by the women I interviewed. Nor have I come across contemporary evidence of Brahmans worshipped by women in *vrats* as is sometimes the case for husbands or brothers (see Wadley 1976).

I met no woman who either always used a priest or pandit in her *vrat* rituals, or never did.[18] Some women among those I interviewed, like Shyamdevi and her niece, said that they could not afford the services of a priest very often. Besides, claimed Shyamdevi, "it doesn't matter . . . they (priests) aren't necessary" [for the majority of *vrats* that women keep].

Almost all women regularly called on a priest to be present at some *vrats*, but not for others.[19] As indicated, most women agreed that when one was ready to end any *vrat*, the pandit should be called to preside over the ending ceremony *(udyāpan)*, formalizing its completion. Weekly *vrats* do not usually involve a priest coming to the home, but women often go to the temple associated with the particular deity worshipped on that day, to take *darśan*, watch a *pūjā* being performed, be involved in a *pūjā* presided over by the temple *pujārī*, or to give money to the temple. On the whole, calling the pandit to the home to perform the *pūjā*, recite the *kathā*, and so forth, renders that *vrat* more śāstric, that is, more like the Purāṇa and Nibandha descriptions. But, in many *vrats* performed only by women, women preside over the whole rite themselves, acting as both officiant and participant, as in the Jiutiyā Vrat described at the end of this chapter.

Some researchers have suggested that women always have acted as their own ritual officiants for the *vrat* rites observed exclusively by women. P. K. Maity, for example, takes what seems to be the typical position among scholars of Bengali "folk" religion, following the lead of Abanindranath Tagore (1919), that "*bratas*" originated and remain in large part "primitive" folk rites performed only by women. Therefore, "no Brahman priest is needed for performing a customary *brata* and it is the womenfolk themselves who conduct the priestly functions. . . . However, nowadays a few customary *bratas* are performed with the assistance of the Brahman priests due to the influence of Brahmanical Hinduism" (1989, 170). Sandra Robinson has also argued this position, noting in regard to the Itu Vrata as practised in Bengal that only recently have priests started to offer their services to women clients. She writes: "The traditional priestly disdain for *vratas* as a collection of trivial women's customs has recently given way to priestly appropriation of the practices" (1985, 209). Others, on the other hand, have argued that women are just *starting* to be their own priests because of the wide availability of *vrat* pamphlets in which the details of the procedure for the rite are provided, including appropriate mantras, allowing literate women to bypass priestly involvement, if they so choose.[20] In my view, the existence of both the long Sanskrit textual tradition on *vrata* (where *vratas* are anything but disdained[21]) and of the plethora of *vrats* (or *vrat*-like rites) that women have been observing on their own for generations (described by Tagore, Gupta, Luschinsky and others) must be taken into account and balanced against each other when addressing the question of women's "priestly roles" in their performance of *vrats*. Certainly, many of the descriptions of the Bengali *bratas* bear only superficial resemblances to the *vratas* depicted in the śāstras and in these women clearly play "priestly roles," but without Sanskrit mantras and rituals like *homa*, no male Brahman pandit, at least, would regard women's officiating functions or actions as truly efficacious. Not so the women themselves, although this is a situation which is evidently fluid and changing. The issue of women's status as "priests" (a word which in English is charged with Christian connotations not present in Hindu contexts) or as "ritual officiants" in their observance of *vrats*, then, must be interpreted with attention to both perspective and semantics.

The *Vrat Dān-Dakṣina*

Dān is the practice of giving of gifts to one's ritual equivalents or superiors, such as Brahmans, usually for services rendered. The practice of *dān* (Sanskrit *dāna)* has a long history in the religious traditions of India.[22] There seems little doubt, however, that the range and number of gifts prescribed in the Purāṇas (often in the contexts of *vrats*) are significantly higher than that prescribed in earlier texts.[23] The later Smṛti and Nibandha writers go into much more detail than earlier writers concerning the qualifications of the donor and donee, the kind of gifts that were appropriate and inappropriate according to various circumstances, the place and time that were suitable, and the merits that could be accrued by the doner.[24] Some of the *mahādānas* (great or major gifting rites) described in the Purāṇas themselves sound like *vratas*.[25]

The making of donations was considered an important way of leading a religious life in the present Kali age (see *Kurmapurāṇa* 1,28,17). The recipients of *dāna* were often monastic institutions *(maṭhas)* or temples, and donors were kings, queens, landowners or merchants who wished to patronize a certain *maṭha* or sect or who simply desired to acquire the merit associated with generous donations. However, in the purāṇic *vratas* it is the Brahmans who are the most frequently cited recipients of the gifts and often the word *brāhmaṇa* is qualified by "good" or "free from hypocrisy" or "learned in the vedas."

In the Purāṇa and Nibandha texts the votary is warned not to be miserly in his giving. One resorting to spending less money than what is allowed by one's income *(vitta śāṭhya)* "with regards to gifts is doomed to hell" (Banerjee 1964, 37). Yet some leeway is allowed for many of the descriptions of the gifts are appended with a statement of the sort "or according to his means," or "unless the votary is poor, then one (e.g., cow) is enough."

All the women I spoke with indicated that the giving of *dān* was an important feature of one's religious life (a *dhārmik karm*) in the context of *vrat* rites as well as on other occasions.[26] Several women referred to the act of giving *dān* as *"dān puṇya"*—meritorious giving. Mira told me that there are certain days on which the giving of *dān* (in the general sense of donation) is especially meritorious, and she listed Makar Saṅkranti (the winter solstice festival), Acala Saptamī, Vāman Dvādaśī, and Rāmnaumī. She said that on Rāmnaumī some wealthy people give *dān* for decorating the temple and for *prasād*, to be distributed after the *pūjā*. Other women also mentioned the winter solstice and the period of an eclipse as occasions (other than *vrats*) for *"dān puṇya."*

The majority of women expressed the view that it was necessary to give *dān* for all one's *vrats*, but especially such *vrats* as Ekādaśī, Pūrṇimā, Tīj and Karvā Cauth. Other women felt that one should give *dān* in some *vrats*, but it was not necessary in others, such as Jiutiyā and Ḍala Chaṭh (both women's *vrats* performed for the sake of children). One woman said that it was not "mandatory" though the "straight" (i.e., orthodox) always give it during *vrats*. Though I did not pursue this line of questioning, it should be mentioned that an underlying theme in the act of gifting in many ritual contexts is, as villagers from Pahansu in northern Uttar Pradesh told Gloria Raheja, "'to move away inauspiciousness' . . . from the donor and transfer it to the recipient, who is thought of as a 'receptacle' . . . for the inauspiciousness contained within the gift" (Raheja and Gold 1994, 80). Such inauspiciousness (in the form of "hindrances," "faults," "afflictions," "disease," "danger," or "evil"), Raheja explains, "may afflict persons, houses, and villages at many times in the yearly cycle and at many times of one's life, and each time it must be 'moved away' by being gifted to an appropriate recipient [who 'digests' it] if well-being is to be achieved" (Raheja and Gold 1994, 80-81). Since the *vrats* that women perform are almost always concerned with increasing auspiciousness and well-being in the family, one of the functions of gifting in a *vrat* is to give away any accumulated inauspiciousness. Brahmans are considered most able to digest the ritual pollution and inauspiciousness of others.

In discussing a particular *vrat* that they observed women would tell me specifically what they would give as *dān* (and to whom). Common items were grain, lentils, ghee, fruit, sweets, cooked food (either as a meal—*bhojan*—or to take away), and money. Nothing more elaborate was usually given during the regularly occurring *vrats*. For the formal ending ceremony, of course, more expensive and imperishable as well as perishable items are given. With respect to the kind and amount of *vrat dān* in general, a few women said that there were specific rules to follow, while others said that what was important was to "follow your feelings," to "follow one's heart's desire."

Most women gave the *dān* to "the pandit" or to "a Brahman." However, one woman remarked: "but nobody is brahman these days . . . [so] one should give to the poor, disabled and worthy Brahmans." That is, in this woman's view, just because a person is a Brahman by caste does not necessarily mean that he or she is of upright character, spiritually "superior," or a true custodian of the *dharma*—as the ideal would have them be. Thus one must be discriminating in determining who ought to be the recipient of *dān*, as the Purāṇas themselves advise. Others also added that one should (or that they did) give to the poor or disadvantaged. Twenty-two-year-old Veena expressed the view that "we should give *dān* to the blind, the disabled, the lame, and to poor Brahmans too. In this way [the giving of] *dān* is fruitful. If you give alms to such people you will be benefited by their blessings. There won't be any benefit from giving *dān* to rich people." Similarly, Sandhya was of the opinion that what was really necessary in a *vrat* was for the richer votary to help the less fortunate. She herself gave cooked meals to the needy on most Thursdays when she kept the Bṛhaspati Vrat. Finally, Savitri emphasized that while it is necessary to give *dān*, "to me what is more important is that one derives satisfaction from it and that the giving is sincere." While some of these qualifications to the giving of *dān* are noted in the Sanskrit texts, others, like giving *dān* to the "needy" irrespective of caste, are not. This concern to give gifts to those who could most visibly benefit from them may well be a relatively recent (perhaps twentieth-century) introduction to the *vrat* tradition, perhaps influenced by the rise of charitable organizations like the Ramakrishna Mission, which is prominent in Banaras.

Pāraṇ and *Udyāpan:* The *Vrat*-Ending Ceremony

The *vrat pāraṇ* is the ritual that marks the conclusion to the fast. The ceremony usually involves the feeding and giving of gifts to Brahmans. The *Vratarāja* suggests that "At the end of a *vrata* one may feed fourteen, twelve, five or three Brahmans according to one's means and offer *dakṣina.*" In practice, other recipients are possible, depending on the *vrata*, such as neighbors, poor people, Brahman boys, unmarried girls *(kanyā)*. The *udyāpana* is a more elaborate ceremony when one has completed a cycle of a *vrat* that one has vowed to undertake, or when one no longer has the ability to carry on the *vrat*.

Again, virtually all the women whom I interviewed agreed that in order to leave a *vrat* one must perform an *udyāpan* ceremony. Many of the younger women had not yet performed one because they were still keeping the same *vrats* which they had started. They were thus somewhat vague about the details and said that when the time came they would call the pandit and he would direct them; "whatever things will be required I will collect, and I will have the ceremony performed through him." Women who had performed an *udyāpan* gave general or specific descriptions for particular *vrats*. One woman who had stopped all her *vrats* said: "There is a big *pūjā* in which having brought together all of the *vrat* things [a priest] performs *hom-havan*, . . . and one gives clothes and *dakṣina* to a Brahman, feeds him and in front of the fire one says to the Brahman, 'now I am not [continuing] this *vrat*.' Then the Brahman gives you permission to stop doing it. This itself is the *udyāpan*." For her Santoṣī Mā Vrat *udyāpan* one woman said that she fed seven Brahman boys with *pūrī*, curried chick peas, rice pudding and bananas. She said that no money is given for *dakṣina* because the boys may go to the bazaar and eat sour foods and therefore ruin the effect of the *udyāpan*. Her comment about sour food refers to the central fasting requirement of this *vrat*—the avoidance of all "sour" foods, because, as she said, Santoṣī Mā does not like sour foods. In another example, Gulab told me that for the Karvā Cauth *udyāpan*, which she performed at the first Karvā Cauth day after her husband's death, she gave paise in a *karvā* (pot) to fourteen Brahman women. To one of these women she also gave earrings, a nose-ring, anklets, a sari, blouse and petticoat.

The *Vrat Upavās*

The term "*upavās*" is conventionally translated as "fast," but it has always had an additional ritual or religious significance. The word is made up of the verbal root *vas* meaning "to dwell" plus the prefix *upa* meaning "near." It originally referred to certain actions of the *yajamāna* (the sponsor of the sacrifice) during the performance of the sacrifice. Specifically, it referred to the requirements that he stay near the sacrificial fire at night and fast.[27] However, the fast did not only mean refraining from food and drink—it also meant refraining from sensual gratification in general. This more general sense of fasting was reinforced and amplified in the context of *vratas* by the Smṛti writers, such that by the time of the *Vratarāja* one finds a section called the "*dharma* of *upavāsa*" with the same sorts of ethical injunctions governing the faster's behavior that one finds under the "*dharma* of the *vratin*." (Indeed the words are often used interchangeably in the *Vratarāja.)* For example, the *Vratarāja* (p. 12) says, "Now we will explain the *dharma* of *upavāsa* according to Kātyāyana and Vāṣiṣṭha: [he] who avoids bad actions and lives by good qualities [*guṇa*], [who] is not attached to worldly things is called *upavāsah.*" The author then explains what is meant by *guṇa* according to various sources before adding that "living without eating" *(nirahārā-vasthānamātram)* is also the meaning of *upavāsa*. The *Vratrāja* (pp. 12-13) also discusses the sorts of people the faster should avoid (liars, depraved people, and so forth); more or less the same list as that for the votary.

The same Nibandha (pp. 13-14) describes the actions and items that break and do not break a fast according to various Smṛti writers' opinions. For instance: "According to Devala an [*upavāsa*] is broken if one takes water many times, chews betel leaf once, sleeps in the day and engages in sexual intercourse. But if feeling very weak one can drink water once, because otherwise one might risk death." (The Dharmaśāstras never encourage extreme asceticism in the context of householder *vratas*.) And, "These eight things do not break a *vrata* [fast]: water, root vegetables, fruit, milk, ghee from *havan*, the request of a Brahman, the words of a guru and medicine." "According to the *Viṣṇurahasya* one should not 'remember' [think about] food, nor look at it, nor smell it, nor talk about it, nor have the desire to eat. One should refrain from putting on oil after the bath, [from using] fragrant powder and oil in the hair, [from] chewing betel leaf, and one should avoid all that leads to energy [*bal*] or lust [*rag*]."

There are specific kinds of fasts that are detailed in the Dharmaśāstras such as *nakta* (eating only at night), or *ekabhakta* (eating only one meal a day, usually at noon), and sometimes *vrata* descriptions will specify one of these sorts of fasts as the requirement for the particular *vrata* under discussion.[28] Other times such details concerning the nature of the fast to be undertaken are left out entirely, especially among the Purāṇa *vrata* descriptions.

When I asked women to tell me about the relationship of *vrats* to fasting requirements they would often resort to giving me a list of *vrats* and then specifying their particular fasting foods. "Take the Ṛṣi Pañcamī Vrat," said Bimla, "in this [*vrat*] there is a special green leafy vegetable that one must eat, and one special kind of rice and curd; only these are to be eaten. In Haritālikā Vrat nothing is eaten, not even saliva is swallowed. Janmāṣṭamī also requires a strict fast. So for each *vrat* the manner of fasting is different." Others described kinds of fasts first, and then gave examples. "There are several ways of fasting," explained Lelauti.

> In some *vrats* we keep a twenty-four hour fast, as in Tīj or Jiutiyā. In other *vrats* we keep a waterless fast [*nirjalā upavās*] during the day and in the evening after performing the *pūjā* we eat some fruit or items prepared with grain [*ann*], as in Karvā Cauth. In some *vrats* we eat fruit but not grain, as in Ekādaśī and a few other *vrats*. In some *vrats* we don't take any salt, such as in Ekādaśī, Pūrṇimā, Sunday Vrat, Tuesday Vrat.

In some cases women were not able to tell me the meaning or significance of particular fasting requirements. Others did offer explanations: "In Bahulā Cauth," Sitadevi commented, "we can eat *besan laḍḍu* [sweet balls made from gram], banana and other fruit, plums, sugarcane, black sesame, and halva prepared from water chestnuts. Water chestnuts grow in water, so they are very pure." She continued:

> Observing a *vrat* is religious, ethical action. Therefore one doesn't eat grain on Ekādaśī, so that [during this period] no sentient being should be killed [because of the insects or their eggs]. . . . During Ekādaśī life comes in the grain. If you eat grain you will incur sin [*pap*]. . . . You should eat fruit and give gifts of grain to a Brahman. That way you will get benefit, spiritual merit.

Kiran offered the medical-health view that "the reason for not eating *anaj* [grains] [during certain *vrats*] is that it is good for the stomach to have a break from the harsher foods." Others too, like Kamala and Hardevi, made similar claims about the health benefits of regularly refraining from certain "harsh" (difficult to digest) foods. The most frequently mentioned food to be avoided in *vrats* besides grains was salt. "In whatever *vrat* one does one should abstain from salt. In this place (Banaras), people eat rock salt (instead)." Vindhya explained that avoiding salt was "for the peace of blood."

In sum, the most common fasting requirement among the women I spoke with is for the votary to avoid salt and/or *ann* or *anāj* (wheat, barley, rice and lentils) or, put differently, to take only "fruit-food" *(phalāhar)*. The anthropologist Jonathan Parry has noted that *phalāhar* is "the food par excellence of the ascetic," which

> typically consists of fruit, as the term itself suggests; but the category also includes wild rice *(teni caval)* and wild vegetables, as well as preparations made from the flour of water chestnuts (which are rated as a kind of cereal), or to which naturally occurring rock salt *(sendha namak)* has been added. The crux of the matter is that *phalāhar* excludes all crops cultivated by the plough.[29]

There are at least four reasons for the votary to avoid foods cultivated by the plough:

1. The act of ploughing kills insects, and, as Parry suggests, is an act of violence against the earth.

2. Grains can contain insect eggs.

3. The traditional requirement of the ascetic, once he had renounced the domestic hearth, was to forage for food—to subsist on the wild roots and fruits that could be gathered in the forests. This was one way in which the votary was to imitate the ascetic life-style.

4. Finally, as Parry puts it, "Cultivated grain (and more especially rice) is the proto-typical food, and abstention from food is above all an abstention from grain" (1985, 613).

Hindus interviewed in Banaras also considered fresh milk and milk products, ghee, sugar, potato, and *caulai* (grain from the amrinthus plant) as *phalāhar*. *Phalāhar* is preeminently *sattvik* food and is therefore also conducive (in a substantial way)[30] to the spiritually attuned state appropriate to the votary. These foods are considered "cool" foods that "dampen" the passions and the appetites. Altogether, then, fasting foods serve to purify, pacify, and clarify the mind and body of the votary. As Hardevi said to me: "I never take *anāj* on *vrat* days, only fruit and milk. It keeps the stomach healthy, it purifies the body, and mentally too we get peace of mind, we can concentrate better and our thoughts become pure."

Many *vrats* are ended with special festive preparations which will usually have been offered during the *vrat pūjā* and which are then distributed to family members as *prasād*. These commonly include fried wheat bread *(pūrī)*, and one or more of such sweet preparations as halva and rice pudding *(khīr)*. A votary who breaks her fast with *prasād* will still retain her state of purity and even enhance it because *any* food that is offered to the gods and returned as *prasād* is "solidified grace" and transcends the usual cultural categories.

The *Vrat Kathā*

A good deal of the Purāṇa *vrata* literature actually rests in the form of the *kathā*, the "story" of the *vrata*. This is true of some Nibandhas as well, including the *Vratarāja*. Some of the recent *vrat-kathā* literature, printed in vernaculars, is closely based on the Purāṇa-Nibandha *vrata-kathās*. The Hindi books of this type that I have examined employ a Sanskritic Hindi with periodic references made to Purāṇas and other "authoritative" works. It represents an extension of the Smṛti-Nibandha literature into vernacular language, and it maintains a certain stiffness in presentation of the ritual, *dāna* and *kathā*. Other paperback books reveal a folksy, simple and parochial Hindi presumably aimed at a less literate audience. It sets in writing and captures the flavor of localized *vrat* rites that have been orally transmitted from one generation of women to another. These booklets may contain both local variants of the Purāṇa *vrata-kathās* and folk stories that do not have such Sanskrit textual referents.[31]

The *vrata-kathās*, which in these texts may run to several pages or be no more than a paragraph, serve a number of functions. In the first place they may provide the details for the procedure of the *vrata* in the context of the narrative; details such as when to begin the *vrata*, how and to whom to perform the *pūjā* and ancilliary rites, which are not otherwise given. Second, the *kathā* may provide an etiology for the *vrata*. The transmission of the *vrata* may be traced back circuitously from one god or goddess and set of events to another, finally reaching its source. In the process familiar myths are explained in a new way, and the elements of the *vrata* given mythological significance. The divine bona fides of the *vrata* is established and the votary presumably made to feel confident of its divine origin.

Third, *vrata-kathās* often recount one example or episode of the particular *vrata*'s performance which serves to demonstrate the efficacy and even more, the potential "transformative power" of the *vrata*.[32] Frequently, it also serves to eulogize the god to whom the *vrat* is directed. Here the stories read like fairy tales.[33] The time is vaguely in the past, the setting "some village" or forest or kingdom. The story may illustrate the great merit obtainable by performing a particular *vrata*, or the calamity that befalls one who ignores worshipping a deity or ignores performing the deity's *vrat* customarily performed in his or her family or who breaks the vow, even if inadvertantly. Through the (regular) performance of such and such *vrata*, a simple householder, a courtesan or king wins (or, in some cases, gains back) power, prestige and wealth; a mistreated daughter-in-law (the Hindu Cinderella) wins merit and good fortune for the family as well as the permanent affection of her husband. Underscoring the efficaciousness of the *vrata* itself, sometimes the protagonist of the *kathā* is described as performing the rite by accident and despite the lack of intention, the (inadvertent) votary reaps all the benefits of the *vrata* anyway.

In some cases the general story line and its protagonists are taken directly from the epics or other well-known story literature. Though there may be no mention of a *vrata* in the older story, the *vrata-kathā* version places the vow into the center of the plot, where it becomes the solution to overcoming a seemingly insurmountable problem. One such example is the "Rukminī *vrata-kathā*," which can be found in the *Kalkipurāṇa* (chap. 31). This *vrata kathā* is based on the story of two women—Devayānī and Śarmiṣṭhā—found in the Adiparvan of the *Mahābhārata* (chaps. 71–78). In the epic version of the story the two women are portrayed as educated, feisty and independent-minded. Through a series of events and circumstances, they are moved from friendship to rivalry, and they become alternately disadvantaged one to the other. Both women refuse to acquiesce submissively to their disadvantaged state, and they find ways to overcome it, notably by quoting religious law in their favor. Like Sāvitrī, they use logical reasoning and a knowledge of tradition to get what they want. When the story turns up in the *Kalkipurāṇa*, the forcefulness of the women's personalities is toned down, and their place as hapless victims of circumstance is underscored. The Rukminī *vrata-kathā* focusses on Śarmiṣṭhā, the underdog, and it shows how she who was sonless because of events beyond her control, was able to bear sons and achieve happiness and fulfillment through observing the *vrata*, taught to her by some village women. Observing the Rukminī Vrata saves Śarmiṣṭhā from "unrighteousness." The didactic function of the Purāṇa-Nibandhas is particularly apparent in the *vrata-kathās* whose main purpose was to show how a prescribed ritual like a *vrata* serves to help women (or householders in general) fulfill their dharmically mandated duties, while at the same time modelling for the votary the form and proper attitude toward these duties.

Whatever its place in the past, today, among the *vrats* that women observe in Banaras and North India, *vrat-kathās* are almost as central to the performance of a *vrat* as are the *pūjā* and the fast. Under the rubric *"vrat-kathā"* women I interviewed included the type of purāṇic story described above, folk tales (*kahānī*—literally, "that which is told") which, while recounted regularly for certain vows, may have nothing directly to do with those vows, as well as the formal Sanskrit text-based *stotra* (eulogistic) genre (e.g., the *Śivastuti Calīsa*, the *Hanumān Calīsa*, and the *Durgāsaptaśatī*). Laxmi Tewari, whose book, *The Splendor of Worship* (1991), provides accounts of some fifty-five *vrat* stories he recorded from Kanyakubja Brahman women in the village of Sheoli and the city of Kanpur in central Uttar Pradesh, states that: "Telling and listening to stories during the fast are considered acts of worship, and thus moral obligations the devotee must fulfil" (1991, 14). Given its status as an "act of worship," it is not surprising to find that the reading or telling of the *kathā* usually takes place during or immediately following the *pūjā*, the primary act of worship during a *vrat*.

Many women made a distinction between those *vrats* in which a pandit had to be called to recite the *kathā* (and perform the *pūjā*) and those in which women themselves told the stories. Examples of the former included Tīj, the Satyanārāyaṇ Vrat Kathā and Mahālakṣmī Vrat. In these cases the pandit reads the *kathā* in Sanskrit (often, as I saw, from one of the rectangular booklets which feature one *vrat* [see plates 15–17]), and then translates the story into Hindi for the benefit of the women present. In other cases women either read the story out loud themselves from a similar booklet or, if they are illiterate, have someone else read it.

Or, again, the story will be recounted from memory, perhaps by the senior *vrat*-observing woman in the family, as often happens in the Karvā Cauth, Bahulā Cauth, Jiutiyā, and Ḍala Chaṭh Vrats. Here the storyline remains consistent and recognizable to everyone present. As one woman put it, "when some story is being told then the saying of 'yes, yes' is necessary" (there must be agreement between story-teller and listeners). Nevertheless, the *kathā* reciter may add her own flourishes and embellishments consonant with her story-telling talents.

Among the women's *vrats* there is usually more than one story connected with each particular *vrat*, and women, if celebrating the *vrat* together, may take turns telling the stories. The oral stories women tell are often very short—a few minutes in duration. Again, they may be versions of Sanskrit purāṇic stories, or more local tales.

When I asked some women to explain to me the difference between a *vrat kathā* and a *vrat kahānī*, some designated the oral tales that they themselves tell as "*kahānīs*" and the stories that the pandit tells as "*kathās*," irrespective of the story's source. The act of reading from a printed text, whether in Sanskrit or Hindi, seems to give the story a more authoritative stamp. And the pandit, of course, is also a transmitter of authority. The elderly Sitadevi, whose own son was a pandit, conveyed the following reflection: "Whether you call it *kathā* or *kahānī* there is no difference when you listen"; that is, it is the act of hearing or telling a *vrat* story that is the important thing. She then continued, "in a *kahānī* it is like this: 'there was some daughter-in-law' or 'there was some girl' . . . then they did such and such and that happened. A *kathā* is about God. It is a religious story, [about] belief in God."[34] It is especially the *kahānīs* that, while associated by votaries with a particular *vrat*, may have no obvious connection to the vow. Many of these stories feature animals such as one finds in the Sanskrit story collections like the *Pañcatantra* and the *Hitopadeśa*, tales which are about *nīti*, "the wise conduct of life."[35]

One could say, following Geertz' terminology with respect to religion and religious symbols, that *vrat-kathās* provide both "models of" problematic realities of Hindu culture, and in their resolutions, "models for" orientations toward those realities (see Geertz 1973). The problematic realities described in the *kathās* include individual and collective lack of control over disease, infertility, death, the workings of *karma* and fate. When women are featured as protagonists, the problematic realities are often set in the context of the partriarchal and patrilineal social structure—for instance, the traumatic move from natal to affinal home; the necessity of producing heirs; a young wife's general lack of autonomy and authority along with the problems presented by her greater impurity and lower ritual status (than male and older female kin). In the śāstric *vratas* (like the Rukminī Vrata) the immediate solution to the particular predicament (e.g., sonlessness) is the performance of the *vrat;* the strategic orientation toward the problem is embodied in the behavior the female protagonist (votary) demonstrates: dutifulness, obedience, perseverance and devotion. In the face of injustice or cruel fate, the heroine of the *vrat kathā* models the appropriate female/wifely behavior and her dutifulness, through the agency of the *vrat,* is rewarded. In other scenerios, a woman is shown to be "sinful," that is, rebellious, or self-centered, or one who has caused trouble through carelessness in ritual procedure, and she reaps the results of those sins by losing her husband to another woman, or to death, as well as all her belongings, or by turning into a leprous, tortured creature. Then, through the performance of the particular *vrat,* she is transformed into a virtuous wife and daughter-in-law and she recovers her beauty, her husband and his wealth.

In the hands of the women votaries who tell the *vrat* stories, without the mediation of a priest or the use of vernacular translations of Sanskrit *vrata kathās*, the problematic realities depicted in the stories are similar, though often limited to the domain of the home, and they can be more patently moralistic (as one finds in the *Pañcatantra):* acts of good will and genuine piety are rewarded; false piety and material greed are punished. Importantly, the stories told, or in some cases songs sung by women are also less conservatively ideological in their "models for" orientation to the problems women face. Gloria Raheja, in analyzing songs sung by women during the *vrat/*festival of Tīj, found that kinship norms were subverted such that a man's loyalty to his wife was valued over his loyalty to natal kin, and the untrustworthiness of mother-in-law and sisters-in-law set against the true fidelity of the (wronged) wife (Raheja and Gold 1994, 130-33). One Tīj song recorded by Raheja challenges the discourse of the ideal wife by depicting, in an approving manner, a wife who resorts to extreme violence when her husband brings home a second wife against the wishes of the first wife. "In the Tīj song the appeal made by the wife to 'sisters,' the women listeners who hear her tale, makes it evident that the wife's actions are indeed valorized. . . . [It is] the ability to act decisively when a wife is treated unjustly" that is being extolled (Raheja and Gold 1994, 146). In her analysis of the Itu Vrata *kathā*, a story told by women to women, Sandra Robinson has pointed out that "values taught through this story include sororal loyalty, bravery, commitment and faithfulness" (1985, 208). To these more woman-affirming values one could add resourcefulness, cleverness and a certain amount of defiance. Such attributes are characteristic of some of the women found in the epics, like Sāvitrī, Devayānī and Śarmiṣṭha. These stories can serve as sources of positive self-valuations for women in the sense that they offer models of women who have confidently achieved ends of their own choosing, without waiting, as Raheja argues in reference to the Tīj songs, "for a son or brother or father to rescue them from their predicaments" (Raheja and Gold 1994, 14).

Ritual Art

One element that appears to be distinctive of women's *vrat* traditions is the making of decorative and symbolic designs out of such ephemeral substances as powdered rice, wheat flour, rust-colored chalk and tumeric. In different regions of India such designs are called *ālpanā* (in Bengal and Bihar), *mandna* (in Rajasthan), *cauk-purṇa* (in U.P.), *rangoli* (in Maharashtra and Karnataka), and *kolam* (in Tamil Nadu). This art, of course, is not only connected with *vrats*. In southern states, for example, such designs ("threshold paintings") are made by women daily on the doorstep to invite auspiciousness. Maithili women (from eastern Bihar) are well known for the quality of the designs they create on their walls and floors for such occasions as weddings. Nevertheless, many of the *vrats* that women perform on their own all over the country are accompanied by some sort of ritual art even if of the most simple and fleeting sort.

There are very few references to such forms of art in the Purāṇa-Nibandha *vrata* descriptions. When we do find directives to make a ritual diagram[36] the instructions resemble (or depict) a tantric *maṇḍala*[37] or *yantra* rather than the *vrat ālpanā* that we see today. Tantric religious rites have used ritual diagrams for worship and meditational purposes for many centuries. Though the *maṇḍalas* and *yantras* are generally more complex and esoteric in their symbolism and use than the *vrat ālpanā*, they do have certain characteristics in common. They both demarcate "sacred space." They are both often drawn with rice powder, and feature an intricate geometry of line and space. They share such symbols as the lotus to represent the deity. Over *maṇḍala* or *ālpanā* the adept or votary utters mantras or prayers to invoke the deity.

S. K. Ray, in his study of the ritual art of *vratas* in Bengal, notes that "in the religion of *brata*, art is an indispensable means of communication between the devotees and the gods" (1961, iv). Each *brata*, he says, "has its own *ālpanā*, which at the time of its performance, is drawn with fingertips on the ground. . . . The *ālpanā* related to a *brata* must clearly depict the object the bratee [votary] desires to have, otherwise its performance will be meaningless and impossible" (1961, 42). He suggests that "the purpose of these *ālpanās* was originally to keep dwelling place, city, or village safe and prosperous, and to make the cultivated land fertile and fruitful, by magical performance" (1961,42). Laxmi Tewari proposes that the making of this form of art may also be viewed as "an act of pilgrimage." "The preparation of materials," he writes, "and the process of painting or sculpting symbolize the journey to the place of pilgrimage. Worshipping and offering food to the painting or sculpture are acts of *darśan* . . . by which a devotee experiences the presence and power of the deity. At the conclusion of the worship, the offerings . . . are distributed as *prasād* (1991,15).

Most of the women that I interviewed had drawn *ālpanās* for at least some of the *vrats* they kept or for other occasions such as on Dīvalī (the festival of lights), Annakuṭ (the food mountain festival) and Bhaiya Dūj ("Brother's Second"). "Only women make *ālpanās*," said Gita, "they always have." "All the girls know," Rani, an elderly Brahman explained. They had all learned them from mothers or other female relatives. Other women I spoke with felt that *ālpanās* are not so common in Banaras as in other areas "like Bengal." "My grandparents did many *ālpanās*—for all festivals—but nowadays fewer are done," said Sudha. I certainly did not see as many of these ritual designs in Banaras as I expected to, and those that I did see were not as elaborate as ones I had seen in Bihar and in the South.

Materials used for the *ālpanās* are ground rice, wheat flour *(aṭa)*, limed tumeric *(roli)*, plain tumeric, and red ochre *(gehru)*. They may be used in a dry form or mixed with water to make a paste. A red spot *(sindūr bindi* or *tilak)* is sometimes applied (by a married woman) to the *ālpanā* after it is made, to bless it with the auspiciousness of a married woman. Though white and red are the traditional colors used, nowadays other colors are being introduced from commercial sources. The designs are most commonly drawn on the ground, but also may be done on the wall "near a *pūjā* place," on a door, or on a clay or wood board. Women were in agreement that there are a few standard *ālpanā* patterns (or "traditional forms") for different *vrat*s that one could then improvise upon or embellish as one pleased. Some *ālpanās* are wholly abstract in form, others contain specific symbols representing the deity, certain rivers, the moon and the sun, auspiciousness, the married couple, children, animals, household objects and can include decorative motifs such as flowers and birds. Now one can also buy lithographs of "ready made" *ālpanās* in the bazaar, a situation which will serve to further homogenize *vrat*s in India in a way that *vrat-kathā* booklets are doing. A few women I interviewed had bought these lithographs, others disdained them because of their "cheap quality."

According to the women who make them, *ālpanās* serve several purposes. Decoration is always a concern. In addition, *ālpanās* may promote auspiciousness, "benefit the outcome of the *vrat*," "for example for children," "for sons." Some *ālpanās* are also specifically "for the *pūjā*." Karvā Cauth was mentioned most often as the *vrat* during which one "had" to draw an *ālpanā*, on top of which the *karvā* (pot) would be placed for the *pūjā*. One woman explained that for her Karvā Cauth *ālpanā* she drew an image of Cand-Surāj (the moon and sun) signifying "the world," then stick figures of men and women signifying "the continuation of life," images of mountains and trees signifying "nature," and a svastik, the symbol of auspiciousness. "We apply a *tika* of *sindūr*, and on top of that we place the *karvā*. Then we perform the *pūjā* when the [full] moon is up."

In addition to or instead of paintings, women may fashion objects out of cowdung or clay for certain *vrat*s (like Bahulā Cauth and Baḍī Ekādaśī) or other observances (like Bhaiyā Dūj, Govardhan, and Annakūṭ). The objects, which may be intricately decorated with seeds, grains, shells, and so on, depict the deities, animals, or other characters featured in the *vrat*'s story. Like any ephemeral *mūrti*, the figures are blessed or made sacred and worshipped with food offerings, incense and lights, and then are thrown away or allowed to disintegrate after the *vrat* is over. The practice of this kind of art seems to be far more common in rural than in urban areas where clay and cowdung are less available (and where the mess they involve is less tolerated!).[38]

TWO VRATS

Having examined eight features common to the performance of a *vrat*, we are now ready to see how these features fit together in two currently observed *vrats* and how they orchestrate the goals of these *vrats*. The two *vrats* which I have selected for a detailed description are both annual *vrats* observed by women in Banaras: Haritālikā (Tīj) and Jīvitputrika. Of the annual *vrats* performed by women in Banaras, these two stand out for their difficulty (a twenty-four-hour waterless fast is required), and for their popularity (in terms of the sheer number of women who keep these vows). Large groups of women can be seen bathing and performing *pūjā* on the banks of the Ganges in the early hours of the morning, when it can be quite cool, as well as at sunset during the days on which these *vrats* occur. Conventionally, Tīj is performed by married women for the sake of their husband's long life, and Jiutiyā for the sake of a woman's children, in particular, sons. While *vrats* for husbands may have the full weight of cultural (gender-ideology) sanction behind them, I found that *vrats* for children carry the strongest emotional commitment for women.

The Haritālikā (Tīj) Vrat

The Haritālikā Vrat is described not only in most of the modern Hindi *vrat-kathā* books but also in many Sanskrit sources.[39] In Banaras, the *vrat* is observed on the third (hence *"tīj")* of the waxing fortnight of Bhādrapad (August/September), although in other parts of Uttar Pradesh it is the third day of the previous month, Śravaṇa, that the *vrat*/festival of Tīj is observed.[40] The texts say it is incumbent on all married women to keep the fast. However, young unmarried girls can keep it to get a "good husband," or, as Kamala put it, "to try to guarantee a long-lived groom," and in practice a few widows continue to observe it ("so that in the next life one won't become a widow"). The Haritālikā Vrat is probably the most common annual *vrat* for husbands kept by women in Banaras, as Karvā Cauth seems to be in western Uttar Pradesh, and Vaṭ Sāvitrī Vrat is in Kerala.

One Brahman family invited me to attend their Tīj Vrat *pūjā*. This family consisted of a husband who worked in an office at Banaras Hindu University and is a son of the publisher of the Hṛṣikeś Pañcāṅga, his wife, Usha, who was twenty-nine at the time and their three-year-old daughter. Usha was well educated, with a master's degree in Sanskrit. They were both relatively orthodox and firm believers in the efficacy and importance of *vrats*. The husband was particularly enthusiastic about my interest in the *vrat* tradition and seemed proud that his wife was involved in it. Usha told me that the Tīj Vrat was observed in her birth family and in her village (in Ghorakpur district) but that it was done differently there from the way her husband's family performed it. There was no priest involved in this *vrat* as observed by the women in her village, and the *pūjā* was very simple. Since it received so much attention in her husband's family, she learned how to do it the "śāstric" way. The way in which this family observes the Tīj Vrat corresponds fairly closely to textual descriptions (though the *pūjā* described in some Sanskrit texts is more elaborate).[41]

I arrived at their home in the early evening. Usha and her newly married sister who had come for the day from another part of the city were keeping the *vrat*. They had bathed in the river in the early morning, at which time they prayed to Pārvatī stating that they were undertaking this *vrat* and asking that it be fulfilled with her help and blessings (their informal *saṅkalp*). After, they returned home to wash and oil their hair. Their last meal had been the evening before and they would not eat again until the next morning. In the late afternoon the two women started to decorate themselves with the "sixteen *ṣṛṅgār*"—the prescribed sixteen "adornments," including items of jewelry and clothing, that represent the auspicious signs of the married women. They put red lac *(alta)* on their feet and elaborate henna designs *(mehndi)* on their hands. They put on gold earrings and a nose-ring, toe-rings, new glass bangles, and new saris of yellow and red which had been given to them by their in-laws for the occasion, according to the usual custom.

Around seven in the evening the family pandit came and sat on the floor of the *pūjā* room, near a small wood table *(piṛi)* upon which stood an unpainted clay image of Śiva and Pārvatī which had been purchased in the bazaar the day before. The pandit began reciting Sanskrit mantras and verses *(ślokas)* and paused periodically to tell the two women to sprinkle first Ganges water on themselves and on the image *(mūrti)*, and then sprinkle flowers and unhusked rice on the image. Incense was lit and they each took a lit stick and circled it around the *mūrti*. Then the pandit put the sticks in an incense burner while continuing to recite *ślokas* from memory. Each woman then presented the *mūrti* with offerings of fruit (apples, bananas, and cucumber), sweets, and items associated with the *suhāgin:* a mirror, comb, *kuṁkuṁ, bindis* (the modern store-bought stick-on variety), hair pins, bangles, and cloth. They each then performed *ārati* in front of the image.

Next the pandit started to read the Haritālikā *vrat-kathā* from one of the flimsy rectangular pamphlets one finds in the bazaar. He first recited a few sentences of the Sanskrit story (taken from the *Śivapurāṇa*), and then explained the story in Hindi to the seated women. This lasted about twenty minutes. Afterwards, all stood up and a last *ārati* was performed with concluding Sanskrit mantras. The women remained silent throughout. The pandit left after being given some of the food that had been offered to Śiva and Pārvatī. The women kept an all-night vigil *(jagaraṇ)* typical of certain *vrats* like Tīj and Śivarātri. They sang *bhajans* (songs of praise) about Śiva and Pārvatī, accompanying themselves on a drum. The songs they had learned from their own mother. At around five in the morning the *vrat*-ending ceremony *(pāraṇa)* began. The pandit returned and the women presented him with *dān-dakṣina* consisting of a kilo or two of lentils and rice, and some money. The pandit blessed them, giving the women permission to break their fast. The women then took another bath, offered soaked chickpeas to Śiva and Pārvatī and broke their fast by eating some of this chickpea-*prasād.*

The Tīj *Vrat-kathā*

The *kathā* which the pandit narrated to the two women is the version which is to be found in many sources, Sanskrit and Hindi, with few variations. It is a well-known story which highlights the extreme asceticism Pārvatī underwent in order to win Śiva as her husband. The fasting women listening to the story are presumably meant to identify with Pārvatī's grueling austerities. Despite his matted hair and indifferent behavior (of which Pārvatī's father Himāvan [or Himāchal] thoroughly disapproved), Śiva is considered an ideal husband because of his faithfulness and, though this is not usually stated explicitly, because of his virility. Similarly, Pārvatī often figures prominently as a protagonist in the *vrat-kathā* literature because, among other things, she is an exemplary *pativratā* and *saubhāgyavatī.* The story starts with Pārvatī asking Śiva to recount to her how she won him as a husband. Śiva proceeds to remind her of the very difficult *tapasyā* that she underwent on the banks of the river Ganges for many years with the object of gaining his favorable attention.[42]

Pārvatī's austerities included living on smoke for twelve years, dry leaves for another twenty-four years, staying in water in the cold month of Māgh and surrounding herself by fire in the hot month of Vaiśākh. Eventually, Pārvatī's father, Himāchal, gets very worried about her and when the sage Nārad comes to him with an offer from Viṣṇu for Pārvatī's hand, he readily accepts. But Viṣṇu backs off when he realizes that Pārvatī was connected to Śiva in a past life as Satī and that she is intent on again marrying only Śiva. Partly to test her resolve, Nārad tries various means to dissuade Pārvatī from her terrible austerities, but she remains firm. Her father also has no luck in dissuading her. After some time, when Pārvatī begins to feel she is no closer to her object of desire, she complains to a friend, "If I don't obtain Śivji as my husband then I will give up my life." Her friend advises her to continue her austerities in another forest where Śiva will certainly take notice and be pleased. She does this and also performs a full *pūjā* to Śiva after making a Śiva-*liṅga* out of sand. This day happens to be the third of the bright half of Bhādrapad. Śiva at last notices Pārvatī and decides to oblige her by offering her a boon. She asks him to accept her as wife. He does so. All the gods are relieved that she has finally ended her powerful asceticism. A joyous wedding ensues.

The lesson for women observing this *vrat* is clear: steadfastly adhering to the difficult fasting requirement will eventually result in the fruition of one's desire—for young girls, to get a good husband like Śiva, and for married women, to win or better preserve their *saubhāgyavatī* state. Indeed, this is made explicit in one *vrat-kathā* text which states at the end of the narration that, "By observing this *vrat* the *saubhāgya* of women remains permanent." And women are warned that: "The *saubhāgyavatī* women who do not observe this *vrat* or do not continue after having observed it for a few years, or eat and drink during the fast—will suffer severe troubles in this life and in the next life" (Tripathi 1978, 145).[43] But another lesson for women from this *vrat-kathā* is that by observing austerities one gets power not only to achieve one's goals but also to control one's own life, rather than be controlled by others (notably by men). While some versions of the story play up the element of destiny (i.e., Pārvatī was Satī, Śiva's first wife, and so was destined to be his wife again), all versions capture Pārvatī's defiance of her father's and Nārad's attempt to direct her life and her strong sense of self-determination. The ascetic power she accumulates through her terrible austerities becomes a source of fear and anxiety to the gods who, in Tripathi's version, importune Śiva to take notice of Pārvatī and stop her.[44]

Most women I talked with affirmed that this is one *vrat* that once started one should try to keep all one's married life as long as one is physically able. Moreover, once one decides to stop it, then certainly a formal ending ceremony *(udyāpan)* should be done with a priest officiating. Mira told me that following the ending *pūjā* one is to give "colorful" saris to three married women. The texts suggest that one should give saris, dhotis, food, and *dakṣina* to a Brahman and his wife, but again, in practice, the details of the *udyāpan* depend on what the family pandit prescribes or on what is normally done in the woman's family. In any case, the giving of gifts (saris, jewelry) to one or some *married* women at the time of the *udyāpan* ceremony is considered essential as is the giving of gifts from mother or mother-in-law or sometimes the husband of items representing the auspicious married state to the daughter, daughter-in-law or wife at the time that she observes Tīj each year. Thus, Lelauti, a well-to-do Thakur in her forties, the matron of a small nuclear family, emphasized that husbands "must certainly bring a new sari for their wives on Tīj, because it is necessary to wear a new sari on this day." Mildred Luschinsky, who described this *vrat* as it was done in a village fifty kilometers north of Banaras in the 1950s, suggested that the giving of gifts from mother to daughter (if the daughter was at her husband's home) or mother-in-law to daughter-in-law (if the *bahū* was visiting her natal family) allowed ties between families and villages represented by marriage to be regularly strengthened. She says further that, "Any family which fails to send Tij gifts when it can afford to do so is loudly criticized by all who hear about it."[45] I would add that the giving of *these* particular gifts to married women reinforces among women the value of the wife in the family as *suhāgin*—the bearer and potential dispenser of auspiciousness. Although the wife is performing the *vrat for* her husband's well-being and long life it is *she* who is being celebrated. Her fast for his sake is an actualization of her protective and life-enhancing power. Interestingly, Luschinsky has noted in regard to the village of the Senapur version of Tīj that, "Women fast on Tij for the welfare of their husbands. *The act of fasting itself* is thought to serve this end. No gods are worshipped" (1962, 658; my emphasis). In other words, recalling the discussion of *tapas* (the "heat" arising from ascetic practice) in chapter 2, the fasting women undertake in the Tīj Vrat can be understood to produce its own creative, transformational power that can effect the wishes of the votary.

The Jīvitputrika (Jiutiyā) Vrat

The Jīvitputrika Vrat (literally, "living son" vow) or Jiutiyā (a contraction of *jīvit-putra)* takes place on the eighth of the waning fortnight of the month of Āśvin (September/October). It is primarily women who have sons who observe this *vrat* and they do so to promote and protect their (male) children's lives and well-being. In his Hindi book describing *vrats*, Tripathi notes that, "the Purāṇas say that women who observe this *vrat* never suffer on account of their sons" (1978,188).[46] *Vrats* for sons are described as early as the *Mahābhārata*, and they are also found in Purāṇas and Nibandhas, though I have not found any description which corresponds to the way women actually perform this *vrat* today. Tripathi goes on to say that, "It is an extremely popular *vrat* among the women of U.P., Bihar, and M.P., and women having limitless love and affection for their children observe this *vrat* with great faith and loyalty. If someone's son is freed from troubles, then women praise the *'jiutiyā'* of his mother." The word *jiutiyā* commonly refers to the red and yellow wool threads women wear on their necks as part of this *vrat*, but in this context it also represents the protective power the votary has garnered by faithfully keeping the *vrat*.

Tripathi (whose book I here use as the śāstric model since his descriptions are usually based on Sanskrit sources) describes the method in this way:

> Having cheerfully arisen in the early morning and after completing the daily chores women (should) purify themselves in a *tīrth* or pool and make their *saṅkalp* out of a desire for the well-being of sons. Having observed a waterless fast the whole day, in the evening time women put on the *jiutiyā* made of cotton or wool and listen to the *kathā*. Then in the night they 'do' (recite) the meritorious story and perform *kīrtan*, and on the second day, after bathing, etc., they give some *dān-dakṣina* to a Brahman woman whose husband is living and who is blessed with sons, and then (the votary) takes food. (1978, 189)[47]

After this, Tripathi recounts the story of noble King Jīmutavāhan and his self-sacrifice to Garuḍa, the half-man, half-vulture king of the birds, for the sake of a Nāg (snake) and his mother. The story bears no obvious relevance to the *vrat* other than that, first, the happy ending occurs on the eighth of the dark half of Āśvin, second, the king may represent the sort of model son whom women hope to have, and third, snakes are thought of as protectors of children, and thus the story may remind women to look out for, if not propitiate, snakes. Tripathi then gives a short "folk-story" about a female jackal and a female kite *(cil)* who both try to keep the Jiutiyā fast. The jackal fails and her children die at birth, while the kite succeeds, and her children flourish. The stories which women tell one another among those I interviewed in Banaras did not include the Jīmutavāhan narrative, but did include a version of the jackal and kite story. Women's Jiutiyā stories always featured an appearance by Śiva and Pārvatī, who give blessings or help to ensure retributive justice. (See appendix D.)

What is significant about Tripathi's description is his omission of the *pūjā* that women do on this day and which is apparently central to the *vrat*. I watched it being performed by hundreds of women at Lakshmi Kund (a rectangular water reservoir adjoining an old Lakṣmī temple off Luxa road), and on the banks of the Ganges. Groups of six to twelve women—neighbors, friends, relatives and strangers—would form a circle near the water and begin the ceremony. They first cleaned the ground with water and then put some tumeric paste (called *lepan)* in a simple swirling *ālpanā* design on the cleansed ground. In the center of each swirl was put a dab of red powder. Then the gathered women started unpacking the contents *(pūjā samāgri)* of their metal plates *(thālīs*), cloth bundles or baskets on top of the designs, directly in front of them, into heaps. The items included cucumbers, bananas, apples, coconuts, white radishes, limes, flowers (including marigold and hisbiscus), *pūrīs*, *kacaurīs*, sweets, incense sticks and ghee lamps. There were also neatly folded saris, mirrors, bundles of yellow and orange wool and some plastic children's toys. The women's piles were of various sizes—perhaps depending on what they could afford. Remaining on their *thālīs* were chickpeas, mung *dāl* and flower tops. When all were ready the women took a handful of the legumes and flowers and one woman began to tell the *kathā* while the other women listened and periodically threw their handfuls on top of their piles. After about ten minutes another woman began a second story, and after another ten minutes a third woman took over. This lasted another five minutes. The story-tellers were the older women in the group (late forties to mid-fifties). Which woman told a story appeared to be a spontaneous decision; I saw no discussion among the women about it. After the third story the women sprinkled water on their piles; hands touched the items, then their forehead and back in an action of self-blessing. After taking blessings from the *prasād* (which I assumed their piles now to be) each woman carefully picked up all the items, every grain, and put them back in the *thālī*, basket or cloth she had brought. Before leaving the site the women put a *ṭīkā* (or *tilak*, an ornamental or religious mark on the forehead) on themselves with some of the *kuṁkuṁ* powder on the ground, again in an act of self-blessing. A new group would then form, clear the ground and proceed in the same manner.[48]

When I asked to what deity the *pūjā* was directed I got various responses: Lakṣmī, Sūrya-Nārāyaṇ, and "Jiutiyā-Mā" (also identified as Pārvatī). Votaries normally worshipped one or the other of these deities during Jiutiyā. The fact that several deities are associated with this *vrat* is interesting and somewhat unusual. The particular deity's association with the vow can be accounted for in various ways. Sūrya-Dev or Sūrya-Nārāyaṇ, the Sun god, is worshipped morning and evening during the Ḍala Chaṭh Vrat, an extremely popular *vrat* in Bihar which has spilled over into Banaras. The *vrat* bears many similarities to Jiutiyā: it is for sons; women perform a similar *pūjā* on the banks of the Ganges; and they tell each other stories. In some *vrat kathā* books it is said that in the Jīvitputrika Vrat one is to "do Sūrya-Nārāyaṇ *pūjā*." Jiutiyā-Mā is clearly the personification of the Jīvitputrika Vrat. She has no iconic form and is said to live in wells or other watery places like *kuṇḍ* and rivers. She has no other function apart from this *vrat*. In Senapur "Jiut Baba" and "Jiutia Mai" are worshipped on Jiutiyā. Luschinsky noted that, "Although women say that they cannot identify many of the gods who are personifications of ceremonies, they do identify Jiut Baba as Siv . . . and Jiutia Mai as Parvati" (1962, 662). (Lakṣmī's connection with the *vrat* will be discussed below.)

As for the *pūjā* offerings (most of which can be purchased from street vendors in the lanes leading to Lakshmi Kund and on the banks of the Ganges), the fruit, flowers, cooked food, sweets, incense, and lamps are, as we have seen, typical items used to feed and honor the deity in any standard *pūjā*. The saris, mirrors and *kuṁkuṁ* represent *saubhāgya*. The children's toys represent the children for whom the *vrat* is being observed.

The legumes (and sugarcane stalks which I saw among women performing the *pūjā* along the Ganges) represent the new harvest, fecundity, and may symbolize the material well-being of the family.

After the *pūjā* women go home as they came—singing songs with their baskets on their heads or held in their arms. At home all the fresh edible things that were offered in the *pūjā* are cut up into small pieces and given as *prasād* to those not keeping the *vrat* (e.g., male family members and children). The women remain fasting. The next morning before dawn they get up, bathe, and break their long fast (in which, Chandravati pointed out, even spittle should not be swallowed). Some women said they simply ate some of the left-over *prasād*. Shyamdevi's niece, Lakshmi, told me that she prepared *pūrīs*, sweet rice, *paraṭhas* stuffed with chickpeas and *laḍḍus*. She invoked Jiutiyā-Mā and touched fingers to food and forehead and back several times to bless herself. Some of this food was taken to the well (beside which she had done the *pūjā* and listened to stories the previous day) and thrown in as an offering. Then she went back to her home and broke her fast by swallowing seven uncooked chickpeas. Finally, she and her family ate the food she had prepared.

Lakshmi also told me that the sixteen red and yellow threads are "worn as *prasād*" after they have been offered to Jiutiyā-Mā. Women will wear these threads around their necks for a few weeks or months, she said. One woman, Chandravati, said that she had silver charms representing the goddess Jiutiyā made for both of her sons. To these she performed a *pūjā* and then tied them to the strings which she then wears each year for two weeks (during *pitṛ pakṣa*).[49] The threads (and charms) are believed to provide blessings and protection for the woman's sons (and indeed daughters, if the woman has no sons or has a daughter that she is concerned about).[50] The tying and wearing of knotted threads is not confined to this *vrat* as the practice is also associated with, for example, the Ananta Caturdaśī Vrat, where one wears fourteen *(caturdaśī)* threads. The sixteen Jiutiyā threads are also evidently connected with the sixteen-day Mahālakṣmī Vrat immediately preceding this *vrat*. During the "Sorahia Mela" (the colloquial name for Mahālakṣmī Vrat), a vow also observed almost exclusively by women for the sake of children and for promoting prosperity, the votary wears red and yellow threads with sixteen knots in it. The knots are tied by one of the priests at the Lakṣmī temple with accompanying mantras. Because Jiutiyā falls on the last day of the Mahālakṣmī Vrat and women observing this *vrat* daily go to the Lakṣmī temple adjoining the same *kuṇḍ* where many women who are keeping the Jiutiyā Vrat go for performing their *pūjā*, it is natural to associate the Jiutiyā Vrat with the goddess Lakṣmī. It is because these two *vrats* intersect in time that certain features of one—the threads and identification of the deity (Lakṣmī)—have passed into the other.[51] In the Jiutiyā Vrat a priest is not involved at all. Women perform the *pūjā*, women bless themselves and women tell the stories. All these aspects distinguish it from the Mahālakṣmī Vrat and the Tīj Vrat where all the *pūjā* rituals, *kathā* telling, and blessing are usually presided over by a priest. Even the all-night vigil, the women's *bhajan* singing and the wearing of the sixteen *ṣṛṇgār* is prescribed in the texts. However, in the Tīj Vrat *laukik* elements also can be and are added. For example, one woman told me that she made an *ālpanā* on the Tīj day, even though it was "not necessary as it is in Karvā Cauth." She made it, she said, for auspiciousness. The simple design which she drew for me prominently featured the svastik, the quintessential symbol of benediction or auspiciousness.

In sum, *vrats* are composed of a number of recurring elements whose particular content and arrangement gives each vow a distinctive stamp. The same *vrat*, however, may be observed differently by different families even of the same caste in the same locale. No doubt incoming *bahūs* may help to introduce minor variations to the practices of an extended family even while they attempt to conform to those practices. Women of urban and nuclear families may feel freer to make modifications "for convenience" or to suit the exigencies of their situation. This is certainly the case among Hindu immigrant women in North America, many of whom want to continue or restart the observance of *vrats* in their new cultural environment.[52] Nevertheless, even within these parameters of change, there is a marked continuity of form in the observance of *vrats* among women I encountered during the period of my field research. The basic constituents of a *vrat* (excepting the ritual art whose traditions themselves are probably very old), elaborated in centuries-old texts, all continue to be found in the *vrats* that women currently keep in India today.

The various individual features of a *vrat* carry a range of significance for women. The *saṅkalp*, stated formally in front of a priest or informally by the woman to herself, reminds the woman of the overall intent of the *vrat*, articulates a commitment to see it through to its conclusion, and beseeches the deity to remove impediments to its fulfillment or to grant the wishes of the votary. Many women emphasized that their resolve gave them added psychological impetus to carry out the *vrat*, especially in the case of the more difficult waterless fasts.

Most of the women I interviewed performed some sort of regular *pūjā* alone at home. But on a *vrat* day, the *pūjā* assumes a special importance because it provides both a social and a devotional context for the *vrat;* the woman's acts of austerity are linked with those of other women and with their acts of devotion to the deity associated with the *vrat*. Pleased by the votary's acts of austerity and by her acts of solicitous devotion in the *pūjā*, the deity to whom the *vrat* is directed (if there is one) may feel inclined, if not compelled, to respond to the votary's desires. If the desires are not expressed in the *saṅkalp* or in the act of *pūjā* itself, they may be represented in the ritual designs the woman creates for the occasion (featuring symbols of children, the husband-wife pair, or auspiciousness in general). Or, the wishes of participants may be expressed more obliquely in the stories following the *pūjā*. That is, the woman listening to the story may identify her wishes and hopes with those expressed by the protagonist.

When a male pandit or *pujārī* oversees the *pūjā*, women undoubtedly assume a more passive role in the proceedings. Yet this passive role may be relatively short-lived. In the case of Usha and her sister, the twenty minute *pūjā* performed by the family pandit was the only point during the twenty-four hour *vrat* when the women were passive. More often, as in my description of the Jiutiyā Vrat, women act as their own officiants during the *pūjās*.

The positive social environment provided by *vrat pūjās* is affirming for women. It was striking to see streams of women carrying *pūjā* articles in baskets, moving slowly or briskly, talking quietly or with animation, gathering numbers as they moved through the narrow streets to the *ghaṭs* or to Lakshmi Kund on several *vrat* days in Banaras. As women form small groups with family, friends and strangers to perform the *pūjā* and tell or listen to the stories, the bonds of solidarity between women as women *(strī-jāti:* "the class of women") are reinforced. Women do not have to tell each other their own personal tales because their stories are told for them in the ritualized setting of the *kathās* and in the songs they sing. In these stories and songs, during the *pūjās*, women in their togetherness find meanings that may be comforting, supportive or subtly critical of normative values and expectations. They may also be empowering, for if they stick to their resolve like Sāvitrī, are as self-disciplined as Pārvatī, and express feelings of true devotion to the gods as other protagonists of the *kathās* do, then any objective may be achieved, anything is possible. As Sāvitrī says in the *Mahābhārata:* "My course shall remain unobstructed through the power of my austerities, my conduct towards my elders, my love for my husband, my vow, and by thy [Yama's] grace."

Why does the *vrat* tradition continue to have such a tenacious hold on Hindu women today? What do women aim to achieve in their *vrats* and why? While we have already begun to see answers to these questions, I will address them more directly in the remainder of the book. In the next chapter I examine how the *pativratā* ideology described in chapter 2 combines with patterns of socialialization to inform and affect the number and type of *vrats* that women observe today and the reasons that women give for performing these rites at different stages of their lives.

6

Vrats and the Life Stages of Hindu Women

When the Dharmaśāstras discuss women they frequently do so according to a tripartite division of a woman's life defined by her relationship to men: the before-marriage phase *(kaumārikā)*, the marriage phase *(vivāha)* and widowhood *(vaidhavya)*. As we have seen, these texts were interested in women primarily from the point of view of how they ought to support and accommodate the prescribed "life-cycle" of men—the four stages and duties (or aims), the *saṃskāras*, and so on. Purāṇa and Nibandha literature sometimes designates particular *vrats* as suitable for (or more explicitly peculiar to) unmarried girls, married women and widows. There is no parallel division for men. Men are rather categorized according to other criteria (e.g., caste or occupation) and so certain *vrats* are singled out as appropriate for kings, others for mendicants, and so forth. The only occupation singled out for women in these texts in which a particular *vrat* is deemed suitable, that I could discover, is prostitution.

Several authors writing on Bengali *brat* have discussed "women's *vrats*" according to this tripartite division of a woman's marital status, for example, S. R. Das (1952) and E. M. Gupta (1984). In Bengal there are clearly a number of *vrats* specific to unmarried girls *(kumarī brata)* and then to married women *(nārī brata)*. In Orissa, James Freeman has described a *vrat* specific to post-menopausal women, the Habisha Vrat (1980). When I went to the field I also planned to divide Hindu women's lives into the three general phases of her life-cycle, for analytic and descriptive purposes. The intention was to determine whether there were *vrats* peculiar to each stage, if so which ones, and the reasons for observing these *vrats* among women in Banaras. However, while a few women I spoke with from other parts of Uttar Pradesh told me about *vrats* which only unmarried (pre-menarche) girls keep, in Banaras, perhaps because of its urban and cosmopolitan nature, I did not discover such strictly segregated marital or age-specific *vrats*. Instead, I found that among the women I interviewed there was a variety of opinion and practice about who does (or should or should not do) which *vrats*, on what occasions and for what reasons they may be performed. Nevertheless, I feel it is instructive to organize and present data on *vrats* according to stages in a woman's life in order to compare Dharmaśāstra notions about women's duty with material from researchers who have written about women in North India from a sociological perspective, and with women's views and personal narratives. Once more, this format allows us to get a sense of the relationship between gender ideology, social norms and actual behavior in the context of women's performance of *vrats*.

Before we begin, it is worth noting that if one looks at the life-cycle from the Hindu woman's point of view, it becomes apparent that while a woman's relations with a man may define her status and set her path, it is the world of women she moves through. On this point, Sylvia Vatuk, in writing about women in an "urbanized village" within metropolitan Delhi, has argued that women do not necessarily, or only, perceive their own position according to the model of the (infamous) dictum found in the *Manusmṛti* (5.148): "In childhood a woman must be under her father's control, in youth under her husband's, when her husband is dead, under her sons'" (Doniger, trans.; see also 9.3).

> They do not see the constraints on their activities as imposed specifically by men, probably because during most of their life control is administered by other women acting either on their own initiative or at the behest of men or of other women who in turn hold positions of authority over them. It is interesting in this connection to note a feminine version of Manu's injunction, volunteered by several of my Raya informants, that sees a woman's life in terms of three successive phases of subordination to other *women*, namely *mā ki rāj*, *sās ki rāj*, and *bahū ki rāj* ("rule of the mother, the mother-in-law, and the daughter-in-law"). (Vatuk 1987, 32)

An effect of this feature of the social structure is that women by and large are the most rigorous defenders of tradition, of normative behavior; especially those who assume the position of matriarch in the family.

KAUMĀRIKĀ—THE UNMARRIED GIRL

In his book *Women in Manu and His Seven Commentators*, R. M. Das writes: "Manu regards the daughter as an object of highest tenderness. . . . She is to be brought up with as much affection and care as is bestowed upon the male child; rather greater kindness is to be shown to her as she is physically more tender and her emotions too are more delicate" (1962, 49).[1] Such sentiments, characteristic of Das' book, reveal more about Das' attitudes than about those of the author of the *Manusmṛti.* For, in fact, the Dharmaśāstra (and the *Manusmṛti*'s) interest in the unmarried girl is minimal. It is centered primarily on ensuring that the girl's virtue is safeguarded under the authority of the paterfamilias, until her transfer, through a properly arranged marriage at the appropriate time, to the authority of her husband.

From a sociological view, researchers (e.g., M. Roy 1975; Kalakdina 1975; Kakar 1978; Vatuk 1987; Minturn 1993) have shown that, in general, a young girl in North India has no authority and little power, but does have a measure of autonomy while residing in her parents' house.[2] The amount and quality of her autonomy depend on myriad factors, bearing on such things as her parents' attitudes toward her, how many and what sex siblings she has, and her economic status, among others. In most cases the daughter's autonomy will begin to be circumscribed between ages six to ten, and she will be more explicitly socialized into her feminine roles, in contrast to her brother who will retain and augment his already greater degree of autonomy. The means of explicit socialization of the daughter include: being given responsibility over younger children; being asked to help older female relatives in household duties, including religious activities like preparing *pūjā* items; not being allowed to go beyond certain boundaries or interact informally with strange men, and then even known men outside the immediate family. The role of *vrats* in the gender socialization of young girls has been noted by some researchers (e.g., Mazumdar 1981; Roy 1975; Kayal in Sen Gupta 1969). A vivid example is the Bengali Daśaputtal Brata, observed by unmarried daughters. Here I quote Mazumdar's description of it:

> The puja and *vrata* more directly involved with the socialization of girls are typically conducted at home—either in a room set aside by the family for worship . . . or in an area designated as

> the altar. The *dasaputtalika* (ten dolls) *vrata*, though no longer as popular as it used to be 30 to 40 years ago, . . . is in many ways the quintessential *vrata* designed for unmarried girls. This is carried out in the first month of the Hindu Bengali calendar. Ten figures, primarily from the epics, are drawn on the ground, and prayers are offered to them in turn, embodying an appropriate wish. These include: a wish for a husband like Rama, a father-in-law like Dasaratha, a brother-in-law like Lakshmana, a mother-in-law like Kausalya; to be chaste like Sita, an efficient cook like Draupadi, to be blessed with children like Kunti (all sons and no daughters); to achieve true womanhood like Durga, tranquillity like the river goddess Ganga, and forebearance like Mother Earth. (1981, 34)[3]

Some of the role models for women in the epics held up all over India and repeatedly reinforced by the observance of *vrats* which bear their name, and in imitation of whom they are performed, were mentioned previously. The Daśaputtal Brata fills out models for the other significant personae in the life of the young wife. Since the girl can expect to marry, she might as well pray for the "best" husband and in-laws; those who will be kind, considerate and fair. The *brata* also makes explicit those qualities that the young woman should aim to achieve in herself: chastity, efficiency, fecundity, strength, tranquillity, forebearance.

Poonam, a middle-aged Brahman woman who was born near Merut (north of Delhi) and then lived in various parts of Uttar Pradesh, told me about two *vrats* that she had observed at the behest of her mother when she was a young girl: Surāj Aṣṭi and Candra Chaṭh Vrat ("sun eighth" and "moon sixth" *vrats*).[4] These are *vrats* only for pre-menarche girls, she said, and she kept them from the age of four to eight, completing them with an *udyāpan*. In the Surāj Vrat one eats one meal before the sun goes down, and in the Candra Vrat one eats only after the moon has come up. These are rather difficult fasting requirements for such a young child, and Poonam said that she was the only one among her four sisters who had been able to complete these two annual *vrats*. The Candra Vrat is marked by a special bath, administered by her mother, in which the *turai* leaf is rubbed on five parts of the body. At the time of breaking the fast, the family pandit came to read the *vrat-kathā*, the details of which Poonam could not remember except that it explained the importance of the special bath. While she could not recall the details very clearly (and did not know anyone who kept these *vrats* today), the ritual and fasting had made a deep impression on her and she took on many more *vrats* with enthusiasm when she got older.

In Banaras, I found that in practice and common opinion, apart from *vrats* for children, unmarried girls could do virtually any *vrat* they wished. In addition to the general familial *vrats*, the girls I met who performed extra *vrats* tended to take on a weekday *vrat* or, among the annual women's *vrats*, Tīj. The weekday *vrats* that were popular were the Monday, Thursday and Friday (including Santoṣī Mā) *vrats*. These were observed by teenagers and women in their twenties for assistance in school studies or work, or for securing a "good" husband. Obtaining a good husband was the only reason given for observing Tīj, and the most frequent reason given for observing the Monday Vrat.[5]

Other *vrats*, of course, can serve the purpose of obtaining a good husband too. Fifty-six year-old Krishna, who came from an observant Brahman family, told me that she started the Śravaṇ Somvār Vrat (Mondays in the month of Śravaṇ Vrat) when she was ten years old for this reason. She said that she saw her mother observing it and was inspired to do so herself. Her mother guided her in the details, but she did not have to spell out to Krishna the purpose for which she should perform the *vrat*. Krishna had already absorbed this lesson in watching her older sisters get married off.

Sudha, unmarried and twenty-four, keeps the Tuesday Vrat, during which she avoids grains, onions, masala and mustard oil, reads verses from a Hindi translation of the *Durgāsaptaśatī* and offers flowers, lights and incense to her *mūrti* of Durgā while silently praying to the goddesss. When I met her she was living at home with her mother while she pursued graduate studies in music at Banaras Hindu University. She observed only two *vrats*, Navarātri and the Tuesday Vrat, both directed to her favored deity, Durgā. In Sudha's case, unlike most of the other women I interviewed who kept this weekly *vrat*, the planet Maṅgal did not have any bearing on the reasons for her observance, and no one had prescribed it for her. She had been observing the *vrat* for one and a half years when I met her and had started it "because I felt a desire to do it." Underlying this desire, it later emerged, was her hope to find a good husband. This hope was all the more poignant because two of her well-educated sisters had burned to death in the homes of their in-laws; victims of so called "dowry deaths." Sudha's mother, a widow as well as a bereaved parent, supported Sudha in her decision to take up this *vrat* as well as

Sudha's desire to carry on with her studies. Despite her marriageable age, no efforts were being made at the time to find Sudha a husband. Sudha asserted that she will try to do the Tuesday Vrat "all my life."

Thirty-four-year-old Chitra said that she started Navarātri—her first *vrat*—some eighteen years previously when she was in tenth standard. Chitra wanted help with her exams, which, at this stage, were very important because they were the "board exams" similar to the British "O" levels. In expressing her concern to her teacher, Chitra's teacher suggested that she try observing the Navarātri Vrat (and thereby secure the goddess' assistance). Chitra agreed to do this and, though her mother and grandparents observed Navarātri, Chitra was the only one in her family to observe all nine days of the *vrat*. Her mother also taught her the details of the ritual. Clearly, obtaining help to pass exams is not a traditional reason for women to keep Navarātri (or any other *vrat*). However, as women's education becomes more highly valued (even if only to render a girl more marriageable [see Jeffery and Jeffery 1994]), doing well in school becomes an important goal and is added to the list of socially acceptable reasons for a young woman to perform *vrat*s. The above example also reveals the perceived nature of *vrat*s (especially "all-purpose" *vrat*s like Navarātri) as potential problem-solvers. Again we may note that this adaptability is one factor that explains the tenaciousness of these rites.

During several Friday morning visits to a small but busy Santoṣī Mā temple in Khojvan (a section of Banaras) I saw teenage girls coming alone, with a friend or with their mothers among the women who came to the temple to take *darśan* of Santoṣī Mā or to perform the *pūjā*, sing her *āratī* song, and to listen to the reading of the *kathā* as part of their *vrat*. I stopped a few of these fourteen- to seventeen-year-old girls as they hurried on their way out to ask them whether and why they were keeping Santoṣī Mā's *vrat*. Some told me they were just going along with their friend or mother. Others said they were keeping a *vrat* and among these the majority told me they were keeping the vow to help them in their school studies. Yet even while they were performing the *vrat* "for school," they could not help but assimilate the messages of this *kathā*. The story features a seventh son and his dutiful wife who are both unfairly treated by his mother, though it is the wife who discovers this unfair treatment (they are only fed leftovers). A subsequent confrontation with the mother results in the son leaving home to make his fortune in the world, promising to return to his wife in twelve years. Without the protection of her husband, the young wife is harassed and overworked by her in-laws. She learns about the Santoṣī Mā Vrat from some village women who tell her that by keeping this *vrat* "poverty will be gone, Lakṣmī will come, all your worries will vanish and you will be very peaceful and happy. If you don't have a son, you'll get one; if your husband is gone, he'll return; if you are not married, you'll get a good husband; if you have a case, it will be over; if you have any kind of problem, it will be solved; you will get happiness, peace, and a lot of money; if you have any disease, you'll get rid of that; and if you have any other wish, it will come true; we have no doubt that all this will happen." The wife performs the *vrat* and asks the goddess to take away her sorrows. Santoṣī Mā gets to work and eventually husband and wife are reunited, they have plenty of wealth, and the in-laws are properly chastened. However, almost all is lost when the wife sets out to perform the ending ceremony for the *vrat* and is tricked into giving some money to the eight boys she is required to feed. The boys, counselled by a jealous aunt, use the money to buy and eat sour fruits, thereby angering Santoṣī Mā who reverses the couple's fortune. The mistake is then redressed and all is restored. But this message is clear: the *vrat* must be done properly to the last detail or not at all.

While the basic story describes the traditional roles and duties of the young wife, it also conveys the message that when treated unjustly women can take matters into their own hands and by demonstrating a pure heart and pious attitude they can access divine assistance. It is interesting too that unlike many Sanskritic *vrata* stories, it is the husband and wife bond and their mutual loyalty that are given primacy and set against the bond of mother and son. It is almost unheard of for a mother to mistreat her son in Sanskritic stories.

As a final example from my own data to illustrate the place of (or attitudes toward) *vrats* in the *kaumārikā* stage, I offer part of the conversation I had with seventeen-year-old Anita, the daughter of a well-to-do army officer:

Do you consider yourself a religious person?
No.

Why would you want to start a vrat*?*
I would want to give a rest to my digestive system.

Mainly for health reasons?

Yes, I like to take a *vrat* on Monday because it is a common belief that if one keeps a *vrat* on Monday then Lord Śiva gives praise and happiness [to the observer of the *vrat*].

If you are not religious then why should it matter what day it was?

Yes, [but] I don't much believe in others [other gods], because God is one.

What kind of fast is required for the Monday Vrat?

My mum told me—I just ask her. Now I don't know.

Is it phalāhar?

Yes, *phalāhar.*

What about your friends, do they also do a Monday fast, or . . .

Some of them take a Monday or Tuesday or Saturday Vrat; whatever day they are told by their mothers. They also can ask their family astrologer what day they should fast.

How many of your friends at school observe vrats?

Most of them—except the daughters of brigadiers and colonels.[6]

So vrats *are quite popular among your friends then . . .*

Yes, quite popular.

Do they *want to keep them or [is it] because their mothers or astrologers told them to?*

They also want to keep them. They have some wishes and ambitions, some *kāmna* [wish or desire]. Mothers also say—if you want to keep then keep [them]. And astrologers also told them [to do *vrats*] according to their horoscopes. "You have to keep this *vrat* to please this god because this god according to the *nakṣatra* is angry with you."

Anita starts off by offering a nonreligious reason for keeping a *vrat*—"giving rest to the digestive system." She then appeals to "common belief," that is, her religious heritage imbibed through her mother, to explain the significance of keeping a *vrat* on Monday, Śiva's special day. Śiva rewards those who devotedly keep his *vrat.* Anita was unclear about the details of the *vrat* because she relied on her mother to guide her through it and prepare the appropriate fasting foods. Undoubtedly, for Anita and all her friends who kept a *vrat,* the mother was the primary guide. Yet, as Anita insisted, there was some autonomy in the girls' choice of whether or not to perform the *vrat* in the first place, and why. This is both consonant with the nature of *vrats* as optional observances, and with this stage in a woman's life: the time before marriage while she still resides in the normally comfortable and supportive atmosphere of home. While traditionally this is the formative period in a Hindu girl's training to be wife and mother, she is at the same time often indulged within the confines of a benevolent if strictly supervised environment.

Most women I interviewed said that they did not observe many *vrats* at this stage in their lives, nor did many take them very seriously. Lapses in fasting or procedural requirements were more easily passed over or excused. Some girls kept them irregularly; they could enjoy imitating their older female relatives and pretending to be grown up. Jyoti said that she started the Tīj Vrat when she was around twelve because other girls were doing it and because one could buy (or have one's parents buy) new clothes and bangles for the ritual. Moreover, "it was fun." At that time, she explained, she did not know the significance of the *vrat.* Mothers or grandmothers were usually the key persons involved in transmitting the details of the procedure, though, as I described in chapter 3, others—teachers, films, school friends, or a family astrologer—could be instrumental in providing the impetus to begin observing a *vrat.* Some girls, like Anita, performed *vrats* even though they did not consider themselves to be "religious"; it was something to do (which their friends did, and, of course, which their mothers encouraged); it was a way to keep the body healthy or figures slim. Others had more specific goals: doing well in school; getting a good husband (when marriage itself was seen to be inevitable). Clearly, however, aside from actually learning how to perform *vrats*, what was (and is) imparted to young girls as they grow up in observant Hindu families is that these rites constitute an important, if not crucial, element of what it means to be a Hindu woman and a supplementary (because they are supposed to be optional) way of fulfilling one's *strīdharm.* Further, the *kathās* which young women hear from the time they are small children provide vivid models for the wifely behavior toward which they should strive, but also give them a repertoire of images of women who have overcome numerous difficulties through their wit, perseverence, devotion and determination.

VIVĀHA—THE MARRIED WOMAN

Once a woman marries, her primary *vrata*, the texts say, is *pati-vrata*—her vow of service and fidelity to her husband-god. But as a married woman, she is also now a *saubhāgyavatī* (or *suhāgin*, or in southern India, *sumaṅgalī*)—all terms signifying "an auspicious married woman"—and it is both her duty and in her interest to take the performance of *vrat*s more seriously than she did before marriage. Since she now has a real husband upon whose welfare depends in large measure her own welfare, she must strive to enhance and protect it, and *vrat*s provide a means by which this can be accomplished. Before I explain how this works, it is necessary to consider the significance of the notions of auspiciousness and *śakti* in Hindu thought and the special relationship that females are perceived to bear to them.

By examining its semantic field in day to day usage, the anthropologist T. N. Madan has demonstrated that auspiciousness (*maṅgala, śubha*) is associated with particular events and configurations of time and place which together promote or ensure well-being, happiness, and fruitfulness for individuals and their endeavors (1985). "The agency which ensures this [state of] well-being," Madan notes, "may be divine grace, the configurations of circumstances and/or human effort" (1985, 12). Frédérique Marglin, in her landmark study of the *devadāsīs* (temple dancers) of Puri, describes auspiciousness as "a state which unlike purity does not speak of states of moral uprightness but of well-being and health or more generally all that creates, promotes and maintains life" (1985, 19). She says further that, "Status seems to be associated on the whole with masculinity and auspiciousness on the whole with femininity, the two intimately intermingling in marriage"; and she calls women "the harbingers of auspiciousness."[7] Neither men nor women are born with auspiciousness, then, but women are called auspicious when they become married (as long as they remain married and preferably chaste) because as feeders and potential (or realized) providers of children they are a source of pleasure and benefit to the family, clan and society. As caretakers of the home and embodiments of the goddess Lakṣmī—the divine ultimate source of auspiciousness—women can mediate the ebb and flow of *maṅgal* in the family. The performance of *vrat*s is an important part of this process because it involves bringing together special time, place, and items considered favorable to the creation of an environment "charged with auspiciousness." Thus it was that several women told me that "*vrats* are for auspiciousness," and that "*vrats* give peace and happiness to the family;" or, as Lelauti put it: "By keeping *vrats* in the home, happiness and calm will prevail. . . . Troubles are kept far away and one's wealth increases. In every way *vrats* are beneficial."

Just as auspiciousness is associated with femininity, so is *śakti*, a term that has received a good deal of attention in recent literature on goddesses, and to a lesser extent, women in India. "Women share in Durgā *śakti*," one woman told me; or, as the husband of another woman I interviewed put it, "women are the *śakti* principle of men." That is, women are perceived to be born with an "enabling," "energizing" force which is manifested most evidently in their ability to reproduce. It is a force or power which, when channeled through a husband and marriage, becomes a "tamed" creative power. *Śakti* has been described as a dynamic, motivational power, the "basis of change" (Minturn 1993), and as a "psychophysiological energy" (Daniel 1980, 89n3). Margaret Egnore has explained that "*śakti*, like our own word 'power' is often defined as the ability to act, to make others act, to make things happen, and as action itself" (1980, 22).[8] It is a force which women share with goddesses.[9] The power of *śakti* is both transformative and transferable to another person or object. One's measure of *śakti* can be increased through chastity and any form of *tapas* (that is, through acts of austerity and self-denial, especially of food), or through suffering and servitude—both associated with women's lot (see Egnore 1980, 15–17). *Vrats* that women perform for the sake of others in the family further augment their "*śakti*," which is then directed to auspicious ends.

When newly married Veena said that, "through *vrats* women do the protection of their husbands" (echoed by other women in so many words), she meant that: (1) the merit a woman accumulates through performing *vrats* can be transferred to her husband—that is, the gods, pleased by the devotion of the votary, answer her prayers by protecting those for the sake of whom the votary acts (the usual *vrat-kathā* scenerio); (2) fasting and self-control increases a woman's *śakti*—her transformative, creative energy which either translates her wishes into reality or is somehow transferred to her husband. Since wives are considered "consubstantial" with their husbands (and to an extent their children), it is not conceptually difficult to accept the notion of the transference of *śakti* from a woman to her husband. In this sense her performance of *vrats* can literally "vitalize" him, therefore lengthening his life and so "protecting" him. I will return to elaborate on the relationship between the performance of *vrats* and the notion of *śakti* from the point of view of Hindu women in the next chapter.

On the one hand, then, the young daughter-in-law's performance of votive rites symbolizes her acknowledgment of and acquiescence to her new role as wife and would-be mother of sons (as well as new member of the family); but on the other hand, it also signifies that her actions have a potentially transformative power insofar as through her regular performance of *vrats* her husband's life may be protected, fertility of the land and crops, as well as her own reproductive fertility may be ensured, and the family wealth and well-being enhanced. Married women's observance of *vrats*, unlike men's or widows', is intrinsically connected to and is a public expression of, their special relationship to auspiciousness.

Let us return to the new daughter-in-law from a sociological perspective. In North India, where arranged marriages and exogamy are still the norm, the newly married woman leaves her natal home and family to join her husband's family, often as a complete stranger. As she comes under the "reign of the mother-in-law," she will find herself on the lowest rung in terms of her (lack of) authority, power and autonomy. In short, her own volition must now, more than at any other stage in her life, be made to bend and adjust to the needs and demands of those around her. One of the most important ways in which she can gain acceptance and status within her new family is to bear a child, especially a son, for her affinal line.[10] So, a newly married woman is expected both to adopt the *vrats* observed in her *sasurāl* (in-laws' family), and to direct her intention for observing those *vrats* to achieving the auspicious ends which serve the well-being of her new family.

There are several factors which can determine how many and which *vrats* a woman will actually perform during her married life. One factor is her own piety. A second factor is pressure from female family members of her *sasurāl* to conform to their practices. A third factor is her personal situation with respect to fulfilling her duties as a wife and provider of healthy male offspring for her husband's family. A woman may feel impelled to resort to keeping new *vrats* or more *vrats* if she is having trouble conceiving, or she had not yet produced a boy. Rekha represents such a situation.

After giving birth to three girls, Rekha, originally from Rajasthan, very much wanted a son. However, on account of a heart condition, she was advised by doctors against becoming pregnant again. Her husband, while wanting a son, did not overtly pressure her either (they both claimed) as he was very concerned about her health. Nevertheless, and not surprisingly given the tremendous value placed on male children in Indian culture, her desire persisted. While visiting her *maike* (birth family), relatives told her to pray to the image of the woman who had been a *satī* (burned herself on her husband's funeral pyre) in their family. "She also has power due to her *sat* (truth/goodness)," Rekha said, "and all the women in her family turn to her in times of want or trouble."[11] Rekha went to her family Satīmātā shrine and drew an inverted *svastik* with cowdung and prayed to the Satīmātā for a son. She made a *manautī* (conditional vow) saying that if she were so blessed she would return from Banaras "to do Satīmā's *pūjā*" and revert the *svastik*. The inverted *svastik*, she explained, represents an incomplete or unsatisfactory state of things (in a woman's life)—and to draw it properly represents a "*saphal*" (literally, "fruitful") situation. Clearly, the inverted *svastik* symbolized the unsatisfactory situation in Rekha's life. Within a couple of months she was pregnant with her son. In addition to this vow, made to her familial Satīmātā, Rekha also kept the Sunday Vrat in order to obtain a son, on the advice of a friend in Banaras. She did this weekly *vrat* until she became pregnant, at which time she ended it with a simple "*havan-pūjā*" ceremony. While pregnant she went to the Durgā *mandir* near her house and prayed to Durgā (her *iṣṭadevtā*): "If my foetus is a son, keep him safe; if a daughter, take her away." Rekha attributes the birth of her son to the combined blessings of all the deities that she propitiated by *vrat* and prayer and from whom she had sought help.[12]

A married woman will also start a new *vrat* if one of her children (especially a male child) is ill or failing to thrive. Chandrakala Devi, age fifty, and originally from western Bihar, told me this story:

> Several years after marriage my one son became quite ill. Later he was diagnosed as having tetanus, and I had no hope of saving him. At that time I made a conditional vow to God that I

> would keep the Ḍala Chaṭh Vrat if my son became well. That son of mine did recover so since then I have been observing the Ḍala Chaṭh Vrat. Now my son is twenty-two years old.

I asked Chandrakala how she had learned about this *vrat*. She replied, "In Bihar this *vrat* is a major celebration—people observe it with great pomp. Everyone learns about this *vrat* just by watching everyone else do it." Thus, though she had not previously kept this *vrat* she knew when and how to observe it.

Both Rekha and Candrakala had inverted the usual format of a *vrat* by transforming the *vrat* into a "*manautī*"—a conditional vow. That is, instead of performing the *vrat* first and hoping for a reward, the vow is undertaken only on condition that the deity propitiated fulfills the supplicant's desire. In my experience (confirmed by McGee's data [1987, 348–49]) conditional vows are most often made when a woman is confronted with an urgent and specific problem for which she seeks an immediate solution. In all cases among the women I interviewed, when a *manautī-vrat* had been undertaken, the reason had to do with the woman's children. In some cases, the woman wanted to conceive a child of a specific sex.[13] In other cases, a child is very ill and medical treatments have not had the desired effect. The mother (or grandmother) look to other means to help the child. Appealing to one or several deities (or deified persons—for instance, Satīmātās and brahms) and offering to perform a self-sacrificing ritual act on condition of a positive outcome is one option. Luschinsky wrote this about such *manautī* vows in Senapur:

> Some village women also turn to Goraya Baba [Senapur village protector spirit] in times of trouble. They vow that they will perform a ceremony for him if he frees them of their difficulties. This kind of mutual give and take arrangement with the gods is very common in the village. Women seldom trust one god to fulfill their request. They usually make their vows to a number of gods, assuming that at least one will be tempted by the promise of offerings and worship. If their demands are satisfied, they worship all the gods to whom they made vows, saying that they have no way of knowing which gods helped them. (1962, 656)

So it was that Rekha, not knowing which deity had helped her, attributed her successful outcome to all the gods, and fulfilled her promises to each.

The Older *Saubhāgyavatī*

Older, post-menopausal women, whose husbands are still alive and who are not required to earn independent incomes, are in a position to observe *vrats* more diligently and frequently than women at other stages in the life-cycle. For post-menopausal women, the restrictions relating to menstruation and childbirth imposed on younger women no longer impede ritual acts such as a *pūjā*. Older married women are usually at the peak of their authority, power and autonomy in the family, and this brings increased freedom to determine their own activities. Those who are financially secure, that is, those whose families can afford a servant to help look after grandchildren, also have considerably more time at their disposal to engage in such activities as *bhajan* groups, pilgrimage, local temple visitation, *kathā* recitations, and the longer (e.g., month-long) *vrats*, such as the Kārtik "*snān-dān-vrat.*"[14] These are all socially approved pastimes for a proper Hindu wife. While all women can engage in these activities, older women predominated in the *bhajan* groups and *kathā* recitations that I attended in Banaras.

Ideologically, the important point in regard to older married women and *vrats* is that as long as she remains *saubhāgyavatī*, she can observe all *vrats* as a *pativratā*. If she has children and they are married off, and if her husband is still alive and well—she has indeed proved herself an "auspicious married woman." Younger women will seek her blessings during such occasions as marriages, festivals and during *vrats* in which women gather together to perform the *pūjā*, tell stories and perform other ritual activities.

VAIDHAVYA—WIDOWHOOD

When a woman is widowed, her situation changes dramatically. "Widows are not supposed to wear makeup," said Mira, "or put on any of the *ṣṛṇgār* [auspicious items, such as bangles and *sindūr*]; [they are to] eat food without spices and stay in cool places, so that their minds can remain fixed on God." Mira has succinctly summed up the traditional expectations regarding a Hindu widow; expectations which are still very much alive among the higher castes in much of India.[15]

From a dharmaśāstric point of view, the woman who becomes widowed ideally ought to commit *sati* as that would not only prove the quality of her *pativratā*-ness in a final act of heroic loyalty to her husband, but practically it would solve the problem of what to do with her.[16] Failing that, the texts variously specify who is responsible for her and how she is to behave. She is most problematic if she is young and has produced no heir, for her still potent sexuality may lead to acts which bring scandal and shame on her affinal family. Though disagreeing on details (e.g., should she be tonsured or not), the Dharmaśāstras are fairly consistent in advocating a life of extreme simplicity in diet and dress, and relative seclusion. She is to focus on "spiritual matters." In short, she is to render herself asexual by acting like an ascetic—without the benefits (and attendant admiration) of having made that choice herself.

Both the texts and more recent observers of Hindu culture never fail to mention the widow's association with inauspiciousness. "It is said that a widow is the most inauspicious. Even a glance at her should be avoided, much less her touch [*Skandapurāṇa* 2.9.22]. . . . The blessing of widows is said to be like the hissings of poisonous serpents. . . . A widow is ordained to spend her time in the worship of Viṣṇu. Decoration or looking into a mirror is forbidden for a widow [*Brahmavaivartapurāṇa* 2.83.94ff.]."[17] The widow is inauspicious essentially because she is no longer (legitimately) sexually active, and so can no longer produce sons and can no longer be a transmitter of well-being to the family. Though in theory she can continue to strive to be the *pativratā* by focusing all her prayers on helping her husband in the next life and on joining him there, she is certainly no longer *saubhāgyavatī*. On the contrary, she bears some measure of responsibility for her husband's death, and so is a potential transmitter of inauspiciousness. In consequence, one is to avoid contact with her as much as possible.

Nevertheless, though widows may be the bearers of inauspiciousness, older (post-menopausal) widows can be "pure." Certainly, Mira conformed in many ways to the expectations of a widow, but she also seemed very concerned about maximizing purity in whatever way possible. Many such widows end up cultivating this quality perforce because of their ascetic regimen.[18] Of course, as we have seen, *vrats* are ideally suited not just to the promotion of auspiciousness, but to the ascetic life and to the cultivation of purity.

According to Vindhya, an elderly Vaiṣṇava Brahman estranged from her husband, widows should keep *vrats* so that their husbands can achieve *mukti*, "and for their own chastity and their own next [lives]." Once more (despite Vindhya's personal circumstances, described below) her response is an ideologically predictable one. The first concern should be for the welfare of the husband. The performance of *vrats* remains a vehicle through which this can be achieved. By extension, a widow must protect her own chastity since chastity remains a key to her *pativratā* status. Again, *vrats* serve the purpose by their focus on sensual abstinence and self-control. Finally, the widow, through her *vrats*, may supplicate a god to ensure that she is not widowed in her next life, and that she may be reunited with her husband.[19]

Usha, the thirty-three-year-old married woman whose observance of Tīj I described in the previous chapter, expressed the view that if a widow was keeping *vrats* before her husband had died then she could continue to observe them for her children. If she had no children, then observing *vrats* was still necessary:

> Some *vrats* are such that they have to be kept for one's whole life; and if a widow prefers to give them up then she has to do the *udyāpan* (for those *vrats*). If a widow has no children then she should observe *vrats* for her next birth. If she will do *pūjā-paṭh* [this includes *vrat*] then in the next birth there won't be such a bad life (as this one was). How it was in the previous birth, what deeds were done that (caused her) to become a widow, who knows? . . . (In short) widows can observe any *vrat*, but they cannot offer *saubhāgya* items in a *pūjā*.

Usha's comments by and large reinforce Vindhya's. What is again impressive is the sense of commitment to *vrats* that these (and other) women express. Once started one ought to keep performing *vrats* despite being widowed. Like Shyamdevi, who gave up most of the *vrats* she observed with reluctance (because she felt physically exhausted by the work involved in making a living and caring for her children), many women feel an attachment to these rituals; rituals that are so closely linked with Hindu women's identity and so expressive of their religiosity.

Gulab is a sixty-six-year-old widowed Brahman who has kept fourteen different *vrats* in her life-time. When she became widowed in her mid-fifties, she left all *vrats* except the semi-monthly Ekādaśī (the quintessential "widow's *vrat*") and the four-a-year Gaṇeś Cauth Vrat which she keeps for her sons, the youngest of whom she currently lives with. Unlike Mira, she does not wear only white saris and she does not stay away from all auspicious occasions; she goes to the Vishwanath temple every day and she likes to participate in *bhajan* groups. Rani (Sarita's older sister-in-law), now sixty-two, was widowed when she was thirty-two, and she is childless. Much of her life centers on religious activities. For example, she performs a daily morning *pūjā* and an evening *āratī* to the "*sanātan devatās*," and every day she bathes in the Ganges and visits the temple. After she was widowed, an astrologer prescribed the Pūrṇamāsī and Ekādaśī *vrats* for her to keep, and she still performs these *vrats*, totalling four per month. She also still keeps Śivarātri, Janmāṣṭamī and Tīj. About Tīj she said: "You don't stop Tīj even if your husband dies"; such is the tradition in Rani's family. The *vrats* she did discontinue when her husband died, because a widow is supposed to, are Karvā Cauth and the Sāvitrī Vrat. (Later she also discontinued Pradoṣ and Śravaṇ Somvār when the astrologer prescribed the other *vrats* for her to take up.) Rani feels that the Ekādaśī and Pūrṇamāsī *vrats* are the most important *vrats* which she now keeps. As she explained: "I have belief in them [*vrats*]. One does *vrats* out of *ārādhanā* [devotion]; it is good *karm* [action]; out of that comes *puṇya* [spiritual merit]; and it is *maṅgal* [auspicious]." Rani never spoke of her husband, and I gather that the fact of her childlessness, and the disappointment, constant worry and sense of failure that this situation precipitated never allowed her to receive acceptance from or form any bonds with her husband's family. (She currently lives with natal relatives.) Clearly, the early death of her husband contributed to her alienation from her affinal family. Though she continues to perform the Tīj Vrat because of a sense of obligation, it is to the other *vrats* that she attributes the most significance, because they are for herself, for nurturing her relationship to God; and, "anything to do with God is *maṅgal.*" Like Sarita, it is Rani's faith (shaped in particular by the teachings of the *Bhagavadgītā*) that has provided her a source of strength, and perhaps a sense of worth and purpose beyond that prescribed by her low and marginal status as a widow.

Reflecting on the relation of *vrats* to the stages in a woman's life, Sarita commented:

> Before marriage, *vrats* are performed out of a desire for specific things and for *bhakti*. Just after marriage, *nitya* and *laukik* *vrats* are done, especially *laukik* [i.e., *manautī*-type *vrats* and

> those for children]. If widowed, then the *laukik vrats* stop and one concentrates mostly on śāstric, *mokṣa*-centered *vrats*.

Mokṣa ("liberation" from the cycle of rebirth) is often included in the Purāṇa-Nibandha *vrata* descriptions as one of the possible rewards or fruits for the performance of a *vrata*.[20] However, there are debates in the Dharma Smṛtis and Nibandhas about women's capacity to achieve *mokṣa*, and these debates were never consensually resolved. Some texts state that women cannot ever obtain *mokṣa* because of their *svabhāva*, their inherent nature. They must wait to be reborn as a male. Others suggest that women can in theory, but this is not an appropriate goal for women as wives. *Strīdharma* dictates that women's goals must always be in relation to their husbands. If such duties are supremely well carried out, then *mokṣa* may be a reward.

Most women I spoke with did not mention *mokṣa* at all when discussing *vrats*. When *mokṣa* was mentioned, it was usually casually, along with other fruits of *vrats*, just as we find in the Purāṇas. Or, it was mentioned in the context of widows' performance of *vrats*, as in Sarita's comments (above). In general, my impression is that *mokṣa* was not a goal that women thought about very much; not because of an acceptance of strictures against their capacity or its inappropriateness for them as women, but because of its abstraction and remoteness from their immediate lives. As dharmic acts, *vrats* are spiritually and socially meritorious; and that is enough, for all dharmic acts eventually contribute to *mokṣa*. Yama and Brahma will decide how well their "good" actions balance against their "bad" actions, and mete out the karmic results.

However, I would suggest that when Sarita, and other women, commented that widows could or should focus on *mokṣa*-centered *vrats*, they are saying that this is the time in a woman's life when she can more explicitly or publicly acknowledge that she is performing religious rituals for her own welfare; just as ascetics who have renounced the social world of duties and obligations are allowed, indeed expected, to pursue their own spiritual development; to aim for *mokṣa*, without concern for the welfare of others. Married women also tend to express sympathy for widows, and allow that a widow should be able to engage in religious activities that will not only help her to secure a better rebirth, or *mokṣa*, but that will provide some solace for her present life.

In sum, how often, how many, and which *vrats* may be observed during a woman's lifetime depends on diverse factors. Family tradition, both natal and affinal, is probably the most important factor; but also important is a woman's own inclination or attitude toward *vrats*. Thus, if a woman's mother, grandmother or mother-in-law observed many *vrats*, she may keep many too. Nevertheless, usually this practice must be sustained, especially when tested by circumstance, by her belief or trust in their efficacy or purpose. Such a belief or trust in *vrats*, however, is often understood reflexively, as giving *her* back something such as "good feelings," "peace of mind," detachment, or a stronger relationship to God. Among those interviewed, I found that in a time of crisis or chronic difficulty one woman will give up *vrats* altogether as being useless while another may observe *vrats* with increased ardour as a source of strength, hope or consolation; or as an outlet for frustration. The following two examples, both of women whose lives have been deeply tried, demonstrate two directions in which personal experience can affect the performance of *vrats*.

Kavita, a fifty-six-year-old Brahman widow, is an example of a woman who gave up on *vrats*. Kavita had finished high school and had been married to a man who became a professor at the university in Banaras. She gave birth to eight children, one boy who is mentally handicapped, and seven girls, two of whom died shortly after birth because they were premature. Two of her daughters are married and one, Sudha, still lives at home. The other two daughters, as I have mentioned before, burned to death at the homes of their in-laws. While formal charges of negligence and murder were lodged with the police, the two husbands have not been indicted and have remarried. These tragedies happened a few years after her husband's death. Without the status, position and support of her husband, Kavita felt unable to revive an investigation of her daughters deaths through the legal system. Kavita used to keep five *vrats*; now she keeps none. She used to keep these *vrats*, she said, "for mental peace"; now the idea of achieving such a state seems to her hopeless. Though she had supported her daughter Sudha's decision to take on the Tuesday Vrat, she has lost interest in performing *vrats* herself. Kavita's only religious activity involves the occasional reading of the *Rāmāyaṇ*.

Vindhya, a Vaiṣṇava Brahman aged seventy-two and estranged from her husband, has also experienced familial trauma.

Her humor and liveliness could not always mask her emotional suffering at the hands of an apparently callous family. At times, she was loquacious in a cheerful way, telling stories, giving anecdotes and reciting verses from the *Gītā* or *Purāṇ*. At other times, she would suddenly become tearful, her voice dropping to a whisper as she talked about the difficulties she has endured. One of her two sons died of fever in adolescence, and her husband used to beat her before he finally left the home when her remaining son and daughter were married. She was left without financial support and now lives with her elderly widowed sister. Vindhya has also been in poor health for some years. She has kept twelve different *vrats* in her life. But, some years ago, after her husband left and when she was about sixty, she gave up all *vrats* except Gaṇeś Cauth (for her children). Two years later she took up the semimonthly Ekādaśī Vrat with a renewed sense of religious conviction, and despite ill-health and advanced age, she remains strongly attached to this *vrat*.

Vindhya has derived much consolation from the *Gītā*, and her reading of the text (much of which she has memorized) seems to have influenced her understanding of *vrats*. Early in our conversation, she made a distinction between two kinds of *vrats*: the "Ekādaśī kind" and the "Śiva-*pūjā* kind." She suggested that in the latter one asks for things in return, whereas "Lord Kṛṣṇa says if you ask for something in return then you are forcing him to give by not eating. Kṛṣṇa says not to ask for anything in return when you perform a *vrat;* ask only for his *bhakti*."[21] Vindhya explained that the Ekādaśī Vrat was especially important to her because "that is the only way to obtain God. People who read the *Gītā* do the Ekādaśī *pūjā* to achieve *mokṣa*. These are the things I want—closeness to God."[22] She said that people who keep *niṣkām vrats* (*vrats* observed without any desire for a reward), as she tries now to do, are "without refuge." "When one is not respected by anyone, when one has been kicked around—then one will keep *niṣkām vrats*; when one is lonely and alone." At this point, in tears, Vindhya told me that when she was younger, she always kept *vrats* and asked God that her sons do well in school, that they won't cheat, and will grow up as good people so that in her old age she could lean on them. But then, after one son died, her other son and daughter moved away, and her husband rejected her, she thought to herself, "Is this what I am asking for? This is all a lie. I can't depend on anyone." Now, she reflected, she is happier because "I don't ask anything from God.

I just do *pūjā* and hope that God will help. . . . It is up to God to decide what He will give."

Vindhya, like other women I spoke with, made many other comments about the correct attitude one should adopt while performing *vrat*s, and about the meaning, spiritual significance and benefits, for themselves as well as for others, of these rites. In the following chapter I will present and examine some of these comments as I summarize meanings and functions of *vrat*s in the religious lives of Hindu women.

7

"Because It Gives Me Peace of Mind": Meanings and Functions of *Vrats* in Hindu Women's Religious Lives

While the women I spoke with were quick to explain why husbands do not need to perform *vrats* for their wives, and why wives and mothers do keep *vrats* for husbands and children, they would hesitate to say that they performed *vrats* for themselves as well. Some women, like Sarita and Padma, denied that they ever kept *vrats* for their own benefit. Yet, in their comments about the meaning and purpose of *vrats* and the benefits that observing *vrats* gives, it is clear that women do get something back for themselves. Indeed, it is apparent that women use *vrats* to express profound spiritual yearnings, and that performing *vrats* gives them "peace of mind," a sense of accomplishment, and further, a sense that they can exercise a degree of control over their bodies and over certain aspects of and events in their lives.

This final chapter draws ideas and material from earlier chapters together with new material to reflect on the functions of *vrats* in Hindu women's religious lives and to form some conclusions about the various factors that can account for the pervasiveness and apparent popularity of the *vrat* tradition among women in India. Specifically, this chapter looks beyond the ostensible reasons for which women perform *vrats* (encapsulated in the phrase "I do *vrats* for *suhāg*") to investigate other explanations of the meaning and significance of *vrats* in a systematic manner. That is, I examine what else *vrats* mean to women besides being a means to maintain or enhance their auspicious married state *(suhāg)*. I review what women get out of *vrats* for themselves, how women use *vrats* to express their spirituality or their religious goals, and what women mean by the phrase "peace of mind." And finally, I explore in more detail the relation of *vrats* to the concepts of purity, *tapas* and *śakti*. As in previous chapters, women's comments and narratives constitute my primary data, and while I have constructed the framework, I have allowed their words to set the agenda and direction of analysis.

Let me first turn to the question which usually marked the beginning of my interview with a woman: What is a *vrat?* Asking women to define the term *vrat* at the start of our discussion would bring the subject matter immediately into focus. As an open-ended question (and one that was generally received as innocuous and nonthreatening), it allowed women to say whatever came to their minds. Some women, like Kamala, seemed to have thought about the nature and meaning of *vrats* before and their comments came easily. Others were hesitant and seemed to be struggling to articulate ideas that had previously been largely inchoate. There is no doubt that the concept of *vrat is* complex and cannot be readily encapsulated. Thus, some women initially responded with a simple statement such as, "a *vrat* is a fast." Or, the purpose of *vrats* would be stated: "We do *vrats* for *kalyān* [well-being]," "for *maṅgal* [auspiciousness]," or, "for *suhāg.*" At other times the procedures of particular *vrats* would be outlined to show what a *vrat* is. Not infrequently, several explanations would be given at once, as in: "A *vrat* is performed for peace; to get rid of problems. It is also duty and [it is] tradition [*saṁskār*]." Later in the interview (or on another day), I would go back to this question or ask it in a different way. Now there had been time for more reflection on the subject. What is interesting to see is how the whole (historical) spectrum of the *vrata* tradition as shaped and recorded in the texts is reflected in women's responses, though reflected in ways which may not have been anticipated by the authors of those texts or by contemporary commentators on *vrats*. That is, texts such as the Purāṇas, Dharmaśāstras and Nibandhas were written primarily by higher-caste men who assumed that any religious practice ought to aim at the proper ordering (or for the betterment) of society in general and for the individual in particular. But the individual is normatively male, as we saw in some of the statements made, for instance, in the context of the issue of entitlement.

The Hindi author Ram Pratap Tripathi, for example, may be considered a modern representative of the Sanskrit Dharmaśāstra tradition. At the beginning of his long introduction to his book on *vrats* and festivals he writes this on the meaning of *vrat* and the reasons for observing these rites:

> The reasons for observing *vrats* are, usually: for obtaining spiritual *(ādhyātmik)* or mental power *(mānsik śakti)*; for purification of mind and soul, and for the firmness [or power] of determination; for the development of devotion to God and for the development of faith; for the purification of atmosphere *(vāṭāvaraṇ)*; for influencing [or leaving an impression on] others; to make the thoughts pure and elevated and so on; and it is done for physical health. (1978, 1)

At the end of his introduction Tripathi concludes that "The meaning of *vrat* is to bind good actions *(bandhanyukt satkarm)*, that is, the fruit from the doer's actions are tied to him. Though humans have to suffer the result of their good and bad deeds, [yet] the reward of solemnly vowed *vrats* is unerring" (1978, 21). There is nothing in these and other general statements made by Tripathi about *vrats* that attend to domestic concerns. Other than two short statements concerning what to do during states of impurity and that women ought to obtain permision from husbands to keep *vrats*, there are here no separate instructions for women, even though it is largely women who purchase *vrat* books and the majority of *vrats* described by Tripathi are ones which women, not men, perform. Of course, in many of the prefaces and final remarks attached to the description of procedures and stories for each *vrat* discussed, there are pronouncements like "by keeping this *vrat* women win good fortune and are never widowed." But, the point is that women have taken seriously the general statements about the *dharma* of *vrat*, and about the overall spiritual self-develpmental aims of *vrats* that are articulated in this book and in the numerous Sanskrit textual sources treating the topic of *vrata*.

Thus it should not be surprising how many of "the ten *niyamas*" (namely, forebearance, truth, compassion, charity, purity, control of the senses, *pūjā*, *homa*, contentment, and not stealing) listed in the *Agnipurāṇa* and other sources as constitutive of the *dharma* of *vrata* have been singled out by women as central to the meaning or purpose of *vrats*. While the *pativratā*/*strīdharma* ideology is a powerful one, it is not the only discourse which Hindu women hear.

MEANINGS OF *VRATS*

Vrat as ordinance or duty

Amma is an elderly Tamil Brahman who had lived in Banaras for many years, and who, through her husband, had much contact with Westerners. She spoke in a mixture of Hindi, English, and Tamil. I begin with her reflections on the meaning of *vrat* because of their resonance with the Ṛgvedic sense of *vrata* as (socio-religiously defined) "function."

> *Vrata* means mostly fasting followed by *pūjā* and offerings [*naivedya*] to the gods. But, *vrata* is also this—my whole life has been a *vrata*. [*Pause*] The Hindu religion is very broad and tolerant. I think it mainly comes under three headings: Smārta, Vaiṣṇava and Virāśaiva. The daily way of life according to these [groups] is itself a *vrata*. For example, a housewife [a *sumaṅgalī*] has to look after her household, the comforts of her husband, children, relatives, et cetera. [She has] to be truthful and dutiful. Reciprocally, the husband also has to look after the comforts of all family members, earn for the family and so on. This is his *vrata*. By being like this [truthfully dutiful] [one] may have *mukti* in this life itself—*jīvan-mukti*. Some say (one) has to be generous, feed the poor and the downtrodden also. . . .
>
> I have not read the scriptures. The family being big—a half dozen children, my husband and myself, people coming and going—I could not find time for extra *vratas* or anything. Whatever I have done is in the routine of family life, side by side with our daily way of life. I was very particular that all our children should study well. In fact, I taught them myself up to the tenth standard—I engaged no tuition. This was also part of my *vrata*. . . .
>
> A Hindu living his daily life is itself an observance of a *vrata*. For instance, a housewife looks after the comforts of her husband, children, and also if there are elders in the family. In the same way a *brahmacarya* keeps his own *vratas*.

While Amma spoke to me in great detail about the particular *vrats* that she observes (seven altogether), she sees these *vrats* as part of a larger *vrata* whose content and form is determined by her identity as a Smārta Brahman married woman and mother. For Amma, the only choice involved in performing her *vrata* is how well she carries it out. Otherwise her *vrata* is ordained by the circumstances of her birth (sex, religion, status) and life (wife, daughter-in-law, mother, mother-in-law). Every Hindu, man or woman, has such a *vrata;* and if they carry out their *vrata* dutifully, truthfully, and conscientiously they may achieve *mukti.* For Amma, then, the central meaning of *vrat* is duty, essentially with the same ramifications associated with the term *dharma;* thus her *vrata* is the primary ordering principle in her life, without which disorder, confusion and inauspiciousness would prevail.

Vrat as *Saṅkalp* (Resolve)

A few days later, across town near the Ganges in a two-storey flat off one of old Banaras' innumerable alleys, a scholarly conservative pandit suggested that a *vrata* is not a duty but an optional observance: "*vrata* is derived from the verbal root *vṛ*, meaning 'to choose,' with the affix *ta*, giving one the noun *vratam.* If you recite something in the mind and accept it, you have made a *saṅkalp.* That is a *vrata. Upavās* came later. It was something different, and later merged with *vrata.* . . . *Vratas* are for *mukti,* and for getting rid of sins and also diseases" (by fasting and so on).

Most men I interviewed, especially pandits, similarly spoke of *vratas* as *saṅkalpa,* emphasizing their voluntary, optional nature. A *vrat* is a vow one chooses to undertake for a specified length of time and for a variety of religious or nonreligious reasons, including both mundane *(bhukti)* and ultramundane or soteriological *(mukti)* goals.[1] Such an understanding of the word *vrata* is essentially no different from the meaning given to it by the earliest lexicographers of Sanskrit and carried through by the Nibandhas treating of *vrata.*

Vrat as Ethical Action

Some of the comments of Premlata, a fifty-six-year-old Brahman widow, on the meaning of *vrat* fit in with *vrat* as resolve. However, in her description (of her mother's usage) *vrat* meant not just a resolve to undertake a course of action for a temporary reason or to achieve a particular goal, but rather to make a choice to alter one's behavior along a certain ethical path.

> My mother used to say, "to be a *vratanī* [fem. for the Sanskrit term for votary] means to have an attitude of service to people. Serve all, feed and give drink, give *dān.* Take the *vrat* of renouncing lying; take the *vrat* of speaking truth—this is the greatest *vrat.*" What she did not do was the cycle of rituals, *pūjā.* . . . I did not see my mother doing *pūjā* for such reasons as her

> marriage, lack of food, personal desires. She did not have any son; she had four daughters. The only *vrat* she kept was Ahoī-Mā Vrat [a *vrat* for children].

Premlata's mother had separated *vrat* from its ritual context and had chosen to focus on the larger ethical principles that have been articulated in the Hindu tradition (and which are clearly not gender-specific). Again, these are some of the injunctions included in the *"dharma* of *vrata"* which the Purāṇas and Nibandhas superimposed on the developing text-based *vrata* tradition as a whole. While Premlata is more "devotional" than her mother—she performs regular *pūjā* and keeps many more *vrats*—she was clearly impressed by her mother's counsel and she tries to be a *"vratanī"* not only when she performs a *vrat*, but during other occasions as well.

Poonam, a thoughtful upper-middle-class Brahman housewife in her fifties, also described one meaning of *vrat* as *saṅkalp* in a manner similar to Premlata. Though she herself took fasting very seriously, she commented that "it is not really necessary that you should go without food; you take a *saṅkalp* that you are going to perform one good thing today—that is also a *vrat."* Vindhya made it clear that ethical action must accompany the performance of a *vrat* in order for it to be fruitful. "Look," she explained, "it amounts to nothing if you are keeping a *vrat* and it [involves] the most difficult fast if at the same time you cheat or kill someone or do bad things. . . . That is what the *Gītā* and *Purāṇ* all say. Doing *vrat* alone won't get you *puṇya* [merit]; you have to [accompany the *vrat*] with good actions."

Vrat as *Sādhanā* (Spiritual Discipline) and *Niyama*

Poonam also made the observation that many *vrats* that women keep today are a form of "ritualized *saṅkalp."* What she meant was that long ago (at some early point in Hindu religious history) women's intentions *(saṅkalp)* for the welfare of their families, shaped and reinforced generation after generation, became surrounded by form, by traditions, by "rituals." By contrast, the Tuesday Vrat, which Poonam has kept diligently for several decades in honor of her favored deity, Hanumān, she called "my kind of *vrat."* "This is my day off"; she explained in English, "[it is my] disciplining, my *sādhanā*. It has nothing to do with my ritual. But the rest of the *vrats*, like Karvā Cauth, Ahoī, Sarad Pūrṇimā are my rituals, because I do these *vrats* with rituals."[2]

When I asked Poonam what she meant by *sādhanā*, she explained: "the worst part of me is my tantrums. I have a bad temper, and I try to get over that aspect of myself through *vrats*. Because *vrat* means that you not only deny yourself food, but also you establish a good routine for yourself, to have good habits." Keeping the weekly Tuesday Vrat, which, for Poonam, involves a long *pūjā* and meditation in the morning and eating one *phalāhar* meal in the evening, helps her to establish a disciplined routine, to inculcate good habits, and to work on controlling her temper. In this way, the *vrat* is her "disciplining." Later Poonam commented that when she first kept *vrats* as a child,

> it was mostly because I was told to do it, so I did it, but without any feeling attached. . . . But gradually, I learned [to use] *vrats* to overcome my shortcomings; then there was some meaning to this. My attitude changed. . . . Anything you are doing concerning God or about disciplining yourself is very *maṅgal* [auspicious]. If you are happy then you are making everyone else happy too. Happiness promotes goodness.

As we talked it became clear that Poonam viewed her Tuesday Vrat in particular, the one *vrat* she has never forgotten to keep, or missed due to illness, as a means of self-transformation. The control of her short-temperedness led to a feeling of peace and satisfaction with herself. "When you master yourself," she reflected, this then "affects those around you, especially as you direct your thoughts and hopes and prayers toward them."

Kamala too spoke of *vrats* as a means to control and discipline the body and mind. But, aware of the multiple angles by which one could explain the significance of a *vrat* and the *vrat* tradition, she had many other things to say as well and she gave a characteristically comprehensive definition of a *vrat*, including a summary of what it can achieve for the votary and what benefits can accrue.

> One does *vrats* for purifying the mind, for steadying it, and to prevent the oscillating mind from becoming less strong. The meaning of *vrat* is: for whatever work we do our mind and senses should be firm and steady. So for as long as we are keeping the *vrat*, we must try to keep our minds fixed. We behave according to the rules of the *vrat*. Do *pūjā*, concentrate—these are the primary meanings of *vrat*. A *vrat* is for giving peace of mind.

> It also gives peace to the senses, heart and intellect. It is for keeping away defilements of the mind. Through *vrats* we get assistance in regulating ourselves. We learn to control hunger, thirst and sleep. In this way we control our desires; for desires, while fluctuating, always increase [unless regulated or checked].
>
> *Vrat* is linked to *dharm*. For example, we may circumambulate some goddess 108 times, and to this *dharm* one may add that God will become pleased; and [because of God's pleasure] one will receive this boon or get that benefit. So we will do such *vrats*. Therefore, we Hindus have related *vrats* to *dharm* so that in the name of God we can observe them easily. We have in our minds and belief so linked *vrat* and *dharm* that to think "*vrat* is separate from *dharm*" is very difficult. This has become our tradition. In other respects, *vrats* are very scientific. If you observe a *vrat* once each week the stomach will get a rest. It is very good for one's health; sleep will come easily. Some *vrats* are like this—they are observed for one's husband; some are observed for one's sons. Jīvitputra, for instance, is observed when someone's child has not continued to live, or when a child dies immediately after childbirth. By performing this *vrat* their children will continue to live—good health will be maintained. Those who have none will get [offspring]. This, of course, is a matter of belief [*viśvās*].

The first half of Kamala's explanation of the meaning of a *vrat*, or rather, of the functions that *vrats* serve, concentrates on the physical and mental or spiritual discipline involved in performing *vrats* and the results or benefits of this discipline to the votary. Kamala's preliminary focus, in other words, is on *vrata* as *niyama*. This emphasis is striking in its articulation. If one did not know the author of these words to be a middle-class Hindu housewife and mother, one might attribute them to an older widow or to a *brahmacāriṇī* (celibate student ascetic); that is, attribute them to one whose stage in life or ascetic vocation encouraged her to use rituals primarily for these purposes. It is interesting to compare Kamala's comments on the mental or spiritual ends (or effects) of *vrats* with a statement made by a Banaras *sannyāsinī* (female renunciate) to an anthropologist: "In the householder life, you know great pleasure and sorrow *(sukh-dukh)*, but you cannot know peace. That life is in a state of constant change *(parivarti*, 'unsteady') and so your mind cannot become still *(sthir*, 'fixed,' 'constant'). In the ascetic life, you are singleminded and so you can achieve salvation" (Lynn Teskey Denton 1991, 215).

Does the "peace" that the renunciate speaks of have anything to do with the "peace of mind" that Kamala referred to? I believe it does. What is this "peace of mind" that is apparently so desirable? On one level, as the English rendering would suggest, peace of mind is simply a state of calmness, or of finding quietude amid the hustle and bustle of daily life (an aim with which anyone who has lived in the relentlessly noisy city of Banaras would find sympathy). One woman described how mundane matters are always diverting a (householder) woman's attention from spiritual concerns this way: "I close my eyes and imagine the figure of God, but then the *dāl* is on the stove and my mind goes there because it starts to burn." *Vrats* provide opportunities for concentration and a more sustained devotional focus. (You may still think of the *dāl* on the stove, but then you are reminded of your hunger, and remember the reason for your fast.)

However, in Kamala's (and other Hindus') usage of the phrase, peace of mind is more than moments of peace or quiet reflection.[3] It is often used to mean spiritual contentment, or more, fulfilment. Ultimately, peace of mind is a state of equanimity, achieved by sustained effort through purifying, steadying and strengthening the "oscillating" mind; by concentrating in one's *pūjā* and by meditation *(dhyān)*. The *sannyāsinī* (above) would go further: such a state can only be truly achieved by renouncing the (values and constructs of the Hindu) social world altogether, freeing oneself to pursue *mokṣa* (presumably, the "Great Peace of Mind"). Nevertheless, even for a householder like Kamala, some degree of equanimity in the midst of the duties and responsibilities of family life is clearly desirable. It can prevent one from falling too deeply into the depths of despair, sorrow, anger, frustration—the *kaṣṭ* (suffering, hardship) and *pareśānī* (worries, problems) of which Shyamdevi and others spoke—that life tosses in one's path; and all the more, it would seem, in the path of women. A level of disciplined equanimity can also prevent one from getting caught up in pleasure or in a happiness whose source may be fleeting—snatched away at any time by the unpredictable forces of fate *(bhāgya)* or the workings of karma. A number of women that I met had suffered a great deal because of poverty, children dying in childhood (or in "dowry deaths"), the premature death of a husband, or husbands who had beaten or abandoned them. While women often perform *vrats* to prevent such occurrences, the regular performance of *vrats* can also build up the inner strength, the feeling of personal ability and confidence and the "presence of mind" needed to better cope with such events.

Lynn Teskey Denton has described how women ascetics see themselves in opposition to householder life *(saṁsār,* the ritually constructed world of human relations).[4] Yet a number of householder women I spoke with have paid attention to values associated with and demonstrably espoused by certain groups of Hindu ascetics—notably the theistic *brahmacāriṇīs* (celibate female ascetics). In fact, Denton has reported householder women as openly admiring the *brahmacāriṇīs*.[5] In other words, while *brahmacāriṇīs* in particular seek to disassociate themselves from the life of the householder, some householder women seek periodically to imitate aspects of the *brahmacāriṇīs*' life-style by adhering to some of the *niyamas* or yogic disciplines during their observance of *vrats*.

Achieving "purity" *(śuddhatā)* is also a concern of many ascetics, as it is for many Hindus in general. T. N. Madan has argued that the "connotation of [the word *śuddha*] is conveyed by invoking images of fullness or completeness in the specific sense of perfection. It thus refers to the most desired condition of the human body or, more comprehensively, the most desired state of being" (1985, 17). The close conceptual relationship between mental and physical purity is evident in the Dharmaśāstra discussion of the *dharma* of *vrata* where the votary is instructed to adopt a physical regimen which aims to maximize purity, but also to adopt a frame of mind conducive to (morally) pure thought. One can observe this free association between bodily and mental purity quite clearly in Tripathi's book on *vrats* where he says:

> There is a special importance of mental and spiritual purification for performing *vrats*. If a man's body and clothing, etc. are unclean, the mind is oscillating and contaminated (by bad thoughts), then he will not receive even a small reward. Therefore, in the first place, our ancestors have given much attention to the purification of bodies, clothing, etc. (1978, 6)

A significant number of women like Kamala spoke of *vrats* in terms of "purifying the mind," and of "keeping away defilements of the mind." The effect of *vrats* in promoting physical purity was certainly mentioned as well, but not as often as the purity of mind and purity of heart. One reason that women may emphasize mental purity is that Hindu women regardless of caste have repeatedly received the message that their bodies are more impure (due to menstrual and birth pollution) than those of men. There is little that pre-menopausal women can do about this impurity. On the other hand, they can do whatever they like with their thoughts. Thoughts, words, and emotions are within their control, so they put an emphasis on the significance of *vrats* in the promotion of mental purity. In addition, the various devotional cults that have been so influential to modern Hindu religiosity have often stressed mental purity over bodily purity. In order to come close to God, one has to cultivate a proper devotional attitude, and this means overcoming any negative thoughts and emotions that are obstructive of one's relationship to God.

According to the women I spoke with the structure of a *vrat* helps one to achieve such objectives as purity, self-control, auspiciousness and peace of mind. Kamala had made a brief but pertinent comment, reiterated later by other women: "We behave according to the rules of the *vrat.*" A *vrat* is rule-governed. There are certain procedures that one must follow with, as we have seen in chapter 5, flexibility built in to each procedure. Bathing, anointing the body with sandal paste, wearing new or fresh clothes, fasting or eating *śuddh* or *sattvik* foods, avoiding "polluted" persons and things, refraining from negative thoughts and actions, and concentrating the mind on God contribute to inner and outward purity. Using tumeric or *roli, sindūr,* wearing the "sixteen items of the married woman" *(ṣṛṇgār),* and making *ālpanās* contribute to auspiciousness. Worship *(pūjā),* muttering the name of God *(japa),* singing hymns, keeping an all-night vigil *(jagaraṇ),* and visits to the temple enhance and exemplify one's devotional attitude. Finally, fasting and other forms of self-restraint, meditation and other mental "*niyams*" like not lying," keeping the *vrat* regularly and carrying through one's resolve contribute to one's self-discipline as well as purity.

Vrats and *Dharm*: *Parampara* and *Pūjā-Paṭh*

Vrats (in particular, the fasting requirements) are often not easy to perform and the results of one's efforts are not usually immediately evident. What incentives are there to pursue them then? I believe that Kamala, having just talked to me about the difficult self-discipline involved in a *vrat,* anticipated that I might be asking such questions. To help explain the attraction or interest of the votive rites, she proceeded to situate *vrats* in the "religious" context: "Hindus," Kamala said, "have related *vrats* to *dharm* so that in the name of God we can observe them more easily. We have in our minds and belief so linked *vrat* and *dharm* that to think '*vrat* is separate from *dharm*' is very difficult." The observance of *vrats*, then, is linked to the performance of *dharm*, and whether they were always linked or not, they have now become so connected that Hindus cannot think of *vrats* apart from *dharm*. This connection makes *vrats* easier to observe. As I discussed in her profile, for Kamala *dharm* primarily means *pūjā-paṭh* and *saṁskār* or *parampara* (tradition). Let us briefly review these two meanings of *dharm* in the context of *vrats*.

Several women started to define *vrats* by explaining that they are "*saṁskār*"[6]—"a traditional thing, handed down from our ancestors. Parents observe *vrats* for their children, then [those] children keep them [for their] own children, and so on." Another woman similarly commented: "It is family practice [that has come down] from very ancient times." Premlata, taking a slightly cynical view, described *saṁskār* as, in so many words, "blind":

> One meaning of *vrat* is that it is our *saṁskār*. . . . In Hindustan we say, "one sheep will go and all will follow." Do they know where they go? No. . . . Take those village people; someone puts a stone in a certain spot and then all start worshipping. Who is it? What is it? Nobody knows. One person drops a flower just there, so another person will go to offer a flower at the same place. One person does a *vrat*, so everyone starts to do that *vrat*. This especially happens among the women of Hindustan.

Pūjā-paṭh refers to the plethora of "religious acts" like performing daily *pūjās*, giving *dān*, and going on pilgrimage *(tīrtha-yatra)* that constitute the core religious practice of most Hindus and whose particular forms are largely determined by family tradition—*parampara*. Most of these religious acts, including *vrats*, are performed within a devotional context. By this I mean that these acts are dedicated to a god or goddess and, while they may be offered as expressions of personal piety and faith alone, such acts may also include (and frequently do include) petitions for help. The relationship between devotee and deity is expected to be in some evident fashion reciprocal. As Kamala said, "we may circumambulate some goddess 108 times—and to this *dharm* [act of *pūjā-paṭh*] one may add that God will become pleased; and one will receive this boon or get that benefit. So we will do such *vrats*." This way of viewing *vrats*—as a form of bartering with higher powers—is one Shyamdevi described. "When we keep a *vrat*," she remarked, "we ask for blessings from the goddess—may our children be healthy, may they outlive us, may our troubles go far away . . . for that itself we keep *vrats*."

According to Kamala, then, in addition to the reasons she put forward for herself, the general incentives for Hindus to observe *vrats* are (1) they are part of tradition, (2) they are part of *dharm*, and (3) as devotional acts, they are a means to petition the gods for boons or assistance. But there are other reasons for some Hindu women to keep *vrats* as well—and one is health.

Vrats and Health

Moving away from the "traditions" that a non-Hindu may not fully appreciate, Kamala mentions the "scientific"[7] aspect of the *vrat*. "If you observe a *vrat* each week, the stomach will get a rest. It is very good for one's health. Sleep will come easily."[8] Just over a third of the women I interviewed cited the health *(svāsth)* benefits of *vrats* in a similar fashion. Centuries-old Ayurvedic ideas concerning the health and medicinal properties of food and fasting have permeated Hindu culture at many levels and no doubt inform the popular understanding of the *vrat* tradition as well. In some cases, however, women were probably responding to me as a foreigner for whom, it was assumed, references to science would lend their explanations credibility. As twenty-two-year-old Veena said: "There is a real scientific basis to *vrats* which the *ṛṣis* (the ancient vedic sages) knew and gave to us . . . so I do them."

The use of the word "scientific" (with its implications of objectivity, verifiability and rationality) to further justify various traditional practices is probably a recent trend among urban, educated Indians. It turns up with remarkable frequency in contemporary Hindu books on Vedic religion. When the term is used as another explanation for the existence and merit of such a popular religious practice as *vrats*, it is not seen as threatening to the basic premise of the rite—which is *viśvās* (belief) in their efficacy. The belief, which is not itself scientific, is not questioned. Rather, the observable effects of the rite—such as more efficient digestion produced by regular fasting—are called scientific. In other words, the *ṛṣis* knew what they were doing when "they gave us these *vrats* to observe," and, even if one does not seem to get one's desires fulfilled, one will at least reap other observable benefits—such as a healthier body. The use of such terms as "scientific," then, need not be viewed as apologetic.[9] Someone like Kamala, who is both highly educated and traditional, is able to make all kinds of adjustments in her mind to accommodate what others might find conflicting points of view. Further, she is able to articulate and blend those varying points of view most persuasively.

Only at the end of her explanation of the meanings of *vrat* does Kamala mention the conventional reasons that women keep *vrats*—for husbands and sons. Yet, it is not a *vrat* for husbands which she illustrates by example, it is a *vrat* women observe for the benefit of one's children: Jīvitputrika. Kamala explains that such a *vrat* is undertaken by women when a child is ill or has died, or to help prevent such circumstances. *Vrats* are a means by which Hindu mothers can positively influence the fate of their children—and this provides an emotionally powerful and sustaining reason for women to keep *vrats*. *Vrats* performed for the welfare of children are usually the last *vrats* women are willing to give up as they age (or after they are widowed). Chandravati, for example, a mother of two sons, talked about how a mother's *vrats* can help her child:

> *Vrats* alone can't stop (the effects of past) karma; can't prevent what is destined to happen. But it can lessen its effects. Say in your karma (or son's karma) it is written that your son will get a very severe injury, but with this kind of ritual, by the *vrat* you are keeping you will definitely make that injury less—he may only suffer a minor cut. But something *will* happen to him.

She went on to explain that an astrologer can predict what problems one will get, and can prescribe measures to lessen the intensity of those difficulties. We may recall that this is how one astrologer also talked about the prophylactic use of *vrats*—they can act as "umbrellas."

Vrats, Belief and Faith

Kamala's final comment, "This, of course, is a matter of belief" *(ye viśvās hi to hai)*, suggests that this is what most Hindu women who perform *vrats* for their children and families accept (believe to be true); *vrats* will help them prevent or solve familial problems, that is why they perform them. "*Viśvās,*" said Shyamdevi and many others, "is necessary to performing a *vrat.*" Simply stated, one has to have confidence that there will be some benefit, that something will arise out of one's observance of *vrats*, otherwise there is no point in keeping them.

For some women, belief or confidence in the efficacy of *vrats* is sustained by an acceptance of the rightness, wisdom or authority of tradition alone. As Poonam put it: "[Women think that] because this has been done [for generations] and we have been told that this *vrat* is for the safety and well-being of our children, then we might as well do it." This is essentially the sort of idea that Kamala was referring to when she said that it was a matter of belief.

"You do, so you do; you shouldn't break [with your traditional] beliefs," the elderly female head of a large, extended Brahman family declared, at the end of series of comments on why she kept *vrats*. "It is just this, that there is a benefit [got] through observing a *vrat;* one's family remains happy. Here itself is the belief in *vrats*." What do you mean?, I asked Sitadevi. "What I meant was that [it is a matter] of *viśvās;* you believe, that is why you do; so that our work will be fruitful. . . . It is this, by observing *vrats* we [enhance] auspiciousness in the family and home. This is a matter of belief . . . and (keeping a *vrat)* gives me peace of mind. What else? In a word, I am saying it is God's *pūjā;* it is one meritorious act."

For many women, however, like Sarita, *vrats* (or certain *vrats*) are preeminently an expression of *bhakti;* both a demonstration of faith in God and a means of getting closer to God. Lelauti, a Thakur married woman in her forties, for example, after first describing *vrats* as *saṁskār*, and mentioning the positive effects that she felt her observance of *vrats* had on the family, ended with: "All *vrats* have this very object—that one worships God."

Jaya, a Brahman woman in her early thirties, felt that having both faith *(śraddhā)* and belief *(viśvās)* in one's heart were "very necessary" in order to keep a *vrat.*

> We people believe that by observing *vrats* our desires [*manokāmana*] will be fulfilled. . . . In our Hindu religion we are taught that if I will do this *vrat* then my *kam* [task, work] will be completed. In such a manner we think. Also, by observing *vrats* our health will remain good. In our hearts we feel happy observing *vrats* because for the sake of God we have refrained from *ann* [grain] for one day; we have sustained ourselves only on fruit. We will receive peace in our *ātma* [soul] and in our heart [*man*].

Likewise, Poonam, in addition to talking about her Tuesday Vrat as her *sādhanā*, also talked about this *vrat* in terms of it expressing her devotion to Hanumān, her *iṣṭadevtā*, and in strengthening her relationship to him. She said that Hanumān "wanted" her to keep his *vrat*. She never asked him for anything specific, as she might for other gods, as that would in some sense diminish the authenticity of her devotion.

Vrats, Devotion and Desireless Action

The pandit I quoted earlier on the etymology of *vrat* went on to say that "*vratas* are for *mukti* and for getting rid of sins and also diseases; [but] only *niṣkāma vratas*, when there are no *kāmanas*, 'wishes,' will lead to *mukti*." "Most women's *vratas*," he proclaimed, "are *sakāma;* especially those relating to desire for 'issue,' or for their [children's] protection, or their [women's] marriage." Later he reflected that some *vrats* can be both *sakāma* and *niṣkāma*, depending on what one intended when one observed them. Nevertheless, it is interesting that, like the texts of which he is an exponent, he immediately identified "most women's" *vrats* with material, worldly, in short, *kāmya* goals. He assumed that these were women's primary (perhaps even only legitimate) interests. On one level, this is a fair, or at least explicable, characterization since women's concerns for their families are evidently manifested in their *vrat* performances. However, I want to pursue this kind of classification in light of my discussion on faith and *vrats*.

The tripartite classification of vedic ritual into the categories *kāmya*, *nitya*, and *naimittika*, which was applied occasionally and sometimes awkwardly by the Nibandha writers to *vratas*, was not a classification normally used by women I interviewed, nor one that was readily understood by them. Rather, women like Vindhya applied the terms *kāmana* or *sakām*, that is, "with desires," and *niṣkām*, or "without desires," to particular *vrats*, or to the votary's attitudes toward *vrats* in general. A few women commonsensically observed that all *vrats* are *kāmana* because there is always *something* that one wants, even if simply wanting to worship God; the desire to worship God, to come closer to God, is itself a wish. Others, like Sarita and her sister-in-law Rani, felt that any *vrat* can be observed in a *niṣkām* way or in a *sakām* way. She explained it this way:

> Some people do the *vrat* to fulfill some wishes; some keep it out of faith. The one who does the *vrat* with wishes makes the

> resolution that "if my wish is fulfilled, then I will stop observing the *vrat.*" [So], there are two [ways of performing a] *vrat.* One way is with wishes, the other without wishes. Those who keep a *vrat* without any [attached] desires, [who] keep the *vrat* only out of devotion, they say this very *saṅkalp* that "I keep this *vrat* only out of devotion; for this [worship] I don't want anything in return."

At this point Rani interjected:

> One should do *niṣkām vrat* because *vrats* with wishes are not good, because you are saying give and take is equal. For example, in the Monday Vrat the specific wish [may be] "may I become rich; may I get sons"—so these things will be obtained, but then whatever worship you did is gone [because it was exchanged for something concrete]. But for the person who keeps the *vrat* out of a feeling of desirelessness . . . no thing is wanted, s/he is following the *yog* of *niṣkāmakarma* [path of desireless action]. Then even God starts thinking, "What should be given to this person who isn't asking for anything?" So God will always remain near the devotee and God gives her/him a place at his feet. This is all written in the *Gītā*, about the *yog* of *niṣkāmakarma*, the *yog* of *bhakti*.

Rani then went on to describe the first chapter of the *Bhagavadgītā* about Arjuna's predicament (to fight or not to fight his relatives and friends at the battle on the field of Kuru) and Kṛṣṇa's teachings. "Then Śri Kṛṣṇa tells Arjuna things in order to make him fight [because it is his *dharma*]—and gives him the teachings about *niṣkāmakarma.*"

I am not certain if Rani had thought through the implications of the teachings of the *Gītā* with respect to the practice of *vrats*. For, if *vratas* are a necessary part of *strīdharma*, and the *dharma* of women is as incumbent upon them as the *dharma* of the warrior is upon the Kshatriya, then *vratas* must be performed—they must be seen as *nityakarma* (obligatory acts), rather than *kāmyakarma* (optional acts). Yet, insofar as *vratas* contribute to the goals of *strīdharma* (service to husband and family), then they need necessarily be accompanied by desires, albeit altruistic ones. But the *Gītā* would seem to say that any (worldly) desires are detrimental to the attainment of God, or of *mokṣa*. "True renunciation," says the *Gītā*, "consists in abandoning the desire for the results [*phala*] of one's actions, while continuing to engage in activity" and "Action without desire is true nonaction, for it does not lead to bondage, while nonaction tainted with longing is equivalent to action that binds."[10] If women's duty-ordained (and no doubt usually genuine) longings for the safety and well-being of families are still classified as desires, then women have no hope of cutting the bonds of *saṁsāra;* no hope of spiritual maturity (or "enlightenment"). The same situation obtains here as it does in the later Nibandhas wherein, as McGee (1987; 1991) pointed out, in labeling all *vratas* performed with wishes attached as *kāmya,* the *nibandhakārins* failed to take into account the situation of women and their (to a large degree socially mandated) altruistic desires.

Nonetheless, I think the message from the *Gītā* which women like Rani, Sartarji, Vindhya and others have taken to heart is that insofar as *vrats* are acts of devotion to God—they ought to be observed with feelings of nonattachment, or in Poonam's words: "as an offering to God." It is significant to remember that Rani had been widowed early in her life and she was childless. Thus from her point of view, keeping *vrats* in a *niṣkām* way is the only legitimate way to observe *vrats* because it is her relationship to God alone which she seeks to nurture; there are no sons, grandchildren or husband whose welfare she needs to protect. Other women, like Poonam, who were married and had children, felt that both *sakām vrats* and *niṣkām vrats* were necessary and each way of keeping a *vrat* had its place in the religious lives of women.

Vrats, the Practice of Austerities and Power

Sarasvati, the middle-aged Brahman matron of a large extended family living on the outskirts of Banaras (whom I introduced in chapter 3), offered a distinctive response to my question about the nature of *vrats*, which brings our focus back to the relationship between *vrats* and the concepts of *tapasyā* and *śakti:*

> *Vrats* are the answer in the Kaliyug to what saints and *ṛṣis* did in olden times. We don't have the power to do *tapasyā* as they did in the past. If one has genuine belief in the *vrats* the gods will certainly listen to you. The gods test people's strength of belief. Purity of motive and strength of belief is very important in the success of the *vrat.* If one starts a *vrat* and then stops because nothing has happened then one has failed the test of faith. . . . Women don't have so much *śakti* in the Kaliyug as they did previously.

> *You mean women like Sītā, Sāvitrī and Anasūya?*
>
> Yes. It is very difficult to be so single-minded as these women were. But, some women, a few, can and do gain spiritual powers. One woman in Pandepur, a householder, has so pleased Mātāji [Devī] that she can give ashes to people as blessings and they will get better.

Sarasvati underscores the importance of performing *vrats* with an attitude of genuine piety for it is the purity of motive and strength of belief that the gods not only reward but, according to Sarasvati, test. Thus one must complete or carry on the *vrats* that one has started if one is to have any hope of success. The necessity of the submissive attitude of devotion and constancy is contrasted with what "the saints and *ṛṣis* did in olden times"—before the present (degenerate) Kaliyug.[11] In the "past" the practice of *tapasyā*, as exemplified in the stories of the famous *ṛṣis* and *munis* found in the epics and popular mythology, could in and of itself accomplish whatever ends the practitioner desired. But, as Sarasvati at first decides, "we don't have the power to do *tapasyā* as they did in the past." So, instead, we have *vrats*—a sort of modified *tapasyā*, dependent for its success on expressions of piety and piety rewarded by the gods.

Almost all the women I interviewed felt that *vrats* are a form of *tapasyā*.[12] In their comments on *vrats* and *tapasyā* (and *siddhis)*, a number of women used phrases almost identical to Kamala's statements about purifying, steadying, and controlling the mind (and senses). "Yes, there is *tapasyā*," Sarita affirmed. "By doing *vrats* the body and mind become one. The mind is bound, [so that say] today I have done this *vrat*—so my mind ought not to go here and there. Through *tapasyā* we increase our *śakti*." Similarly, nineteen-year-old Lakshmi said: "Yes, *vrats* are a form of *tapasyā*. Through observing a *vrat* our mind won't wander about; from this *śakti* grows." In other words, one gets mental (and spiritual) power from concentration; which is precisely what Tripathi named first as one of the reasons that people keep *vrats*, that is, "for obtaining spiritual or mental power" *(mānsik śakti)*.

What did women mean by *tapasyā?* A range of descriptions was offered. Kamala, for example, said that "the meaning of *tapasyā* is restraint of the six senses." Likewise, Sudha felt that *vrats* are a form of *tapasyā* "because they involve *niyams*," that is, self-restrictive rules. Her mother, present during much of the interview, agreed, adding: "because [*vrat*] is a kind of sacrifice."

And Sartarji, whose life in recent years had been difficult and emotionally painful, commented that "The path of religion is itself *tapasyā*."

Shyamdevi's remarks on *vrats* and *tapasyā* reminded me of the principles of homeopathic medicine (indeed modern vaccinations). That is, limited exposure to the disease is held to prevent the worst case of it, if not to cure it; you take on hardship to lessen [present] or to prevent [future] hardship. "*Tapasyā* is this, that I do *tapasyā*. I keep on reciting [the name of God]; I remain hungry—so that my hardships will go far away, my well-being [*kalyān*] will be there. If my children are in distress, let it be removed soon. That is why it is called *tapasyā*. . . . The meaning of *vrat* is also this—no matter which *vrat*."

Annapurna explained the meaning of *tapasyā* simply but graphically: "If I am thirsty, I would not take water; I would burn my own body—that is *tapasyā*." Such a description of *tapas* is arresting for its consonance with the ancient meanings of *tapas*—meanings which metamorphosized from "heat" in the *Ṛgveda* to the powerful and creative heat generated in the body/mind through self-sacrifice. While heat transforms that with which it comes in contact, it also is understood to act as an agent of purification. Thus it is not surprising that several other women, after affirming that *vrats* are a form of *tapasyā*, returned to the theme of purification, describing self-purification as the purpose of the acts of *tapasyā*. Hardevi, for example, asked rhetorically, "So what is *tapasyā*? It is for purification of the mind and thought." She then explained further: "One remains restrained and [achieves] 'self-control of the mind.'"

In the epic literature in particular, an individual's acts of austerity often result in supernormal powers—"*siddhis*." Hardevi's remark suggests that women think that they can obtain such *siddhis* by performing *vrats*. When I commented to Hardevi that perhaps Sāvitrī was able to save her husband from Yama because of her *siddhi* from *vrats*, she interrupted with "*aur kya?*" (lit., "what else?," meaning, "of course"). "Can other women do this with the same result?" I asked. "Not everyone can do this," she replied. "That which Sāvitrī did, not all people can do. . . . Her heart and mind were very pure. . . . Women may obtain *siddhi* or not in that way [like Sāvitrī]. There are all kinds of *siddhi*. [The point is] *vrat* at least makes one strong—here itself is the biggest *siddhi*. 'Self-control'—it makes one's character strong."[13]

When I first asked women about obtaining *siddhis* from *vrats*, I was thinking of the term as it is used in the epics and other Sanskrit literature (meaning "magical powers" that accrue to the performer of strenuous ascetic practice). While this sense is retained in the modern Hindi usage, it is usually a secondary meaning. First, *siddhi* means simply accomplishment, fulfillment, or success. Thus Chandravati exclaimed, "Why not? Women can get *siddhis*. It means, you get what you want from keeping these *vrats*." Annapurna, in a separate interview, concurred: "*Siddhi* is the fulfillment of one's desires. . . . When we observe a *vrat*, we say that 'we will do it for five Sundays, or eleven Sundays,' and if it is successful [i.e., one's wishes are answered], this is the *siddhi*." Finally, Sarita put it this way:

> Yes, certainly, one can obtain any *siddhi*. For whichever god you do *tapasyā* [she or he] will give you [his or her] *siddhi*. You may receive Devī's *siddhi*, Hanumān's *siddhi*, Śaṅkar's *siddhi*—but you have to do [the *pūjā* or *tapasyā*] from the heart. Whomever you worship—if you are able to please him—he will become happy and give you *siddhi*.

Trying to determine more clearly what she meant by *siddhi*, I asked Sarita if women could gain "yogic *siddhis*" by this means. She first suggested that one could get yogic *siddhis* too—since there are female *yogis* as well as male *yogis*. But, Sarita explained, "I'm just a householder."

> In order to obtain [yogic] *siddhi* you have to renounce [being a *gṛhasthin*—"householder"]. By not renouncing, my mind will run about here and there [thinking], "I have to get my husband food, I have to do kitchen work." If the mind [*man*] runs about in all directions, it can't adhere to God. Therefore, first I will have to renounce the "husband-son-householder" stage; then my mind can concentrate on God, and then through doing *tapasyā* I will receive *siddhis*. [But right now] I am a householder. I don't have these *guṇ* [qualities]. We must first serve [the family]; then I can do *vrats*, meditate on God. . . . This isn't enough to obtain *siddhi*.

However, not all women agreed with Sarita. In Sitadevi's view, "with *viśvās* and *bhakti* all is possible," including supernormal powers. Many women that I interviewed, in fact, did interpret the word *siddhi* as "special power." But, while some were of the opinion that people could and did obtain *siddhis* through *vrats*, others, like Sarasvati, were doubtful that it was possible today as it had been in the past because today women's "*śakti* is less strong," they are less "single-minded," or they "have less ability to do difficult *tapasyā*, or to do such long *vrats*—as Pārvatī did." By and large, "women and men just don't do really difficult *vrats* these days—but if they did," Premlata suggested, "they could certainly obtain *siddhis*."

Yet, on reflection, Sarasvati remembered a woman who had gained special powers through her devotion to the goddess; and other women related similar stories. Sudha, for instance, who at the start felt more assured than some others that "it is possible to gain *siddhis* from *vrats* or [from] any kind of *tapasyā*," told me about the unusual abilities of her mother's brother's wife. She was able to anticipate questions that people were about to ask and to provide a response "before they had even opened their mouth." Sudha attributed this ability to her aunt's religious practice and to her powers of concentration.

Like Sudha, Padma affirmed that

> certainly [women] can obtain *siddhis*. All things are obtained when one controls oneself, has determination. If a *sādhak* [spiritual aspirant] loses his concentration/resolve, then he won't achieve anything. The meaning of *sādhak* is he who does spiritual practice for his balance to such an extent that for whatever has been determined, there should not be even the smallest wavering from that. . . . One becomes a true *sādhu* when one has control over oneself.

Women's repeated mention of self-control in the context of *vrats* is highly significant, in my view. It seems evident that women like Kamala, Rekha and Poonam have appropriated elements of the pervasive ideology of abstinence, self-control and self-purification, articulated in the Yogasūtras, the *Gītā* and elsewhere, to lend their observance of *vrats* a wider meaning and more significance for the development of self and individual spirituality than the *pativrata* ideology alone would permit. Aligning themselves with the essentially self-centered values of the ascetic tradition is not an obvious act of defiance for women because, as we have seen, the Dharmaśāstras incorporated self-control and mental and physical self-discipline as integral to the *dharma* of *vrata*. But, given the texts' proscription of any kind of formal asceticism for women, one would expect that women were not supposed to place an emphasis on the *niyama* aspect of *vrata dharma* as ends in themselves. Yet this is where women have seen value and esteem placed by the Hindu tradition at large and so this is where women have chosen to place an emphasis as well.

Further, women's alignment with ascetic practices should not be surprising because it represents an extension of the training in self-denial, self-restraint and self-sacrifice that many women receive as they grow up. It is clear from the work of researchers like Sudhir Kakar, and from the women I spoke with, that women experience the message of self-effacement and self-control much earlier and more bodily than do men and that their lives, by and large, are more constrained than are the lives of men by social rules or conventions dictating their roles and their behavior within those roles, and by the limitations placed on their choices. In short, women are culturally expected to practice self-denial in order to serve the interests of male kin. While restraint is presented as a generalized virtue in the Dharmaśāstras, there is a special emphasis placed on this virtue with regard to women (for example, Manu 9.29). Yet by choosing to identify the significance of their performance of *vrats* more with the non-gender-specific *niyamas* and less with the values surrounding *saubhāgya* and auspiciousness, Hindu women can, in a fashion, dissociate themselves from the ramifications of their gendered status. At times, the responsibilities of family and some of the negative associations with femaleness can feel like onerous burdens and barriers to the development of autonomy and a positive self-image. Through the asceticism involved in the performance of *vrats*, which can be as rigorous as the votary desires, women can transcend their sexuality and limit their degree of pollution, which is already greater than that of men. Both eating and sex are polluting, and these are curtailed in a *vrat*. Abstinence is physically purifying and powerful because of the internal heat it creates. As a form of *tapasyā*, *vrats* increase one's *śakti* to achieve ends of one's own choosing. "*Vrats* make one strong," as Hardevi put it. Strength is manifested in the ability to will into being what one wants. When the body is under control, the mind fixed (steadied), "all things are obtained."

A statement from an anonymous Maharashtrian Brahman woman recorded by Carolyn Slocum (and included with little comment in a volume on religion in Maharashtra [1988, 208–9]) wonderfully and comprehensively reiterates many of the remarks about the relationship between women's practice of austerities and *śakti* made by the mostly Brahman Uttar Pradeshi women I interviewed. I quote the statement in full:

> *Shaktī* [sic] is like steam: if you compress it, steam has the power to pull a whole train. If you don't bottle it up, it simply dissipates—but it could explode if you don't let some out. *Shaktī* is just like that. If you control your will, you can gain *shaktī* or inner strength. If you don't, your *shaktī* will just disappear.
>
> Rituals and fasts are the most important ways to control your will. You have to suppress your desires and do everything for God. Everyone has some *shaktī*, but women have more of it because they do more rituals and fasts. Women also gain *shaktī* because of their place in the family. Husbands and fathers control women's wills. We must always be lower than men. You must control your own desires too. You must have perfect fidelity to your husband even in thought. When women have children, they bear pain and suppress their own desires for their children. That brings *shaktī* too. Young girls now aren't being taught self-control and aren't learning to do rituals and fasts. They won't have as much *shaktī* as older women.
>
> Women use *shaktī* mostly to help their families. In old days, women like Savitri could save their husbands from death. Because this is the Kali Yuga, women can't do that anymore, but we can give our husbands longer lives and bring prosperity to the whole family. Women can make their husband's and sons' businesses go better. Women with a lot of *shaktī* can cure illnesses. All women can bring happiness to their families through their *shaktī*. Women also use their *shaktī* for themselves—to help do all their daily work and to get peace of mind. It can even save you from harm. Sita's *shaktī* saved her from burning.
>
> So a woman's *shaktī* can be really strong in helping herself and others. It's funny that you get more inner strength the more you control and suppress your desires and will. If it's suppressed too far though, it can explode and be a bad force. But mostly it's a good power. So you see, it's a lot like steam.

According to this woman, "rituals" and "fasts" (*vrats*) increase one's *śakti*—one's "inner strength"; so also does women's place in the family and their childbearing, all of which require the suppression of personal desires and a measure of suffering. The accumulation of this power can be used by women to help their families: bring happiness and prosperity, lengthen the lives of husbands and children, and cure illnesses. But, women can use *śakti* for themselves too, to get protection for themselves, help in their work, and peace of mind—which, as I have suggested, often means spiritual self-development. Tellingly, however, this woman recognizes the psychologically fine line between the suppression of ego and affect and loss of "self" when she concludes that too much suppression can result in the opposite effect: a total breakdown in self-control.

In sum, insofar as the regular performance of *vrats* gives women opportunities to develop control of their own minds and bodies and to take charge of their spiritual destinies, *vrats* are sources of empowerment to Hindu women. Women are empowered both in the culturally understood sense of *tapas* and *śakti* and in the sense that women feel a measure of autonomy because they can decide how many *vrats* to perform, how rigorously they will keep them, and to what ends. If anyone in a woman's family is experiencing difficulties, including herself, she can take matters into her own hands and try to solve the problem through *vrats*.

For certain women, like Sarita, Vindhya and Rani, *vrats* are empowering in a different way. Each of these women focused more on the devotional aspects of *vrats*, rather than on the self-disciplinary features. For these women, *vrats* present opportunities to submerge themselves in God, to invest their emotional energy and spiritual longings in regular acts of worship and self-sacrifice—not to husband and family, but to God. Such an investment of emotional and spiritual energy in the Divine allows them to detach or escape from the draining pressures and difficulties of their unhappy familial situations. For them also, *vrats* can bring peace of mind. Thus, while perhaps the majority of women initially perform *vrats* out of convention and social expectation, as they continue the regular, almost habitual practice of these rites year after year, many women start to take charge of these rites; they make them meaningful for themselves personally.

CONCLUSION

A chapter in the anthropologist R. S. Khare's book, *The Hindu Hearth and Home* (1976), contains descriptions and analyses of several *vrats* in terms of their practitioners and aims, and the symbolic significance of food and other elements of the *vrats*' procedure. In this chapter, Khare distinguishes between what he calls "spiritual fasts" (*vrats*), which he suggests mainly men perform, and "women's fasts and festivals" or "familial fasts." He bases this distinction on a conceptual separation of the purity-impurity axis and the auspiciousness/inauspiciousness axis. Spiritual fasts are directed toward augmenting purity in the individual for the ultimate purpose or aim of pursuing *mokṣa*. Familial fasts, on the other hand, are intended to maximize auspiciousness for the social collective, as a way of maintaining *dharma*. The dominant values of the spiritual fast, he says, are austerity, self-control, spiritual merit and devotion; whereas women's "fasts-cum-festivals" underscore social and domestic values and a "collective morality" (1976, 132, 138). He continues:

> Thus though one practices to observe the rules of purity in his [sic] social world, it is worthless if it cannot be ultimately related to the construct of individual moral and spiritual existence. Observances of ritual purity are a network of techniques that, if correctly pursued by the individual, accrue the desired religious or spiritual merit in relation to his own existence. . . .
>
> In contrast come the fasts of women which are meant to be different in morality. Here non-eating or restrictive eating (for a specified period) is directed towards the benefit of those who are near and dear to the woman who is fasting. Here the principle is just the reverse—collective familial and social life and its quality are brought into sharp focus. . . . These women through their households manage and regulate those links with the wider social system that their husbands and brothers try to give up in the hope of reaching their spiritual self. Women in this domain have remained dominant for a long time . . . ; they invent and carry on their body of ritual, generation after generation, overruling priests if they stand in the way. What *shastric* texts do not say these women do with impunity and make it run on a social system that men ostensibly dominate and differentiate. If these women care for ritual rules of purity it is by imitation of their menfolk. (1976, 143–44)

As Marglin has pointed out, Khare was the first researcher since Srinivas (1952) to bring out once again the importance of the value of auspiciousness as a major cultural category among Hindus, distinct from the value of purity (Carmen and Marglin 1985, 2). Khare's work on auspiciousness served as a counterpoint to the dominant attention given to the purity-impurity axis following the influential work of Louis Dumont (1970). His work also directed attention to women's special interest in and manipulation of auspiciousnesss.[14] Khare's description of the role of women's *vrats* in the promotion of auspiciousness has been elaborated in Mary McGee's analysis of the relation of the value of *saubhāgya* to auspiciousness and women's performance of *vrats*. Khare further rightly emphasized women's interest in the "social collective"; and pointed to the fact that women's rites, like *vrats*, often work to overcome barriers which men (by and large) have set up.

However, my work stands as a statement of caution against the trend, particularly in the context of *vrats*, towards what I see as an overidentification of the religious lives of Hindu women with the domestic sphere and the value of auspiciousness. First, I would hope that the material presented in this book would make readers dubious about drawing a hard distinction between so-called spiritual fasts and women's familial fasts. As I have observed, and as women often indicated to me, most individual *vrats* are associated with a particular deity and with an ostensible or prima facie purpose, and together these two factors contribute to the form of the *vrat*. However, as even the texts acknowledge in various ways, any *vrat* can be observed for any purpose(s), and many women observe most or all of their *vrats* with several underlying aims in mind. Prominent among these aims are the expression of personal devotion and piety, and the achievement of spiritual self-development, aims which the textual tradition and its modern exponents elucidate. Thus, to separate, as Khare does, women's fasts from men's on the basis that women's *vrats* are exclusively concerned with familial/collective interests and men's *vrats* with spiritual/self-directed aims is misleading. It would be more accurate to say that auspiciousness and familial well-being are values, albeit important ones, included among the aims and purposes of the *vrats* that women perform.

Second, as long as a person is a householder, there can be no rigid individualism. One could say that men are "allowed" to be outwardly more concerned about their own spiritual welfare and their own salvation than are women because men have the support structure to pursue these goals (including the cooperation of women in the family who will prepare the necessary foods and worship items, in the right utensils, at the right times, and who will "give men the time"). Women, on the other hand, are expected to pursue this concern more indirectly through their actions vis-à-vis others. This does not mean that women are less interested in their own spiritual welfare. Rather, the forms in which they express this interest are circumscribed by the ideologically prescribed roles in which the allocation of spiritual merit is proportionate to the degree to which women adhere to *strīdharm* (of which *vrats* form a part). In other words, while it is true that Hindu women's performance of *vrats* is expressive of a religiosity that is framed within an androcentric gender ideology and patriarchal social structure, I would argue that out of the richness of the *vrata* tradition, women have culled meanings and significance that are supportive of spiritual goals for themselves; that contribute both to a positive self-understanding and to a sense of empowerment.

In the end, even if some of the rituals accompanying particular *vrats* begin to lose their symbolic force because they no longer speak meaningfully to votaries; or if particular goals such as the prevention or amelioration of droughts and diseases become irrelevant; or, finally, if the necessity of having sons, and protecting the life of a husband for fear of widowhood—in short, the conservative ideology underlying gender arrangements—become less compelling, *vrats* will continue to be observed by women. These rites will be observed because they serve so many functions. In addition to the important social interaction with other women—relatives, friends and strangers—that many women enjoy when they perform *vrats* collectively, *vrats* provide opportunities for the preparation of special foods, for the creation of ritual art which many women painstakingly fashion, and for the telling of stories expressive of women's concerns and dilemmas. Then, *vrats* function as problem-solvers—for such traditional but always compelling reasons as the need to secure aid and blessings from the gods for children, as well as for more modern reasons such as securing help for settling a court case, finding a job and performing well in school. For many women, however, *vrats* primarily serve as a means of expressing their faith in God, demonstrating their piety and love through acts of self-sacrifice; of leading a more moral, disciplined and spiritual life. For other women, *vrats* provide the opportunity periodically to imitate the values and life-style of the ascetic. In performing acts of asceticism they can tap into the potent realm of *tapas* and so enhance their purity and power. The women of North India have shown me that it is precisely because they derive a great deal of spiritual significance for themselves from their performance of *vrats*—apart from any concern with duty—that the *vrat* tradition is as vigorous and lively among Hindu women as it is in India today.

Appendix A

HISTORY OF SCHOLARSHIP ON *VRATA*

The first detailed account of the history of meaning of the term "*vrata*" from traditional Sanskrit sources of *dharma* (religious law), from the Vedas to the Nibandhas, is that done by P. V. Kane. This historical overview is presented in the first eighty pages of volume five, part one of his larger work, *The History of Dharmaśāstra*. The remaining few hundred pages are descriptions and lists of various *vrata*s and festivals found in Dharmaśāstras, Purāṇas and Nibandhas. The latter two groups of texts contain the antecedents to many of the *vrata*s in current practice. One significant omission in Kane's overview of the meaning of *vrata* is the important Sanskrit epic literature. On balance, however, a great debt is owed to Kane for his preliminary charting of the *vrata* landscape in dharmaśāstric literature. Subsequent to Kane is Mary McGee's dissertation (1987), the first half of which focuses on *vrata* in the large corpus of Nibandha literature (religio-legal digests written between the eleventh to eighteenth centuries). Her textual analysis is complemented in the second half of her dissertation by fieldwork conducted with women votaries in Pune, Maharashtra. This is a significant contribution to the scholarship on *vrata*, and because it covers fieldwork as well as texts, its contents will be discussed at the end of this survey.

A larger body of scholarly literature exists when we come to the arena of actual *vrat*s performed in different regions of India. One of the earliest references to *vrat*s by a foreigner is that made by the Muslim traveller Alberuni in the eleventh century. Such references may be found in Edward Sachau's translation of Alberuni's journals: *Alberuni's India* (reprint of 1888 ed., Delhi: S. Cand and Co., 1964). There are also accounts in some eighteenth- and nineteenth-century Christian missionary writings, for example, W. Ward, *A View of the History, Literature and Religion of the Hindoos* (Birmingham: W. H. Pearce, 1817), and J. A. Dubois, *Hindu Manners, Customs and Ceremonies*, trans. by H. K. Beaucahmp, 3d. ed. (Delhi: Oxford University Press, 1978 [1897]). Nineteenth-century orientalists occasionally described a *vrat* rite in various journals current at the time. These include such journals as *The Indian Antiquary* and the *Journal of the Royal Anthropological Society of Bombay*. And, in this century, the anthropological journal *Man in India* has featured a number of articles describing *vrats*.

In the twentieth century, one of the first scholars to take a serious look at *vrats* was Abanindranath Tagore. Tagore's main interest was in popular Bengali culture, and the place of the folk arts in this culture. He could not help but notice the omnipresent and lively *brat* (Bengali for *vrat*) traditions, with their rich but ephemeral ritual art *(ālpanā)* and their stories. His book, *Banglar Brata* (1919), describes many of the *brats* he saw performed in Bengal and speculates on their origin. It may be that *vrats* have proliferated in Bengal more than in other parts of India, or that Tagore's research (perhaps given added weight by the stature of his family) sparked scholarly interest among his fellow Bengalis; whatever the reason, the majority of subsequent studies on *vrats* also focus on Bengal (e.g., Bagchi 1922; Rowlands 1930; Banerjee 1946; Das 1952; Mukherjee 1950; Sen 1959; Ray 1960, 1961; Mazumdar 1981; Gupta 1983; Robinson 1985; Maity 1988). With the exception of Ray's and Maity's (in English) and Eva Maria Gupta's (in German) book-length studies on *brata* and their *ālpanā*, these references are to articles or chapters in books. Among these works, E. M. Gupta's and Maity's are the most important contributions to the ethnography of *vrat* in Bengal. Both authors build directly on Tagore's earlier book and both provide short but informative descriptions of a large number of *bratas* for girls and women. Gupta's work also provides an analysis of the content and symbolism of the ritual art, and in fact her book contains probably the largest number of *brata ālpanā* reproductions currently available. Rowlands, Mazumdar and Robinson look at selected *vrats* only within the larger context of Bengali women's religious lives. Rowlands is interested in what we can learn about the lives of medieval Bengali women through Bengali literature, and Mazumdar in how *vrats* are used as agents of socialization for Bengali girls. Robinson's article discusses "cultural constructs of the feminine" in Hinduism and through a descriptive analysis of the Itu Vrata and its *kathā* shows how *vrats* "illustrate salient dimensions of women's religiosity in Hindu devotionalism" (1985, 202). All of these studies, in fact, attend to *vrats* as women's folk rites essentially separate from the Brahmanical Sanskrit tradition.

Apart from Bengal, the state of Uttar Pradesh has received the most attention from scholars writing on *vrats*. Relevant studies include Marriott 1958; Lewis 1958; Luschinsky 1962; Khare 1976; Wadley 1975, 1976, 1978, 1980a, 1983a, 1983c; and Tewari 1982, 1991. Again, Marriott, Lewis, Luschinsky and Khare only look at some *vrats* within the larger context of their studies—the first three on village life, and Khare on the cultural significance of food and food management among Brahmans in an area around Lucknow. Luschinsky's exclusive focus, however, is on women and she provides some valuable ethnographic data in the form of descriptions of ten women's *vrats* set in the context of the daily (and yearly) lives of women in a North Indian village. Both Tewari's 1982 article and 1991 book are helpful in providing quick overviews of the names, dates and purposes of several important women's *vrats* currently observed in central Uttar Pradesh. Susan Wadley, working primarily out of one village near Delhi, has contributed substantially to the analysis of the function of *vrats* in the lives of Hindu women.[1] Wadley was the first anthropologist to take a serious and continued interest in women's performance of *vrats*. Among her contributions, Wadley pointed out the important role that women's rites play in the transmission of Hindu ideas and values, and drew attention to the role of kin as "religious symbols." According to Wadley, a study of these calendrical rituals "can provide new insight into the role of kinship in Hindu ritual behavior and ideology" (1976, 150). Wadley also clearly placed women's *vrats* in the context of women's "duty" *(strīdharm)*, showing them to be a "fundamental aspect of being a *pativratā*" (the ideal Hindu woman) (1976, 164), and at the same time indicated some of the positive aspects for women in these rites through which they express traditional roles (1980a). Both my own work and that of McGee's on women and the *vrata* tradition build in particular on the foundation of research and ideas that Wadley (in the field) and Kane (in the texts) have established.

To complete this survey of literature on *vrata*, a few other works need to be mentioned. Recent studies on selected *vrats* in other parts of India and Nepal include Freeman's 1980 article

---

1. Wadley has also written about the plethora of vernacular *vrat* booklets currently being produced and has described the effects that this written literature is having on the formerly primarily oral traditions found in village settings (see Wadley 1983a).

on the Habisha Vrat observed by post-menopausal women in Orissa, Reynold's 1980 article and a chapter in Duvvury's 1991 book on the role that *vrats* (here *"nonpu")* play in the lives of Tamil married women, and J. Bruce Long's 1982 article on the important Mahāśivarātri Vrat as observed in Madras. Babb, in his book (1975) on popular religion in Chhatisgarh, Madhya Pradesh, discusses some *vrats* that are observed during the annual festival cycle, and McGee (1987) describes, with reference to both texts and practice, many *vratas* that are current among women in the state of Maharashtra. Lynn Bennett (1983) provides a detailed description of the Tij-Rishi Pancami and the Swasthani *bartas* (Nepali for *vrat*) that Brahman-Chetri women from one village in Nepal observe. Bennett also provides a stimulating symbolic analysis of the stories *(kathās)* that accompany these two *vrats*.

Other articles have focused on certain elements of *vrat* rites (elements which are not necessarily specific to *vrats*) such as the ritual art (e.g., Ray 1961; Kramrisch 1985), or the stories (e.g., Wadley 1978, 1986). Tewari's book (1991) contains fifty-five *vrat* stories and variations that are part of fifteen "fasts and festivals" annually celebrated by Kanyakubja Brahman women in the Kanpur region of Uttar Pradesh. This book is especially valuable as a primary source of *vrat* stories that have been orally transmitted by women for generations. Finally, one can find ample mention or description of *vrats* in books or articles on Hindu festivals and on the calendar (B. A. Gupte 1916; Underhill 1921; Sharma 1978; Sivananda 1983), or in works about pilgrimage or pilgrimage centers (e.g., Bhardwaj 1973).

McGee's work provides a detailed, instructive and comprehensive study of the concept and treatment of *vrata* in the Dharmaśāstra (especially Nibandha) literature, a study which essentially expands and amplifies Kane's work. In the textual portion of her dissertation, McGee analyzes how certain *mīmāṃsā* categories[2] are applied by the Nibandha writers to *vrata* in these texts and examines the gender implications of these categories. This analysis sets the stage for her investigation of the roles of *vratas* in the lives of high-caste Hindu women in western Maharashtra

2. The *mīmāṃsā* refers to a school (or method) of vedic textual exegesis. The particular categories referred to here are the *"nitya," "naimittika"* and *"kāmya"* classification, which McGee calls the "motivational categories."

found in the second half of her dissertation. McGee argues that, contrary to the way the Nibandha authors have categorized *vratas* that women perform, women view their *vratas* as "rites of maintenance" rather than "rites of acquisition." That is, women by and large do not see the *vrats* they perform as optional rites that they may choose to perform in order to fulfil a personal desire or to acquire some specific object, but as obligatory rites that help to fulfil their specific dharmic duties. This is an expansion of Wadley's observation that women consider some *vrats* they perform as "necessary"—those for husbands—while others are less essential (1976, 164). Another important contribution that McGee brings to the study of Hindu women is the analysis of the concept of *saubhāgya*—the "state of marital felicity"—and she directs our attention to how *vratas* explicitly contribute to the maintenance of *saubhāgya* as well as to the promotion of the central Hindu values of purity and auspiciousness.

Appendix B

FIELDSITE, RESEARCH POPULATION, AND FIELDWORK METHODS

The city of Banaras was selected as the fieldsite for several reasons. First, its population is predominately Hindi-speaking, a language of which I have a working knowledge. Second, there had not been any substantial research done on *vrat* practices there. And third, Banaras is well known as one of the major and oldest centers of Hindu orthodoxy—and so a place where the observance of *vrat*s would have a long and continuous history, where pandits, priests and astrologers would be well acquainted with them, and where local and pan-Indian *vrat*s would be known. Fieldwork in Banaras was carried out over a fourteen-month period in 1984–85.

My research population consisted largely of women whose native tongue was Hindi, who resided permanently in Banaras or its immediate vicinity, and who regularly observed *vrat*s. The majority of the women interviewed were Brahmans and most lived in the areas between "Chowk" and Banaras Hindu University to the south of the city. The former area is a very densely populated and old part of the city where many long-established and orthodox families live. I tried to include a variety of age groups, marital statuses, and related family members in my interview sample. My research assistant was a Brahman, single and in her early thirties. She had many relatives, friends and acquaintances in the city and I relied heavily on her for my initial contacts. After that I used the "snow-ball" method to find new contacts. I make no claims about having adequately represented even one segment of the *vrat*-observing population of India, Uttar Pradesh or even Banaras. This was not my intention. Rather, my intention was to find women with whom I could establish a climate of trust in which they could share with me their views and feelings on their religious lives in general and on their observance of *vrat*s in particular.

Altogether, during the period of my fieldwork in India, I conducted sixty-two interviews during which I spoke with fifty-eight women in Uttar Pradesh and with sixteen women in the southern state of Kerala. I visited Kerala about one-third of the way through my stay in India and took the opportunity to interview sixteen mostly Nayar and Nambudiri women in the hill town of Kottayam and the capital city of Trivandrum. (Some of these interviews were conducted with several women at once.) The purpose of conducting interviews in the south of India was essentially to obtain first hand comparative data in order to gain a sense of some of the continuities and differences among women's *vrat* observance in a northern state and a southern state in India.

Initial interviews were mostly short and exploratory and served to test out my questions as I sought to prepare a finalized interview schedule. Once the interview schedule was finalized, I used it to conduct longer interviews with women in Banaras, as well as with a few women in surrounding villages and in the northern Uttar Pradesh towns of Dehradun and Mussoorie. Interviews usually lasted about two hours at a time, and in many cases I had to return once or more in order to complete the interview. However, not all questions were either asked of or answered by every informant. The first section of the interview schedule covered basic information such as age, education, marital status, religious affiliation, and common religious activities (pilgrimages, visits to temples, etc.). The remaining sections, consisting of both fixed answer and open-ended questions, pertained to the respondent's *vrat* practices and her reflections on their meaning and benefits. Where time permitted and circumstances were favorable, I would ask further questions from a supplementary list that grew larger as the weeks went by. Most of the interviews were tape-recorded, with the permission of those interviewed. The following sections provide more detailed information than provided in the body of the text concerning the caste, religious affiliation, age and background of the women I spoke with about *vrats* in Banaras.

It was sometimes difficult to elicit specific information about the caste or *jāti* of women. The majority of women interviewed were Brahman, about one-sixth were of Kshatriya *jātis* and the remainder were from other classes and castes. Of forty-four answering this question, thirty-two women said they were Brahmans (about half giving a specific *jāti);* seven said they were Kshatriyas; one was an Ahir (a Shudra caste); two were "Harijans";

one was a Lingayat, and one an Ayyar (both from families originating in Karnataka).

The women's ages ranged from seventeen to seventy-two years, and their educational backgrounds ranged from illiterate to Ph.D. Four women were illiterate, five were home-educated, nineteen women had a few grades of schooling, thirteen women had high school diplomas, and ten had university-level education. Just over two-thirds of the women interviewed were married, and the others were either unmarried or widowed. There were interviews with five unmarried young women, two unmarried older women, twenty-two pre-menopausal married women, twelve menopausal married women, one separated woman, and nine widows. Nine of the respondants had no children.

I often encountered a certain hesitancy and even confusion concerning the question of religious affiliation. For this reason I omitted this question toward the end of my fieldwork. Out of twenty-six positive answers, four women identified themselves as Vaiṣṇava, two women as Śaiva, one as a Śakta, two as Smārta, and seventeen women as "Sanātani"—a category I had not even intially included in my first questionnaire. "Sanātanis" consider themselves followers of the *sanātan* "eternal" *dharm*—the nonsectarian "ancient," "time-honored" or traditional religion of India, wherein no deities, no rituals (except the *saṁskāras*), and no overarching doctrines or dogmas are privileged. Those who identified themselves as Sanātani usually had images (*mūrtis*) or pictures of several deities in their homes—sometimes reflecting the various *iṣṭadevatās* ("chosen" or favored deities) that different family members worshipped.

Appendix C

TABLES OF MONTHS, *TITHIS*, AND *VRATS*

Table 1. Months of the Year According to the North Indian Pūrṇimanta* System

LUNAR MONTHS			GREGORIAN EQUIVALENTS
Sanskrit	Standard Hindi	Variant	
Caitra**	Caitra	Cait	March/April
Vaiśākha	Vaiśākh	Baiśākh	April/May
Jyeṣṭha	Jyeṣṭh	Jeṭh	May/June
Āsāḍha	Āsāḍh	Āsārh	June/July
Śravaṇa	Śravaṇ	Savan	July/August
Bhādrapada	Bhādrapad	Bhādon	August/September
Āśvina	Āśvin	Kvar	September/October
Kārtika	Kārtik	Kārtik	October/November
Mārgaśīrṣa	Mārgaśīrṣ	Agahan	November/December
Pauṣa	Pauṣ	Pus	December/January
Māgha	Māgh	Māgh	January/February
Phālguna	Phālgun	Phāgun	February/March

Notes:

*In the Pūrṇimanta system, each month begins with the day after the new moon.

**New Year.

Table 2. Names of *Tithis*

	Standard Hindi	Variant	Associated Deity(ies)*
First	Pratipadā	Piruva	
Second	Dvitīya	Dūj	
Third	Tritīya	Tīj	Goddesses
Fourth	Caturthī	Cauth	Gaṇeś
Fifth	Pañcamī		Ṛṣis, snakes
Sixth	Ṣaṣṭhī	Chaṭh	Lakṣmī, Sūrya
Seventh	Saptamī	Sat	
Eighth	Aṣṭamī	Āṭhe	Goddesses, Durgā
Ninth	Navamī	Naumī	Rāma, Sītā
Tenth	Daśamī	Daśmī, Dasehra	
Eleventh	Ekādaśī	Gyās	Viṣṇu
Twelth	Dvādaśī		
Thirteenth	Trayodaśī	Teras	Śiva
Fourteenth	Caturdaśī		
Fifteenth	Pūrṇimā (full moon)		usually auspicious
	Amāvasyā (new moon)		usually inauspicious

Notes:

*From Banaras field data and local religious calenders.

Table 3. Names and Dates of *Vrats* and Festivals Mentioned in This Book

Name(s) of *Vrat* or Festival	Time	Associated Deity	Associated Purpose
ANNUAL OR SEMI-ANNUAL			
Navarātri (Nine-Nights) or Durgā Pūjā	Caitra bright 1 to Caitra bright 9	Durgā and Devīs	general/ prosperity
Rāmanavamī (Rām's Ninth)	Caitra bright 9	Rām	general/ prosperity
Nṛsiṁh Caturdaśī	Vaiśākh dark 14	Nṛsiṁh	general
*Vaṭ Sāvitrī	Jyeṣṭh new moon	Sāvitrī	long life of husband and marital felicity
†Nāg Pañcamī (Snake's Fifth)	Śravaṇ bright 5	snakes	propitiate snakes; protect family
*Bahulā Cauth (Abundant Fourth)	Bhādrapad dark 4	cows with calves; Gaṇeś	sons; protection of children
*Halṣaṣṭhī (Plough-Sixth) or Lalahī Chaṭh	Bhādrapad dark 6	'Lalahī Mā'; the sun; 'Ṣaṣṭhī Devī'	sons; protection of children
Kṛṣṇa Janmāṣṭamī (Kṛṣṇa's Birth Eighth)	Bhādrapad dark 8	Kṛṣṇa	general/ prosperity
*Haritālikā or Tīj	Bhādrapad bright 3	Śiv and Pārvatī	long life of husband; marital felicity
*Ṛṣi Pañcamī	Bhādrapad bright 5	Seven Ṛṣis	to nullify effects of bad deeds and menstrual pollution
Lolark Chaṭh	Bhādrapad bright 6	Sūrya; Śiva	human fertility; sons
Mahālakṣmī (Great Lakṣmī)	Bhādrapad bright 8 to Āśvin dark 8	Lakṣmī	prosperity; children
Vāman Dvadaśī	Bhādrapad bright 12	Vāman; Viṣṇu	general
Ananta Caturdaśī	Bhādrapad full moon	Viṣṇu; Ananta	"get rid of troubles"
Candra Chaṭh	Āśvin dark 6	the moon; goddess Ṣaṣṭhī	protection of children

(continued)

Table 3 *(continued)*

*Jīvitputrikā (Living Son) or Jiutiyā	Āśvin dark 8	"Jiutiyā Mā"; Lakṣmī; Pārvatī	long life of sons
Śāradīya (fall) Navarātri or Naurātri	Āśvin bright 1 to Āśvin bright 10	Durgā and Devīs	general
†Daśaharā or Vijayā Daśamī (Victory Tenth)	Āśvin bright 10	Rām; Sītā; Lakṣman	general
*Karvā Cauth (Pitcher Fourth) or Karak Caturthī	Kārtik dark 4	Gaṇeś; the moon	long life of husband
*Aśok Āṣṭamī or Ahoī (Mā)	Kārtik dark 8	"Ahoī Mā";	well-being of sons
†Dīpāvalī (Festival of Lights)	Kārtik new moon	Lakṣmī	material well-being
†Annakūṭ or Govardhan	Kārtik bright 1	Kṛṣṇa	familial well-being
†Bhaiyādūj (Brother's Second) or Yamdvitīyā	Kārtik bright 2	brother/male family members	protection of brothers
*Ḍala Chaṭh (Sūrya Ṣaṣṭhī)	Kārtik bright 6	the sun	sons; children
Prabhodhinī Ekādaśī	Kārtik bright 11	Viṣṇu	general
†Makar Saṅkrāntī (Winter Solstice)	Pauṣ (when the sun enters the Makar zodiac)		
Saṅkaṭā Cauth	Phālguṇ dark 4	Gaṇeś; Saṅkaṭā Devī	children
Mahāśivarātri	Phālguṇ new moon	Śiv	general
†Holī (Festival of Colors)	Phālguṇ full moon	Kṛṣṇa	general

MONTHLY OR FORTNIGHTLY *VRATS*			
Gaṇeś Cauth	semi-monthly on 4th *tithi*	Gaṇeś	general
Ekādaśī	semi-monthly on 11th *tithi*	Viṣṇu	general
Pradoṣ	semi-monthly on 12th/13th *tithi*	Śiv	general
Śivarātri	monthly on 13th *tithi*	Śiv	general
Pūrṇimā	monthly on full moon day		
Amāvāsyā	monthly on new moon day		
SEASONAL			
Śītalā Aṣṭamī	8th in the dark half of Vaiśākh; Jyeṣṭh; Āṣāḍh and Śrāvaṇ	Śītalā	prevent fevers; pox and other "hot" diseases; family well-being
Śravaṇ Somvār	Monday *vrat* in the month of Śravaṇ		
Cāturmās Vrat Niyam (Four-months [monsoon] Vrat)	Āṣāḍh bright 12 to Kārtik bright 12		cleansing; purification; personal well-being
Aśūnya Śayan	2nd in the dark half of Śravaṇ, Bhādrapad, Āśvin and Kārtik		general

Notes:

*Observed by women only.

†Predominately a festival; fasting (or taking a *"vrat"*) is optional.

Appendix D

HARITĀLIKĀ (TĪJ) AND JĪVIT PUTRIKA (JIUTIYĀ) STORIES

In the following I present translations of procedures and stories *(vrat-kathā)* for the Tīj and Jiutiyā *vrats* from Hindi printed and oral sources. I have chosen two printed sources representing two styles of readily available paperback "*vrat* and festival procedure and story" books. One style employs a Sanskritic Hindi and draws primarily from the Sanskrit tradition (Purāṇas and Nibandhas); the other employs a more parochial style of Hindi, capturing current local language, practices and tales (normally orally transmitted from woman to woman). For the Jiutiyā Vrat, I also include two stories told to me by an illiterate woman (Shyamdevi) I interviewed which she said women recounted for this *vrat*.

TĪJ PROCEDURES AND STORIES

1. Source: Rampratap Tripathi, *Hinduoṅ ke Vrat, Parv aur Tyauhār* (1978).

On the third of the bright half of the month of Bhādrapad, the Haritālikā or Tīj Vrat is observed. This is a *vrat* which increases *saubhāgya* and its tradition is being carried on among Hindu women. On this *tithi* married women keep a fast, wear new clothes and give new clothes to daughters, sisters, et cetera. Among women this *vrat* has great importance. Months beforehand they eagerly await and prepare for this festival.

Procedure

Haritālikā is Pārvatī's *vrat*. Its śāstric rules go as follows. In the Hasta Nakṣatra of the third of the bright half of Bhādrapad, one should keep a waterless fast the whole day. Usually, after rising at three or four o'clock in the morning women take food, etc. and clean the home and after applying *ubtan* [a cosmetic paste rubbed over the body for cleaning and softening the skin] of sesame and *amala* [emblic myrobalan] they take a bath. After that, the *mūrtis* of Śiv and Pārvatī are placed in a special enclosure and they are established with the correct utterance of mantras; and *saṅkalp* for following this *vrat* is taken. At the time of making the resolve, having prayed for the destruction of all her sins [a woman] should perform the correct *pūjā* for Gaṇeś. [And] after the Gaṇeś *pūjā*, one should perform *pūjā* to Śiva and Pārvatī [with] the sixteen *upacāras*: invocation, seat, washing feet, water libation, sipping water, bath, clothes, *upavit*, beetle leaf, braziers [*kuṅcukī*], one more small cloth, and ornaments etc., according to one's capacity [*śakti*]. Upon completion of the *pūjā* one should make an offering of flowers with folded hands, circumambulate them and greet them. Then one should listen to this story and at the end, after putting sweets, clothes, *saubhāgya* items, *dakṣina*, etc. in a vessel or bamboo basket, one should give this to the *ācārya* or priest as *dān*. For the whole day and night of the third one should keep a waterless fast and at night keep awake singing. Then on the morning of the second day, on completing the *pūjā* one should perform the ending ceremony. In the night one should also tell other stories of Śiv and Pārvatī, sing their praises and perform *kīrtan*.

Kathā

Pārvatīji asked Lord Śaṅkar who was seated on the crystal rock of Kailaś mountain [which was] well-adorned with charming peaks—"Dev, please tell me about some such *vrat* which is the best among *vrats* and may be achieved with little effort. Please also tell me, by your kindness, about that great *dharm* by doing which I got you." Mahādevji said—"Devī! Just as among *nakṣatras* the moon is best, among planets the sun, among *varṇas* the Brahmans, among gods Viṣṇu, among rivers Gangā, among ancient writings the *Mahābhārat*, among Vedas the *Sāmaveda* and among the senses the mind; in the same way the Haritālikā Vrat is the best among all *vrats* for women. You have obtained me by following the ritual of this *vrat*."

Pārvatī said—"Lord! In what manner did I do the ritual of that *vrat*—please tell me this also." Upon Pārvatī's asking this question, Śivji said: "Pārvatī! There is a great mountain called Himalaya in the north of India. All around there are many rivers, pools, ascetic groves and ashramas of *ṛṣis*. You performed hard *tapasyā* for several years while living on that mountain. For many days you lived by eating only leaves, therefore people called you by the name *'aparṇā.'* Facing downwards you inhaled fire for twelve years. In the [hot] month of Vaiśākh you served Agni [god of fire], and during the cold days of Māgh you lived in water. Your father Himālaya started to become very worried because of your hard *tapasyā*. One day in the middle of this, the Devārṣi Nārad[3] approached Himālaya and said—'O King of Mountains! I have come to you to ask your daughter to be married to Lord Viṣṇu.'"

Himālaya became very pleased with what Devārṣi Nārad had to say. In an overwhelmed voice he said—'Devārṣi! If the Lord himself wants to marry my daughter then there is nothing more fortunate [*saubhāgya*] for me than this. I give my approval.' After receiving Himālaya's approval, Nāradji set out for Viṣṇu's abode and told [him] the whole story. Lord Viṣṇu thought for some time. Then, in a serious tone, he said—'Devārṣi, the daughter of Himālaya is in the past of Lord Śiv. She had the name Dakṣāyanī Satī in her previous life. In this life too she is performing difficult *tapasyā* to obtain Śivji. My marriage with her will not be proper. But also her *tapasyā* is not completed yet. She has to perform more difficult *tapasyā.'*

Nārad went to Pārvatī and said to her—'your beautiful body is not for all this *tapasyā*. What is the use of making your body emaciated? As the daughter of the king of mountains, what is the meaning of doing such extreme *tap?'* Pārvatī said to Nārad—'I am performing this hard *tap* only to obtain Lord Śaṅkar as my husband.' Nārad made extreme efforts to mislead her, thereby testing her so that he could see how deep Pārvatī's loyalty for Śiv was. But Pārvatī held her own in Nārad's test. This was her pledge—'Either I will be able to get Śivji as my husband or I will remain unmarried throughout my life.'

After Devārṣi Nāradji had gone, Himālaya himself came to take Pārvatī back home in order to talk her into marrying Lord Viṣṇu, but Pārvatī remained steadfast to her purpose. When Himālaya returned without hope, Pārvatī related her agony to her friend—'If I don't obtain Śivji as my husband, then I will give up my life.' The friend reassured Pārvatī and said—'If it is like this then you go to another forest to do *tapasyā*. One day or other Śaṅkarji will become pleased by your hard *tap* and [he] will certainly come to take you.'

---

3. Nārad is the notorious celestial "busy-body" who is always involving himself in the affairs of the gods and humans.

Going to another forest, Pārvatī again engaged in hard *tapasyā*. There, she made Śiv-*liṅg* out of sand, [and] she performed *pūjā* according to the rules on this date, the third of the bright half of Bhādrapad. Pārvatī's hard *tapasyā* had become a matter of concern to all the gods. Through the inspiration of the gods, Śaṅkarji felt compelled to decide to oblige Pārvatī. He asked Pārvatī to request a boon. Pārvatī said—'O Master [*nath*], if you are pleased with me then accept me as a wife.' Śivji said to Pārvatī obligingly—'Devī, your *sādhanā* is completed. I accept you as my wife [*ardhāṅganī*].'

Upon Lord Śiv's acceptance of Pārvatī's request, the gods showered flowers of *parijit*[4] from heaven. The *apsaras* [female celestial dancers] danced and the *gandharvas* [male celestial musicians] sang songs. When Himalaya heard about Pārvatī's success he became overjoyed. For many days he had been worried and searched for Pārvatī, but there had been no trace of her.

Then the marriage of Pārvatī with Śaṅkarji took place with great pomp and show. All the gods were members of the wedding party. The residents of the Himalayas were awed on seeing the various appearances of Śiv's *gaṇa* [horrific retinue].

The day on which the friends of Pārvatī carried her from the residence of Himālaya and took her to the grove and the day when Śivji conferred a boon on her was the day that became famous by the name *haritālikā*—due to being *'harita'* [kidnapped] *'alibhih'* [by the friends].

There is a special glory to hearing the Haritālikā story as well. By observing this *vrat* the *saubhāgya* of women remains permanent. The *saubhāgyavatī* women who do not observe this *vrat*, or who do not continue after having observed it for a few years, or who eat or drink during the fast—they will suffer severe troubles in this life and in the next life; this is also said in the *mahātmya*. If for some reason some *saubhāgyavatī* does not manage to keep this *vrat*, then she could have the *vrat* completed by some Brahman woman or by her husband.

4. *Parijat* — the coral tree (erythrina Indica); the name of one of the five trees said to exist in paradise.

2. Source:[5] Aśa Bahan and Lado Bahan, *Hinduoṅ ke Vrat aur Tyauhār: Vidhi, Vidhān, Kahāniyoṅ aur Citroṅ sahit* ["Hindu *Vrats* and Festivals: With Rules, Procedures, Stories and Pictures," n.d.]

"The Hartālikā Tīj Vrat"

This *vrat* is to be performed on the third of the bright half of Bhādra. On this day the women who want *suhāg* should make an image of Śaṅkar and Pārvatī out of sand and should perform *pūjā* to them. Women should decorate their homes with beautiful cloth placed around pillars, and should keep an all-night vigil, singing auspicious songs. Those women who perform this *vrat* become happy and dear to their husbands, like Pārvatī, and go to the abode of Śiv [after death].

Kathā *[Śiv narrating to Pārvatī]*

One time you went to the Himalaya mountains because you wanted me as your husband, you started to undertake very severe *tapasyā* on the bank of the Ganga. During your *tapasyā* Nārad-ji came to Himālaya and said to him—"Viṣṇu Bhagwan wants to marry your daughter. Viṣṇu sent me for this task [bearing this proposal]." Your father accepted this false-talking of Nārad. After this Nārad went to Viṣṇu and said—"Himālaya has decided to arrange your marriage with his daughter Pārvatī. Give your consent for this."

After Nārad left, your father Himālaya told you about your marriage with Lord Viṣṇu. When you heard this unexpected talk you became very sorrowful and cried out loudly. When you started to cry loudly one friend came and asked you what happened and you told her the problem. "Here I have started very hard *tapasyā* to get Śaṅkar as my husband, but my father wants to arrange a marriage with Viṣṇu. If you can help me then you save me. Otherwise I will commit suicide."

That friend consoled you and said—"I will go with you in one forest where your father will not find you." This time you took your friend's advice and went to a dense forest. Your father Himālaya searched for you here and there in the house but he did not find you. He became very worried because he was ready to

---

5. The last name of these two women authors is a Gujarati name; but the authors employ different dialects of Hindi found in U.P., Bihar and M.P.

arrange your marriage with Viṣṇu according to Nārad's [advice]. Incoherent, worried talk lead to him fainting, and then all the mountains came to know about this matter; they started to search you out. There in a cave on the bank of the Ganga, with your friend, you started to perform hard *tapasyā* in my name. On the third of the bright half of Bhādrapad, you kept a fast, made a Śiv-*liṅg* out of sand, performed *pūjā* and also kept an all-night vigil. Due to this difficult *tap-vrat* I was not able to remain sitting [in an ascetic posture] and I immediately had to come to your place of *pūjā*. According to your request and desire, I had to accept you in the form of my *ardhāṅganī* [as my wife]. After that I went at once to Kailash mountain. In the morning, when you were throwing out the *pūjā* material in the river, King Himālaya arrived at that place. He saw both of you and began tearfully to ask—"Daughter! How did you come here?" Then you told the story about Viṣṇu's [proposed] marriage. Your resolve being fulfilled, he [Himālaya] called you back to your home, and then you were married to me according to the procedure of the śāstras.

I will also tell you about the reason for the name Haritālikā Vrat. Because of the friend you were kept away [in the forest] [*harat*—friend + *alika*—kept away]. Śaṅkarji also told Pārvatī that whichever woman will do this *vrat* with great devotion will get endless *suhāg* just like you.

JĪVITPUTRIKA PROCEDURES AND STORIES

1. Source: Rampratap Tripathi, *Hinduoṅ ke Vrat, Parv aur Tyauhār* (1978).

Jīvitputrika Vrat is observed on the eighth of the dark half of Āśvin. It is primarily women with sons who observe this *vrat*. This *vrat* is performed for the long life of sons and for their well-being. The Purāṇas say that women who observe this *vrat* never suffer [on account of] their sons. It is an extremely popular *vrat* among the women of Uttar Pradesh, Bihar, Madhya Pradesh, etc., and women having limitless love and affection for their children observe this *vrat* with great faith and loyalty. If someone's son is rid of dangers then women will praise his mother's *jiutiyā*.

Procedure

Having cheerfully arisen in the early morning and after completing the daily chores women [should] purify themselves in a *tīrth* or pool and make the *saṅkalp* [expressing] their desire for the well-being of sons. In the evening time, having kept a waterless fast all day, women put on the *"jiutiyā"* made of cotton and listen to the *kathā*. Some rich women wear a *jiutiyā* made of gold or silver. Then in the night they tell the meritorious story and perform *kīrtan* and on the second day after bathing, etc., they give some *dān-dakṣina* to a Brahman woman whose husband is living and who is blessed with sons, and they take food.

In connection with Jiutiyā there are many folk stories current among women, but this following story has been given in the Purāṇas.

Kathā

In olden times there was a king named Jīmutavāhan. He was extremely religious, beneficient, kind, just and loved his subjects as if they were sons. One time, he went to the valley of Malayagiri to hunt deer and there he met a very beautiful princess named Malayavatī who had come to a temple to do *pūjā*. As soon as they met their eyes locked and they became spellbound with each other. The brother of Malayavatī had also come there. For a long time Malayavatī's father had thought about marrying his daughter with Jīmutavāhan, so, when Malayavatī's brother came to know that Jīmutavāhan had come there and that he had also fallen in love with her, he became very happy. Jīmutavāhan and Malayavatī did not lapse in their duties to protect the royal glory, even after feeling the pains of extreme love. The princess returned to her father's residence with her friends, and in vain Jīmutavāhan made efforts to console his heart while he wandered around in search of deer.

After some time, while wandering on the peaks of Malayagiri, King Jīmutavāhan heard in the far distance the sound of a pathetic cry of some woman. His compassionate heart became overwhelmed. He followed the sound of the crying and came to the vicinity of the woman. Upon humbly asking, he found out that according to a previously-made promise, her only son Śaṅkhacurṇ had to go this day as food for Garuḍ.[6] According to the compromise agreement that had been made between the Nāgas [snakes] and Garuḍ, one snake was to regularly present himself on the peak of Malayagiri as food for Garuḍ. Upon hearing the distress

6. Garuḍ is the animal vehicle of Viṣṇu; represented as a half-man, half-vulture.

of Śaṅkhacurṇ's mother, Jīmutavāhan's heart was filled with sympathy and compassion, for Śaṅkhacurṇ was the only support she had in her old age. Because of the death of his father at the beginning of his youth, the mother had brought him up with great hope and fondness.

Jīmutavāhan assured the mother of Śaṅkhacurṇ saying, "Mother, I myself am ready to go as food for Garuḍ in place of your son. You should abandon this worry and sadness." Having said this, Jīmutavāhan took the red cloth from the hands of Śaṅkacurṇ that was worn for that occasion, put it on himself, bowed to the mother and asked permission to depart. The snake mother was wonderstruck. Her heart became more heavy from compassion. She made great effort to stop Jīmutavāhan, but how could he be stopped? He promptly took the path toward the prescribed mountaintop to be food for Garuḍ, while the mother and son remained staring at him with sadness and amazement.

When Garuḍ came to his food peak at the fixed time, eagerly scanning here and there, his strong beak collided with the food and the whole peak reverberated. His beak got a big shock when it collided with the strong body of Jīmutavāhan and a frightening noise was produced from the impact. Garuḍ's head whirled, being stunned with much pain. [Soon,] he became quietly stable while there King Jīmutavāhan remained, lying still as before, wrapped in red cloth like the other snakes.

After some time, when Garuḍ became cool and composed, he asked—"Brother, who are you? I have been doing this action continually for years but I have never encountered such a strong body. I am eager to make you acquaintance." King Jīmutavāhan, lying wrapped in the cloth, replied in this way—"O king of birds! I am Jīmutavāhan. I could not bear the pathetic cry of the snake Śaṅkhacurṇ's mother; therefore I have come here to fill your stomach in place of him. You can eat me without uncertainty."

The moonlit glory of Jīmutavāhan spread all over the three *lokas* [earth, heaven and the nether region]. The king of the birds, Garuḍ, had already heard stories about his honor. His rigid heart started to melt from the fire of this great model who was a remover of others' troubles and a most righteous king. He raised the king with great respect and entreated him to ask for a boon while begging forgiveness for his faults.

King Jīmutavāhan had no scarcity of material things in the three worlds but he did not want to make the grace of the bird king Garuḍ fruitless. He said humbly and in a voice with contentment and gratitude—"O bird king, I am very much obliged for your unerring kindness. My wish is that as many snakes as you have eaten up until now please return them to life through the power of the knowledge of revivification so that no other mother should have to suffer like the mother of Śaṅkhacurṇ."

The beneficent voice of King Jīmutavāhan was filled with so much pain that the bird king Garuḍ became restless. With a choked throat he granted the boon to be fulfilled upon the king's word. He made the snakes come back to life through the unfailing knowledge of revivification. In the world of the snakes an endless sea of happiness surged due to the king's compassion and beneficence. From all directions a shower of blessings fell for his achievements and the scent of nectar was spread through his moonlit glory which pervaded the three worlds.

At this time, the father and brother of Princess Malayavatī had also arrived there searching for him. They arranged the marriage of Malayavatī and Jīmutavāhan with great pomp and show.

This blessed event took place on the eighth of the dark half of Āśvin. Since then, the importance of this festival has been spread among the whole of women's society [*strījāti*]. All women complete this *vrat* with great faith and devotion for the sake of the long life of their sons.

A Folk Tale *(Lok Kathā)*

Many stories are current in relation to Jiutiyā. One of them goes as follows.

In a certain jungle a kite used to live on a *samar* [cotton] tree. At a little distance from there, in a ditch covered with bushes, was the lair of a female jackal. They lived together in harmony. Whatever the kite hunted, she gave a share of it to the jackal, and the jackal also used to pay back the kite's generosity. Everyday the jackal would save something or other for the kite. In this way, their days passed by happily.

Once, in this very jungle, the neighboring women were observing the Jiutiyā Vrat. The kite saw this. She had the memory of her past life. She took an oath [*pratijña*] to complete this *vrat*, and, following her, the jackal also took an oath to complete this *vrat*. They both observed the *vrat* with great faith and devotion. The whole day they both kept a waterless fast, remaining without food, and wished for the welfare of all creatures. But, when night came, the jackal began to become restless with hunger and thirst. It became difficult to pass the time. She went quietly toward the jungle and finding some left-over flesh and bones from the remains of wild animals she brought them back and began to eat as silently as possible. The kite was not aware of what was going on; but, when while chewing a bone, the jackal made a cracking noise, the kite asked—"Sister, what are you eating?"

The jackal said—"Sister! what should I do? Because of hunger my bones keep on cracking. How can there be hearty food and drink while keeping such a *vrat?*" But the kite was not so stupid. She realized everything. She said—"Sister, why are you speaking lies? You are chewing a bone and saying that your bones are cracking because of hunger. You should have considered before whether you would be able to fulfill this *vrat* or not."

Becoming ashamed, the jackal went far away. She felt overwhelmed by hunger and thirst so, after proceeding some distance, she ate and drank until her stomach was full. But the kite remained in the same state [fasting] the whole night.

The outcome too was befitting. All the children that the kite had were healthy, beautiful and good, while each child of the jackal died within a few days of birth.

Jiutiyā Stories Told by Shyamdevi

(a) There were seven brothers who went for pilgrimage, or to do business. So the wives drove their [the brothers'] sister out of the house and said to her, "Bring pounded rice without using a mortar and pestle." Having gone to the jungle, she sat down and cried. The birds came from above and asked, "Why are you crying?" Her name was Soncirai. Soncirai said, "What to do? My sisters-in-law have given me rice to pound. How can I pound it?" So the birds pounded the rice with their beaks. She took the rice and returned home. Then they [the sisters-in-law] said, "Bring a strainer filled with water." So she kept on pouring water in the strainer and it kept on flowing out. Then again she started to cry. At that time, Śiv and Pārvatī were passing by. They asked, "Daughter, why are you crying?" She said, "They have asked me to fill this sieve with water but it keeps flowing out." They [Śiv and Pārvatī] gave such a curse *(śrap)* that the holes were closed. Then she carried the water and returned. [Thus] one should say the name of Mahādev [Śiv] daily. This is a story that is told [during Jiutiyā].

(b) There was a kite and a jackal. The kite asked, "O sister, why are you not eating today?" She replied, "I am the votary of Jiutiyā Mā." So the jackal said, "I will also do that." And the kite said, "So be it." So the jackal stayed there the whole day, did *pūjā-paṭh* and returned to its hole when midnight came. It had stored the bones of some animal [in its hole]. At night it started chewing the bones and made sounds. The kite asked the jackal, "What is that sound coming from your hole?" The jackal said to herself, "What shall I do?" "O sister, did I not keep the *vrat?* When I just turn, all my bones crack!" When a long time had gone, Śiv and Pārvatī were passing by, and the jackal fell at their feet and said to them, "I was a *vratin*—but I ate. So I couldn't maintain the Jīvit (Vrat)." So they gave a curse [boon] that she become well [that absolved her].

NOTES

INTRODUCTION

1. According to E. Klinger, "In the broadest sense, vows are unconditional promises to do something specific—good or evil. In the narrower sense, they are unqualified pledges to do good, not evil, and as such they are directed solely to God" (1987, 303).

2. There are other words in Hindi which refer to taking "pledges," such as *praṇ*, which used with the verbs *karnā* or *rakhnā* means "to take a pledge," "to keep a vow." The words *pratigñā* and *bhujā uṭhānā* also mean to resolve, to swear (to do a thing).

3. See William Christian, Jr. (1972, 119–28). When *vratas* are turned into conditional vows, they are usually called *manautī;* from the Urdu word *manaut*, "to resolve." Examples of these are described in chapter six.

4. Santoṣī Mā and her *vrat* is documented, for example, by A. L. Basham, 1976; and M. Robinson, 1979.

5. See, for example, Prabhati Mukherjee's *Hindu Women: Normative Models* (1978); Lynn Bennett's *Dangerous Wives and Sacred Sisters* (1983); Julia Leslie's *The Perfect Wife* (1988); and Vanaja Dhruvarajan's *Hindu Women and the Power of Ideology* (1989).

6. For an interesting application of Bynum's insight, see Lynn Bennett's description of a cycle of goddess myths shared by men and women in ritual contexts in which she argues that the image of Durgā "reflects a predominately male view, focused on the problematic woman, while Pārvatī presents Hindu women's own idealized perceptions of themselves and the problems they experience" (1983, 274).

7. One exception is Kathryn Hansen, who in a 1992 essay explores the relationship between *tapas* and *strīdharma* while surveying forms of "heroic" behavior among Hindu women. However, since *vrats* as such are not the subject of her study, she does not detail how rites like *vrats* can be used by women to pursue their own spiritual goals.

1. SIX WOMEN

1. Accordingly, much has been written about Banaras, Kashi or Varanasi, over the centuries by both Hindus and foreigners. For example, see Havell 1933; Vidyarthi et. al. 1979; Eck 1982; Freitag 1989; and Hertel and Humes 1993. Hertel and Humes write that "[m]ore than any other *tīrtha* (pilgrimage site) it [Banaras] is looked to as representing the essence of Hindu place, values, and customs; that is, its claim to supremacy lies not in its uniqueness but in the fullness with which it embraces and portrays Hindu places, values and ways" (1993, 7).

2. For more information on the women I interviewed and on my fieldwork methods, see appendix B.

3. As is the case in many patriarchal cultures, men commonly speak on behalf of their female dependents (especially wives) in India.

4. The criteria for selecting the six women's interviews from among the total full interviews conducted were that the woman was based in Uttar Pradesh, preferably from Banaras; that the interview was complete or at least contained a large amount of information on *vrats* and the woman's religious life in general; that the interviews selected represented a range of age, caste, marital and educational status; and that there was one family (affinal or consanguinal) related pair, such as mother and daughter, for comparative purposes.

5. See also T. N. Madan (1987) where he notes in his introduction (p. 8) that "the interpretive endeavour knows no finality. . . . Each understanding is a preface to yet another, each 'arrival' a 'point of departure.' As the questions change, so do the answers, and the completeness of description is inevitably deferred."

6. Lakshmibai (d. 1854) was the Brahman-born queen of the princely state of Jhansi. She has been compared to Joan of Arc because some time after her husband died and she became regent, she donned warrior's clothes and led her troops into battle against the British during the disturbances which spread over North India in 1857. She was killed while defending one of the forts and immediately found a permanent place as a heroine in the early history of India's struggle for independence.

7. There can be more than one *kuldevtā* in a family. Among the women I interviewed in Banaras, *kuldevtās* are invoked, worshipped and propitiated with their "share of blessed food" (as one woman put it) before such occasions as the *upanāyaṇa* and marriage *saṁskāras*, and before such significant events as "house openings" *(gṛha praveś)*. In some areas like Rajasthan a *kuldevtā* seems to be both more often a localized deity (or deified personage) and to play a more significant role in

the family's worship practice and ancestral/religious identity than I found to be the case in Banaras. (On the significance of *kuldevtās* in Rajasthan, see Harlan 1992.) A person's "chosen" deity *(iṣṭadevtā)*—which may or may not correspond with the *kuldevtā*—seemed to be more significant than the *kuldevtā* in the devotional lives of the mostly Brahman women I interviewed in Uttar Pradesh.

8. That is, they are of pan-Indian importance, as opposed to being of regional, local or sectarian importance. Agehananda Bharati has asserted that: "Basically there are two types of occasions which mark the Hindu, Buddhist and Jain pilgrimage. One of them is the fulfillment of a *vrata* [here Bharati mostly means a conditional vow] . . . , the other is [for] *darsan*. . . . The latter is more diffuse and less urgent. . . . *Vrata*, 'vows,' are often highly specific and they usually require a visit to one place only. It is the place where a deity [usually a goddess] specializes, as it were, in repairing damage, or balancing some need of the pilgrim who seeks remedy" (1970, 94).

9. S. Kakar says of these ghosts that: "The malignant spirits . . . are collectively known as *bhuta-preta*, though Hindu demonology distinguishes between the various classes of these supernatural beings. The *bhuta* . . . originates from the souls of those who meet an untimely death, while a *preta* is the spirit of a child who has died in infancy or was born deformed (1982, 56).

10. There are parallels between some of Sarita's comments here about women's natural compassion (softness) contrasted with men's "hardness" and Margaret (Trawick) Egnore's statements concerning perceptions of Tamil women. She writes: "*Bhakti* is religion of emotion, of feeling . . . and without it all religion is empty. . . . Women are regarded as inherently more religious than men, because they have naturally this power of feeling, of suffering for others, of love. It is often said that male worshippers who seek union with the deity must 'soften,' that is, they must become like females, before their desires will be consummated" (1980, 20–21).

11. I did not pursue her relationship with her guru or the circumstances in which she met him. However, it is not unusual for older women especially to acquire a guru (see next profile).

12. Banaras is teeming with small street shrines, but I saw more Hanumān shrines, with florescent orange-painted reliefs of Hanumān, than those of any other deity. Many of them had been recently erected.

13. Unfortunately, the English words "belief" and "faith," as the anthropologist Rodney Needham and the historian of religion W. Cantwell Smith have demonstrated respectively, are probably even more

mercurial than their Hindi equivalents *viśvās* and *śraddhā*. Nevertheless, though I proceed with caution, and would not want to rest any important conclusions solely on this semantic distinction, I think examining a distinction in usage between the two words can help to elucidate aspects of women's relationship to *vrats* and/or some of the functions that *vrats* play in Hindu women's lives.

14. Luschinsky writing about Senapuri women, notes: "A man or woman who is very religious-minded can become the disciple of a . . . *guru*. Such a person is then known as a *gurumukh*. A number of village women become *gurumukhs* in their later years. Very few young women do so. The procedure is this. A woman chooses a person devoted to religious pursuits, usually a Brahman, whom she would like to have for her personal *guru* and this person whispers some sacred verses of scriptures in her ear. He cautions her never to repeat these verses to anyone. He also tells her when and and how often she should recite these verses, which god she should worship and how, what she can eat and cannot eat, and how she should behave. . . . Most of the men whom Senapur women have selected for *gurus* give their disciples ethical counsel. They tell them not to lie or steal . . . that it is sinful for them to have sexual relations with anyone except their husbands. They also usually tell them that it is wrong for them to think too much about worldly affairs. Instead they are advised to keep their minds constantly on their tutelary god" (1962, 731–32). For a description of householder women seeking gurus (in Bengal) and on the emotional and spiritual relationship they often develop with him, see Manisha Roy (1975, 138–45).

15. Such pilgrimage tours are now commonly arranged by travel companies and the former hardship of getting to a distant *tīrtha* has been considerably reduced for many. As most people in North America would choose a holiday destination based on "sea, sand and sun," Indians (especially middle-class Indians) often choose one or several of hundreds of pilgrimage sites in which to spend their holidays or even "honeymoons."

16. For descriptions of Karvā Cauth in U.P., see Marriot 1955, 203–6; Wadley 1975; Khare 1976, chap. 6. A Banaras bangle-seller whom I got to know told me that every Karvā Cauth day his shop was thronged by women from western U.P. and the Panjab, buying bangles for the *vrat* day.

17. See, for example, *The Times of India* (20 October 1984, p. 1) newspaper reports about the celebration of Karvā Cauth by huge numbers of women in the capital and its environs.

18. *Āṅvla* is "emblic myrobalan," a tree which produces small, plumlike, green, and very sour fruit, full of iron and vitamin C.

19. The Satyanārāyaṇ Vrat has become quite popular in North India. It can be undertaken at any time, although the full moon day, because of its natural auspiciousness, seems to be the favored day for it. The Satyanārāyaṇ Vrat is often a sponsored occasion marking for the sponsor a time of special difficulty or special prosperity (as Raheja and Marriott have noted in their translation of the *kathās* for this *vrat* for use in courses at the University of Chicago). This *vrat* is always officiated by a priest who performs or guides the *pūjā* and recites the *kathā*. In Shyamdevi's case, she liked to fast on the full moon day and then go down, often with her niece, to the Ganges to bathe and to sit on the *ghaṭs* with others as a local *pujārī* read out the story.

20. This is a very well-known pilgrimage circuit around Banaras. As Eck notes: "To follow the Panchakroshi Road around Kashi [Banaras] is, they say, to circle the world. The pilgrims who circumambulate Kashi on this sacred way take five days for the trip and visit 108 shrines along the way" (1982, 42).

21. She has observed: Jyeṣṭh and Kārtik (Nirjal) Ekādaśī, Mahāśivarātri,the first and last day of Naurātra, Kṛṣṇa Janmāṣṭamī, Tīj, Lalahā Chaṭh (which she kept for only a couple of years, and performed it the same way as Jiutiyā), Jiutiyā, Karvā Cauth, and Pūrṇimā.

22. The Gāyatrī mantra is found in RV 3.62.10 and is addressed to the Savitṛ (the sun). According to N. N. Bhattacharyya (*A Glossary of Indian Religious Terms and Concepts* [Delhi: Manohar, 1990], 63), it "is interpreted as a prayer to the source and inspirer of everything. Literally it is: 'we contemplate that esteemed refulgence of the divine Savitṛ who may inspire our intellects.'"

2. *VRATA* IN THE HINDU TEXTUAL TRADITION

1. In the nineteenth century the Indologist F. Max Müller testified that *vrata* "is one of many words which, though we may perceive their one central idea, and their original purport, we have to translate by various terms in order to make them intelligible in every passage where they occur" (1964 [1891], 236, n.2).

2. For a full discussion of this controversy, see Kane (1974, 5,1:1–21; and Apte (1947, 407–88). Max Müller (1964, 236) took *vrata* to be derived from the root *vri* meaning "originally what is enclosed, protected, set apart," whereas the Sanskritist W. D. Whitney held that *vrata* derived rather from the root *vṛt*—"to proceed, turn"—thus meaning "procedure, course, line of movement, course of action, conduct or behaviour, obligatory actions imposed by religion or morality" (Apte 1964, 411). Later, the lexicographer V. S. Apte, accepting the *vṛt* derivation, focused on

"route or circular path." Apte held that the divine *vratas* mentioned in the *Ṛgveda* mean the heavenly routes, the divine rounds, the periodical movements around the sky closely adhered to by the gods themselves (Kane, 1974, 5,1:3). Finally, Kane refuted Apte on the grounds that Apte's derivation of the meaning does not at all account for the way the term is used in many passages in the *Ṛgveda*.

3. O. Böehtlingk and R. Roth, Sanskrit Wörterbuch, 7 vols. (St. Petersburg: Buchdruckerei des Kaiserlichen Akademia der Wissenshaften, 1855–75).

4. Kane suggests that choosing involves willing and thus the root *vṛ* can also mean "to will," and *vṛ* with the suffix *ta* can mean "what is willed," and by extension "law or ordinance" (1976, 5,1:5). Thus, he continues: "the several meanings of the word '*vrata*.' which I derive from the root *vṛ*, are command or law, obedience or duty, religious or moral practices, religious worship or observance, sacred or solemn vow or undertaking, then any vow or pattern of conduct" (1974, 5,1:6). Other scholars take the word *vrata* in its early vedic context to mean simply laws in general or ordinances of the *ṛta* (Banerjee 1946, 35). The *ṛta* is "cosmic order," or the universal absolute and eternal "code" which W. Norman Brown describes as "impersonal in itself and entirely objective and mechanistic in its operation" (1978, 111). J. Gonda takes *vrata* to mean fixed and regular behavior, and personal function (1975, 1:97,167).

In the *Ṛgveda*, the gods are spoken of as having their own *vratas*, and as ruling over the *vratas* of the animate and inanimate world; (RV 3.4.7) "Praising the Ṛta they (the gods) proclaim the Ṛta; observers of their duty *(vrata)* they concentrate upon their duty *(vrata)*" (Brown 1978, 112). The god most often (though not exclusively) mentioned in connection with both the *ṛta* and with *vratas* in the *Ṛgveda* is Varuṇa. He is portrayed as the "trustee of *ṛta*," in Bloomfield's words. He also has a direct influence in human lives through his role as a divine punisher and rewarder of those who violate or observe the *vratas* ordained by the gods (see Day 1982, 32 and chap. 2, n.5). The following RV prayer is a recognition of human inclination to break the gods' *vratas*, and it is to the god Varuṇa that the plea is directed: "Whatever . . . [vrata] of thine, O Varuṇa! we may break day to day as people (subjects) . . . do not reduce us to death" (RV 1.25.1–2, quoted in Kane 1974, 5,1:9). It is in this role that Varuṇa is sometimes addressed as "*dhṛta-vrata*" (upholder of the *vratas*). The gods Agni and Sūrya are often called "*vratapaḥ*" (protector or lord of *vratas*) in the *Ṛgveda* and later Saṁhitās.

Vrata and the word *dharma* are also semantically connected in the *Ṛgveda* and in some usages their meanings "appear to have coalesced," as Kane puts it. Among other passages he cites RV 7.89.5 to illustrate his claim: "when we destroy (or violate) your *dharmans* through heedlessness . . . , do not harm us, O Varuṇa, on account of that sin" (1974, 5,1:20 and n. 31). There are also passages where the three words *ṛta, vrata* and *dharma* occur together and appear to mean much the same thing. For example, the three terms appear in RV 5.63.7: "'O Wise Mitra and Varuṇa! according to your fixed rule of conduct *(dharman)* you guard your ordinances *(vrata)* with the wonderful power of an *asura;* you rule over the whole world according to the principle of cosmic order *(Ṛta);* you establish in the heaven the Sun that is a brilliant chariot.' In RV 5.72.2 and 6.70.3 *vrata* and *dharman* occur together, while in RV 1.65.2; 2.27.8; 3.4.7; and 10.65.8, *Ṛta* and *vrata* occur together in a manner which suggests that they carry equal force with *vrata*, according to Kane" (cited in Day 1982, 256, n.6).

5. I did not come across any references to specific gender related *vratas*. It is entirely possible that in vedic literature women's maternal functions could have been called their *"vrata,"* as their wifely functions came to be called in later Smṛti literature.

6. For example, the verse RV I.22.19: "'Mark the deeds of Viṣṇu, the helpful friend of Indra, whereby he watches over his ordinances [*vrata*]' occurs also in TS I.3.6.2, AV VII.26.6, Vajapeya Saṁhitā VI.4" (quoted in Kane 1974, 5,1:22).

7. Kane (1974, 5,1:23) cites TS 2.5.5.6 "this is his vrata (vow); he should not speak what is untrue, should not eat flesh, should not approach a woman (for sexual intercourse), nor should his apparel be washed with water impregnated with cleansing salt; for, all these things the gods do not do." And, TS 5.7.6.1: "birds are indeed fire; when one who has performed Agnicayana [an important vedic fire sacrifice, the altar for which is in the shape of a bird] eats the (flesh of) birds, he would be eating fire and would meet with disaster (or distress); (therefore) he should observe this vrata (not to eat bird's flesh) for a year, for vrata does not extend beyond a year."

8. The "other secondary meaning of *vrata,*" Kane writes, "seems to be *upavāsa* (i.e. Yajamāna's passing the night in the Darśa-iṣṭi and the Pūrṇamāsa-iṣṭi near the Gārhapatya [central home fire] and other fires, or [and?] reducing his intake of food or fasting): 'that he performs *upavāsa* in Darśa and Pūrṇamāsa iṣṭis is so because the gods do not partake of the offerings made by one who has not undergone *vrata;* therefore he undergoes *upavāsa* with the thought 'the gods may partake of my offering' (Ait.Br. VII.II)" (1974, 5,1:26).

9. A. B. Keith and A. Macdonell 1912, 2:342. References cited include: AV 6.133.2; TS 6.2.5, 3.4; ŚB 3.2.2, 10.17; 4.2.15.

10. See Eliade 1958, chapter on *dīkṣa;* also Vesci 1985.

11. Chakladar 1962, 2:569. For more descriptions of these now obsolete *vratas* that every student of the Veda had to undergo, see Kane 1974, 2:370–73.

12. This important two-day ritual, called the *agnyādhāna* (or *agnyādheya)* was performed when the young head of a family considered "himself capable of assuming responsibility for his own household and of celebrating the prescribed rites in his own name" (Vesci 1985, 150).

13. In describing the *agnyādhāna* ceremony (based on the Bhāradvāja Śrauta sūtras of the Taittirīya school), Vesci (1985, 159) writes: "During his *vrata* the new *yajamāna* must make a vow not to eat meat, not to have sexual intercourse with any woman, not to sit on high stools and not to sleep. Finally, on the eve of the day when the fireplaces have to be erected, the *yajamāna* ends his period of *vrata* by observing, together with his wife, the prescribed fast and by keeping vigil the whole night playing the *vina* and watching over the provisional fire lest it should die out. The fast and vigil are explained by the texts both as a form of *tapas* to strengthen the *yajamāna* and as a way of paying honour to the Deities who are present at the ceremony and of thus fulfilling one's duties of host in their regard."

14. Ap.DS 2.1.1ff., cited in Kane 1974, 5,1:27.

15. McGee 1987, 22. She provides specific references to these rites from the Gṛhyasūtras in note 17. Anyone familiar with the *Atharvaveda* would note the similarity of these rites with some of the "magical" formulas and charms for the same sorts of purposes, as McGee herself comments. See also Margaret Stutley 1980.

16. For a detailed discussion of *prāyaścitta*, see Kane 1974, 4:1–30; and Bhattacharya 1962.

17. Bühler, trans. See also Manu 11.170, 182.

18. M. N. Dutt, trans. (1978 [1908]). See also Yāj.Sm. 3.251, 252, 267, 270, 283, 301.

19. Neither a single author nor a single date can be assigned to the *Mahābhārata*. It was a popular work that underwent numerous changes in style and language before it was committed to writing. The oldest portions, the core Bhārata story, are hardly older than 400 B.C.E. The last books, the Śanti and Anuśāsana *parvans*, an introduction to the first book and later dharmaśāstric material (redacted into various parts of the epic) were added between 200 B.C.E. and 200 C.E. The complete text according to current views cannot be later than the fourth or fifth century C.E. Kane believes that the extant *Mahābhārata* is later than the extant *Manusmṛti* because, among other things, there are vers-

es in the epic which correspond exactly with verses in Manu (Kane 1974, 1:344).

20. It has been noted by numerous scholars that while there are a number of contradictory views in the epic, reflecting its history and the interests of its multiple redactors, one central tension is that between *dharma* and *mokṣa;* or, more specifically, between the duties and responsibilities of this-worldly life, on the one hand, and on the other, the abandonment of dharmically-ordered society for the pursuance of personal power and/or *mokṣa* through ascetical practices. Thus in the epic *dharma* and the practice of austerities are alternately shown to be antithetical to each other and necessary to each other. An example of the futility and potential dangers of asceticism is illustrated in the well-known Jaratkāru story (1.13.8ff., 1.41.5ff.), the central message of which is that there is no point in being "of strict vows" if one does not beget (male) offspring to fulfill one's debts to the ancestors.

21. This praiseworthy behavior is at various points in the epic contrasted with the "fallen" state of Brahmans and humanity in general in the decadent Kali Yuga. For example, in Mārkeṇḍeya's description of the Kali Yuga (3.188.25ff.) he says: "Men who had always been firm in their vows at a śrāddha or sacrifice will be harnessed with greed and exploit one another. . . . The brahmins shall find fault with the veda and abandon their vows. . . ."

22. Another reference, however, provides a different possibility. Adiparvan 121.24 says: "The Bhargava voiced his assent and gave him the weapons, and all his lore of weaponry with its secrets and vows" *(sa rahasya vratam ca iva).*

23. Kane 1974, 5,1:55. See also *Rāmāyaṇa* 5.28.5, 7.76.2, 7.75.25 where Shudras are forbidden vedic instruction and also the right to "practice religious austerities or penance" (Bhagat 1976, 253).

24. Just one example of demons performing such ascetic *vratas* is in the story of Sunda and Upasunda (1.201.5–7).

25. Both Jayal (1966) and Bhagat (1976) mention and provide references for penances and austerities performed for the birth or well-being of children. Jayal (p. 152) says: "For the well-being of sons mothers performed various penances, kept fasts and offered prayers. Kausalya and Kunti propitiated the deities with fast, penances and various rites and ceremonies" (Ramāyaṇa 2.20.48; 25 [whole sec.]; Mbh. 5.83.37ff.). Bhagat adds (p. 257): "It was common to perform austerities with a view to having a son."

26. It is called the Vaṭ Sāvitrī Vrat, and is observed over the new moon day in the month of Jyeṣṭh (in North India). For textual references,

see Kane 1974, 5,1:91–94; for textual descriptions, see AP chap. 194, MP chaps. 208–14; for descriptions of this *vrat* in practice, see: B. A. Gupte 1919, 238–45; McGee 1987, 469–75; Tewari 1991, 40–43; Duvvury 1991, 198–200.

27. Mbh. 3.281.18. The Sanskrit reads: *niyama vrata saṁsiddha mahābhaga pativratā*. While this clause could be translated in a different (and less dramatic) way than van Buitenen has done, I am accepting his rendering as close to the overall intent of the author.

28. The word *tapas* is derived from the root *tap* meaning to "irradiate heat," to "shine," to "consume by heat," to "suffer." In its early vedic context, Vesci writes: "As the heat of the sun or of fire, *tapas* penetrates, without leaving any immediately visible traces, into the depths of those things on which it alights and transforms from within. As a verb, or as a verbal participle *tap* is . . . linked with *śṛta*" (meaning cooked, boiled, especially as in boiled milk: Monier-Williams, *A Sanskrit-English Dictionary*, 1088). "Its effects," Vesci continues, "are psychologically felt by the person who experiences it and who exerts it on any given object, as, e.g., the ritual implements to which the priest transmits energy, not only through the direct action of the fire but also through his internal ascetic power." Thus the term *tapas* assumed a bipolarity, "which includes both the end to be achieved and the means to achieve or produce it" (1985, 21) and which has remained characteristic of it to the present day.

On *tapas* see, for example, C. Blair, *Heat in the Ṛgveda and Atharvaveda* (New Haven: AOS, 1961); D. K. Knipe, *In the Image of Fire—The Vedic Experience of Heat* (Delhi: Motilal Banarsidass, 1975); Vesci 1985; and Bhagat 1976, especially pp. 14–27.

29. Vesci 1985, 58. Vesci later argues that in the *Atharvaveda*, "one can observe a new phase in the cosmicization of the Sacred Action in the fact that specific tasks hitherto reserved for the Divinities have transferred to the ritual implements," like the sacrifical pot (*gharma*, also lit. "heat") which as it is heated and the milk inside bubbles over is said to "milk" out the present, the past and the future, discharging "all the duties (*vrata*) of the Gods" (AV 4.2.2, quoted in Vesci, 66).

30. Vesci describes this point of view in the context of the AV, the TS (e.g., 6.2.2.7), and the ŚB.

31. "Without the help of a Supreme Divinity which, no matter how capricious in its favours, knows also how to be merciful, the task of the priest engaged in an Action without appeal, far from having been facilitated, has become terribly complicated. . . . Now it is the rite itself which has to overcome the obstacles and it can only do so by itself through the help of its own creative principle: the heat" (Vesci 1985, 83).

32. This idea of the potential destructiveness of excess heat persisted in various forms and contexts in Indian history. Besides the havoc-provoking excess heat generated by severe asceticism attributed to various yogis, *asuras*, and so forth, in the epics and other literature, diseases, fever, emotions (rage, passion), and of course sex are either effects or producers of "excess heat."

33. For example, the woman Ahalyā is described in the *Rāmāyaṇa* (1.49.17) as "magnificent, flaming in ascetic energy" after practicing austerities (see Bhagat 1976, 15).

34. "*Satyavat*" also means, according to Monier-Williams' *Sanskrit-English Dictionary* (1135–36), "sincere," "pure," "virtuous," and "effectual."

35. See W. Norman Brown's article, "Duty as Truth" (1978).

36. For example, in the Mbh., truth-vows are made by Damayantī (3.54.17–20), the "frog princess" (3.37.79), Draupadī (3.252.20), and Sītā (3.275.20).

37. A comprehensive overview of the form and concept of *vrata* in this corpus of texts has been undertaken by P. V. Kane (1974) and, more recently, by Mary McGee (1987). McGee's treatment is more thematically developed and critical than Kane's (and she also pays attention, as Kane does not, to gender as a category of analysis).

The Purāṇas ("ancient stories") are compendia of Hindu religious lore—ritual, philosophy, myths, genealogies—gathered and edited primarily between c. 400 and 1400 C.E. There are conventionally eighteen "major" *(mahā)* and eighteen "minor" *(upa)* Purāṇas, though there has been no full consensus on which Purāṇas qualify for which designation. Unlike the Dharmaśāstras and Nibandhas, the Purāṇas are not particularly systematic in their presentation of materials. They also tend to be slanted towards one of three sectarian directions: Śaiva, Vaiṣṇava or Śakta.

The Nibandhas were written in Sanskrit by Brahman pandits between the twelfth and eighteenth centuries. (The term *nibandha* means a "binding together"; in this case, of explanations and examples of *dharma* [see McGee 1987, 41].) Surviving Nibandha texts number in the hundreds; some of them are mammoth works, comprising five or six volumes. What the *nibandhakāras* (writers) did essentially was to gather information on a variety of dharmic topics from a myriad of sources including the early Dharmasūtras, epics, Dharmaśāstras and commentaries, Purāṇas, as well as local practices and customs, and organize all this (often contradictory) information into systematic presentations. At the same time, the *nibandhakāras* would add their own learned opinions. These treatises tend to be nonsectarian.

38. An example is the Bhīmadvādaśī *Vrata* described in the *Matsyapurāṇa*, chap. 69.

39. *Amantravat* means one who does not have the authority to says mantras because of his or her lack of vedic education and because of ritual impurity.

40. The *Vratarāja* Nibandha was composed in Banaras. It is a relatively late Nibandha that incorporated sections from many earlier works, and, as the title suggests, it focuses entirely on the subject of *vrata*.

41. *The Garuḍapurāṇa*, trans. by a board of scholars, ed. J. L. Shastri, vol. 12, chap. 116 (Delhi: Motilal Banarsidass, 1978). Further references in the text to the *Garuḍapurāṇa* are to this translation.

42. As in the Purāṇas, some of the *vratas* sound so contrived (the purpose, merits and procedure being tediously repetitious) that they appear to be concocted fillers devised to ensure that there is at least one *vrata* under each time category.

43. The rite of *nyāsa*, obscure in origin according to Eliade, is a "practice of considerable antiquity but one that Tantrism revalorized and enriched. The disciple 'projects' the divinities, at the same time touching the various areas of his body; in other words, he homologizes his body with the Tantric pantheon, in order to awaken the sacred forces asleep in the flesh itself" (1962, 210–11). An example of the rite of *nyāsa* required in a *vrata* is the Ajachita *Vrata* described in the *Garuḍapurāṇa*, chap. 133.

44. McGee has argued carefully and repeatedly in her dissertation that *vratas* are "dharmic" acts (see, especially, 1987, 55–58). She follows the arguments of Candeśvara (14th cent.) and Hemādri to show how they demonstrate that *vratas*, as intentional acts of self-discipline and devotion, are dharmic; they cause one to act virtuously.

45. See section on "entitlement" in chapter 4.

46. Monier-Williams (1984, 1126) defines *saṅkalpa* as: "conception or idea or notion formed in the mind or heart (esp.) will, volition, desire, purpose, definite intention or determination or decision or wish for; . . . with the root *kri*, 'to form a resolution, make up one's mind'; . . . a solemn vow or determination to perform any ritual observance, declaration of purpose." See also Kane on *saṅkalpa* (1974, 5,1:28–30), and McGee (1987, 52–55).

47. For details on this latter application, see chapter 6, where ritual *saṅkalp* is described in the context of the procedure of a *vrata*.

48. Quoted in B. N. Sharma (1972, 105).

49. Quoted in Kane (1974, 5,1:30).

50. Bhagat notes: "The *Yoga-sūtras* describe yoga as consisting of eight limbs *(aṅgas):* the various forms of abstention from evil doing *(yama),* the various observances *(niyama),* posture *(āsana),* control of the breath *(prāṇāyam),* withdrawal of the mind from the sense-objects *(pratyāhara),* concentration *(dharma),* meditation *(dhyāna)* and absorption in the Purusha *(samādhi)*" (1976, 54). Yardi adds: "Of these, the first five are known as external aids to conscious contemplation, as they merely facilitate the mood of contemplation and aid yoga only indirectly. The last three are known as internal aids, as they constitute the very core of conscious contemplation" (1979, 42).

51. Some people translate *brahmacarya* as "celibacy," which it clearly does mean in some contexts. However, Patañjali's own commentators were divided on its intent, as Yardi has noted (1979, 44–45). That is, some held *brahmacarya* to mean complete abstention from sex (or such things as remembering or looking at a woman); others held it meant sexual restraint.

52. Ideally being an ascetic would facilitate this path, but I am not convinced that Patañjali intended his work to be applicable *only* to ascetics or renouncers, for his version is a rather moderate form of asceticism, easily adapted to *gṛhasthins* (householders).

53. *Agnipurāṇam,* trans. M. N. Dutt (1967). Other Purāṇa and Nibandha texts also have such lists of *niyamas* or *vrata-dharmas*. For example, the *Vratarāja* (p. 9) quotes Hemādri (who probably took it from the AP itself) as listing these same ten common features *(dharma)* of *vrata.*

54. If one examines the dictionary definitions of these terms, one will find that they are often given the same or similar series of meanings. For example, in Apte's Sanskrit- English dictionary (1965), the term *niyama,* in addition to its primary meaning of "restraints," is given the meanings "vow," "obligation," "penance," "devotion," and "religious austerity."

55. See AP 175; GP 128; LP 24. The VR (p. 13) quotes Hārita as saying that the faster *(upavāsaḥ)* or votary should avoid these sorts of people: one who does bad things, a scoundrel, a show-off, a nonbeliever, a liar, one who speaks pruriently. Viśvanātha Śarma then adds: "one who speaks and does not act, one who does not control [his/her] senses, and one who eats forbidden foods" should be avoided. Finally added to this list are: menstruating women, a *caṇḍāla* (of very low caste), a *dobhi* (washerman), a woman who has just given birth, and those who do not wash their mouth after eating. The latter list consists of people whose condition or employment render them extremely "polluting"; and

the others listed are all, of course, people who act in nondharmic *(adharmik)* ways.

56. The *Agnipurāṇa* gets even more detailed in later verses in its various prohibitions and requirements of the votary. It says: "The man who bathes every day, practices moderation in all his acts . . . and worships the gods, the Brahmanas and his preceptor, should abstain from taking alkaline substances, small grapes, salt, wine and meat. Grains such as wheat, kodruva, and all other grains except sesamum orientale and mudga, gram, devadhanya . . . constitute alkaline food. . . . Seeds such as vrihi [black sesame], jasthika, mudga, pulse, barley and sesamum should be used in vows and penances, while vegetables such as gourd, alavu, eggplant and palanki must be avoided. . . . Water, edible roots, milk, ghee, the fervent prayer of a Brāhmaṇa, and the ambrosial words of one's spiritual guide, are the . . . things which can never vitiate a vow."

57. Hārita, quoted by Kane (1974, 2:651).

58. See Gonda 1970, 82.

59. In fact there is a great deal of interest in toothbrushes in Indian texts. According to Gonda (1970, 176n66), "There are manuals (see, e.g., *Agitāgama*, 19, 22ff.) which expatiate upon the bits of wood to be used or avoided, their length (if it has the breadth of eight fingers it may contribute to final liberation) and other qualities." *Dantadhāvan* (brushing the teeth) is one of the *āhnika* rituals (daily duties) from the Vedas (p. 68).

60. See chapter 3.

61. Quoted in Kane 1974, 5,1:49.

62. See S. C. Banerjee 1946, 42.

63. R. S. Khare uses this distinction when discussing men's and women's performance of *vrats* in his book *The Hindu Hearth and Home* (1976), chapter six, *passim*.

64. Most of the Nibandhas and some Purāṇas arrange (and so in this sense, classify) their presentation of *vratas* according to time categories. The earliest *nibandhakāra* to arrange *vratas* according to time categories *(tithi*, day [*vāra*], *nakṣatra*, month, year) during which the particular *vrata* was to be performed was Lakṣmidhāra in his *Kṛtyakalpataru*. Others later followed suit. For example, Hemādri arranges his description of *vratas* into ten groups, each group of which is named for an astrological or seasonal category, except the last which is *prakirṇaka* or miscellaneous. A minority of Nibandhas arrange *vratas* according to the deity to whom the *vrata* is to be directed.

65. Examples of other observances deemed *nitya* are the "*nitya karmas*" enjoined on twice-born men: daily morning and evening prayers, bathing *(snāna)*, *japa*, *homa*, *deva-pūjā*, and the receiving and honoring of guests *(atithi pūjā)*. See McGee 1987, 301–2; also Kane 1974, 5,1:56–57.

66. See McGee 1987, 302.

67. "In the broader category of *naimittika* occasions fall events such as births and marriages, and unusual astronomical occurrences such as eclipses and conjunctions" (McGee 1987, 303–4). While most *naimittika* occasions are auspicious, some are inauspicious (e.g., a death) and others are highly ambivalent with potential for both benefit and harm, such as eclipses.

68. See Kane on Ekādaśī (1974, 5,1:96ff.).

69. See chapter 4, section on entitlement.

70. As A. B. Keith (1925, 259) puts it: "The nature of the ordinary offerings to the gods is expressly stated to be an offering made to the god for the purpose of attracting his attention and goodwill, so that, delighted himself, the god may reward in the appropriate way his worshipper. This is essentially the standpoint of the Ṛgveda where the sacrificer is promised wealth both temporal and in the world to come in return for his sacrifice."

71. An examination of the plethora of vernacular *vrat (kathā)* books and pamphlets reveals the continuity in the treatment of *vrata* in the textual tradition. It is largely from the Purāṇas and Nibandhas that a number of the current popular *vrat* booklets draw their material.

72. Vanaja Dhruvarajan (1989, 96) quotes two Kannada folk sayings which are pertinent: "If the son dies, the family is destroyed, but if the daughter-in-law dies there will be a wedding;" and "we cry the day a woman is born and the day she is married but we heave a sigh of relief on the day she dies."

73. See Julia Leslie 1989, 107ff. for a description of women's role, historically, in the sacrifice, and p. 36ff. for an excellent summary of the process by which women were disenfranchised from vedic education.

74. Besides the work of J. Leslie, see: A. S. Altekar, *The Position of Women in Hindu Civilization* (Delhi: Motilal Banarsidass, [reprint] 1973); M. A. Indra, *The Status of Women in Ancient India*, 2d rev. ed. (Delhi: Motilal Banarsidass, 1955); B. S. Upadhyaya, *Women in the Rigveda* (Bombay: S. Chand, 1974).

75. Manu 9.18; also Baudhāyana Dharmasūtra 1.11,7 and Mbh. 12.40.11–12. Quoted in J. Leslie 1989, 38.

76. While several of my informants (male and female) proclaimed that "woman is Śrī," Leslie (1989, 62) points out that, "It is quite obvious that 'fortune' [*śrī, lakṣmī*] is personified as female quite simply because it is held to possess such 'female qualities' as fickleness and instability."

On the other hand, K. Young (1987, 63) has argued that the direct point of transmission of many of the (positive) values and images of women's role (etc.) contributed by the vedic Saṁhitās to traditional Hindu women even today "was the marriage ceremony itself, which was based on Ṛg-Veda 10:85ff. Through the centuries, woman as maiden, wife, and mother was esteemed as fortunate (sumaṅgalī; subhagā) and auspicious (śivā). Her association with wealth, prosperity, beauty, grace, charm, and splendor became enshrined in a later age by the idea that she was Lakṣmī, goddess incarnate. Moreover, the visible expression of these qualities in the aesthetics of feminine form, clothing, jewelry, sweet-smelling unguents, and flowers continued to connote the well-being of the family as a whole, which in turn was a reflection of the fact that the deities had blessed the family."

77. Leslie 1989, 267; e.g., *Smṛticandrika* of Devanna Bhatta, 3.2.582; Mbh. 1.68.40.

78. Unlike Hindu men, however, a Hindu female's *varṇa* (caste) becomes relevant only at the time of marriage—to ensure a same caste or *anuloma* marriage ("following the grain"; includes lower-caste women marrying upper-caste men) and avoid a *pratiloma* ("against the grain") marriage. Otherwise, it is her sex that determines her *dharma.* Hence, women as a class are to follow *strīdharma* (rather than *varṇāśrama-dharma).*

79. Leslie 1989, 38, quoting Manu 2.6–7.

80. In the remarks that women offered to me in answer to my question about what *they* considered *strīdharm* to be, there was a remarkable degree of consensus (and accord with McGee's findings), suggesting that women are well familiar with conventional notions of what women as wives ought to do or how they ought to see their role. For example, Lelauti said: "*strīdharm* is—one accepts the orders of one's husband, one follows *dharm.* One should bring up one's children in a good way; one should serve one's husband. One should give respect to one's elders." She ended by asserting that "*strīdharm* is very significant (lit."big"—*baṛa) dharm.*" Others, like Shyamdevi, stressed sexual fidelity, or, like Sarita and Mira, conflated serving one's husband with housework.

81. S. A. Dange (1989) in his *Encyclopaedia of Purāṇic Beliefs and Practices* lists numerous purāṇic references to the *pativratā* under his section on "women" (vol. 5). For example, from the *Brahmavaivarta-*

purāṇa he quotes passages about how the "excellent wife" is to behave, behavior which underscores her structurally inferior position as devotee to god: "Getting up early in the morning . . . she should bow to her husband with joy and greet him with praise. Thence she should start her household duties. After bath, wearing [clean] clothes, she should worship her husband with a white flower. . . . She should attend to the bath of her husband, wash his feet and give him [clean] clothes. After arranging a seat for him, and asking him to sit there, she should apply sandal paste to his forehead and the whole body; she should place a wreath [*mālā*] in [*sic*] his neck. . . . [And then, contradicting women's supposed *amantravat* status:] With *mantras* from the *Sāmaveda*, she should worship him and bow down to him with these words 'Om, obeisance to the lustrous one, the calm one, the resort of all the gods; hail! . . . ; after this she should offer him a flower and sandal-paste, place offerings at his feet; wave incense and a lamp with a wick; she should also offer to him water made fragrant with ingredients and read (or mutter) a . . . *(stotra)* in front of him" (83.110–42). An earlier passage in this same Purāṇa makes explicit that the wife is to see Viṣṇu in her husband as she worships him. Similarly, she is to eat his leftover food and to drink the water in which his feet were bathed *(Brahmavaivartapurāṇa* 84.15–17). The practice of a wife eating her husband's leftovers (or at least eating whatever is left after everyone else has eaten) is still common in India.

3. *VRATS*, THE SEASONS AND THE FESTIVAL CALENDAR

1. When my colleague Hillary Rodrigues returned from studying a Durgā temple in Banaras in 1991, he told me that many men as well as women fast during Navarātri; not only devotees of Durgā, but also others who seek empowerment from the goddess during this time of year. Their vows (*vrata*) may consist of sleeping on the ground, not sleeping at all, or only sleeping for three hours a day. Sexual continence is common. These acts are often combined with daily recitations of the *Durgāsaptaśatī*. Votaries either recite the text themselves in their own homes (if they are literate), or listen to it being recited at the temple.

2. Hardevi used the well-known version of the *Durgāsaptaśatī* found in the sixth-century Śakta devotional work, the *Devīmahātmya*. This text describes the different occasions when the goddess (in her warrior—as Durgā, and terrifying—as Kālī, aspects) was summoned by the gods to save them (and humanity) by defeating various demons who had usurped the gods' powers and were terrorizing the universe. "Interspersed between these heroic episodes are hymns of praise to the goddess *(stotra)* in which the gods beseech her protection" (Bennett 1983, 263).

3. Navarātra Devī temple circuit in Banaras: (1) Śailaputrī Devī, (2) Brahmacāriṇī Devī, (3) Citraghantā Devī, (4) Kuṣmāṇḍā Devī, (5) Skanda Mātā Devī, (6) Kātyāyanī Devī, (7) Kālarātri Devī, (8) Durgānavamī (or Mahā-) Gaurī, (9) Siddhidātrī Devī.

4. For a more detailed description of the yearly cycle of festivals and observances in Banaras, consult Eck 1982, chapter 6, "Seasons and Times"; Judy Pugh 1983; and Vidyarthi et. al. 1979.

5. For the month of January 1986, for example, these predictions included: predicted rainfall (normal); wheat, oil, gram flour will be more expensive; there is a greater than normal possibility of war, plane crashes, and important people dying; countries governed by white people will have more problems; white metals, rice, vegetables and mustard oil will be cheaper; and "yellow things" will be more expensive.

6. As Kane wrote, "There are separate treatises on Ekādaśī written by Medieval writers, such as the Ekādaśī-viveka of Śulapāṇi and the Ekādaśītattva of Raghunandana. Besides, such . . . digests as Kālaviveka . . . , Hemādri on Kāla . . . , Kālanirṇaya of Madhava . . . , *Vratarāja* . . . devote hundreds of pages to discussions on Ekādaśī" (1974, 5,1:95). Kane himself discusses it in his *History of Dharmaśāstra* (1974, 5,1:95–100, and 103–15). For Purāṇa descriptions, see GP, chaps. 123, 125, 127; AP, chap. 187; *Naradapurāṇa*, chap. 23.

7. Rampratap Tripathi (1978) describes a Cāturmās *vrat* in his book, reiterating in his prefatory comments some of the points just made. He gives a *saṅkalpa* for the *vrat* which includes: "I will also observe a *vrat* of not eating pulses in Kārtik, milk in Āśvin, curd in Bhādrapad and green vegetables in Śravaṇa." Tripathi then mentions that, "In the Dharmaśāstra many things to eat have been prohibited during the Cāturmāsa Vrat and amazing results have been recounted. During the Cāturmāsa Vrat:

if these are abandoned . . .	these results are obtained:
gūr (raw sugar)	melodious voice
tel (oil)	beauty
betel leaf	*bhog* (physical pleasure), a sweet voice, a smooth body
śak (geen, leafy vegetables)	(one becomes) an enjoyer of cooked delicacies
curd, milk, buttermilk	Viṣṇu *lok*

The recommended practices during this *vrat* are keeping *brahmacarya*, sleeping on the floor with *kuś* grass, and *pūjā*.

8. Adding up the number of *vrats* for each *tithi* over a year from the Hṛṣikeś calendar, one finds the 4th, 11th, and 12th with the most number of *vrats* (12–24), followed by the 13th and 15th with 10-12, the 8th with nine, the 6th with seven, the 2nd, 3rd, 5th, 9th and 14th (variety of deities designated) with two to four, the 1st with one, and the 7th and 10th *tithis* with none.

9. Rāhu means "seizer" and is the vedic name of the demon *(dānava)* responsible for lunar and solar eclipses. Ketu is the personification of any unusual celestial phenomena such as a comet or meteor, and also of the descending node of the moon.

10. The VR (p. 3) quotes the *Ratnamālāyam* (Nibandha) as saying with respect to the qualities of the solar weekdays: "On Monday, Wednesday, Thursday and Friday all good actions will be fulfilled—therefore these days are called *siddhitā* (conferring success). On the three days of Sunday, Tuesday and Saturday, only prescribed *vratas* can be done (will be successful)."

11. Among the women I interviewed the Friday *vrat* was the most commonly observed weekly *vrat.*

12. Religious book sellers stationed outside major temples in Banaras told me that the Santoṣī Mā *Vrat-Kathā* booklet had been their "best seller" in recent years.

13. I found that the most "testimonials" regarding the fruit or results of a *vrat* came within the context of a discussion of the Santoṣī Mā Vrat.

14. One of the astrologer-pandits I spoke with viewed the majority of these *vrat* books that have sprung up in the hundreds in the last two or three decades with disdain. Like many other educated and high-caste people, he made a distinction between *"pakka"* (from the verb *paknā* "to cook," meaning "perfected," that is, "proper") and non-*pakka* ways of doing things (rituals) and texts. He considers most of the *vrat* books and pamphlets sold in the bazaars and outside temples to be of the latter sort. He said that people who write them are not learned and are just out to make some money. The authors "just put the material together from various sources, add their own ideas and pass the results off as their own" (products of scholarship).

4. PRECEPT AND PRACTICE: THE CONTOURS OF A *VRAT*

1. In the Purāṇas and Nibandhas, *vratas* are often conflated with both *prāyaścittas* (expiations) and *utsavas* (festivals). This is because the terms were interchanged in some of the early Dharmasūtras and the rites continued to share some of the same characteristics in their

observance such as eating or abstaining from certain foods, ritual bathing, performing *pūjā*, observing restraints *(niyama)*, reciting mantras and giving gifts *(dāna)*. Also, writers on *vrata* were no doubt aware that the intention, if not the circumstances of the celebrant or votary could determine whether a *vrata* was being observed as a *prāyaścitta*, or a festival as a *vrata*. Thus one cannot always clearly demarcate the boundary between these three rites from textual descriptions alone. Generally, what most distinguishes *vratas* from *utsavas* is that the latter are public secular or religious observances often occuring annually, such as the celebration of the birthday of a deity or a saint in which a whole family or community participates, while *vratas* are usually performed by individuals for specific purposes, and often for delimited periods of time. Another distinction is that whereas *vratas* can be part of the observance of a festival (as in the case of Kṛṣṇajanamāṣṭamī, the annual celebration of the birth of Kṛṣṇa during which many celebrants will keep a fast [*vrata*]), a festival (as opposed to festivities) would not be part of a *vrata*.

Vrata was associated with *prāyaścitta* in Manu, Yājñyavalkya, and other Smṛtis of around the turn of the Common Era. However, in the later Smṛtis, the Purāṇas and the Nibandhas *prāyaścitta* and *vrata* are treated as separate topics, though many of the well-known *prāyaścittas* (e.g., Cāndrayāṇa, where one takes one morsel of food on the first day of the bright half, or waxing moon, of the month, on the second day two morsels, and so on until the day of the full moon fifteen morsels are taken; then on the first day of the dark half fourteen morsels are taken, one being reduced on each succeeding day) have been integrated into the purāṇic *vratas* whose primary purpose is indicated as expiatory. As well, terms like *ekabhakta* (one meal per day), *nakta* (one meal per day to be taken at night) and *ayacita* (subsisting on food got without begging) used originally with *prāyaścittas* were adopted into the purāṇic *vratas* (see Kane 1974, 5,1:103).

What differentiates a *vrata* and a *prāyaścitta*, then, is that the latter is a prescribed observance to nullify or moderate the effects of some transgression from a *mahāpataka* ("major offence") like Brahman-killing to an *upapataka* ("minor offence"—these are innumerable) like stealing. Doing something intentionally or unintentionally to break a *vrata* is itself considered an *upapataka*, for which a *prāyaścitta* is prescribed: "If one gets angry or shows greed about anything during this period [the duration of the *vrata*], he commits a breach of vow [*vratabhaṅga*]; and the expiation for this is not taking food for three days or tonsuring the head. He may start his vow afresh thereafter" *(Agnipurāṇa* 174.40, quoted in Dange 1990, 1525. Note the masculine orientation of this injunction, although some texts make allowances for women. For example, a certain length of hair should be cut off rather than shaving the head altogether). The purpose of *prāyaścittas* is essentially to purify oneself, to redress one's "karmic" balance, and to pay back society (the dharmic order) for one's transgressions. A *vrata* may be undertaken as an expiatory rite, but it may be undertaken for many other reasons as well, usually determined by the individual. *Prāyaścittas*, on the other hand, are usually imposed from without, by a family priest, the village council, or even by a king.

2. Nāgpañcamī (Śravaṇ bright 5) is an old festival, still popular in Banaras, celebrated for the purpose of appeasing snakes. Mira said: "By doing Nāgdevtā *pūjā* the benefit is that a snake won't bite us. He [the snake] knows that 'these people have done *pūjā* to us;' we won't disturb the snake and he will protect us." See Kane (1974, 5,1:124-27) for textual references to and descriptions of Nāgapañcamī.

3. The Ṛṣi Pañcamī Vrat takes place on Bhādrapad bright 5. This is a very interesting *vrat* with respect to women because it is specifically for eliminating or mitigating the "sin" (of brahmanicide committed by the god Indra that women "agreed" to take on, along with trees, rivers, etc.) represented by women's menstruation. See McGee (1987, 368), Kane (1974, 5,1:149-51), and Bennett's descriptive analysis of this *vrat* as observed by high-caste women in Nepal (1983, 215ff.).

4. About one-third of the women that I asked agreed with Bina that there was a difference in the way one community observed *vrats* from another; but more than half of the women I spoke with said there was no difference or no significant difference.

5. Kiran, for example, felt that around Mussoorie there is little difference in the way her family observes some *vrats* compared to the way other people do. "Even Harijan *vrats* are not significantly different—they all follow the same basic Hindu philosophy," she asserted.

6. This also may be true in Maharashtra (or at least among high-caste women in Pune) according to my reading of Mary McGee's thesis. Further research would have to corroborate these impressions as well as discern what happens at lower caste levels.

7. While there is no śāstric restriction on a Shudra's observing such a *vrat* as Ekādaśī (see Kane 1974, 5,1: 99), it may well be possible that they were not in fact encouraged to keep it because of the association of Ekādaśī with the higher castes. The necessity of time and expense, employing a Brahman pandit, and so on, may also have discouraged (and may continue to discourage) poor, lower castes from keeping this semi-monthly *vrat*.

8. Luschinsky (1962, 700) also mentions that she saw several women fasting on cloves during certain *vrats*.

9. These two views are represented by various scholars. On the one side, S. R. Das has argued that the Purāṇas succeeded as popular texts because they absorbed and integrated many "non-Aryan" elements, thus appealing to a large population. Many "popular rites and practices including certain *vratas* were given new interpretations and eventually incorporated into the Brahmanical system" (1952, 222). Das contends that a large proportion of the *vratas* found in the Purāṇas were of non-Aryan origin before they and their accompanying *kathās* were "brahmanized," and that the original folk *vratas*, still practised in many parts of India, "are nothing but primitive magico-religious rites, [that] do not find any mention in our sacred lore or hieratic Brahmanical literature." Similarly, others like J. Helen Rowlands (1930, 50-51), Eva Maria Gupta (1983) and Maity (1989) have argued that "śāstric" *vratas* were introduced in imitation of popular rites. They have followed Abanindranth Tagore's thesis (spelled out in his 1919 book) that the term "*anyavratas*" found in the Vedas referred to the "different rites" of the autochthonous peoples. Among these, Gupta argues, the only rites to survive were those of the girls' and women's because the "world of men" (the exterior, public world) was more strongly subordinated to the acculturation process of the Aryans than the world of women, the world of the household (1983, 4). Eventually, many women's (or indigenous) and "Vedic *vratas*" (brought in by the Aryans and performed primarily by men) were changed into the "śāstriya *vratas*"—forming the basis of the Purāṇa-Nibandha *vratas*, although Gupta claims that the "maiden" *vratas* remain unadulterated to this day. New gods were introduced, new *vratas* were invented, the role of priests' "esoteric wisdom" increased and a certain disjunction between the names or goals of the *vratas* and their ritual procedures occured. While women's folk *vratas* have continued to survive (though influenced to greater or lesser extents by "śāstric *vratas*"), the "Vedic *vratas*" disappeared or were completely amalgamated. What we have left then according to this view, are women's essentially "folk *vratas*" widely practised in Bengal (and virtually everywhere else in India), and "śāstric *vratas*," known by pandits mostly through Nibandha texts and prescribed for and practised by a much smaller segment of the population, male and female.

In the second view, rather than arguing that *vratas* and other popular folk rites were included in the Purāṇas (and Nibandhas) as a concession to their prevalence at a popular level, P. V. Kane, the Purāṇa scholar R. C. Hazra, and S. C. Banerjee, among others, maintain that the inclusion of *vratas* (as well as *dāna*, *upavāsa*, *tīrtha*, etc.) and their glorification in the Purāṇas represented a popularization of Smṛti material. That is, these rites were basically "made up" or created out of the components of vedic rituals. As evidence, Hazra cites the following elements of a *vrata:* "selection of a proper tithi, determination of taking the vow, lying on the ground, bath, japa, . . . (homa), keeping awake during the night, and listening to tales" (1975, 240). All these, he says, have their parallels in vedic rituals. In trying to account for why the Brahmans took such an interest in promoting the Purāṇas, Hazra propounds a theory which states that during the early centuries of the Common Era certain heterodoxies (Buddhism, Jainism) had become influential rivals to orthodox Brahmanism. The lower castes and women were especially prone to these influences because (1) they were less educated and (2) they were debarred from a significant role in the vedic religious rites and so had less interest at stake in them (1975, 240). As more people strayed from the Brahmanic fold, the Brahmans began losing power, income and prestige. They realized that the revitalization of the *varṇāśramadharma* and the authority of the Vedas and śāstras was essential to the reestablishment of their own authority and well-being. Thus, the orthodox "brahmanists," Hazra suggests, began to preach the performance of *gṛhya* rites through Smṛti works and the more numerous "Smārta-Vaiṣṇavas and Smārta-Śaivas . . . introduced Smṛti materials into the Mahābhārata and the Purāṇas to preach Vaiṣṇavism and Śaivism as against the heretical religions" (1975, 213-14, 226, 257). To attract more followers, then, the exclusivity of vedic rites was relaxed to allow more people to participate in them, the importance of these rites for the well-being and harmony of society was emphasized, and personal devotion to a single god as a way to *mokṣa* began to be propounded by the sectarian Brahmans through the Purāṇas and Smṛtis. Kane (1974, 5,1:43ff.) and Banerjee (1946, 34-35) support the above view and suggest that the success of this popularization of Smṛti rites was ensured by the promises of heaven or "otherworldly and spiritual rewards [made] to those who performed *vrata*s that were comparatively easy and within the reach of all instead of sacrifices (Kane 1974, 5,1:43).

Having both studied the texts on *vrata*s and conducted fieldwork on women's practice of *vrat*s, I would argue that neither view is sufficient. The accounts based on Tagore's thesis of the "*anyavrata*s" betray an inappropriate and anachronistic use and understanding of the term *vrata*. Our review of the history of the term *vrata* in the earliest texts suggests that while *vrata* may translate as "ordinance" or "function" in some contexts, *vrata* did not refer to votive rites as such before the beginning of the Common Era. It is misleading to speak of "vedic *vrata*s" as if we knew what they were. But we can be even less certain of what the "original" rites of autochthonous peoples were like, and we cannot say with any certainty whether women's and girls' *vrat*s of today are the direct descendents of these rites. The views of Kane and Hazra, on the other hand, tend to downplay the extent to which "elite" traditions borrow from "folk" traditions (the opposite process of "Sanskritization," or, to use McKim Marriott's term, the process of "universalization"). The whole range of *vrata*s—both those described in the texts and those practised in villages and cities today are, in my estimation, an interweaving of "folk" and "elite" traditions, and both of these sets of traditions occupy different parts of the same continuum. Thus some *vratas*, especially many of those observed by women, are performed in such a way that they bear scant resemblance to the nibandhic prescriptions, while others are performed with all the accoutrements of the text format.

10. Altogether, women listed twenty-four different *vrats* (or kinds of *vrats*, like "weekly") as being either śāstric or *laukik*. Among these, five *vrats* ended up on both sides (i.e., different women named these five *vrats* as either śāstric or *laukik*). Those that were designated most often as śāstric tended to be the pan-Indian and annual "family" *vrats*; e.g., Ekādaśī, Pūrṇimā, Janmāṣṭamī, Śivarātri and Rāmnaumī. Those that were named *laukik* tended to be ones that are traditionally associated with women; e.g., Karvā Cauth, Jīvitputrika, Har Chaṭh and Bahulā Cauth. Bina said *laukik vrats* are those which are local to the area, whereas śāstric *vrats* "are those *vrats* observed all over India, like Mahālakṣmī."

11. However, Sarasvati was not finally certain about the status of the Santoṣī Mā Vrat because she heard that some people had received good results from observing this *vrat*.

12. On the various layers of meaning of "*adhikāra*" and its relation to *vrata* and women's performance of *vrata*, see McGee 1987, 72-87. I have relied on some of this material in this section, as indicated.

13. For example, the Anaṅyadau Vrata (MP ch.70). In this *vrata* for courtesans, though the prostitute is promised removal of all her sins and eventually a place in Viṣṇu Loka, she was still required in this life to maintain her role, and further, to be especially obliging toward Brahmans desiring her favors.

14. Two-thirds of the women I asked said "no," less than a third said "yes," and a couple of women said that it depended. McGee, who asked the same question of her respondents in Pune with the same intent, received virtually the same range of responses that I did in Banaras (see McGee 1987, 83-87).

15. The *vrat*, however, may be just one element, albeit an important one, in an arsenal of remedies. Such an arsenal may include the use of amulets, herbs, stones, and other remedies of which women avail themselves.

16. See McGee 1987, 110-20, for a discussion of these textual stipulations.

17. McGee (1987, chapter 6) found that most of the women she interviewed in Maharashtra kept the fast when menstruating, but did not

perform the *pūjā*, and other actions potentially capable of transferring pollution.

18. See Kane 1974, 5,1:54; also McGee 1987, chap. 6. In my sample, husbands were mentioned most often as substitutes, followed by Brahman women or girls, and then by other male family members.

19. Less than a third of the women I questioned had actually used a proxy.

20. Prepubescent girls are ritually equivalent to Brahmans; as premenarche virgins, they are "pure" and so not likely to sully the *vrat* in any way.

21. The positive self-affirmation that women express about their duty and special ability to protect their husbands and families through forms of service, self-sacrifice, rituals and vows is thoroughly and illuminatingly documented by Lindsey Harlan in her book on Rajput women (1992).

5. PRECEPT AND PRACTICE: THE CONSTITUENTS OF A VRAT

1. Each of these "features" can be elaborated at length, both from textual sources and from anthropological research. I indicate through footnotes where some of this work has already been done.

2. Technically, it is preceded by the *svativācana* (the benediction), the *karmārambha* (the commencement of the rite), and the *snāna* (the ritual bath).

3. Because Ekādaśī is usually a *nitya* rite for Vaiṣṇavas, no references to particular desires are made in this *saṅkalpa*.

4. This is the second meaning given for "*saṅkalp*" in the Chaturvedi and Tiwari Hindi-English dictionary (1978, 756), viz. "*Saṅkalp karnā*—to resolve; to gift away."

5. *Homa* is one of the five daily *yajñas* to be performed by a Brahmana. On *devapūjā*, see Kane 1974, 2:705–12. For one of the earliest descriptions of *devapūjā* (from the *Viṣṇudharmasūtra*), see Kane 1974, 2:726–27.

6. Kane 1974, 2:730. Down through the centuries the formal honoring of any guest *(atithi pūjā)* was (and is) considered a sacred duty incumbent on all householders.

7. Anything from one to thirty-eight are mentioned, though five and sixteen are the most common numbers cited.

8. Panditji, whose comments on various *upacāras* will constitute the next three notes, also said this, among other things, about the significance of water: "Water cools, calms and refreshes—so should we be to ourselves and to others. And water always returns to its source—so it is the natural path from the self to God."

9. "A lamp emits light all around, giving clarity while destroying itself. We too should sacrifice ourselves while giving light to others. The thoughts, especially desires, are the oil which is burned up to 'free' us to give to others."

10. "God should be offered the best foods—foods that are beautifully cooked and beautifully presented in the best vessels—as symbols of our devotion. Sweet things are especially appropriate because they represent the quality of *madhu* (honey)—the sweetest *bhāvanā*." "God does not actually eat the foods, but in the act of offering, they are infused with God's blessings."

11. "Three rounds are offered to Lord Śiva, and five rounds to Lord Viṣṇu. When performing *ārati* one should trace (in the air with the lamps) the figure of *aum* in front of the *mūrti*—between its chest and head.

12. Kane 1974, 2:730. There are, however, detailed rules about the use of flowers, as with other *upacāra* items. The *Viṣṇudharmasūtra* (66.5–9) "prescribes that flowers emitting an overpowering smell or having no smell whatever are not to be used, nor flowers of thorny plants unless the flowers are white and sweetly fragrant" (quoted in Kane 1974, 2:732–33). There are different grades in the merit of offering certain flowers, and these grades depend on the deity to whom they are offered.

13. The pandit (above) referred to *pañcagavyam* (cow urine and dung, ghee, milk, curd) as the "soap" used to bathe the deity and *pañcāmṛt* (ghee, curd, milk, honey, sugar) as the "rinse." Each item of these two mixtures is separately added and "charged" by mantras.

14. Mataji's husband is the priest of a small Lakṣmī-Nārāyaṇ temple. He performs the twice daily *pūjā* to the temple's *mūrtis* and Mataji helps him out by, for instance, holding the pot as he sprinkles water on the images. She prepares all the *pūjā* items and later carefully cleans the pots, sweeps the floor, and so on. She said that assisting her husband in his religious duties was her religious duty, and she took pride in the fact that they performed these important religious ceremonies together.

15. Besides my own descriptions, women's *pūjās* in the context of *vrats* and other calendrical rites are described by Luschinsky (1962, 644–718); Wadley (see bibliography); E. M. Gupta (1983); Maity (1988, chap. 4); S. Robinson (1985); Duvvury (1991, chap. 7); and Tewari (1991).

16. Kane (1974, 2:134ff.), Gonda (1965, 203–4), and Hazra (1975, 257–59) cite a number of passages which describe Brahmans as gods in vedic and sūtra literature. Gonda also notes the following in his discussion of the position of Brahmans: "In the *Ṛgveda* the brahman is the mighty figure who by the ritual word he pronounces and the ritual acts he performs is able to achieve supernormal and highly important objects. . . . He is moreover the seat par excellence of speech (1.164.35), the expert in the knowledge of ritual texts (2.39.1) and of important facts, events, phenomena, or connections (164.45; 10.85.3, 16)" (1965, 202).

17. As an example of Purāṇic identification of Brahmans with gods, Hazra cites the *Varāhapurāṇa* chaps. 125 and 169. Hazra also notes that the "later the Purāṇa the greater the claim to their divinity" (1975, 259). Examples of the worship of Brahmans in purāṇic *vrata*s include the Sarasvata *Vrata* (MP, chap. 66) and the Anaṅyadau *Vrata* (MP, chap.70).

18. This is with the exception of my research assistant, who for complicated reasons (her influential father being a Marxist and atheist, her being unmarried at the age of thirty-two) felt ambivalent about Brahman priests and about her *vrat* observances in general.

19. The Satyanārāyaṇ Kathā (Vrat) was specifically mentioned by several women as an occasion when the pandit needed to be called in order to say the *kathā*, the *"pradhāna"* of this particular observance.

20. McGee writes that *vrat* pamphlets "are enabling more men and women to act as their own ritual priests, and are thus opening up new possibilities and ritual roles, especially for women" (1987, 379).

21. Further, if one accepts Tagore's thesis about the origin of *vrata*s among the autochthonous people of India, one could say that "priestly appropriation" of these rites began many hundreds of years ago.

22. On the history of *dāna* consult Kane 1974, 2:837–88; Gonda 1965, 222–26.

23. The multiplication of gifts in the purāṇic *vrat*s, Hazra contends, "stands in striking contrast to the simple priestly fee prescribed in the ṣaṣṭhi-kalpa of the Manava-gṛhya-sūtra. . . . This ṣaṣṭhi-kalpa, which is almost a regular *vrata* . . . is meant for the attainment of progeny and wealth, and in it the priestly fee is only a cow and a bull" (1975, 256).

24. Devala quoted by Hemādri (see Kane, 1974, 2:847), classifies gifts into three groups: (1) "best"—food (ghee, sesame, curds, honey), protection, cows, land, gold, horses and elephants; (2) "middling"—learning, house for shelter, domestic paraphernalia (like cots), and medicine; and (3) "inferior"—shoes, swings, carts, umbrellas, vessels, seats, lamps, wood, and fruit.

25. For example the Gosahasra-Mahādāna involves a three-day fast on milk, the donation of ten painted and ornamented cows, the making of a golden image of Nandi and the uttering of mantras glorifying the cow. The merit of performing this *mahādāna* is that the donor "would dwell in the world of Śiva and would save his pitrs and his maternal grandfather and other maternal relatives." (See Kane 1974, 2:871–77.)

26. Gifting can be quite a complicated matter in contemporary practice, even more so than a reading of the śāstras would reveal. Gloria Raheja writes that "[e]ach potential act of giving is always subject to multiple strategic possibilities concerning, for example, the quality and quantity of items to be given, whether the gift is presented through an intermediary or by the donor himself, whether the donor gives freely or only after much expedient calculation of his own interests and prerogatives, and the relationship of the gift in question to the whole history of gift giving engaged in by the parties to the exchange" (Raheja and Gold 1994, 79).

27. M. Monier Williams, *A Sanskrit-English Dictionary*, s.v. *"upavāsa"* (206); and McGee 1987, 189n113.

28. On *nakta* and *ekabhakta*, see Kane 1974, 5,1:100–3.

29. Parry 1985, 613, ft.1. Parry's article contains much interesting information on Indian food categories and codes, as do the books by R. S. Khare: *The Hindu Hearth and Home* (1976), *Culture and Reality: Essays on the Hindu System of Managing Foods* (Durham: Carolina Academic Press, 1976), and *The Eternal Food* (Albany: State University of New York Press, 1992).

30. "One who eats not only absorbs the qualities of the cook, but also the intrinsic properties of the food itself. In Hindu culture, a man is what he eats. Not only *is* his bodily substance created out of food, but so is his moral disposition" (Parry 1985, 613).

31. Several of Susan Wadley's articles describe the vernacular (Hindi) *vrat-kathā* books and pamphlets that have been published with increasing abundance since the early sixties by many small presses specializing in religious books. Her article, "Popular Hinduism and Mass Literature in North India: A Preliminary Analysis" (1983) describes and compares the contents of nine *vrat* books. Wadley concludes in this article that "the variety of ritual behavior presented in these guides far outweighs any apparent concern for standardization, or we must assume, any consensus on 'correct' ritual behavior" (p. 100). On *vrat-kathās*, see also Wadley 1975 (chap. 4); 1983c; Kaushik (n.d.); McGee 1987 (appendix B); and Tewari 1991, all of which have translations of *vrat*-kathās.

32. Wadley describes how *vrats* are depicted as being able to transform the votary's karmic destiny in her article "*Vrats*: Transformers of Destiny" (1983). McGee uses the phrase "transformative power" in her dissertation (1987, 382).

33. Wadley formally situates the *vrat-kathā* in the genre of "myth" in her article, "The Kathā of Sakaṭ: Two Tellings" (1986, 200).

34. Tewari found that his informants used the words *kathā* and *kahānī* interchangeably, but he also observes that a "*kathā* is always a religious discourse, while a *kahānī* can be either religious or secular" (1991, 19n7).

35. See Arthur Ryder, 1949, *Panchatantra* (Delhi: Jaico Publishing House), 4. Some scholars have argued that the *Pañcatantra* is the source for Aesop's fables.

36. For example, in the Kalyāṇīni Vrata—a thirteen-month *vrata* to Sūrya to be observed every seventh *tithi*, described in the MP, chap. 74—an eight-petalled lotus with eight suns around it is to be drawn. The eight suns around the lotus probably signify the "eight directions": the four cardinal points and the four intermediate points over each one which presides a *lokāpala* or guardian. In many *vrata* descriptions, the votary is to worship or pay homage to the *lokāpala* of each direction, beginning with the eastern direction, then south-eastern, and so on.

37. Eliade describes a *maṇḍala* as a "circular border and one or more concentric circles enclosing a square divided into four triangles; in the center of each triangle, and in the center of the *maṇḍala* itself, are other circles containing images of divinities or their emblems." The *maṇḍala* is both an image of the universe and a theophany. It also serves as a "receptacle" for the gods who are invoked to enter the sacred area and are contemplated and interiorized by the initiate (Eliade 1969, 219–20). One *vrata* (GP 126) prescribes such a psychic diagram to be meditated upon as "over the mystic nerve plexus of the heart." Only the very beginning and the ending of this *vrata* description fall into the usual pattern of Purāṇic *vratas*, suggesting that these sections were appended to a tantric ritual already in practice.

38. For detailed information on and especially for examples of *ālpanās*, consult E. M. Gupta 1983 on Bengali *brata-ālpanā;* see also Tewari 1991 for photographs of *vrat* "folk-art" from central U.P.

39. For example, in the Uttara Khaṇḍa of the *Bhaviṣyapurāṇa*, the *Nirṇayasindhu* (p. 133), and the VR (pp. 103–10). See Kane's description of the *vrata* from digest sources (1974, 5,1:144–45).

40. It is possible that the Bhādrapad "Haritālikā" Tīj and "Hariyālī" or "Kajalī" Tīj observed in Śravaṇa have been conflated. The Tīj festival in Śravaṇa, occuring at the beginning of the rainy season, is associated with women swinging on swings and with a host of "swinging songs" called *kajalī*. These songs celebrate the joy of the rainy season and its association with conjugal (and erotic) love, the reunion of lovers and fertility in general. (See Wadley 1983; and for translations of Tīj songs, Raheja and Gold 1994.) Women are supposed to wear green clothes on this day. There is also another festival celebrated in the Banaras and Mirzapur districts on the third of the "dark" half of Bhādrapad called "Kajrī Tīj," also associated with swinging and singing songs about the rainy season; and instead of swings, there is a tradition of getting in boats on the Ganges river.

41. The *Vratarāja* gives the Tīj Vrat *saṅkalpa* as follows: "I perform the Haritālikā Vrat so that my sins will be removed for seven births and (so that) my *saubhāgya* will remain unbroken and increase, and for (the sake of) love [or devotion] of Umā-Maheśvara." The Nibandha instructs the votary to first perform a *pūjā* to Gaṇeśa, then to Gaurī and Maheśvara (Pārvatī and Śiva). The *pūjā* described is very formal, involving all the *upacāras*. Each *upacāra* is to be done with mantras which are mostly verses of praise to the goddess and prayers soliciting her blessings for *saubhāgya*. All the items associated with *saubhāgya* are to be offered to the goddess: for example, tumeric, *kuṁkuṁ* or *siṅdūr, kājal* (collyrium). Each part of her body is to be worshipped. The description of the *pūjā* ends with the statement to be recited by the votary asking the goddess to fulfill all her desires.

42. The version of the story I summarize below is from Rampratap Tripathi's *Hinduoṅ ke Vrat, Parv aur Tyauhār* (1978, 141–145), which follows fairly closely the *Vratarāja* version. (The full story and other variants are found in appendix D.)

43. One woman quoted a saying about the Tīj Vrat to the effect: "If you drink water you will be born as a fish; eat sweets you'll be born as a fly."

44. It is significant that several women told me that it was male relatives (fathers and husbands) who at certain times told them to stop keeping *vrat*s because they were "worried" about the effects of the *vrat*s on the women. No woman I spoke with ever mentioned a female relative telling her to stop performing *vrat*s that she was already keeping.

45. Luschinsky describes the Tīj Vrat as it is done in Senapur this way: "Women who married into Senapur fast and bathe in their homes. Daughters of the village assemble and go to a tank where they brush their

teeth, bathe, dress in clean clothes. After the dressing, each girl is expected to sing the name of her husband . . . [a ritually charged event because women in most parts of India do not normally ever speak their husbands' names.] In the evening, those who have fasted eat some sweet preparation so they will not feel faint, but they do not regard the fasting period as over until the next morning when they swallow some soaked chickpeas. . . . Women receive many gifts on Tij or just prior to Tij. The gift parcels usually include one or more saris, blouse pieces, glass bangles, some vermilion and perhaps a comb, mirror and other beauty aids" (1962, 657–58).

46. Tripathi does not specify which Purāṇas mention this story, but, versions of this *vrat*'s *kathā* and other stories about its hero, King Jīmutavāhan, may be found in the *Kathāsaritsāgara*, among other Sanskrit medieval story collections.

47. See Appendix D for a full translation of Tripathi's account of the *vrat* and the *kathā*.

48. I was told that if a woman has children she does the *pūjā* sitting, if not, she will do it standing. Men are not involved at all, though I saw a few standing around looking on. Children of various ages hung behind their mothers or scampered about waiting for the proceedings to end.

49. Scholars have suggested that there is a link between ancestor worship and the obtaining of progeny. Veena Das has noted that while ancestors "have the power to cause great harm, they also have the potential and the interest to bestow wealth and progeny on their descendents" (quoted in Marglin 1985, 78).

50. In reference to the Senapur version of Jiutiyā, Luschinsky also found that "the word Jiutia refers to strands of red cotton thread on which small metal charms are strung. Each woman has as many charms on her cord as she has sons." And in a footnote she comments, "A woman who has strong affectionate feelings for her daughters may celebrate Jiutia for her daughters as well as for her sons. In this case she will string on her Jiutia metal charms representing each of her daughters. This is not a common practice, however" (1962, 663).

51. This may be a current example of the movement that has been taking place between śāstric rites that are overseen by a priest and women's own rites.

52. My current project involves investigating continuity and change in the practice of *vrat*s among Hindu women immigrants in southern Ontario.

6. *VRATS* AND THE LIFE STAGES OF HINDU WOMEN

1. Das goes on: "Manu makes every effort to see the position of the daughter exalted to its highest. According to him no householder should pick any quarrel with her [4.180]. Medhatithi and Kulluka say that no sort of unpleasant dealing, . . . is to be entered into with her. This, they think, will tell upon her tender emotions. It is probably for this reason that they are not allowed to undergo the strenuous exertions of the Vedic studies."

2. 'Power' may be defined as the ability to influence or control the actions of others and 'authority' as socially legitimated power (see Louise Lamphere 1974). Vatuk has defined 'autonomy' as "the ability to determine one's own activities and actions, free of the control (by virtue of either legitimate authority or power) of another person" (1987, 24). For a description of the socialization process that takes place among girls and boys in one South Indian village (in Karnataka), see Dhruvarajan 1989. Dhruvarajan's book on the whole is a rather bleak evocation of the lives of women. She emphasizes women's lack of self-development, maturity, autonomy and power, and their cooperation with their own subordination. She explains how through songs and sayings and parental instruction girls are taught that "the qualities of docility, shyness, patience and tolerance are . . . the most important qualities of a woman" (1989, 66).

3. A close variant of this *brata* is described in Kayal, "Women in the Folkore of West Bengal," in *Women in Indian Folklore,* ed. Sen Gupta (Calcutta, 1969), 190.

4. These are the same two *vrats* which Kiran had mentioned as *vrats* for young girls, though she had only heard about them. Poonam could not recall in which months these *vrats* were performed, and I have been unable to identify them in my collection of Hindi *vrat* books.

5. Both M. Roy (1975) and S. Mazumdar (1981) mention the (Monday) Śiva Brata as being especially popular among young, unmarried girls in urban Bengal. Roy (pp. 37–38) provides a long first-hand account of a college girl performing the Śiva Brata with about fourteen other girls from her dorm "to get a Siva-like husband." At the end of her account this young woman told Roy: "If you ask me whether I believed in the whole things, I have no answer. I liked doing it and, unlike my friend who jeered about it, I felt good in doing it. I always liked Siva, and knowing the story of Siva and Uma I thought a marriage like that would not be bad" (38).

Among the women I interviewed in Kerala, the Monday Vrat was the most commonly observed short-term vrat. (Half of the sixteen women I interviewed had kept this *vrat* before they married, and several continued after.) For example, Radha, thirty-nine, told me she kept the Monday Vrat every week for two years because she wanted a good husband and on the advice of her mother (who had also kept it). Initially Radha told me that she thought this *vrat* did help her to get a good husband, but then she confided that she has doubts about whether the *vrat* was really responsible or whether her ability to adjust to her husband is more responsible for the satisfactory marriage.

6. Unfortunately, I did not ask her why the daughters of brigadiers and colonels did not keep *vrats* because we were interrupted, and I did not return to this point.

7. Marglin also characterizes the role of the wife as the "feeder of the household"; she is the "life-maintainer par excellence" on whose proper behavior depends the welfare of the group (both the living and the ancestors) (1985, 53).

8. Additionally, Daniel reports that the villagers in Tamil Nadu she interviewed held that "although males also possess a measure of *śakti*, it is believed that this is because they embody a small portion of the female principle" (1980, 78). For further discussions of the concept of *śakti*, see Wadley 1975 and the various contributions to Wadley's edited volume *The Powers of Tamil Women* (1980); also Mitter 1991, chapters 7 and 10, O'Flaherty 1980, and S. Gupta 1991. In commenting on a long statement on the meaning of *śakti* from one of her female informants from the village of Khalapur in Uttar Pradesh, Leigh Minturn writes: "The complexity of this description of Shakti is primarily concerned with reproduction, but its power extends to many aspects of behavior. Since it is earned by good or bad karma, it can be good or bad in nature. It is embodied in the earth. Childless women have none, but mothers lose theirs by giving to children through acts of birth or teaching. It can return from children through their earnings, so it may be embodied in wealth and secular power. It can be lost through pride, and greatly diminished by a saint's curse" (1993, 205).

9. Just as Śrī/Lakṣmī is the divinized form of fortune, luck, auspiciousness, so Śakti is the divinized philosophical principle of "enabling energy" (from the verbal root *śak*—"to be able to"). Śrī/Lakṣmī is the consort of Viṣṇu who is usually depicted as the preserver and ruler. Together they represent kingship, wealth, abundance and stability. The goddess Śakti is often referred to as the "consort" of Śiva. However, Śakti also is used by Hindus to refer loosely to all goddesses, whether they are depicted as consorts or not. Together, Śiva and Śakti create; alone, in their "terrible" aspects—as Bhairava and Kālī—they can be destructive.

10. On this topic, see, e.g., Wadley and Jacobson 1977.

11. On *satī*, *satīmātās*, and the concept of *sat* (which in many ways resembles the notion of *śakti)* among Rajput women, consult Harlan 1992.

12. When I met her, her three-year-old son was a healthy cherished child, but Rekha's heart condition had seriously worsened and she was awaiting surgery.

13. Lakshmi, Shyamdevi's niece, gave a similar account to Rekha's. In her case she had three boys and strongly desired a girl, even when "people told me that I should stop having children." She prayed to Jiutiyā Mā saying, "If you will grant me a girl then I will do your *vrat.*" Lakshmi too was successful.

14. As Freeman (1980, 124–25) has described in relation to the Habisha Vrat in Orissa, longer *vrats* may involve pilgrimage, as well as story-telling, singing and dancing or dramatic reenactments of scenes from the *kathās* in cases where the *vrat* is performed by a group of women. Pre-menopausal women cannot observe the month-long Habisha Vrat because their period might come in the middle and compromise the *vrat.*

15. The respected national news magazine *India Today* featured an in-depth report on the plight of widows in India which starkly revealed that the terrible social and economic conditions for (many) high-caste widows have not significantly changed in recent years. Unless financially independent and either educated or very determined, the widow's fate largely depends on the attitudes of her in-laws or her birth family ("Widows: Wrecks of Humanity," *India Today*, 15 Nov. 1987, 68–75).

16. In the famous story of Śakuntalā in the *Mahābhārata*, there is a passage where Śakuntalā lectures Duḥṣanta when he has refused to recognize her and their son (Adiparvan 68.39–46). She eloquently speaks of the *pativratā*, and among other things, says: "Only a faithful wife follows even a man who has died and is transmigrating, sharing a common lot in adversities, for he is forever her husband. A wife who has died before stands still and waits for her husband; and a good wife follows after her husband if he has died before" (van Buitenen tr.).

17. Quoted in Dange 1989, 1615.

18. Marglin has noted this too (1985, 54): "Old widows—i.e. after the child-bearing age—are pure. They fast all the time; they never eat fish, meat and other 'hot' food, they wear white (colour of purity) garments and in general live an austere life. It is only by disassociating inauspiciousness from impurity that one can understand why it is only old widows who can become temple attendants."

19. There is another possibility. Annapurna, married to a poor and domineering pandit, told me bluntly that she prayed to be reborn as a man. For her, life was hard enough without the added burden of being a woman.

20. Actually, instead of *mokṣa* or *mukti*, the Purāṇas often specify a, one could say, "pre-final liberation" state as the reward. As McGee notes (1987, 63–64), philosophical schools recognized different levels of *mokṣa* (that is, leading up to *mokṣa): salokya* (reaching one of the gods' heavens); *samīpya* (nearness to God); *sarupya* (identical form with God); and *sayujya* (absorption in God).

21. Vindhya apparently associated Śiva-*pūjā* with animal sacrifices, which she felt were wrong. "People who do this kind of *pūjā* are blind in their mind and heart. . . . It won't work if I sacrifice my finger to strengthen yours!"

22. Vindhya's understanding of the term *mokṣa* seems to correspond to the concept of *samīpya* (nearness to God); one of the "levels" of *mokṣa.*

7. "BECAUSE IT GIVES ME PEACE OF MIND"

1. For example, one gentleman gave this example for a "nonreligious" *vrat:* "Say you wanted to stop smoking or stop chewing *pān* (stuffed betel leaves)—then you can take a *vrata* to accomplish that goal."

2. By "rituals" she meant the special clothes worn, the fasting and fast-breaking foods, the stories told, songs sung, ritual art made, that are dictated by family tradition, and which are not an important part of her Tuesday Vrat.

3. Wadley has pointed out that for Hindus *śānti* (which she translates as "calmness") is one of the prerequisites or indicators of good psychological health. She writes: "Physically, a person is in good condition if he is in good health *(tanurustī)* and not in ill-health *(bīmarī, rog).* Psychologically, a person's condition is good if he has happiness *(sukh),* calmness *(śānti)* or contentment *(santoṣ)"* (1983, 51).

4. A world "which, from the ascetic perspective, is the foremost social expression" of the cycle of life, death and rebirth (see Denton 1991, 215).

5. Denton writes: "householders regard [the *brahmacāriṇīs*] highly: when they see the women celibate students of their neighbourhood (on the occasion of a religious festival, for example), they point them out with a mixture of pride and awe" (1991, 230).

6. *Saṁskār* as it is used here does not refer to the specific Hindu "sacraments," but rather, as I indicate, to the body of rituals inherited from one's family.

7. Kamala used both the English word "scientific" and the Hindi word "*vaijñanik*" which, according to the Chaturvedi & Tiwari Hindi-English dictionary, means "scientific," and in Apte's Sanskrit-English dictionary means "clever, skillful, proficient."

8. One of my astrologer informants explained in more detail: "Observing, say, four *vrats* per month reduces blood pressure, balances the humours in the body. [This is] especially [the case] when one avoids eating salt and eats only when the sun goes down."

9. The Hindu author R. Tripathi, however, does get a trifle defensive about the depiction of *vrats* in the Sanskrit literature against possible criticisms based on logic and science. He writes: "The importance (given to) *vrats* [in the Dharmaśāstras] seems so exaggerated, unnatural and absurd that it cannot be stuffed in any way into today's logical mind; but, on these occasions we need sympathy and a little profoundness. . . . As it is ridiculous to set about researching the beautiful poetical fancies and similes of some poems in today's science labs, in the same way we should also say that it is improper to test the spiritual thoughts and religion on the touchstone of logic and scientific criticism." Tripathi goes on in similar words to argue the point that science cannot render *vrats*, festivals or the gods irrelevent (1978, 4–5).

10. *Bhagavadgītā* 18.11, quoted in Patrick Olivelle (1978, 31). My discussion on the implication for women's performance of *vrats* from the teachings of the *Gītā* are to some extent in dialogue with Olivelle's article, though he mentions neither women nor *vratas*.

11. This view that in the "golden past"—the Kṛta Yuga—everyone was spiritually stronger and society was peaceful (because ordered), whereas today we are in the midst of the Kali Yuga, the age of decline and disorder, is one shared by a great many Hindus and serves as an explanatory paradigm for all events perceived as violent, unfortunate, immoral, and so forth.

12. Of the twenty-five Banarasi women to whom I specifically asked the question whether they thought *vrats* were a form of *tapasyā*, twenty-four replied in the affirmative.

13. I also asked Kamala about Sāvitrī when we were discussing *tapas* and *siddhi* and she quickly replied: "Yamrāj was tempting Sāvitrī [by offering many things], but she had made her own resolve that she only wants the life of her husband. So then she obtained that *siddhi*. Her father had no son but she was not tempted by that offer. She remained

firm in her goal. She did not get angry. The kingdom, etc., all these she contemptuously rejected. She only wanted [the return of] Satyavan's life. So if everyone could act like that [then] it is possible that [all] could obtain *siddhis*. But that is not how it can be. This is a matter of great self-discipline. To be able to control the mind is very difficult. Concentration is most necessary. Complete restraint is essential for obtaining *siddhis*."

14. A number of scholars have since written about the special relationship between Hindu women and the value of auspiciousness, as well as further investigated and conceptually refined the relationship between auspiciousness and inauspiciousness and purity and impurity (see especially Marglin 1985).

GLOSSARY

akṣat Literally, "unbroken" ; unhusked rice used for ceremonial occasions, such as in *pūjās*.

ālpanā Ephemeral ritual art often, though not exclusively, made by women in the context of a *vrat*.

anāj Grain; a type of food often proscribed during the observance of a *vrat*.

āratī The rite of circling a small, lit oil lamp in a clockwise direction in front of a deity, holy person or guest as a form of honor or worship.

bahū Daughter-in-law; son's wife.

bhakti Devotion; an attitude of surrender or worshipful love toward the divine.

bhajan Devotional hymns or songs.

brahmacarya Period of studentship; the first of the four ideal stages of life or *āśramas*; celibacy, sexual restraint.

dāl Pulse, such as lentils; a staple food of India.

bhūt-pret Unhappy ghosts and spirits.

dān Ritual gifting usually to person(s) of equal or higher status. The giving of *dān* usually occurs at the end of a *vrat*.

dakṣina A payment given to Brahmans for for their ritual service.

darśan Auspicious mutual viewing between a devotee and the divine or a holy person or sacred place.

dharm Religious or moral law; righteousness; one's prescribed duty according to age, sex and caste; religion or any religious tradition in general.

dhārmik Any act or activity that accords with *dharm*, thus meritorious.

dīkṣa Initiation into vedic rituals. Mantra *dīkṣa* is to be intiated into or with a mantra.

dīp Lamps, usually in the form of small clay vessels filled with clarified butter or oil and a cotton wick used during *pūjā*s and during *āratī*.

Gaṅgā-jal Ganges water; considered sacred and often used in *pūjā*s.

ghaṭ Stone or mud steps or bank leading down to a river or a tank adjoining a temple.

guṇ Quality characteristic of or inhering in a thing or person.

gṛhastha The householder or second "stage" in a man's life and the stage most closely associated with females.

hom (Skt. *homa*) Offering made to fire with mantras in the name of different deities performed on numerous ritual occasions by a Brahman priest or male house holder who has undergone the *upanāyaṇa* or sacred-thread initiation ceremony. It is also called Agni *havan*. Because in orthodox circles women do not have the right to say mantras, they have not had the right to perform *hom*.

iṣṭadevtā An individual's chosen, preferred or favored deity.

jap Meditational recitation; repeating or muttering the name of a guru, mantra or deity by the devotee; considered a means to spiritual attainment.

jāti Caste; a Hindu's birth group which conventionally determined occupation and ritual status. There are thousands of *jāti*s and the term is now usually distinguished from *varṇa* or the fourfold "classes."

kāmanā Desire; wish.

kāmya	Desire; with vrata signifies a voluntary vow undertaken with the object of obtaining specific wishes or (often material) desires.
khīr	Rice pudding; a common fasting or fast-breaking food.
kīrtan	A song expressing the glory of a deity.
kuldevtā	Family or lineage deity who has a protective interest in the welfare of the particular family.
kuṁkuṁ	Red powder used as a symbol of auspiciousness in Hindu ceremonies.
laukik	Worldly, mundane, secular.
liṅga	The aniconic (and phallic) representation of the god Śiv, suggestive of both his transcendence and his progenetive power.
loṭa	A small, round, metal vessel used in the household.
manautī	A conditional vow or vow of offering pledged to a deity on fufilment of a wish.
mandir	A temple.
maṅgal	Auspiciousness, well-being; the planet Mars; Tuesday.
mantra	An incantation, mystical verse or magical formula.
mokṣa	Liberation or release from the cycle of rebirth; one of the four aims *(artha)* of life.
mukti	Salvation, liberation, deliverance, release.
mūrti	Form or likeness; the material image of a deity and locus of worship and *darśan.*
naimittika	Occasional; an occasional or periodic ceremony or rite.
nakṣatra	Lunar asterism or mansion; constellation through which the moon passes.
nirjal (Skt. *nirjalā)*	Literally, "Waterless"; the most rigorous form of fasting.

nitya — Perpetual, constant, obligatory; applied to vrata, nitya refers to those considered ritually necessary for certain categories of Hindus.

niyam — A rule, law, principle.

niyama — Bodily and mental self-restraints; a rule or course of discipline or voluntary penance.

pakṣa — Literally, "wing"; a half of the lunar month.

pañcāṅga — Literally, "five limbs"; a religious almanac used to determine the proper time and date for observing a rite.

pāp — Sin or evil.

parvan — Literally, "knot" as in the knots of a bamboo stick; refers to regularly occurring festal days, such as the new and full moon days on which a ritual observance (not necessarily a *vrat)* may be kept.

pativratā — A woman vowed to her husband in service; the ideal Hindu wife.

phalāhar — Literally, "fruit-food"; a diet consisting of fruit alone. A common fasting requirement during a *vrat.*

prasād — Grace; blessed food or the leavings of food distributed among devotees after it has first been offered to a deity or holy person.

prāyaścitta — A rite of expiation or atonement.

pūjā — Worship; devotional service to a deity in a home shrine, public temple or other place.

pujārī — A priest who performs devotional worship; a temple attendant.

pūjā-paṭh — The various rituals and observances *(pūjā*s to household deities, visits to temples, keeping of *vrat*s and festivals, etc.) that constitute the central religious practice of many Hindu householders.

punarjanma — Rebirth.

puṇya — Meritorious, propitious.

ṛṣi Seer; a sage or hermit.

sādhanā Spiritual exercise, endeavor or training; course of discipline.

śakti Power (energy, will) of the gods or the Godhead; the divine consort of a god; female creative (generative) power.

saṅkalp A statement of intent, formal or informal resolve taken before starting a *vrat* (or other ritual); a rite accompanying ritual gifting.

sannyāsa The last and renunciate stage of the idealized four stages *(āśrama)* of man.

sannyāsinī A female renouncer (ascetic).

śāstrik From or according to the śāstras (Sanskrit Brahmanical religious texts).

sasurāl Husband's household.

sattvik That which participates in the qualitiy *(guṇ)* of *sattva*, a quality characterized by purity, light (in both senses), tranquility, etc.

saubhāgya Good luck, fortune; the auspicious state of the married woman.

siddhi Accomplishment, fulfillment; miraculous or supernormal power arising from the practise of austerities.

siṅdūr Vermilion, decorative red powder placed in the part of the hair by married women.

smārta Followers of the Smṛtis.

smṛti Tradition; body of authoritative texts on traditional Hindu law.

snān Ritual bathing; a purificatory bath essential at the start of a *vrat*.

śraddhā Faith in God (and sometimes also includes faith in the "scriptures").

śruti The body of vedic texts containing the repository of unquestionable divine knowledge or revelation.

strīdharm The normative code of behavior for high-caste Hindu women.

strīsvabhāva Women's "inherent" nature.

śubh Auspicious, good.

śuddh Pure, clean, uncorrupt; proper, correct.

suhāg Hindi version of *saubhāgya* (the auspicious married state).

suhāgin A woman whose husband is alive.

tapasyā Heat generated by rigorous ascetic disciplines; the practice of austerities.

tithi Time or period required by the moon to gain twelve degrees on the sun to the east, corresponding more or less to a day. Many *vrat*s (and other ritual occasions) are supposed to begin and end at precise times defined by the parameters of one to three *tithi*s.

tyauhār A festival.

tīrth A "crossing"; a holy or sacred place, place of pilgrimage.

tulsī The basil plant; sacred to Viṣṇu.

udyāpan The concluding rite of a *vrat* when undertaken once or when a final cycle of a given *vrat* has been completed.

upacāra Ritual "attendance" or rites honoring a deity during pūjā; there are up to thirty-two distinct upacāras.

upavās A fast; fasting as a means for physical and spiritual purification.

viśvās Belief, confidance or faith.

yajña Sacrifice, offering, act of worship.

yajamāna Sacrificer; the person sponsoring the sacrifice.

BIBLIOGRAPHY

Agnipurāṇa. 1900. Edited by the pandits of the Ānandāśrama. Ānandāśrama Sanskrit Series 41. Pune: Ānandāśrama Press.

Agni Purāṇam. 1968 [1908]. 2 vols. Translated by M. N. Dutt Shastri. 2nd ed. Varanasi: Chowkhamba Sanskrit Series Office.

Apte, V. M. 1947. *Bulletin of the Deccan College Research Institute* 3:407–88.

———. 1965. *The Practical Sanskrit-English Dictionary.* Delhi: Motilal Banarsidass.

Altekar, Anant Sadashiv. 1983 [1956]. *The Position of Women in Hindu Civilization from Prehistoric Times to the Present.* Varanasi: Motilal Banarsidass.

Babb, Lawrence. 1975. *The Divine Hierarchy: Popular Religion in Central India.* New York: Columbia University Press.

Bagchi, P. C. 1922. "Female Folk-Rites in Bengal: The Suvachani-Vrata-Puja." *Man in India* 2:52–57.

Bahen, Aśa, and Lado Bahen. n.d. *Hinduoṅ ke Vrat aur Tyauhār: Viddhi, Vidhān, Kahāniyoṅ aur Citroṅ Sahit.* Haridvar: Randhir Book Sellers.

Banerjee, S. C. 1946. "Purāṇic Basis of the Vratas Mentioned in Bengal Smṛti." *Indian Culture* 8, no. 1 (July–September): 35–44.

Basham, A. L. 1976. "Santoshi Mata: A New Divinity in the Hindu Pantheon?" In *Proceedings of the 28th International Congress of Orientalists,* Canberra. Wiesbaden: Otto Harossowitz.

Bennett, Lynn. 1983. *Dangerous Wives and Sacred Sisters: Social and Symbolic Roles of High-Caste Women in Nepal.* New York: Columbia University Press.

Bhagat, M. G. 1976. *Ancient Indian Asceticism.* Delhi: Munshiram Manoharlal.

The Bhagavadgita. 1948. With an introductory essay, Sanskrit text, English translation and notes by S. Radhakrishnan. London: George Allen and Unwin Ltd.

Bharati, Agehananda. 1970. "Pilgrimage Sites and Indian Civilization." In *Chapters in Indian Civilization*, vol. 1., ed. J. Elder. Madison: University of Wisconsin.

Bhardwaj, S. M. 1973. *Hindu Places of Pilgrimage in India: A Study in Cultural Geography.* Delhi: Thomson Press.

Bhattacharya, Dinesh C. 1962. "Penances and Vows." In *Cultural Heritage of India*, vol. 2, ed. S. K. De and a Board of Scholars, 381–89. Calcutta: Ramakrishna Mission.

Brown, W. Norman. 1978. "Duty as Truth in Ancient India." In *India and Indology: Selected Articles by W. Norman Brown*, ed. R. Rocher. Delhi: Motilal Banarsidass.

Bühler, George. 1975 [1886]. *The Laws of Manu.* Translated with extracts from seven commentaries by G. Bühler. Sacred Books of the East, vol. 25. Reprint. Delhi: Motilal Banarsidass.

Burghart, Richard. 1983. "Renunciation in the Religious Traditions of South Asia." *Man*, n.s., 18:635–53.

Bynum, Caroline Walker, D. Harrell and P. Richman, eds. 1986. *Gender and Religion: On the Complexity of Symbols.* Boston: Beacon Press.

Carman, John and Fréderique Marglin, eds. 1985. *Purity and Auspiciousness in Indian Society.* International Studies in Social Anthropology, vol. 43. Leiden: E. J. Brill.

Caturvargacintāmani of Hemādri. Vrata Khaṇḍa. Bibliotheca Indica Series, vol. 2, pt. 1, 11. Calcutta: Asiatic Society of Bengal, 1878–79.

Chakladar, H. C. 1962. "Some Aspects of Social Life in Ancient India." In *The Cultural Heritage of India*, ed. by a Board of Scholars. 2nd. ed. Calcutta: Ramakrishna Mission.

Christian, Jr., William A. 1972. *Person and God in a Spanish Valley.* New York: Academic Press.

Clifford, James, and George Marcus, eds. 1986. *Writing Culture: The Poetics and Politics of Ethnography.* Berkeley: University of California Press.

Dange, Sadashiv. 1989. *Encyclopedia of Purāṇic Beliefs and Practices.* Granby, Mass.: Bergin & Garvey Publishers.

Daniel, Sheryl B. 1980. "Marriage in Tamil Culture: the Problem of Conflicting Models." In *Powers of Tamil Women*, ed. S. Wadley. Syracuse: Maxwell School of Citizenship and Public Affairs.

Das, R. M. 1962. *Women in Manu and His Seven Commentators*. Varanasi: Kanchana Publications.

Das, S. R. 1952. "A Study of the Vrata Rites of Bengal." *Man in India* 32, no. 4: 207–45.

Day, Terrance. 1982. *The Conception of Punishment in Early Indian Literature*. Canadian Society for the Study of Religion (CSSR). Waterloo: Wilfrid Laurier University Press.

Denton, Lynn Teskey. 1985."Dharma, Mokṣa and Hindu Asceticism." Unpublished paper.

———. 1991. "Varieties of Hindu Female Asceticism." In *Roles and Rituals for Hindu Women*, ed. J. Leslie, 211–31. London: Pinter Publishers.

Diehl, Carl G. 1956. *Instrument and Purpose*. Lund: C. W. K. Gleerup.

Dhruvarajan, Vanaja. 1989. *Hindu Women and the Power of Ideology*. Granby, Mass.: Bergin & Garvey Publishers.

Doniger, Wendy, trans., with Brian K. Smith. 1991. *The Laws of Manu*. With an introduction, and notes. London: Penguin Books.

Dumont, Louis. 1970. *Homo Hierarchicus: The Caste System and Its Implications*. Trans. by Mark Sainsbury. Chicago: University of Chicago Press.

Duvvury, Vasumathi K. 1991. *Play, Symbolism and Ritual: A Study of Tamil Brahmin Women's Rites of Passage*. New York: Peter Lang.

Eck, Diana. 1982. *Banaras: City of Light*. New York: Alfred Knopf.

Egnore, Margaret. 1980. "On the Meaning of *Śakti* to Women in Tamil Nadu." In *The Powers of Tamil Women*, ed. Susan Wadley. Syracuse: Maxwell School of Citizenship and Public Affairs.

Eliade, Mircea. 1958. *Birth and Rebirth: The Religious Meaning of Initiation*. New York: Harper & Row.

———. 1969 [1958]. *Yoga: Immortality and Freedom*. Trans. from the French by W. R. Trask. Bollingen Series LVI. New York: Princeton University Press.

"Fairs and Festivals in Uttar Pradesh." 1966. *Census of India*, 1961, vol. 15, part 7-B. Delhi: Manager of Publications.

Freed, Ruth S., and Stanley A. Freed. 1964. "Calendars, Ceremonies and Festivals in a North Indian Village: Necessary Calendric Information for Fieldwork." *Southwestern Journal of Anthropology* 20 (Spring): 67–90.

Freeman, James. 1980. "The Ladies of Lord Krishna: Rituals of Middle-Aged Women in Eastern India." In *Unspoken Worlds: Women's Religious Lives in Non-Western Cultures*, eds. N. Falk and R. Gross, 110–26. San Fransisco: Harper & Row.

Freitag, Sandria B. 1989. *Culture and Power in Banaras: Community, Performance, and Environment, 1800–1980.* Berkeley: University of California Press.

Gandhi, M. K. 1957. *An Autobiography: The Story of My Experiments with Truth.* Boston: Beacon Press.

Garuḍa Purāṇam. 1903. Edited by Vāsudeva Lakṣmaṇaśāstri Paṇśīkar. Bombay: Nirnayasagara Press.

Garuḍa Purāṇa. 1978. Translated by a board of scholars and edited by J. L. Shastri. Ancient Indian Tradition and Mythology Series, vol. 12. Delhi: Motilal Banarsidass.

Geertz, Clifford. 1973. *The Interpretation of Cultures.* New York: Basic Books.

Gonda, Jan. 1965. *Change and Continuity in Indian Religion.* The Hague: Mouton & Co.

———. 1970. *Viṣṇuism and Śivaism: A Comparison.* London: The Athlone Press.

———. 1975. *Vedic Literature Saṁhitās and Brāhmaṇas.* Wiesbaden: Otto Harrossowitz.

Gupta, Eva Maria. 1983. *Brata und Ālpanā in Bengalen.* Wiesbaden: Steiner.

Gupta, R. K. 1961. "Hindu Vratas (Fasts)—A Sociological Study." *Indian Cultures Quarterly* 19, no. 4: 1–11; 19, no. 5: 16–25.

Gupte, B. A. 1916. *Hindu Holidays and Ceremonials: With Dissertations on Origin, Folklore and Symbols.* 2nd. rev. ed. Calcutta: Thacker, Spink & Co.

Hansen, Kathryn. 1992. "Heròic Modes of Women in Indian Myth, Ritual and History: The *Tapasvinī* and the *Vīrāṅganā.*" In *The Annual Review of Women in World Religions*, vol. 2, eds. A. Sharma and K. Young, 1–62. Albany: SUNY Press.

Harlan, Lindsey. 1992. *Religion and Rajput Women: The Ethic of Protection in Contemporary Narratives*. Berkeley: University of California Press.

Hazra, R. C. 1975. *Studies in the Purāṇic Records on Hindu Rites and Customs*. 2nd. ed. Delhi: Motilal Banarsidass.

Heckaman, Curt. 1980. "Towards a Comprehensive Understanding of Ṛta in the Ṛgveda." M.A. thesis, McMaster University.

Hertel, Bradley, and Cynthia Humes, eds. 1993. *Living Banaras: Hindu Religion in Cultural Context*. Albany: SUNY Press.

Jacobson, Doranne. 1978. "The Chaste Wife: Cultural Norms and Individual Experience." In *American Studies in the Anthropology of India*, ed. S. Vatuk, 94–138. New Delhi: Manohar.

Jayal, S. 1966. *The Status of Women in the Epics*. Delhi: Motilal Banarsidass.

Jeffery, Patricia, and Roger Jeffery. 1994. "Killing My Heart's Desire: Education and Female Autonomy in Rural North India." In *Women as Subjects: South Asian Histories*, ed. Nita Kumar, 125–71. Charlottesville: University Press of Virginia.

Kakar, Sudhir. 1981. *The Inner World: A Psycho-analytic Study of Childhood and Society in India*. 2nd ed. Delhi: Oxford University Press.

———. 1982. *Shamans, Mystics and Doctors*. Delhi: Oxford University Press.

Kalakdina, Margaret. 1975. "The Upbringing of a Girl." In *Indian Women: Report on the Status of Women in India*, ed. Devaki Jain. New Delhi: Ministry of Information and Broadcasting.

Kane, P. V. 1974. *History of Dharmaśāstra*. 5 vols. 2nd ed. Poona: Bhandarkar Oriental Research Institute, 1941–62.

Kaushik, J. N. n.d. *Fasts of the Hindus around the Year: Background Stories, Ways of Performance and Their Importance*. Delhi: Books for All.

Khare, R. S. 1976. *The Hindu Hearth and Home*. Durham: Carolina Academic Press.

Kieth, A. B. 1925. *The Religion and Philosophy of the Veda and Upanishads. Harvard Oriental Series*, vol. 31. Cambridge, Mass.: Harvard University Press.

Kieth, A. B., and A. Macdonell. 1958 [1912]. *Vedic Index of Names and Subjects*. 2 vols. Delhi: Motilal Banarsidass.

Klinger, E. 1987. "Vows and Oaths." In *Encyclopedia of Religion*, ed. Mircea Eliade. New York: Collier Macmillan Publishers.

Kramrisch, Stella. 1985. "The Ritual Arts of India." In *Aditi: The Living Arts of India*, 247–57. Washington: Smithsonian Institute.

Kṛtyakalpataru of Bhatta Lakṣmidhāra. 1942. Vrata Khandam. Edited by K. V. Rangaswami Aiyangar. Gaekwad's Oriental Series no. 98. Baroda: Oriental Institute.

Kumar, Nita, ed. 1994. *Women as Subjects: South Asian Histories*. Charlottesville: University Press of Virginia.

Lamphere, Louise. 1974. "Strategies of Cooperation and Conflict among Women in Domestic Groups." In *Women, Culture and Society*, eds. M. Rosaldo and L. Lamphere. Stanford: Stanford University Press.

Leach, Bernard. 1984. "Two Essays Concerning the Symbolic Representation of Time." In *Reader in Comparative Religion: An Anthropological Approach*, eds. William Lessa and Evon Vogt. 4th ed. New York: Harper & Row.

Leslie, Julia. 1983. "Essence and Existence: Women and Religion in Ancient Indian Texts." In *Women's Religious Experience*, ed. Pat Holden. London: Croom Helm.

———. 1988. *The Perfect Wife: The Status and Role of the Orthodox Hindu Woman as Described in the* Strīdharmapaddhati *of Tryambakayajvan*. Oxford: Oxford University Press.

———. ed. 1991. *Roles and Rituals for Hindu Women*. London: Pinter Publishers.

Lewis, Oscar. 1958. *Village Life in Northern India*. New York: Vintage Books.

Liṅga Purāṇa. 1973. Translated by a board of scholars and edited by J. L. Shastri. Ancient Indian Tradition and Mythology, vol. 6. Delhi: Motilal Banarsidass.

Long, J. Bruce. 1982. "Mahāśivarātri: The Śaiva Festival of Repentence." In *Religious Festivals in South India and Sri Lanka*, eds. G. Welbon and G. Yocum, 189–218. New Delhi: Manohar.

Luschinsky, Mildred. 1962. "The Life of Women in a Village of North India: A Study of Role and Status." Ph.D. diss., Cornell University.

Madan, T. N. 1985. "Concerning the Categories *Śubha* and *Śuddha*." In *Purity and Auspiciousness in Indian Society*, eds. J. Carmen and F. Marglin. Leiden: E. J. Brill.

———. 1987. *Non Renunciation: Themes and Interpretations of Hindu Culture.* Delhi: Oxford University Press.

Mahābhārata. Critically edited by V. S. Sukthankar et al. 19 vols. Pune: Bhandarkar Oriental Research Institute, 1933–69.

Maity, Pradyot Kumar. 1988. *Folk Rituals of Eastern India.* New Delhi: Abhinav Publications.

———. 1989. *Human Fertility Cults and Rituals of Bengal: A Comparative Study.* New Delhi: Abhinav Publications.

Mani, Vettam. *Purāṇic Encyclopedia.* Delhi: Motilal Banarsidass, 1964. English edition, 1975.

Marglin, Frédérique Apfel. 1985. *Wives of the God-king: The Rituals of the Devadasis of Puri.* Delhi: Oxford University Press.

Marriott, McKim. 1955. "Little Communities in an Indigenous Civilization." In *Village India,* ed. M. Marriott, 171–222. Chicago: University of Chicago Press.

Matsya Purāṇa. Translated by a Taluqdar of Oudh. Sacred Books of the Hindus, vol. 17, 1916–17. Allahabad: Sudhīndra Nāth Vasu. (Reprint 1974, New York: AMS Press.)

Mazumdar, Sucheta. 1981. "Socialization of Hindu Middle-Class Bengali Women." *U.C.L.A. South Asia Bulletin* 1 (Winter): 30–37.

McGee, Mary. 1987. "Feasting and Fasting: The Vrata Tradition and Its Significance for Hindu Women." Th.D. diss., Harvard University Divinity School.

———. 1991. "Desired Fruits: Motive and Intention in the Votive Rites of Hindu Women." In *Roles and Rituals for Hindu Women,* ed. Julia Leslie, 71–88. London: Pinter Publishers.

Merry, Karen. 1982. "The Hindu Festival Calendar." In *Religious Festivals in South India and Sri Lanka.* eds. Guy Welbon and Glenn Yocum, 1–25. New Delhi: Manohar.

Minturn, Leigh. 1993. *Sita's Daughters—Coming Out of Purdah.* New York: Oxford University Press.

Mitter, Sara. 1991. *Dharma's Daughters: Contemporary Indian Women and Hindu Culture.* New Brunswick: Rutgers University Press.

Monier-Williams, Sir Monier. 1984 [1899]. *A Sanskrit-English Dictionary.* Oxford University Press. Reprint. Delhi: Motilal Banarsidass.

Mukherjee, Charulal. 1950. "Bratas in Bengal (A Cult of Beauty)." *Man in India* 30 (April–September): 66–72.

Mukherjee, Prabhati. 1978. *Hindu Women: Normative Models.* London: Orient Longman.

Müller, F. Max. 1964 [1891]. *Vedic Hymns.* Sacred Books of the East, vol. 32, part 2. Delhi: Motilal Banarsidass.

Olivelle, Patrick. 1978. "The Integration of Renunciation by Orthodox Hinduism." *Journal of the Oriental Institute* 28, no. 1 (September): 27–36.

Ortner, Sherry, and Harriet Whitehead, eds. 1981. *Sexual Meanings: The Cultural Construction of Gender and Sexuality.* Cambridge: Cambridge University Press.

Parry, Jonathan. 1985. "Death and Digestion: The Symbolism of Food and Eating in North Indian Mortuary Rites." *Man* 20, no. 4 (December).

Pearson, Anne M. 1983. "A Study of the Purāṇic Vratas." M.A. thesis, McMaster University, Hamilton, Canada.

Personal Narratives Group. 1989. *Interpreting Women's Lives: Feminist Theory and Personal Narratives.* Bloomington: Indiana University Press.

Pugh, Judy. 1983. "Into the Almanac: Time, Meaning, and Action in North Indian Society." *Contributions to Indian Sociology* 17, no. 1: 27–49.

Pusalker, A. D. 1963. *Studies in Epics and Purāṇas of India.* Bombay: Bharatiya Vidya Bhavan.

Raheja, Gloria Goodwin, and Ann Grodzins Gold. 1994. *Listen to the Heron's Words: Reimagining Gender and Kinship in North India.* Berkeley: University of California Press.

Ralph, T. H. Griffith, trans. 1896–97. *The Hymns of the Rigveda, Translated with a Popular Commentary.* 2 vols. 2nd ed. Banaras: E. J. Lazarus and Co..

Ray, Sudhansu K. 1960. "A Study of Brata Rituals of Bengal." *Folkore* (Calcutta) 1 (March–April): 93–136.

———. 1961. *The Ritual Art of the Bratas of Bengal.* Calcutta: Firma K. L. Mukhopadhyay.

Reynolds, Holly Baker. 1980. "The Auspicious Married Woman." In *The Powers of Tamil Women*, ed. Susan Wadley, 35–60. Syracuse: Maxwell School of Citizenship and Public Affairs.

Robinson, Margaret. 1979. "Santoshi Ma: The Development of a Goddess." Unpublished project for the University of Wisconsin College Year Abroad Program (Banaras).

Robinson, Sandra P. 1985. "Hindu Paradigms of Women: Images and Values." In *Women, Religion and Social Change,* eds. Y. Haddad and E. Findlay, 181–215. Albany: SUNY Press.

Rowlands, J. Helen. 1930. *La Femme Bengalie dans la Littérature du Moyen Age.* Paris: Librairie d'Amérique et d'Orient, Adrien Maisonneuve.

Roy, Manisha. 1975. *Bengali Women.* Chicago: University of Chicago Press.

The Śatapatha Brāhmaṇa According to the Text of the Mādhyandina School. Translated by Julius Eggling. Sacred Books of the East, vols. 12, 26, 41, 43, 44. Oxford: Clarendon Press, 1832–1900.

Schechner, Richard. 1993. "Crossing the Water: Pilgrimage, Movement, and Environmental Scenography of the Ramlila of Ramnagar." In *Living Banaras: Hindu Religion in Cultural Context,* eds. Bradley Hertel and Cynthia Ann Humes. New York: SUNY Press.

Sen Gupta, Sankar, ed. 1969. *Women in Indian Folklore—A Linguistic and Religious Study.* Calcutta: Indian Publications Folklore Series no. 15.

Sharma, B. N. 1978. *Festivals of India.* New Delhi: Abhinav Publications.

———. 1972. *Social and Cultural History of Northern India 1000–1200* A.D. Delhi: Abhinav Publishers.

Shastri, M. N. Dutt, trans. 1978 [1908]. *The Dharam Shastra: Hindu Religious Codes.* With Sanskrit text. New Delhi: Cosmo Publications.

Sivananda, Swami. 1983. *Hindu Fasts and Festivals.* 4th ed. Shivanandanagar: Divine Life Society.

Slocum, Carolyn, recorder and translator. 1988. "Shakti: Women's Inner Strength." In *The Experience of Hinduism: Essays on Religion in Maharashtra,* eds. Eleanor Zelliot and M. Berntsen, 208–9. Albany: SUNY Press.

Srinivas, M. 1965 [1952]. *Religion and Society among the Coorgs of South India.* Reprint. London: Asia Publishing House.

Stutley, Margaret. 1980. *Ancient Indian Magic and Folkore: An Introduction.* Delhi: Motilal Banarsidass.

Tagore, Abanindranath. 1919. *Banglar Brata.* Bholpur: Visvabharati Publications.

Tewari, Laxmi G. 1991. *A Splendor of Worship: Women's Fasts, Rituals, Stories and Art.* New Delhi: Manohar.

———. 1982. "Women's Fasts and Festivals from U.P.: Their Art, Ritual, and Stories." *Journal of South Asian Studies* 5, no. 1: 42–50.

Tripāṭhi, Rampratāp. 1978. *Hinduoṅ ke Vrat, Parv aur Tyauhār.* Allahabad: Lokbharti Prakasan.

Underhill, M. M. 1921. *The Hindu Religious Year.* London: Oxford University Press.

Upadhye, P. M. 1972. "Vows in the Purāṇa Literature." *Bharatiya Vidya* 32: 13–19.

Van Buitenen, J. A. B., trans. and ed. 1972–78. *Mahābhārata.* 3 vols. (Books 1 to 5). Chicago: University of Chicago Press.

Vatuk, Sylvia. 1987. "Authority, Power and Autonomy in the Life Cycle of the North Indian Woman." In *Dimensions of Social Life: Essays in Honor of David G. Mandelbaum,* ed. P. Hockings. Berlin: Mouton de Gruyter.

Venkateswaran, C. S. 1962. "The Ethics of the Purāṇas." In *The Cultural Heritage of India,* vol. 2. Ed. by a board of scholars. Calcutta: Ramakrishna Mission.

Vesci, Uma Marina. 1985. *Heat and Sacrifice in the Vedas.* Delhi: Motilal Banarsidass.

Vidyarthi, L. P., B. N. Sarasvati, M. Jha. 1979. *The Sacred Complex of Kashi: A Microcosm of Indian Civilization.* Delhi: Concept Publishing Co.

Vratarāja of Viśvanātha Śarma. 1984. Compiled at Banaras in 1736. Edited with an introduction and commentary in Hindi by Pandit Madhavācarya Śarma. Bombay: Śri Venkateśvar Press.

"Vratetsavaṅk." 1952. *Āryamahilā* (Banaras), April–July.

Wadley, Susan Snow. 1975. *Shakti: Power in the Conceptual Structure of Karimpur Religion.* University of Chicago Studies in Anthropology. Series in Social, Cultural, and Linguistic Anthropology no. 2. Chicago: Department of Anthropology, University of Chicago.

———. 1976. "Brothers, Husbands and Sometimes Sons: Kinsmen in North Indian Ritual." *Eastern Anthropologist* 29, no. 1: 149–70.

———. 1978. "Texts in Contexts: Oral Traditions and the Study of Religion in Karimpur." In *American Studies in the Anthropology of India*, ed. S. Vatuk. New Delhi: Manohar.

———. 1980a. "Hindu Women's Family and Household Rites in a North Indian Village." In *Unspoken Worlds Women's Religious Lives in Non-Western Cultures*, eds. N. Falk and R. Gross, 94–109. San Francisco: Harper & Row.

———, ed. 1980b. *The Powers of Tamil Women*. Syracuse: Maxwell School of Citenzenship and Public Affairs.

———. 1983a. "Popular Hinduism and Mass Literature in North India: A Preliminary Analysis." In *Religion in Modern India*, ed. Giri Raj Gupta, 81–103. Main Currents in Indian Sociology, vol. 5. New Delhi: Vikas.

———. 1983b. "The Rains of Estrangement: Understanding the Hindu Yearly Cycle." *Contributions to Indian Sociology* 17, no. 1: 51–85.

———. 1983c. "Vrats: Transformers of Destiny." In *Karma: An Anthropological Inquiry*, eds. Charles Keyes and E. V. Daniel, 147–62. Berkeley: University of California Press.

———. 1986. "The Kathā of Sakaṭ: Two Tellings." In *Another Harmony. New Essays on the Folklore of India*, eds. S. Blackburn and A. K. Ramanujan, 195–232. Berkeley: University of California Press.

Wadley, S., and Doranne Jacobson. 1977. *Women in India: Two Perspectives*. New Delhi: Manohar Book Service.

Ward, W. 1817. *A View of the History, Literature and Religion of the Hindoos*. Birmingham: W. H. Pearce.

Welbon, Guy, and Glenn Yocum, eds. 1982. *Religious Festivals in South India and Sri Lanka*. New Delhi: Manohar Publications.

Yājñavalkyasmṛti, with the *Mitakṣara* commentary of Vijñaneśvara. 1887. Edited by Shivarama Janardan Shastri Gore. Bombay: Janardan Mahadev Gurjar.

Yardi, M. R. 1979. *The Yoga of Patañjali*. With an introduction, Sanskrit text of the Yogasūtras, English translation and notes. Pune: Bhandarkar Oriental Research Insititute.

Young, Katherine. 1987. "Women in Hinduism." In *Women in World Religions*, ed. Arvind Sharma, 59–103. Albany: SUNY Press.

Zimmerman, Francis. 1975. "Ṛtu-satmya: The Seasonal Cycle and the Principle of Appropriateness." Translated by McKim Marriott and John Leavitt. *Puruṣārtha* 2: 87–105.

INDEX